THE X-FILES™ BOOK OF THE UNEXPLAINED VOLUME II

by

JANE GOLDMAN

Based on the series created by Chris Carter

SIMON & SCHUSTER
A VIACOM COMPANY

First published in Great Britain by Simon & Schuster, 1996
An imprint of Simon & Schuster Ltd
A Viacom Company

Simon & Schuster Ltd.
West Garden Place
Kendal Street
London W2 2AQ

Simon & Schuster of Australia Pty Ltd
Sydney

A CIP catalogue record for this book is available
from the British Library.

0 684 81634 2

Design, Typesetting and Repro by
The Imaging Business Ltd
Unit 39, The Kings Exchange
Tileyard Road, Islington
London N7 9AH

Printed and bound in Great Britain by
Butler & Tanner Ltd
The Selwood Printing Works
Caxton Road
Frome
Somerset BA11 INF

*The opinions and interpretations contained
in this book do not necessarily reflect
those of Chris Carter, The X-Files' creative
team and Twentieth Century Fox*

Dedication

This book is dedicated to Anne Solomon, to Betty and Harvey, and to the little human growing inside me – four people who remind me that love transcends the boundaries of past, present and future.

Acknowledgements

This book could not have been written without the love, support and assistance of my heroic and perfect husband, Jonathan. Truly I am blessed.

The generosity I encountered, across the board, whilst working on this book was little short of astounding. To be so warmly welcomed by the *X-Files* team, during an astonishingly busy period when I'm sure the last thing anyone needed was a Britishy writer lurking around, was something for which I shall be eternally grateful. My profuse and sincere thanks go to Chris Carter, Mary Astadourian, Howard Gordon, Darin Morgan, Frank Spotnitz, John Shiban and Vince Gilligan for their invaluable time, assistance and kindness. (And to Cindy and Angelo who also made me feel ever so welcome on the 20th Century Fox lot).

I am wildly indebted, too, to Jennifer Sebree at Fox for her incredible support, and to the wonderful, tireless folks at Simon and Schuster – Martin Fletcher, Gillian Holmes, Sally Partington and Michelle Hughes.

Thanks also to the ever-diligent Cleo Paskal.

Not a day goes by without my reflecting on my good fortune in having so many generous and loyal friends, many of whom provided both loving support and practical assistance – including my beloved parents, Amanda Goldman and Stuart Goldman, the preternaturally kind and talented Jack Barth, Toula Mavridou (the best sister anyone could wish for) and Monica Rivron, a very special friend indeed. My love and gratitude goes out to them all, as it does to Jacqui Deevoy, Max Ellis, Emily Dean, Rowland Rivron, Debbie Marrow, Frank Skinner, Michelle Alexander and David Baddiel.

Enormous thanks are due to all who gave so generously of their time, wisdom and assistance, including Loren Coleman, Bob Rickard, James Randi, Wade Davis, Dr Susan Blackmore, Colonel Robert Ressler, Professor Michael Persinger and Brenda Dunne.

Thanks also to Penn Jillette, Tom Paskal, Philip Levine, Professor WMS Russell and Claire Russell, Laura Najman, Mrs. Ressler, Professor R.A. Gardner, Suzanne McClintock, Special Agent Rex Tomb at the FBI, Cathy Mahoney, the guys at The Sound Company, Mark Mason, Derek Dawson, Marinda Van Dalen, Jeannie Samuel and Dr Kim Kachanoff.

Additionally, I would like to express my respect and appreciation to William R. Corliss and Leonard George, whose books provided especially valuable reference.

I do hope that I have not left anyone out, and that if I have, they will forgive me, and accept my belated thanks.

CONTENTS

Dedication iii
Acknowledgements v

Life Outside the Mortal Form

Hallucinogenic Journeys 9
Perchance to Dream 21
Between Two Worlds 33

Human Enigmas

Miraculous Wounds 51
Looking Into the Abyss 59
Physical Anomalies 77
Psychic Detectives 93
Lake Monsters 105

Weird World

More Weird Nature 115
Electric Skies 127
Is There Intelligent Life on Earth? 141

Ancient Beliefs

Native American Wonders 149
The Night Stalkers 161
A Dark Collusion 173
Voodoo 185
Written in the Stars 203

20th Century Threats and Paranoias

Conspiracy 213
Mind Control 233
Urban Legends 247
Mass Hysteria and the Belief Engine 267
The Frontiers of Reality 279

A Cosmic Conundrum

The Search for Extra-Terrestrial Intelligence .. 289
Alien Abduction 307

Investigating the Unexplained

Inside the FBI 319
In Search of the Truth 331

Episode Guide 340
The X-Files Mythology 342
Bibliography 346

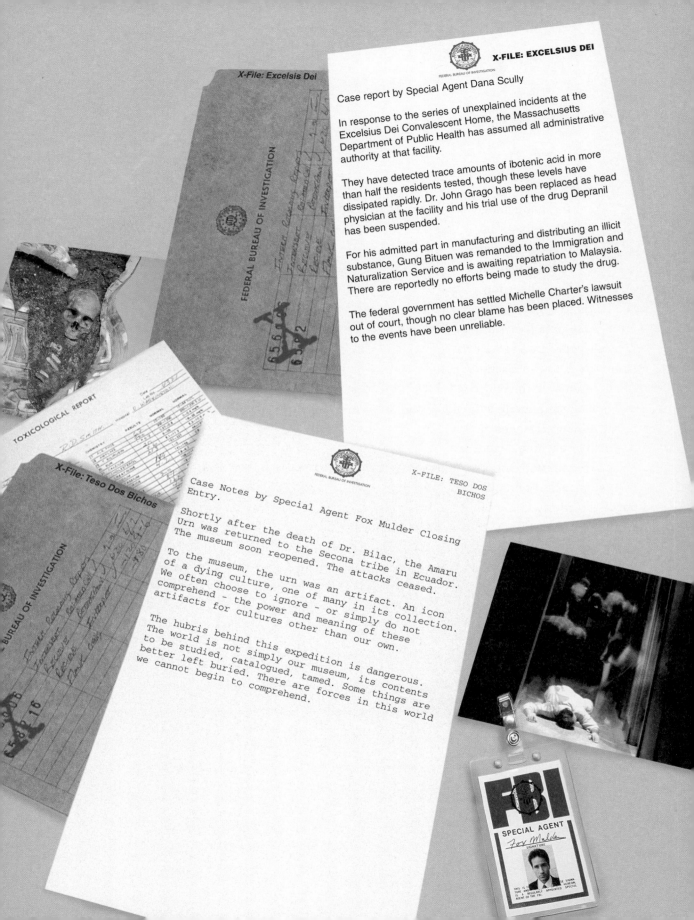

HALLUCINOGENIC JOURNEYS

Do the hallucinogenic powers of mushrooms and plants simply permit the mind to roam its own fantastical inner realms? Or do they allow users to enter another dimension of reality? The effects of hallucinogens have intrigued mankind for centuries, and inspired two very different episodes of *The X-Files*.

In the first, *Excelsius Dei*, a nurse's claim that she has been raped by an invisible entity brings Mulder and Scully to the grim Excelsius Dei old people's home. The residents are thriving despite harsh treatment and a dismal environment; even those registered as being in the advanced stages of Alzheimer's – an incurable brain disease whose degenerative effects are irreversible – are bursting with vigour and in remarkably sharp mental form. The key to this miracle seems to be the remedy secretly handed out daily by an altruistic orderly, Gung Bituen, hand-made according to his native Malaysian traditions from the crop of psychoactive fungi that he cultivates in the basement.

Scully is surrounded by the restless spirits of the Excelcis Dei rest home

But what of the nurse, and the unexplained deaths of other members of staff? Could it be, as Bituen suggests, that when the door to the spirit realm was opened by the patients on their hallucinogenic journeys, the vengeful spectres of mistreated former residents flocked through?

A season later, *Teso Dos Bichos* finds Mulder and Scully investigating the disappearance of two archaeologists. Both had been involved in the recovery of artifacts from an Ecuadorian tribal burial ground, including a sacred burial-urn containing the remains of an Amaru – a female shaman.

Scully's suspicions fall upon Dr Alsonso Bilac, who had served as the project's liaison with the Secona Indians until he had been forced to quit over his belief that the ancestral remains should not have been taken away from Ecuador. Mulder, meanwhile, is prepared to consider that interference with the remains may have invoked a curse: the wrath of the Jaguar Spirit.

Among the tribal societies of South America the existence of spirits is unquestioned, and most individuals will have witnessed 'proof' first hand through the ritual imbibing of a hallucinogenic drink known as Yaje. Pronounced ya-hay, this concoction acts as a ticket to a vast immaterial world. And the plot thickens when Mulder and Scully discover that Dr Bilac has been spending a great deal of time there.

> ### 'Personally, if someone digs me up a thousand years from now, I hope there's a curse on them, too'
>
> #### MULDER
>
> #### *Teso Dos Bichos*

Writer John Shiban, who joined the *X-Files* team at the start of the show's third season, reveals that his initial inspiration was a book by Tony Hillerman, the popular author of mystery novels set in and around the Native American reservations of the American Southwest.

'I can't remember what it was called,' says Shiban, 'but it was about the whole issue of the return of ancestral bones; an issue which I found fascinating. In the States, The Smithsonian Institute has probably got about 20,000 Indian skeletons. Over the last hundred years, people dug them up and they live in a museum. So the idea is, this is somebody's family member, somebody's great-grandfather . . . And I believe that they have a right to make legitimate claims for those remains.

'Until very recently it was a felony to disturb a white person's grave, but not a felony to disturb an Indian's grave. That issue started me thinking, because I also believe in the mission of science and the mission to understand our world; I do think that's important. So the whole story came out of Doctor

Bilac: a character who is caught between these two worlds. In a way, he's like Mulder, who is on the one hand grounded in psychology and in law enforcement, and on the other, believes in these far-out things. I found that idea of inner conflict very interesting.'

'The Secona believe great evil will befall anyone who disturbs the remains of an Amaru, a woman shaman. That they will be devoured by the Jaguar Spirit'

MULDER

Teso Dos Bichos

Shiban began to read up on the traditions of South America's shamanic societies, where he found plentiful inspiration for the rest of the story, and developed an impressively authentic background.

'I did a lot of research,' he says, with wholly legitimate pride. 'And so did the art director and the costumers . . . the paint on the faces and the look of the costumes were actual things we pulled from real sources.'

Snowy weather and a distinct lack of jungle terrain in Vancouver, where *The X-Files* is filmed, meant that the story could not be set in the rainforests, as Shiban had hoped, but beyond this adjustment Shiban found that the rich and fantastical culture he was exploring left him little need for artistic license. 'The Amaru (woman shaman), the urn, the spirit of the shaman and the Jaguar Spirit are things that supposedly really exist in that culture,' he explains. 'And the whole Yaje ceremony was genuine. The "Vine of the Soul" is a real hallucinogen. And it's pretty wild. We even toned down some of it.'

'What is that?'

STUDENT ARCHAEOLOGIST MONA WUSTNER

'The Vine of the Soul'

DR BILAC

'Yaje? You're drinking Yaje?'

MONA

Teso Dos Bichos

In the rain forests of the Amazon and the Orinoco basins, in Columbia and in Ecuador, grows a species of large climbing vine which botanists call *Banisteriopis Caapi*. When its bark is boiled or soaked in water and combined with other natural ingredients, it produces what

An example of hallucinatory art by the Huichol Indians of Central Mexico. This picture depicts the dangerous path of initiation that every shaman-in-training must take

may be the most widely used and significant hallucinogenic substance in the world: Yaje or Ayahuasca – the 'Vine of the Soul'. In large doses, it effectively becomes what one psychopharmacologist has described as a 'chemical door' to another world.

In tribal societies, unlike western ones, hallucinogenic drugs are not regarded as a way to get your kicks or to take a mind-expanding trip just for the heck of it. They form the core of spiritual belief and ritual tradition and are sacred: as such, they are regarded with reverence. Yaje in particular demands this kind of approach.

Harvard ethnobotanist Wade Davis spent more than a year in the Amazon at the behest of Professor Richard Evans Schultes, a near-legend in the field and revered pioneer of psychopharmacology – the study of hallucinogenic substances. Before his departure, Davis asked Schultes for some tips. Davis recalls: 'He said "wear a pith helmet", because in 15 years he'd never lost his bifocals, "don't wear big boots because all the snakes bite at the neck", and "don't come back without trying Yaje".'

'Yaje is many things,' says Davis, 'but pleasant isn't one of them.' Even amongst more experienced users, the ingestion of Yaje is usually followed by one or more of the following: dizziness, sweating, convulsive shaking, nausea, elaborate vomiting, violent diarrhoea, mucous streaming from the nose, creeping terror and aggressive urges.

But what happens next is remarkable. The user is transported to a boundless and wondrous realm that he perceives as clearly as everyday reality.

It seems that his soul is released from the corporeal body so that he may freely explore without the need for physical movement. Here, he is able to see and communicate with his ancestors, with the gods, with animal spirits and with the first human beings. All knowledge is available to him; from an understanding of the universe and man's place in it, to the answers to specific puzzles.

A shaman will learn what ails a sick patient who has come to him, the identity of someone who has committed an unsolved crime, the whereabouts of a lost item, the location of game to be hunted or the solution to a problem within the community: he is even afforded glimpses into the future. A shaman's training allows him to control not only his own visions, but to conjure up specific visions for an apprentice, or for other members of the tribe partaking of Yaje at the same time.

'*What is it that the Secona Indians believe? That the spirit of a jaguar devours those who would despoil the burial place of a holy woman. Essentially, transmigration of the soul into animal form, achieved through a ceremony. Where they drink that Yaje to summon these spirits*'

MULDER

Teso Dos Bichos

A shaman may also, if he wishes, take advantage of his freedom from his mortal form to leap into the body of a beast or bird. It is this aspect that inspired Shiban to write the denouement of *Teso Dos Bichos*, in which it appears that the perpetrator of the attacks is not the Jaguar Spirit, but the spirit of the shaman, first entering the body of a jaguar, and then, back in the USA, a herd of cats.

A hag brings a light snack to the witches sabbath. Fortunately for babies everywhere, the flight and bacchanal took place only in the minds of witches, thanks to an ointment containing natural hallucinogens

The shaman is also able to fly. Not literally, of course – although the subjective experience is so convincing that it may as well be so.

Hallucinogenic flight is an ancient phenomenon, common to every culture, and is responsible for a potent image which endures today: the witch on her broomstick. During the Middle Ages and the Renaissance in Europe, witches were believed (and believed themselves) to be able to fly to strange and far off places for a night of dancing and wanton sex with demons.

The power of flight was achieved by the use of a magic ointment, containing natural substances such as Belladonna, rubbed liberally over the body. When the ointment entered the body through a wound on the skin, it induced hallucinations – and the witch was in flight. The uncertainty – what if there was no broken skin for the preparation to enter? – was overcome by applying the ointment internally. The taste prohibited oral use, leaving the witch with one alternative . . . which is where the broomstick (specifically its handle) comes into the story. Hence the popular image of a witch sitting on a broomstick; an image which has transmuted over the centuries into one more acceptable for illustration in children's stories.

'I spent the last six months living with the Secona. Learning from them. Coming to understand the nature and depth of their culture'

DR BILAC

Teso Dos Bichos

Transcendent experience is not the exclusive privilege of the shaman. In some communities, most people will imbibe Yaje, on all sorts of occasions, for a wide variety of purposes. It is often regarded as a great medicine, equally potent for physical and spiritual ailments. Its aggressive influence is useful to warriors, and hunters often take small quantities to enhance their instinctual ability and night-vision. (This latter effect is no mystery: Yaje dilates the pupils.) The highly skilled hunters of the Amahuaca tribe attribute their enhanced sensitivity to the spirit animals they see in Yaje visions, which enables them to study their quarry's movement and habits. The Tukanoans

The life-force represented as sun shining over a cornfield. The shaman, at upper left, is directing the force

use Yaje to communicate with their ancestors, and to explore the heavens. Documenting Richard Evans Schultes's studies with the Kofan tribe, Wade Davis writes: '(Yaje) is the source of wisdom itself, the ultimate medium of knowledge for the entire society. To drink Yaje is to learn. It is the medium by which each person acquires power and direct experience of the divine.'

'I've seen the Amaru. Coming out of the jungle, with the eyes of a scorpion, the claws of a jaguar. She leaps down from the trees. She tears at my flesh'

FROM DR BILAC'S JOURNAL

Teso Dos Bichos

Much of what its users experience under the influence of Yaje can be explained by cultural beliefs and potent subjective expectations. But there are several aspects which remain extremely peculiar.

Most hallucinogens induce visions (though few as powerfully 'real' as those induced by large doses of Yaje and other drugs from the same family). But the nature of those visions will vary dramatically from one person to the next. Yaje is different. Even amongst subjects who have not been exposed to South American cultural traditions, Yaje commonly induces visions of large felines, and of snakes. This fact has long intrigued psychologists, and remains unexplained. Some have suggested that these visions could be 'genetic memories'; primal 'fear cues' imprinted deep within the human genes and triggered by the drug.

Members of shamanic societies, on the other hand, have no doubt that these things are commonly seen simply because they are there – residing in the alternative dimension to which Yaje is a passport.

Native artists will frequently make paintings depicting their Yaje-induced experiences, and the commonality of visions is so marked that one ethnobotanist observed: 'Someone watching a man at work or finding a drawing would say: "This is what one sees after three cups of Yaje."'

The apparent collective nature of its visions also forms part of another strange aspect of Yaje use: the conviction – which again occurs cross-culturally – that one can experience the thoughts of others. When biochemists first isolated the compound now called harmine, in the Banisteriopsis vine, they dubbed it telepathine.

'The chemists heard that the shamans could conjure up animals in the forest for the initiates,' explains Wade Davis, 'and I don't really have any problem believing that they can do that.'

That an individual could project his thoughts in such a way that another could receive them is, under these particular circumstances, not as outrageous as it may sound. Many hallucinogens are known to induce varying degrees of synaesthesia: a clear mental sense-impression induced by the stimulation of another sense. In other words, the ability to 'hear' colours, or to 'taste' shapes or 'see' sounds. During a Yaje ritual, a shaman will often sing or chant. Through synaesthetic responses, others present may vividly see his utterances come to life.

Psychopharmacologists who have studied the drug dimethyltryptamine, or DMT (which is present in other plants used in making Yaje, and becomes orally active when combined with harmine), have logged numerous reports of 'visible languages' – the effective conveyance of thoughts, concepts and words through three-dimensional images.

Wade Davis has committed his fascinating investigations in the Amazon to paper in his latest book *One River*. When asked to describe his own experiences of Yaje, he retrieves a copy of his manuscript and reads an entire chapter of intoxicating prose. 'There's really no other way, no easy way to describe what Yaje is . . .' he apologises. 'It's not like taking LSD or other hallucinogens that people do recreationally these days. I don't use drugs, but I have in my work experimented on a few occasions with almost every conceivable hallucinogenic that comes from plants – because you can't work with shamans without doing so – and I've always found it very illuminating and not at all fearful. Whereas with Yaje, I think it is an awesome realm . . . When the Indians talk about facing down the jaguar they're not joking.'

'Exactly what kind of mushrooms are they?'
DR GRAGO, THE EXCELSIUS DEI PHYSICIAN
'From my prefecture, in my country. They have been used for centuries'
GUNG BITUEN
Excelsius Dei

There is evidence that early man believed that hallucinogenic plants and mushrooms themselves were divine gifts, and that supernatural forces resided within them.

In tribal societies, this belief endures. Pondering the origins of the strange psylocybin mushroom, Terence McKenna – psychopharmacologist, contemporary philosopher and outrageously provocative thinker – has updated the theory, suggesting that the mushroom may be some form of extra-terrestrial communication device which allows the people of the planet Earth to communicate with a higher intelligence. (Unfortunately, many of McKenna's ideas sound somewhat implausible when stripped of his dazzlingly eloquent arguments.)

Whatever their origin, it seems certain that hallucinogens act as triggers for perceptive experiences and abilities of which the human brain is already potentially capable.

Shamanic practice, for instance, does not rely solely on drugs: many shamans induce the altered mental state desired for their work simply by drumming. Prolonged repetitive rhythm disrupts the brain's circuits and results in a perceptive shift not too far removed from that induced by psychoactive substances. Adherents of other religions practice meditation, frenzied dancing or spells of isolation and sensory deprivation in order to transcend their everyday mental states. Many of the experiences and perceptions associated with hallucinogens like Yaje can also occur spontaneously, without external stimuli.

The pretty and deceptively innocuous-looking Banisteriopsis *vine*

> *'There are forces in this world we can't begin to comprehend'*
>
> MULDER
>
> *Teso Dos Bichos*

For a small number of people, synaesthesia is a permanent faculty, a range of 'additional' senses that they are born with. These are not mere individual quirks of perception. In studies of synaesthetites, as they are called, it was found that the sensory impressions were the same for all of them. The musical note B-flat, for example, always evokes the colour green, while A-sharp is experienced as yellow. Synaesthesia often runs in families, but researchers are some way from understanding exactly what is being passed on in the genes. One intriguing possibility is that synaesthesia is not some odd gift, but a universal human potential: it may be not so much that synaesthetites are born with an exceptional ability, but rather that they are born without whatever it is that blocks the ability in the rest of us.

Altered modes of consciousness also occur in various sleep-states. As we slip from wakefulness into sleep, we enter the Hypnogogic state, a mental no-man's land in which the most common experience is seeing geometric shapes and patterns. These are known as form constants and are a typical factor in the hallucinogenic drug experience, caused in both cases by the random firing of cells in the neural system – a natural result of disruption in the brain when the normal waking state begins to dissolve. Many people see fleeting images of faces or hear their name called out just before they fall asleep. Some hear random noises or snatches of music, conversation or poetry, and a few even report experiencing smells, usually flowers or food.

In the period between sleeping and becoming fully awake again the mind is in an equally unusual condition, known as the Hypnopompic state, and people who report precognitions – visions or 'waking dreams' which seem to predict future events – usually experience them whilst in this state.

Beyond the obvious fact that many hallucinogens bring a 'dream-like' quality to the world, many dreams include experiences typically associated with psychedelics, such as enhanced sensory perception, and some dreams even induce a feeling of ultimate wisdom, understanding and 'oneness' with the universe.

The phenomenon of drug-like dreams has been called 'high dreaming',

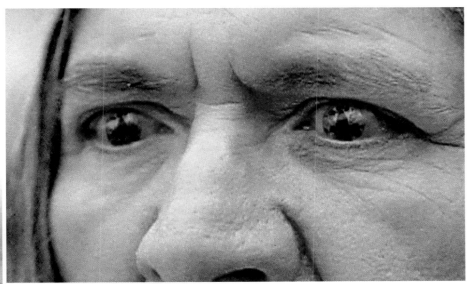

The shaman becomes at one with the jaguar, in Teso Dos Bichos

and was at first assumed to be limited to people who had at some time used psychoactive drugs – in other words, who were simply re-living their drug experiences in their dreams. Further research revealed a number of cases in which 'drug virgins' reported high dreams. Those who tried hallucinogens afterwards reported little difference between the two experiences – further supporting the notion that drugs do not 'give' experiences but simply trigger the potential that already exists within the mind.

It is common to write off both hallucinogenic experiences and dreams as somehow inferior to 'real' experiences. But others have suggested that these altered states are ones in which we are freed from our rigid ways of thinking, and in which we may therefore be capable of accessing all sorts of hidden abilities whose measure we have yet to understand.

Many anthropologists believe that the early use of hallucinogens was what introduced mankind to the concept of mystical experience, of spirit realms, of magical abilities and other-worldly knowledge. It is not out of the question that religion itself was born from the marriage of the human mind and the hallucinogen.

Others believe that natural hallucinogens played an even greater role. Terence McKenna has posited that the 'mind-expanding' nature of psychedelic experience may have been the key to our mental evolution: 'the light at the beginning of history that pushed the animal mind onto the human stage . . . The skeleton in the closet of human origin.'

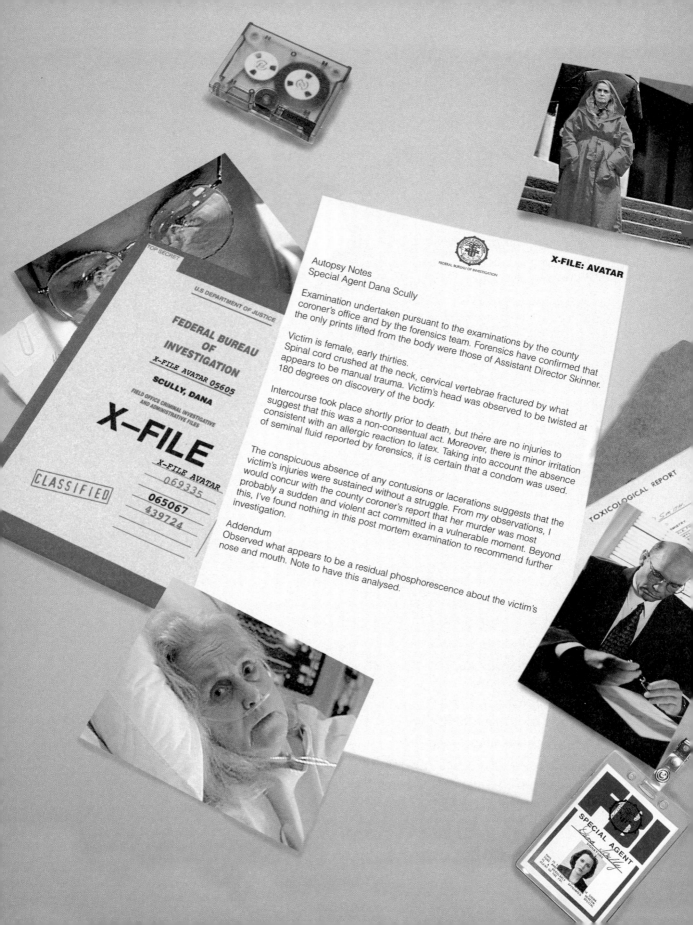

X-FILE: AVATAR

FEDERAL BUREAU OF INVESTIGATION

Autopsy Notes
Special Agent Dana Scully

Examination undertaken pursuant to the examinations by the county coroner's office and by the forensics team. Forensics have confirmed that the only prints lifted from the body were those of Assistant Director Skinner.

Victim is female, early thirties.
Spinal cord crushed at the neck, cervical vertebrae fractured by what appears to be manual trauma. Victim's head was observed to be twisted at 180 degrees on discovery of the body.

Intercourse took place shortly prior to death, but there are no injuries to suggest that this was a non-consentual act. Moreover, there is minor irritation consistent with an allergic reaction to latex. Taking into account the absence of seminal fluid reported by forensics, it is certain that a condom was used.

The conspicuous absence of any contusions or lacerations suggests that the victim's injuries were sustained without a struggle. From my observations, I would concur with the county coroner's report that her murder was most probably a sudden and violent act committed in a vulnerable moment. Beyond this, I've found nothing in this post mortem examination to recommend further investigation.

Addendum
Observed what appears to be a residual phosphorescence about the victim's nose and mouth. Note to have this analysed.

TOP SECRET

U.S. DEPARTMENT OF JUSTICE

FEDERAL BUREAU
OF
INVESTIGATION

X-FILE AVATAR 05605

SCULLY, DANA

FIELD OFFICE CRIMINAL INVESTIGATIVE
AND ADMINISTRATIVE FILES

X-FILE

X-FILE AVATAR
069335

CLASSIFIED

065067
439724

TOXICOLOGICAL REPORT

SPECIAL AGENT

PERCHANCE TO DREAM

*A*vatar plunges the Agents' supervisor, Assistant Director Skinner, into a living nightmare when, lonely and confused over his pending divorce, he has a one night stand with a woman he meets in a bar. Skinner dreams that his partner has become a gnarled old woman – an image which has been haunting him for some time – and wakes to find her dead beside him. Already in a state of emotional turmoil, his sleep persistently disturbed by nightmares, Skinner's torments are now compounded by a murder charge . . . and a nagging uncertainty as to who strangled the woman he bedded.

The episode arose from an idea suggested by *X-Files* star David Duchovny. 'He and I wrote the story together,' explains Howard Gordon. 'And it's interesting because it's sort of oblique . . . It's very different from anything we've done before because it's very elliptical: nothing is defined too neatly.'

A melancholy Walter Skinner wrestles over whether or not to sign his divorce papers in Avatar

Indeed, although we discover that Skinner is the victim of a set-up, the identity of the spectral old woman who haunts him remains teasingly obscure. For once, both Mulder's suggestion (that an amorous spirit-being may have become attached to Skinner) and Scully's rational counter-argument (that he is suffering from a rare sleep disorder) turn out to be incorrect.

'In fact it's a sort of manifestation of Skinner's own wife; the spirit of his wife reaching back and protecting him because he's being set up . . .' Gordon clarifies. 'So the spirit, we discover, is not an evil thing but a good thing; a benevolent thing who was in Vietnam with him 25 years ago, escorting him back from the light . . . when he had his out-of-body experience.'

The oblique nature of *Avatar* gives the episode a dream-like quality highly appropriate to its theme of nocturnal mysteries.

'I've always been interested in sleep and dreams . . .' says Gordon, who has researched the subject widely. 'I've read most of the articles in Scientific American and other journals and some assorted books on the stages and nature of sleep. And I've read a lot on the mysteries of sleep and dreams from Freud to Jung . . . Mythology, Chaucer . . . Whatever I've come upon.'

'The clinical term is REM sleep behaviour disorder. Although rare, dozens of cases of sleep-related violence have been related to it . . .'

SCULLY

Avatar

For a long time, sleep researchers denied that REM sleep behaviour disorder existed. It has always been accepted that people do things in their sleep, from simple walking and talking to preparing and eating substantial meals. (The latter is known as sleep-related eating disorder. Its sufferers, who are rarely habitual overeaters, are usually first alerted to their disorder by mysterious weight-gain and the baffling discovery that their fridge has been emptied overnight.) But as every sleep researcher knew, somnambulism took place only during dreamless sleep – once REM kicks in, the motor functions are paralysed.

But nature seldom makes rules without exceptions, and it was discovered that a very small number of people are *not* in fact paralysed during the REM stage – and they do 'act out' their dreams.

'So you think Skinner killed the victim in his sleep?'

MULDER

Avatar

Sleepwalkers and people who suffer from night terrors rarely injure others. More often, they accidentally injure themselves. Sufferers from REM sleep disorder are another matter. The cases on file are astonishing. A mother dreamed that her house was on fire and threw her children from

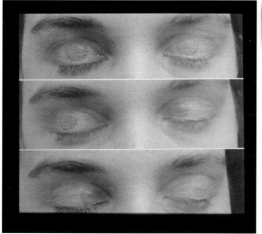

an upstairs window in the belief that she was saving them. A man bludgeoned his wife to death during a dream about a burglar. A 16-year-old girl from Kentucky had a nightmare in which her family were being murdered, but she had saved them by shooting the attackers. She woke to discover that she had retrieved both of her father's guns and frantically discharged them, injuring her mother and killing her father and six-year-old brother, who had got up to investigate the noise.

And in a case which reads like something out of a film script, a French police detective interrupted his seaside holiday to help the local law enforcement investigate the apparently motiveless shooting of a man on the beach close to where he was staying. He discovered footprints at the crime scene made by a man who had one toe missing . . . and it dawned on him in horror that, during one of his frequent, fitful, work-related dreams, he himself had been the killer.

It was cases like these which led Howard Gordon to look into REM sleep behaviour disorder. 'That these people are actually phsyicalising a response to their dreams . . . I just found that really interesting,' he muses, adding that although sleep-related violence is a genuine phenomenon, it is clearly subject to abuse as a legal defence. 'Now everyone's going to be saying, "I was asleep! I didn't know what I was doing!"'

Dr Meir Kryger, director of a prominent Sleep Disorder Clinic in Winnipeg, Canada agrees. Kryger believes, however, that in bona fide cases of sleep-related violence, the perpetrator is genuinely *not* responsible for his actions, and should be acquitted – though not returned to society until the sleep disorder has been successfully treated.

Psychiatrists and neurologists have found no evidence of mental illness underlying cases of sleep-related violence. Decent, stable people can and do unwittingly kill and injure people in their sleep – and sadly, the victims are usually those most dear to them.

'According to his psychiatrist, Skinner's been experiencing a recurring dream in which he's confronted by an old woman. Sometimes she straddles his chest, suffocating him . . .'

SCULLY

Avatar

'I'm not sure what it was that made me wake up. But right away I had this horrible feeling, just feeling really scared and like there was someone else in the room, and it was a few seconds after that that I realised I couldn't move . . . actually couldn't move at all. By then I was panicking, and at the same time I felt there was someone leaning right over me: not touching me at that point, but really close, looming. And I saw this face coming quickly out of the dark, just for a second; really horrible, ugly, old, and just . . . I can't really describe how frightened I was. And I realised I couldn't breathe properly, it felt like someone was pushing down really hard on my chest. And I was staring at my chest and it was like I couldn't believe that there was nothing on me, no one on me. I honestly couldn't breathe, I thought I was going to die . . . I'm not sure if the pushing on my chest stopped before I could suddenly move again, or afterwards.'

This account, strikingly similar to Skinner's experience but for the fact that the victim was awake, was related by David Musson, a 29-year-old architect from Croydon. According to Jerome Clark, one of the most meticulous and level-headed anomalists in the United States, 'There is reason to believe that one American in six has had this kind of experience; yet it is so little discussed in our culture that it has no name.'

Virtually identical accounts can be found stretching back throughout history and spanning the globe. Anomalists file them under the title *Old Hag* – a term coined in Newfoundland, where such experiences are commonly acknowledged and, in more superstitious eras, were thought to be the work of witches, or hags. In German-speaking countries, the phenomenon of Old Hag was known as *Mare* – the word from which our own 'nightmare' is derived.

Traces showing brain and muscle activity during the various stages of sleep

Sleep researchers recognise Old Hag as what is called Non-REM sleep paralysis. During REM sleep the body automatically de-activates the muscles as a safety measure. Without this function, we would thrash about, acting out whatever we dreamed we were doing (as do those suffering from REM Sleep Behaviour Disorder). Usually, muscle function is restored as soon as we wake up – but occasionally there is a delay. Often this will be so brief that we don't even notice it, but sometimes it lasts longer – a minute or so: time for the alarming realisation to dawn that you are awake but unable to move.

As for the crushing sensation on the chest, one theory points to the 'diving reflex' – an ability of aquatic mammals to slow down breathing and heartbeat in order to increase the amount of time that can be spent under water. It seems that humans too once had this function, and that remnants of it remain in our genetic code, not yet entirely atrophied by evolution. Working on this assumption, it has been suggested that the diving reflex can kick in during deep, dreamless sleep. Essentially, the body's life support system is being suppressed: Old Hag's crushing sensation and breathing difficulties – not to mention attendant feelings of fear and panic – may be similar to the effects which accompany cardiac arrest.

The diving reflex has also been mooted as a possible cause of sudden infant death syndrome (SIDS or cot-death), and as a trigger for the myoclonic jerk – the common experience of being sound asleep and then waking abruptly with a feeling of stumbling or landing after a fall. The latter is caused by a large electrical pulse sent to the muscles from the brain, and it has been suggested that this is a safety mechanism, jolting the body back into action if breathing and circulation become too slow.

Science has even offered a theory for the sense of presence in the room. Pioneering neurophysicist Michael Persinger explains that just as our sense of 'self', the awareness of who we are, is a function of the left half of the brain, 'so we argue that there must be something equivalent for most people on the *right* temporal parietal area. What would happen if we stimulate it?'

In his experiments, Persinger found that stimulating the right-brain gave his subjects a definite sensation of someone else being there in the room with them, uncomfortably close. 'The sense of the presence is the intrusion of the right hemispheric equivalent of the left hemispheric sense of self,' he explains. 'Usually it's quite aversive, very scary.

'Now, what enhances the capacity to have the sense of a presence is the amount of interactivity between the left and right hemispheres, so therefore anything that enhances that interconnectedness should increase the sense of a presence. You would expect that people who have had a traumatic brain injury where (the area separating the two hemispheres) has been sheared would have more of a sense of presence. And in fact over 80% of our clinical patients that have traumatic brain injury report a sense of a presence. They think they're going nuts, but in actual fact that's a normal process that takes place when the normal exclusion of right hemispheric input of this type is broken down because of the injury.

'The point is,' concludes Persinger, 'we have shown that the brain itself is doing it . . .'

So is Old Hag no more than a concoction of tricks that our brains and bodies play on us? If so, why do they all occur together? And how do we explain the remarkable consistency of the things that are seen, especially since the witches and demons for whom Old Hag was named are no longer an everyday part of the popular imagination. As yet, those questions remain unanswered – and largely ignored. In his book, *The Terror That Comes in the*

Night, behavioural scientist David Hufford expresses bafflement at the lack of serious attention given to Old Hag. After all, he points out, Old Hag is 'an experience with stable contents which is widespread, dramatic, realistic and bizarre', and one that has been reported 'by large numbers of our fellow humans.'

'It's not such a strange story . . . It's age old, actually. You may have heard it – although in slightly less clinical terms. In the Middle Ages, a visitation like the one Skinner described would have been attributed to a Succubus. A spirit that visits men during the night in the form of an old woman'

MULDER

'Visits them for sex?'

SCULLY

'Usually'

MULDER

Avatar

The legend of the Succubus and her male equivalent, the Incubus, is undoubtedly related to the Old Hag experience. These amorous but malevolent spirits were said to make nocturnal visits to people's bedrooms, mount the victim's chest – commonly inducing a crushing sensation – and then have intercourse with him or her.

A succubus surprises her unsuspecting victim

Moreover, the term 'Incubus Nightmare' began to be applied to Old Hag experiences and is still used occasionally today.

So were incubi and succubi imaginary beings? Were they nightmares which followed disturbing Old Hag experiences? Or were they merely a convenient medieval label for unusually vivid sexual dreams? Now and again, the odd report of succubus activity still surfaces. Authors Colin and Damon Wilson succeeded in tracking down a few, including one from psychologist Stan

Gooch. Gooch called his nocturnal 'visitor' a succubus, but noted that, in appearance, she was a combination of several women he knew. Whilst insistent that he was awake, not dreaming, during the encounter, Gooch was prepared to accept the idea that, in some unspecified way, the presence he perceived as a physical one had come from his own psyche.

In his own book, Gooch cites cases of people who, under hypnosis, are able to touch, as well as see and hear, things that the hypnotist suggests. Certainly induced hallucinations are not limited to the visual and the auditory. Most of us have seen those stage acts where a hypnotist persuades someone that an onion is a delicious apple. Tactile hallucinations can exist, and it is not out of the question that they might, on rare occasions, occur spontaneously.

There again, it is not impossible that succubi and incubi are the products of the sleeping mind. Absurd as it may sound, it is not always easy to distinguish dreams from reality, and for good reason: there is in fact very little difference between the two experiences.

Technically, our conscious, everyday experience is simply a reality that we construct for ourselves from the firing of neurons in our brains. All our sensory input – everything we see, hear, or touch – is processed by the brain. In some sense, everything we experience is subjective. Our dreams are constructed in exactly the same manner, only without the sensory input. By most criteria, at least, they are no less 'real'.

Demons were often blamed for the chest-crushing sensations associated with the peculiar Old Hag syndrome

Innovative sleep researcher Steven LaBerge has done a great deal of work illustrating this point. One series of his experiments demonstrated that the responses displayed by the brain and body when we perform activities in our dreams – anything from solving maths problems to making love – are little different to the physiological and neural responses we have to those activities when we perform them physically.

A Stanford-trained scientist who completed a university degree in mathematics at the age of 18, LaBerge has found himself hailed as something of a new-age guru in recent years, thanks to his ongoing study of a phenomenon in which the ultimate blurring of the boundary between dream and reality takes place: lucid dreaming.

A lucid dream is one in which the dreamer is fully aware, in a state of waking consciousness, and able to do as he pleases. The only valid difference between a lucid dream and reality is that the dream environment is weirder and more wonderful, and the dreamer is able to achieve the physically impossible (such as flying). And unlike the real world, nothing you do during during a lucid dream is subject to any repercussions – no matter what you get up to, you know you're going to start with a clean slate next time.

Not surprisingly, lucid dreams are extremely enjoyable.

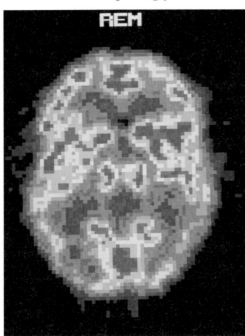

A Positron Emission Tomography (PET) scan of a brain during dream-filled REM sleep shows cerebral activity similar to that observed in the waking brain

'They're wonderful!' enthuses Howard Gordon, who has had a few. 'The erotic ones are my favourites,' he admits playfully, relishing the notion of an encounter entirely without consequences, 'sort of like, sex-lite, infidelity-lite!'

Like LaBerge, Gordon questions mankind's confidence in separating the 'real' from the imagined. 'Ultimately . . . does the fact that it's a dream make it any less real? To what extent is it not? It *feels* real. You haven't exchanged fluids with someone, but you've had that experience with them. It's a very interesting area.'

The term 'lucid dreaming' was first coined in 1913 by Dutch psychiatrist Frederik van Eeden, but accounts of the phenomenon date back to Aristotle. In most surveys, more than half the respondents report having had a lucid dream at least once and around 10% have them regularly.

For some time, it was believed that lucid dreams occurred during 'micro awakening episodes' – the tiny periods of wakefulness that most people experience around five times a night and usually don't recall the next morning. In other words, a 'lucid dream' is actually more like a daydream, perhaps running on from a real dream, except that you're so groggy from sleep that you're not aware you're awake. This suited traditional sleep researchers, who insisted that if you are aware, you can't be dreaming, and that a lucid dream is, by definition, a paradox.

LaBerge started by proving that lucid dreaming is a genuine phenomenon.

Under controlled conditions, he and other subjects were able to communicate to the outside world (using complex, pre-arranged eye-movement signals), confirming that they were conscious and aware, while machines monitoring their body functions confirmed that they were in the REM stage of sleep.

LaBerge believes that lucid dreaming has many positive benefits, and that within a lucid dream, freed from the waking state which, he feels, constrains our mental abilities, we can achieve all sorts of useful personal goals. Most are remarkably similar to traditional shamanic skills – resolving dilemmas, addressing health problems, obtaining creative inspiration and gaining better understanding of ourselves, our fellow man, and the universe. LaBerge also points out that lucid dreaming is wonderful entertainment, likening it to virtual reality, as generated by 'the best computer you can get – your brain.'

However eccentric this may sound, we should not be tempted to dismiss it out of hand. The *Skeptical Inquirer* (the quarterly journal of CSICOP – the Committee for the Scientific Investigation of Claims of the Paranormal), which takes no prisoners in its mission against pseudo-science looked into LaBerge's work in 1992, and pronounced his methods suitably scrupulous, remarking that it 'forces us to ask questions about the nature of consciousness . . . and the nature of imaginary worlds.'

> *'It seems no one will believe her story'*
> SCULLY
> *'Why's that?'*
> MULDER
> *'Because she claims to have been raped by an invisible entity.
> A spirit being'*
> SCULLY
> *Excelsius Dei*

In their research into incubi and succubi, Colin and Damon Wilson found a number of claims of unwelcome and violent visitations like the one experienced by nurse Michelle Charters in *Excelsius Dei*.

One which echoes *Excelsius Dei*'s ethereal intruder (and, coincidentally, *Teso Dos Bichos*' warning that sacred artifacts are best left alone) is the report of a young American woman named only as Marcia. A university graduate with a masters degree in psychology, Marcia, on holiday in Sao Paulo, was sufficiently unsuperstitious to pocket a small plaster effigy of the sea goddess

Yamanja which had clearly been left on the beach as a ritual offering – despite her religious aunt's warning to leave it be.

Not long afterwards, Marcia became ill, and narrowly escaped injury in two domestic accidents: the explosion of a pressure cooker and later an oven. But Marcia's most bizarre claim is that, whilst lying in bed one night, she sensed a presence in the room, followed by the clear physical sensation that someone or something climbed onto the bed and raped her. Marcia claimed that these noctural attacks continued until her aunt consulted an expert in Umbanda (a faith similar to Voodoo) and returned the statue to the beach.

> **'Observed what appears to be a residual phosphorescence about the victim's nose and mouth. Note to have this analysed'**
>
> SCULLY'S AUTOPSY NOTES

Avatar

Michelle Charters' injuries convinced even Scully that the attack on her was not a figment of her imagination. And in *Avatar* it seemed that Skinner's elderly spirit visitor may have left some proof of her existence in the form of the mysterious phosphorescent substance that Scully found on the dead woman's body. Such physical evidence is almost always lacking from 'real' cases.

One exception was a bizarre spate of nocturnal attacks which took place in 1985 on girls in a small boarding school in Rietfontein, Botswana. The girls reported that vicious male and female entities tore their clothes, cut off their hair and scratched them – and they had the injuries to prove it.

Medical examinations ordered by the police revealed needles deeply embedded beneath the scratch marks on the victims' legs. But despite investigations (and continuing attacks), the police were unable to find a culprit or an explanation, returning the open-minded but somewhat inconclusive verdict that the case was supernatural.

Here, the subject of nocturnal

Skinner catches a disturbing daylight glimpse of his nocturnal visitor in Avatar visitations begins to cross over with alleged cases of poltergeist activity – the cause of which is still a matter of much debate. Most believe that 'intrusions' of this kind – usually involving a lot of noise, and furniture and crockery flying around, and occasionally mild injuries – are unlikely to be the work of spirits. Rather, it has been suggested that somehow the person who is the focus of the disturbance is causing it to manifest. Certainly many such episodes have come to an end when the 'victim' undergoes psychotherapy.

In the case of Romanian teenager Eleanora Zugun, researchers observed what appeared to be scratches and bites

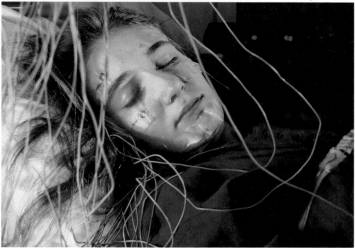

appearing spontaneously on her face and arms. However, this would only occur when Eleanora felt defensive about things that other people had done or said – which was often. The 'attacks' stopped as she grew older and less neurotic.

It is well known that the majority of 'focuses' in poltergeist cases are adolescents, and many researchers have suggested a link between the manifestations and repressed sexual tension. The victims in three of the best known poltergeist cases were all found to have passionate crushes on famous people (the sisters in the famous Enfield case were obsessed with TV cops Starsky and Hutch), prompting theorists to wonder whether large concentrations of unreleased emotional energy could somehow be discharged in bizarre ways that we don't yet understand.

The same theory could conceivably account for alleged visits from incubi and succubi. With maturity, the ability to keep sexual tensions under control increases. But in all sleep states (bar lucid dreaming) a certain degree of emotional control is lost.

Understanding the sleeping human mind could be the key to solving any number of mysteries. For there is no doubt that simply by closing our eyes we enter a realm that is, by definition, paranormal.

Electrode-connecting wires festoon the head of a sleeping subject at the Henri Mondor Hospital sleep research unit, in Creteil, France. Monitoring the brain and muscle activity of sleepers helps us to understand the physiological processes of sleeping, but the secrets of the sleeping mind remain fiendishly enigmatic

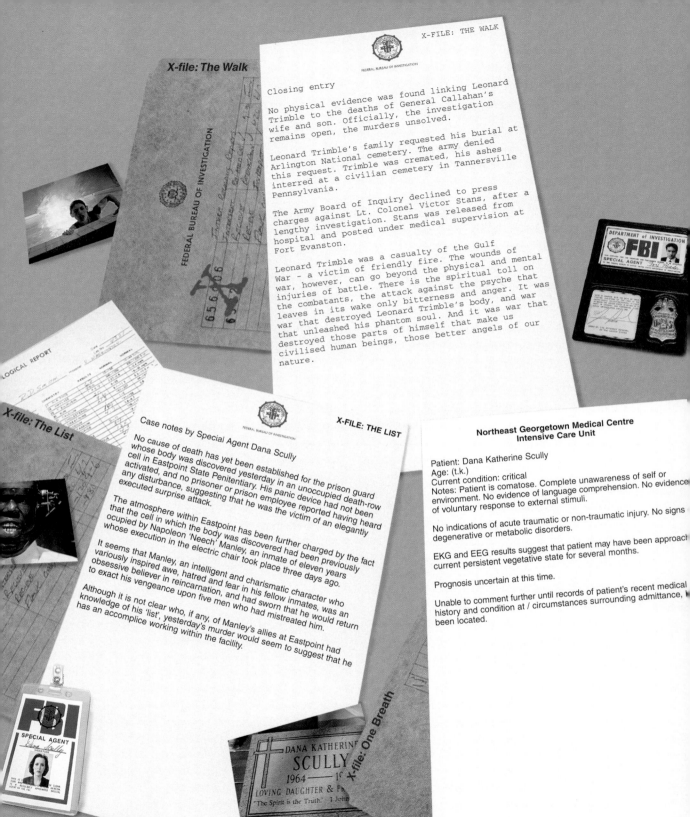

X-file: The Walk

X-FILE: THE WALK

FEDERAL BUREAU OF INVESTIGATION

Closing entry

No physical evidence was found linking Leonard Trimble to the deaths of General Callahan's wife and son. Officially, the investigation remains open, the murders unsolved.

Leonard Trimble's family requested his burial at Arlington National cemetery. The army denied this request. Trimble was cremated, his ashes interred at a civilian cemetery in Tannersville Pennsylvania.

The Army Board of Inquiry declined to press charges against Lt. Colonel Victor Stans, after a lengthy investigation. Stans was released from hospital and posted under medical supervision at Fort Evanston.

Leonard Trimble was a casualty of the Gulf War - a victim of friendly fire. The wounds of war, however, can go beyond the physical and mental injuries of battle. There is the spiritual toll on the combatants, the attack against the psyche that leaves in its wake only bitterness and anger. It was war that destroyed Leonard Trimble's body, and war that unleashed his phantom soul. And it was war that destroyed those parts of himself that make us civilised human beings, those better angels of our nature.

DEPARTMENT of INVESTIGATION
FBI
SPECIAL AGENT

X-file: The List

X-FILE: THE LIST

FEDERAL BUREAU OF INVESTIGATION

Case notes by Special Agent Dana Scully

No cause of death has yet been established for the prison guard whose body was discovered yesterday in an unoccupied death-row cell in Eastpoint State Penitentiary. His panic device had not been activated, and no prisoner or prison employee reported having heard any disturbance, suggesting that he was the victim of an elegantly executed surprise attack.

The atmosphere within Eastpoint has been further charged by the fact that the cell in which the body was discovered had been previously occupied by Napoleon 'Neech' Manley, an inmate of eleven years whose execution in the electric chair took place three days ago.

It seems that Manley, an intelligent and charismatic character who variously inspired awe, hatred and fear in his fellow inmates, was an obsessive believer in reincarnation, and had sworn that he would return to exact his vengeance upon five men who had mistreated him.

Although it is not clear who, if any, of Manley's allies at Eastpoint had knowledge of his 'list', yesterday's murder would seem to suggest that he has an accomplice working within the facility.

FBI
SPECIAL AGENT
Dana Scully

DANA KATHERINE
SCULLY
1964 —
LOVING DAUGHTER & F
"The Spirit is the Truth." 1 John
X-file: One Breath

Northeast Georgetown Medical Centre
Intensive Care Unit

Patient: Dana Katherine Scully
Age: (t.k.)
Current condition: critical
Notes: Patient is comatose. Complete unawareness of self or environment. No evidence of language comprehension. No evidence of voluntary response to external stimuli.

No indications of acute traumatic or non-traumatic injury. No signs of degenerative or metabolic disorders.

EKG and EEG results suggest that patient may have been approach current persistent vegetative state for several months.

Prognosis uncertain at this time.

Unable to comment further until records of patient's recent medical history and condition at / circumstances surrounding admittance, been located.

BETWEEN TWO WORLDS

L earning that a patient at a military hospital is being tormented by a 'phantom soldier', the Agents begin the terrifying investigation that is *The Walk* – the first episode by new *X-Files* recruit John Shiban, and one with few rivals for good old-fashioned hide-behind-a-cushion scariness.

Shiban conceived the idea after watching *The Men*, in which Marlon Brando played a paraplegic World War II veteran. 'It just occurred to me that if I were in a wheelchair, the one thing I would

Rappo, in astral form, prepares to attack an unsuspecting victim

want to do is walk. Its the one thing you can't have. And out of imagining that frustration came the idea: *well, what if he could get out of his body?*

'Then I brought in Gulf War Syndrome and all those issues; all the bitterness. Rappo – the guy with no arms and legs – really wanted people to look at the world like he sees it. What was interesting to me was that here's a guy who's a bad guy, but you can't help but feel sorry for him.'

Rappo overcomes his immobility by astral projection, leaving his material body behind in order to wreak his revenge in disembodied form. Shiban dreamed up this unusual M.O. by expanding on the well-known phenomenon of Out-Of-Body-Experience (OBE).

'I knew a couple of people who had told me stories about it. One of them was my wife. She told me that when she was a teenager, she was very sick and she wanted to talk to her sister, but she couldn't even reach out to touch the phone. Then suddenly she felt she was there, in her sister's bedroom, and it was very creepy. She told me she assumed it was a dream or something. But then her sister called her, and said: *Are you okay? Because I thought you were here.* She had woken up and thought for a minute that my wife was in the room.'

OBEs are surprisingly common. Surveys have found that a quarter of respondents have had at least one. They can happen under unpleasant circumstances like illness, pain, stress, trauma or fear; or during altered states of consciousness created by hypnosis, meditation or drugs (one survey of marijuana users found that 44% had had an OBE). And they frequently occur during more natural altered states – those just before, after and during sleep.

'I came down here wondering if it could be true. That what Lieutenant Colonel Stans was describing was a case of astral projection'

MULDER

The Walk

Some people enjoy their spontaneous OBE so much that they strive to have more. This deliberate sneaking out of the body has been recorded since history began, but came to be known as Astral Projection after the publication at the turn of the century of *Practical Astral Travel*, a book by Frenchman Marcel Louis Forhan, who called himself Yram.

Astral travellers claim to defy the laws of physics with impunity – speeds, distances and solid objects pose no obstacle to their adventures. Yram himself reported that his travels included visits to the home of a woman he eventually married. Later Yram and his wife would travel together, and even claimed to have out-of-body sex.

Robert Monroe, a former broadcasting executive, set up an OBE study centre named The Monroe Institute for Applied Sciences in Richmond, Virginia. Like Yram, Monroe was no poster-boy for objective science. He claimed that, whilst out of his body, he often bumped into other astral travellers (he too had astral sex), met strange entities, visited a parallel universe and once accidentally re-entered a corpse instead of his body.

'Every major religion, every culture has got some sort of out-of-body experience,' John Shiban reflects, 'whether it's shamans or astral projectors. So you start to wonder: *well, maybe there is some logic to it*. Then you read something that makes you think: *uh-oh* . . . On the World Wide Web there's an astral projection page, and you start reading people's methods of how to do it . . . people would put their little tips on there. One guy ate high-protein foods. Someone else would watch a certain TV show . . . It was very amusing.' Shiban found one astral projector who used postcards and letters as a kind of homing device – which provided him with the inspiration for Rappo's technique.

The most extensive study of OBEs has been carried out by highly-respected British parapsychologist Dr Susan Blackmore. 'We don't understand them,' she says. 'But they might not be paranormal.

'There's no doubt that lots of people have the experience of lying in bed at night, floating up to the ceiling, looking down . . . They can see everything, they fly around town, they visit their friends or whatever, then they come back. Or they may even see spiritual beings. I don't doubt those experiences for a minute because I've had them myself and I've talked to countless people who've had them. But the paranormal bit would be if they really could see accurately out-of-body, and all the evidence I have suggests that they can't.'

Dr Blackmore was determined to give her subjects every opportunity. 'When people say: "I can't do astral projection in your lab, I can only do it at home in bed", my answer was to say: Fine, okay, I will put a target somewhere of your choosing, and you go astral projecting whenever you like, and then come back and tell me what that thing is . . .

'I recently tested a guy who makes fantastic claims, and he was very cooperative and helpful. We ran a series of experiments for six weeks with objects in my house. There were twelve objects and he got two out of twelve right. You'd expect one by chance. Not very good. He was very nice and said "Oh well, I've failed . . . but I can predict bombings, you know."'

The fact is that no matter how an astral travel experiment is constructed, it *never* yields positive results. One oft-cited experiment involved a female college student who, whilst wired up to a brain monitor and other equipment in bed at home, successfully read the number 25132 which was placed on a high shelf behind her. What you don't often read is that the result was invalidated when it was realised that the subject could have seen the number reflected in her clock. There was no evidence that she *had* done this, but it meant that the experiment was flawed.

Nor would a successful experiment necessarily prove that the subject had been out-of-body. It might just as well be said to prove ESP or clairvoyance. Indeed, people who study and practise what they call 'Remote Viewing' make essentially the same claims as astral travellers: that they are able to 'project' to designated targets. All that's missing is the astral body.

(Remote Viewing itself forms an uncommonly fruitful corner of psychical research. The PEAR laboratory at Princeton University, for instance, has had some very consistent results, and, beginning in the 1970s, the US Government funded research into it under the auspices of the CIA, who hoped to put it to use for espionage.)

'Practitioners claim that during a self-hypnotic trance the astral body can detach itself and travel virtually anywhere, sometimes invisible, sometimes appearing as an apparition. They even claim the astral body has psychokinetic abilities'

MULDER

The Walk

The one other factor that, if proved, could demonstrate that astral projectors are genuinely out-of-body is the claim that the astral body can be sensed, seen or can affect its surroundings.

An artistic rendering of the non-physical body within the astral plains

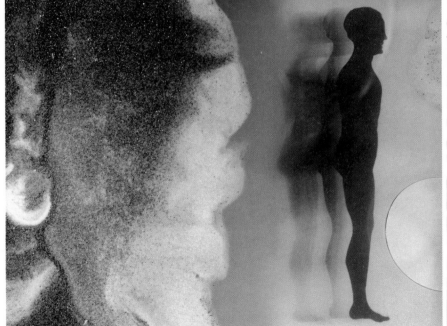

Fortunately, no one has even attempted the out-of-body feats achieved by *The Walk's* Rappo. But Robert Monroe claims to have travelled to see a woman friend while she was talking to two other women, and pinched her on the waist. He reported that later, when he asked the woman what she had been doing at the time of his visit, she told him that, yes, she had been talking to her friends, but she had not sensed Monroe's presence. However, according to Monroe, his friend then showed him a mark on her waist, and reported that she had thought at the time that her brother-in-law had snuck up and pinched her.

But in science, anecdotal evidence counts for nothing. And under controlled conditions, no astral traveller has ever been able to affect his surroundings. Professor Robert Morris tried an experiment where his subject, Keith Harary, would project into a building half a mile away and try to affect two kittens whose behaviour was being precisely monitored. Although the experiment is often reported in books as a success, Dr Morris himself reported in the journal of the American Society for Psychical Research that there had been no significant results. A similar experiment with a snake was more exciting – the snake was said to have suddenly reared up and bitten at the side of its enclosure – but the result failed to replicate on subsequent attempts.

Dr Blackmore feels that no amount of lab-test failures will convince everyone who has had an OBE that they did not leave their body. 'I think it's because the experience itself is so compelling, you're so convinced in your own mind that you are out of the body, that you're just not interested in science. The only explanation people can think of is that they got out of their body and then left.'

Dr Blackmore's own theory is that the human mind is able to construct different viewpoints of reality and, given an appropriate trigger, may shift from our regular viewpoint to another – one which gives us the impression that we are floating and looking down. What we see is a constructed image of what we know or imagine to be there.' She cites the experience of one man 'who said he always believed he really astrally travelled, until one night he looked down on the bed, and saw every little detail as usual, studied the colour and the pattern on his pillows and duvet . . . and then when he woke up in the morning he realised that his wife had changed the pillow cases the night before, and they were different. He'd seen the ones that he *thought* were there.'

Dr Blackmore can understand why many people are not persuaded. 'In order to understand that explanation, you have to have gone a little way into thinking about your own consciousness, and you have to be prepared to let go of the common sense idea that you are a little person inside your head pulling the strings. Now that view is very natural, that you are running your body. But science shows that you are not. The brain is doing it itself. But if you can't take on board that first step then it doesn't sound like a very good explanation. I can't blame people for not accepting it.'

And *The X-Files'* John Shiban offers another reason why so many are reluctant to give up on their ideas about the OBE: 'It is tied in with life

Keith Harary, the subject of numerous scientific studies of astral projection

after death, because if there is a spirit that can exist outside the body, it leads you naturally to the idea that the deterioration of your body needn't mean the end. And that's a universal desire.'

'I told you once what happened to me in Vietnam. That I was caught in an ambush'

SKINNER

'You were the only survivor. You also described having what sounded like a near death experience'

MULDER

Avatar

More suggestive still of life after death is the Near Death Experience (NDE). The term came into popular usage after the 1975 publication of *Life after Life*, in which author Raymond Moody brought the phenomenon to public attention.

The typical NDE involves some of the following experiences: a sense of stillness, or being 'dead'; an OBE during which the experiencer sees his own body and watches, with a feeling of detachment, people fussing around it; cessation of pain and distress; feelings of peace and even extreme joy; a journey through a dark tunnel towards a warm, bright light; meeting dead relatives and friends; encountering a 'being of light', sometimes personified by a stranger, an angel or Jesus; a 'life review', during which the experiencer sees scenes from his past; glimpsing an indescribably beautiful landscape, sometimes inhabited by happy, welcoming people and accompanied by exquisite scents and music; and finally, either being told or realising that it is not yet time to die, and a return to life must be made, perhaps for some specific purpose (for the sake of children or other needy relatives; to complete some task).

According to a 1982 Gallup Poll, eight million Americans have had an NDE. Perhaps it is not surprising, then, that in *The X-Files* universe, Scully, Mulder *and* Assistant Director Skinner are all among that number.

> *'Mulder, when they found me, when the doctors, even my family, had given up, I experienced something I never told you about. Even now, it's hard to find the words. But one thing I'm certain of, as certain as I am of this life: we have nothing to fear when it's over'*

SCULLY

Dod Kalm

Scully was certainly affected by her experience in the typical manner. In nearly every case, an NDE leaves the experiencer profoundly changed. They no longer fear death – some even look forward to it – and yet they have an increased appreciation of the value and importance of life.

> *'Her soul is here. Dana's choosing whether to remain . . . or move on'*

MELISSA SCULLY

One Breath

In the poignant *One Breath*, we find Scully in limbo between life and death, and trespass in her mind as she lies comatose. Here she is visited by her late father, whose profoundly touching words encourage her to fight on.

Although most NDEs take place in a matter of minutes, there are accounts of patients who, like Scully, recover from the coma state with extended memories of time spent in a strange mental no-man's-land. Mulder's experience in *The Blessing Way* also seems to fall within this category. As he fights for his life under the care of Navajo elder Albert Hosteen, he too is visited by those who care for him and who have passed on: his ally, Deep Throat and his own father.

'Dana, honey . . . I'm here to take care of you sweetheart. To watch over you. To help you find the way home. I know you are far from home tonight. And that where you are is peaceful. It would be nice to stay . . .
but your time is not over'

NURSE OWENS

One Breath

In common with the classic NDE, however, Scully is guided by a gentle and benevolent stranger – Nurse Owens, whom Scully at first erroneously believes to be a real nurse – intruding on her consciousness from the outside world.

It seems to make perfect sense that a woman such as Scully, who puts her faith in science and medicine, would meet an otherworldly nurse. The ethereal figures encountered during an NDE are usually wholly appropriate to the experiencer. Devout Christians often meet Jesus, children tend to see pretty Christmas-tree-type angels and atheists encounter anonymous-looking guides whom they perceive as being profoundly good and kind and wise (although biblical-style clothing is frequently mentioned – perhaps because it brings to mind those qualities, regardless of religious belief. Flowing robes and sandals are common, and one NDE experiencer has described a guide wearing 'a blue blanket thing'.)

*'During my fever . . . I left here and
travelled to a place –'*
MULDER
*'– this place, you carry it with you. It is inside you.
It is the origin place'*
HOSTEEN
'It wasn't a dream?'
MULDER
'Yes'
HOSTEEN
The Blessing Way

Like Albert Hosteen's reply to Mulder's question, the real-life puzzle of the NDE is open to interpretation. Let's look at what might be going on . . . The strongest argument for a literal interpretation of the NDE would be if some of the experiencers really had 'come back from the dead'. But death is, by definition, irreversible. Doctors tend to agree that if someone 'comes back' after being declared dead, they could not have been clinically dead in the first place. Even in the absence of vital signs of life, the body can be in the process of winding down. Forty minutes after the heart stops

beating, electricity can still be detected in it. According to Dr Julius Korem, a Professor of Neurology at the New York University School of Medicine, 'the "moment of death" is a fiction'.

The NDE could still be interpreted as telling us what it is like to approach death's door. But this leaves room for other explanations besides a literal journey towards the beyond. Neurologists have suggested, for instance, that an NDE could be a side-effect of disrupted brain function. Computer simulations have even shown that a tunnel with a light at the end of it is exactly the image created by faulty neuron transmissions.

Other scientists believe that the NDE could be a natural trick of the mind which kicks in as the body approaches death; a peaceful, reassuring experience we create for ourselves to reduce the trauma of dying.

But if the human mind did have such a capacity built in, it would seem remarkable that it should include a function allowing it to go smoothly into

reverse – an image of someone telling you that your time has not come, for instance. Opponents of this theory also wonder how on earth such a function would have evolved in the first place. Easing the passage towards death serves no obvious purpose. Mental functions that helped us to deal with, say, bereavement or with the pain of childbirth would, arguably, be much more useful – yet we do not have them.

But let us imagine for a moment that this theory is the right one. Psychiatrists Bruce Grayson and Nancy Evans Bush have collected numerous accounts of *unpleasant* NDEs, ranging from feelings of discomfort, fear and unhappiness, to hellish landscapes peopled by terrifying entities, to dreadful voids and a sense of eternal nothingness. Where do these fit in to the picture?

(And for those who are tempted to suggest that the two kinds of NDE support the classic notions of heaven and hell, there is nothing to indicate that those who experienced bad NDEs were deserving of eternal damnation. Those who judge suicide a sin are out of luck, too – failed suicides are accompanied by good NDEs, bad NDEs and no NDEs at all.)

All the theories which assume that the NDE is a preview of what happens at the point of death face a major problem in the fact that not everyone who comes close to death has an NDE. Moreover, no element of the NDE is unique to the near-death state. OBEs happen spontaneously to perfectly healthy people. The 'life-review' is so common in situations of peril that the phrase 'my life flashed before me' has become a cliché. Other elements of the NDE can occur in religious visions, lucid dreams and hallucinogenic trips. Many people have also had classic NDEs in circumstances when they are not actually in danger of death – during non-life-threatening illnesses or after narrowly escaping an accident, for instance.

And while NDEs are similar enough from person to person for the phenomenon to be recognisable and intriguing, they may not be similar enough to support the weight of these hypotheses. Dr Peter Fenwick, President of the International Association for Near Death Studies points out that no two NDEs are exactly alike. There are elements which appear frequently in one culture and are completely absent from another. Japanese experiencers, for instance, often report seeing a wide river, and in India many NDEs involve a rather bizarre scenario in which the experiencer is told that there has been a clerical error, and in fact there is someone else by the same name who is supposed to die today instead.

These discrepancies lead to suggestions that the NDE is an artifact of cultural conditioning. But how, then, do we account for the NDEs of young children with no prior knowledge or expectation of the phenomenon? There are plenty of them, and they differ little from those of adults. British investigator Jenny Randles met a five-year-old boy who woke from an operation asking: 'Mummy, why wouldn't the doctors speak to me when I was floating up by the ceiling?', and in the US, researchers met Ricki Enriquez, a two-year-old girl from a non-religious family, who recalled a beautiful angel looking after her before she made a miraculous recovery from a coma.

Hallucinations triggered by oxygen deprivation or anaesthetic have been suggested as one possible cause of the NDE. But many people who have NDEs are *not* deprived of oxygen, nor under anaesthetic. And, conversely, many who are do not have NDEs.

Those who oppose the all-in-the-mind theory often cite cases in which NDE experiencers are able to recall things that it seems impossible for them to have experienced – details of operations performed under anaesthetic, conversations held by relatives or by emergency workers whilst the experiencer was unconscious.

Author Martin S. Caidin interviewed a Florida man named William Larson, the victim of a motorcycle accident in June of 1987, who awoke in Cape Canaveral Hospital to be told that he had been without vital signs before being resuscitated by paramedics.

Larson remembered seeing his body lying on the road, and listening to those around him. When a witness to the accident – a stranger – visited to see how he was, Larson recalled hearing the man tell one of the paramedics that his own son had died in an accident a year and a half earlier. The man was astounded by Larson's memory, since Larson had not been breathing, let alone conscious, at the time.

Larson recognised other people from the scene, and correctly recalled the names of two whom he heard talking to one another. One was a paramedic who confirmed that Larson's heart had stopped.

But even cases like these cannot be said to prove that our consciousness is capable of leaving the body. They may equally be said to suggest that we can gather sensory input even when our brain is unable to process it, and store it in some kind of 'back-up' memory bank.

There *are* a number of frequently-cited cases in which people have seen things they couldn't have seen even if they had been conscious. But as Dr Peter Fenwick remarks in his book, *The Truth in the Light*, 'Nearly always, when [these cases] are examined in detail, it proves hard to substantiate the claims that are made. One of these has become so well known that it is often quoted to "prove" that information really can be acquired by someone who is out of his or her body.'

In this case, a woman named Maria recovered from a cardiac arrest in a Seattle hospital and described an NDE during which she floated out of the window. Whilst aloft she saw an old tennis shoe hidden on the corner of a high window ledge, out of the range of normal sight. The shoe was discovered to be where she had 'seen' it, and to match Maria's detailed description.

'The only problem,' notes Dr Fenwick, 'is that no one who has tried to follow up this story has ever actually been able to find this particular woman and talk to her. So we still have to regard it as hearsay rather than hard fact.'

Most paranormal subjects are fiendishly hard to get to the bottom of, but the NDE may well be the hardest of all. The subject is impossible for experts to study first hand, because no one can have an NDE on demand. NDEs undoubtedly happen, but for now, they remain stubbornly inexplicable.

'Allah said the spirit shall rise again and be reborn in this life. The Soul shall be recast, borne unto new flesh'
NAPOLEON 'NEECH' MANLEY
The List

One of the few paranormal beliefs that can rival the NDE for sheer emotional investment is reincarnation, or the transmigration of the soul (see *The X-Files Book of the Unexplained* Volume One.)

First addressed on *The X-Files* in season one's *Born Again*, Chris Carter tackled it from a different angle in season three's *The List*, which he wrote and directed. An unsettling and powerful episode, brimming with horrors both visceral and psychological, *The List* introduces Mulder and Scully to Napoleon 'Neech' Manley, a charismatic and erudite death-row prisoner who vows that his execution will not prevent him from wreaking vengeance on five men who have mistreated him. And Manley keeps his promise.

'I had been reading an article about death row,' Carter recalls, 'and the fact that belief in reincarnation on death row is almost absolute, for obvious reasons. So I was very interested in the idea that if you *believe* you could be reincarnated, and if you had been so mistreated, what would you be reincarnated as? And so I expanded it, and found ways to tell a story that I was interested in both as a writer and as a director.'

'You think he's back, don't you?'
MULDER
'Y'know, I think if anyone could come back, it'd be Neech'
DANIELLE MANLEY
The List

'I'd like to meet someone who could make me think they could come back,' muses Carter, 'and I'd like to think that people can come back. I'd like to see my Mom and my Dad again, so I think this is some sort of semi-conscious hope that there is a chance that you can make it back.'

Carter has read a great deal about reincarnation and other phenomena suggestive of some kind of afterlife. And he is intrigued by the single, crucial question that links them, the one raised by *all* the subjects in this chapter: is the human consciousness – our personality, the part of us that is thinking and wondering right now – something separate from the human body? Or, more poetically: *is there such thing as a 'soul'?*

'I give thought to it a lot,' says Carter 'and I think the deeper experiences you have in life – whether they be tragedy, happiness, fear, pain, all these things that tend to transform you or just transcend everyday existence – make you believe the idea that there might be psychic energy that would be transferable or transmutable. If you've ever been in a battle of emotional turmoil in your life, or a desperate situation of any type, I think you start to realise that there are levels of existence and experience, and energies that seem as if they almost exist outside of you, separately. I'm not doing a very good job of explaining, and I don't understand it . . . but I have sensed something outside of myself.'

The nature of the soul has been debated by theologians since time immemorial, but within this decade it has also become one of the hottest subjects of scientific debate. Either there is such thing as a soul, or whatever we choose to name the intangible life-force for which our bodies would be a mere vessel; or there is not, and consciousness – our sense of identity, our delights and sorrows, our loves and hates, our hopes and fears – is no more than a peculiar product of the machine that is the human brain.

Francis Crick, who co-discovered the double-helix structure of DNA (for which he received a Nobel Prize) outlines the latter theory, the reductionist argument, in *The Astonishing Hypothesis: The Scientific Search for the Soul*. Crick admits that we are a long way from understanding how the brain works, but predicts that we will eventually learn enough to discover exactly what it is that gives us a sense of free will and awareness; enough to dismiss the idea of a mind or soul separate from the brain. 'I myself find it difficult at times to avoid the idea of the homunculus – a little man in our head directing it all. One slips into it so easily,' he told *Omni* magazine, adding that 'as Lewis Carroll's Alice might have phrased it, "You're nothing but a pack of neurons."'

As Scully lies comatose in One Breath, *she perceives herself in a series of strange environments in which she is guided by a kindly stranger and visited by her late father*

'Duane Barry was shot in the line of duty, the bullet piercing the bilateral frontal lobes . . . A hundred years ago there was a famous case – a man named Gage had a blasting rod pierce the same region. He became a pathological liar . . . His behavior was characterized as bizarre and violent.'

SCULLY
Duane Barry

Some support is provided for the reductionist argument by cases in which people undergo bizarre personality changes after sustaining damage to the brain: cases like the one cited by Scully in *Duane Barry* – which, incidentally, is genuine.

Francis Crick has studied many such cases himself, including one in which a woman appeared temporarily to lose her 'free will'. She understood perfectly what people said to her but could not communicate with them because her mind felt 'empty', and she had nothing to say. The damaged region of her brain, the *anterior cingulate sulcus* is also associated, Crick points out, with 'alien hand syndrome' – a state in which a patient has no control over the actions of one of his hands, which appears to act in a controlled manner of its own volition.

But Crick admits that study of such cases will only take us so far, since accidental brain damage is rarely specific enough to help teach us which areas serve which functions. 'If we could make nicely controlled brain damage on people, we could find out how the brain works,' he notes, 'but we're not allowed to do that – quite rightly.'

Not all scientists agree with the reductionist argument. Many are dualists, who believe instead in the 'ghost in the machine' – some intangible spark that makes us more than just organic robots.

And if the reductionist view of consciousness sounds depressing, it is heartening to consider that even if it is correct, there may still be a route to immortality. If all that we are and all that we experience is created by, and stored within, the squishy computer we call the brain, there is no reason, according to many scientists, why we should not one day be able to download every last byte of data into an *actual* computer. And no reason why, in this state, we should not continue to be just as alive and aware as we are right now. And since all that we experience is processed by the brain, there is no reason why, with a few adds-ons to receive input, we could not

Nobel Prize-winner Francis Crick – a highly vocal proponent of the reductionist argument who believes that continued study of the brain will lead us to discover that what we perceive as consciousness and free will are merely the products of electrical activity in the infinitely complex biological machine that is the human brain

continue to see, hear, feel, smell and taste things just as we do now.

According to science writers Frederik Pohl and Hans Moravec, 'If the mind-transplant procedure can be done at all, as seems at least theoretically plausible, it is at least a good gambling bet that something like it will be real within the next few computer generations.' At a rough estimate, that's fifty-odd years.

Outside of the scientific community, most people (besides those with a robust faith in a religion) are resigned to the fact that the soul remains a mystery.

'I was raised Catholic and I was raised to believe that this body is just a temple for something else,' says *The X-Files'* John Shiban. 'Then I went to school, I took science – I wanted to be an astronomer at one point in my life – and you become grounded. You think: *that can't be true*. But part of me instinctively feels that it must be true, that there must be more. Part of me says: I can't believe that just the corporeal parts of my body can feel all these things, can do these things, can . . . come up with an *X-File* ! There must be something else. But I can't put my finger on it. I can't say: it *is* an astral body, or it *is* a soul.'

And for as long as the soul remains a mystery, so too will we continue to ponder all the phenomena that seem to hint at clues. Muses Chris Carter, 'Anybody who is a deep thinker has had things happen that rattle them, or things that seem to defy rational explanation. I just think that that's where the mysteries lie: in the mind. An all-encompassing idea of the mind, that is, because in fact the mind could be the spirit, the soul, the intelligence, God; all those things.'

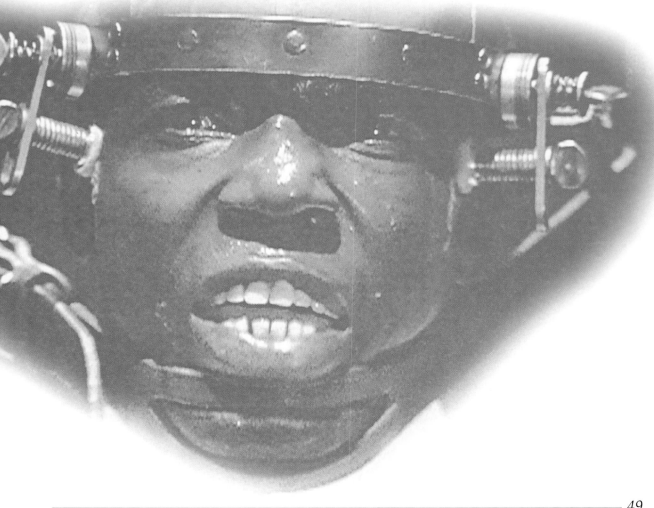

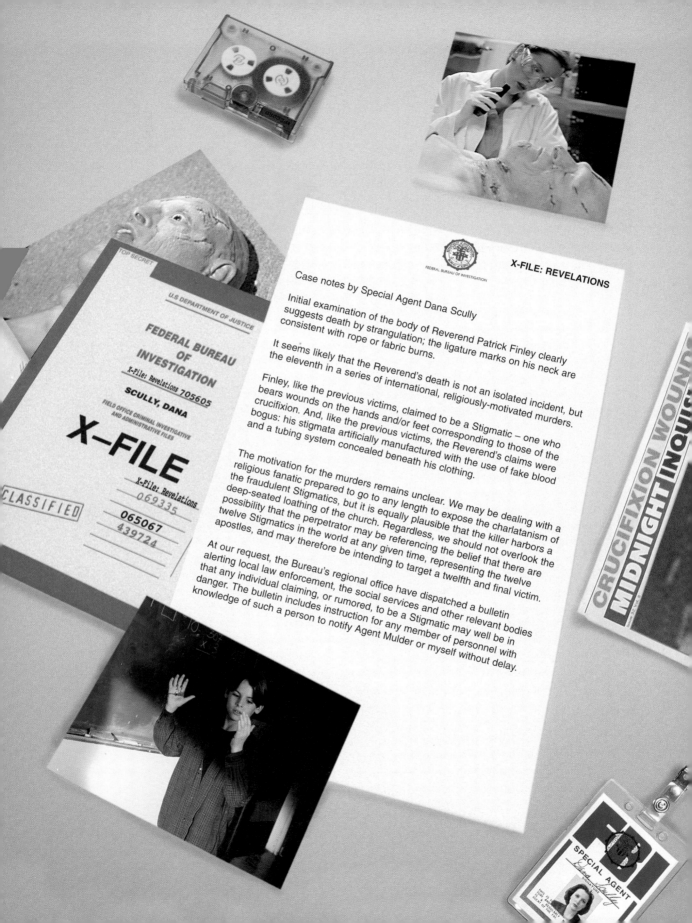

X-FILE: REVELATIONS

Case notes by Special Agent Dana Scully

Initial examination of the body of Reverend Patrick Finley clearly suggests death by strangulation; the ligature marks on his neck are consistent with rope or fabric burns.

It seems likely that the Reverend's death is not an isolated incident, but the eleventh in a series of international, religiously-motivated murders.

Finley, like the previous victims, claimed to be a Stigmatic – one who bears wounds on the hands and/or feet corresponding to those of the crucifixion. And, like the previous victims, the Reverend's claims were bogus: his stigmata artificially manufactured with the use of fake blood and a tubing system concealed beneath his clothing.

The motivation for the murders remains unclear. We may be dealing with a religious fanatic prepared to go to any length to expose the charlatanism of the fraudulent Stigmatics, but it is equally plausible that the killer harbors a deep-seated loathing of the church. Regardless, we should not overlook the possibility that the perpetrator may be referencing the belief that there are twelve Stigmatics in the world at any given time, representing the twelve apostles, and may therefore be intending to target a twelfth and final victim.

At our request, the Bureau's regional office have dispatched a bulletin alerting local law enforcement, the social services and other relevant bodies that any individual claiming, or rumored, to be a Stigmatic may be in danger. The bulletin includes instruction for any member of personnel with knowledge of such a person to notify Agent Mulder or myself without delay.

TOP SECRET

U.S. DEPARTMENT OF JUSTICE

FEDERAL BUREAU OF INVESTIGATION

X-File: Revelations 705605

SCULLY, DANA

FIELD OFFICE CRIMINAL INVESTIGATIVE AND ADMINISTRATIVE FILES

X-FILE

X-File: Revelations

069335

065067

439724

CLASSIFIED

FEDERAL BUREAU OF INVESTIGATION

CRUCIFIXION WOUND

MIDNIGHT INQUIS

SPECIAL AGENT

MIRACULOUS WOUNDS

Following the death of a somewhat theatrical preacher, Mulder and Scully must hunt down a murderer who is targeting stigmatics, and protect Kevin Kryder, the little boy who looks likely to be the next victim. The miraculous and mysterious events that take place in the episode *Revelations*, the strange pronouncements made both by Kevin's devout father and by family friend Owen Jarvis, force Scully to ponder her religious upbringing and re-evaluate her own beliefs.

'His parishioners said the Reverend Finley's hands were
bleeding. Like the wounds of the crucifixion . . .'

MULDER

'Stigmata?'

SCULLY

'A sign from God bestowed on the righteous'

MULDER

Revelations

In the thirteenth century one Brother Leo, a contemporary of Saint Francis of Assisi, announced that a strange event, a 'great joy . . . even a new miracle' had come to pass.

'From the beginning of ages there has not been heard so great a wonder, save only in the Son of God . . . For, a long while before his death, our Father and Brother [St Francis] appeared crucified, bearing on his body the five wounds which are verily the stigmata of Christ. For his hands and feet had, as it were, piercing made by nails fixed in from above and below, which laid open the scars and had the black appearance of nails; while his side appeared to have been lanced, and blood often trickled therefrom.'

St. Francis of Assisi

Francis of Assisi (1181/2–1226) was the first reported stigmatic and was, in the words of stigmata expert Ian Wilson, 'what might be popularly described as an oddball.'

Born into a well-off family, Francis at first led the typical life of a boisterous young rake. He caroused and frolicked and, as young men do, chose to let off steam in a small local war alongside some of his friends. Unfortunately for Francis he found himself on the wrong side in the skirmish, was arrested and thrown in jail.

When he was released a few months later, he was a changed man. He was frequently ill, possibly with recurrent malaria. But, stranger still, he had begun to be . . . well, saintly. He heard unearthly voices, visited lepers, and gave away the clothes off his back.

For his father, Pietro Bernadone, a rich cloth merchant, the final straw came when Francis sold some expensive bolts of cloth and gave the money to an impoverished priest to rebuild a ruined church. Francis said that Christ had told him to do it. Pietro was so furious that he called Francis to account in front of the local religious leader, Bishop Guido. In 1206, before an assembled throng, Francis returned the money to his father. Then he stripped himself naked, abandoned his fancy clothes in the street and officially renounced his father Pietro in favour of Our Father, who art in Heaven. From that day on, Francis led a life of extreme austerity.

In 1224, whilst fasting and praying on Monte Alvernia, Francis saw a vision of the crucified Christ. Soon, what we now consider to be classic stigmatic wounds appeared on his body: one in each palm, one on each foot, and one in his side. They caused Francis considerable pain and embarrassment and they stayed with him until he died. A miracle? A hoax? Subsequent studies of stigmata suggest that it was neither.

'But I see no wounds here, on his hands or otherwise'
SCULLY
'No, I think this is a case of too much faith . . .
(Mulder dips his finger in the Reverend's blood and tastes it)
and too much sugar . . . It's a fake'
MULDER

Revelations

There have unquestionably been many fake stigmatics over the years. Some have been motivated by a desire for fame, religious status or money. Some have been mentally ill. A number of hoaxers have been shown to be severely masochistic and would indulge in bouts of violent self-flagellation. Others were eventually convicted of fraud.

Not every case, however, has been so easy to debunk. Every era likes to believe itself more sophisticated than the last. The twentieth-century sceptic will say, 'if I'd been around in the time of St Francis, *I* could have proven him a charlatan . . .' But the fact is that *every* age has had its intelligent, inquisitive investigators. And some have been very thorough.

Padre Pio

In 1875, Dr Warlomont encased the right arm of 25-year-old Belgian stigmatic Louise Lateau in a glass cylinder. The cylinder was angled so that nothing could be poked inside it to inflict injury, and just to make certain, Warlomont sealed it with wax. Nevertheless, Louise bled from a puncture in her palm, just as she did every Friday.

Nor has the Roman Catholic Church been all that keen to acknowledge the authenticity of stigmatics. The most famous stigmatic of this century, the Italian priest Padre Pio (1887–1968), was visited by Papal investigators and forbidden to deliver mass or receive confession. The Vatican also tried to have him removed from his monastery, until local villagers threatened to take up arms to defend him. Eventually, under public pressure, the Church gave in and Padre Pio was allowed to perform one mass a day, at 5 a.m., and to hear confession. So many people attended his confessional that the queue to be heard sometimes lasted for days.

If stigmatics are closely examined both by the scientists of the age and by the Church itself, and if some are exposed as a result, why aren't they all debunked? Perhaps because some in fact do bleed spontaneously from wounds that resemble those of the Biblical Christ.

In many ways St Francis was the archetypal stigmatic. Many of the components we see in his case recur throughout the most convincing instances of stigmatisation. For example, a history of severe physical and emotional stress: the same sort of stress that is known to cause multiple personality disorder.

Stigmatic Georgio Bongiovanni (below and right) bleeding profusely at his home near Ancona, Italy, in 1993. Bongiovanni developed his stigmata after a visit to Fatima and has delighted the members of his vast cult following by oozing copiously on a daily basis ever since. He is noted for his additional interest in UFOs, and claims to have had numerous visions in which Jesus and the Blessed Virgin Mary show up in flying saucers.

'Isn't a saint or a holy person just another term for someone abnormal?'

SCULLY

Revelations

Francis was deeply affected by his time in prison (a common circumstance for religious conversions) and afterwards never fully regained his health. Louise Lateau was gored by a bull when she was eleven. Later she almost died of angina, and was frequently unwell. Padre Pio was similarly often ill. All three saw visions, conversed with invisible spirits and would pass out from the intensity of their religious ecstasies.

Stigmatics also share a tendency to writhe uncontrollably and to speak in tongues. The vast majority are women, and most bleed on a day of specific religious importance, such as Fridays, or Lent. This is not normal behaviour, even by the standards of religious fanaticism. In the words of Ian Wilson, 'many stigmatics have been known more for their neuroses than their sanctity.'

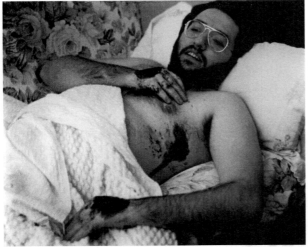

'I've been watching you, Kevin. You're a very special boy'

OWEN JARVIS

Revelations

What we are dealing with, in fact, is extremely suggestive and imaginative people: the same sort of people who are highly susceptible to hypnosis.

According to Dr Michael Persinger, a behavioural neurologist at Laurentian University, the spontaneous appearance of a wound without physical injury is not impossible – particularly under hypnosis. 'If you take the individuals that have the greatest creativity, which means the same population of people who are prone to religious conversions, and you suggest to them that the metal you just placed on their hands ... is hot and burning, you can induce reactive erythema (reddening and/or blistering of the skin) and the actual infiltration of cells. If you put that together with the powerful effects of suggestibility, then you can see why stigmata would be a predictable phenomenon.'

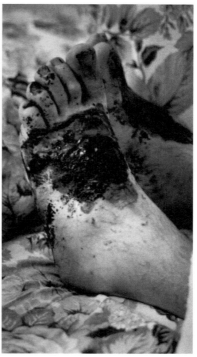

Those who react the strongest to the burning metal test, writes Ian Wilson, 'fascinatingly, turn out to be of the ... highly stressed type common among stigmatics and multiple personality sufferers. According to a study by psychologist Gordon Paul of the University of Illinois, those who have genuinely exhibited the blister reaction have included a victim of shell shock, a student who had a sleep-walking problem, a man who suffered hysterical blindness as a result of wartime experiences, [and] several women specifically labelled hysterics.'

'He's bleeding again, isn't he?'
MICHAEL KRYDER
(KEVIN'S FATHER)

Revelations

'The releasing of fluid is not unique to stigmata,' says Dr Persinger. 'Some people who dissociate very often will show other kinds of lesion. When epileptics seizure at night, even without massive movement ... they will often end up with erythemic responses and rending of the skin.'

Persinger suggests that many anomalous experiences are mediated by the same kind of brain activity, and that marks on the skin which have been attributed to encounters with demons or with evil aliens may in fact be a natural consequence of seizures.

'It's a normal feature of certain kinds of seizure activity to influence the vascularity (of tissue containing veins and blood vessels). "Demon's marks" were commonly referred to in the pursuit of witchcraft. Remember "looking at Satan's marks"? They were looking for the prick marks. There was a whole group of people that were called Common Prickers, who went around specialising in finding these marks.'

Hypnotism goes even further in unravelling the mystery of stigmata. Liverpool hypnotherapist Joe Keeton regressed one of his patients, Pauline McKay of Ellesmere Port, to a 'past life'. McKay announced that she was a Devon woman named Kitty Jay, who had hanged herself. Those who were present during the hypnosis session say that, as McKay re-lived Kitty's suicide, they saw a livid red mark, not unlike a rope-burn, appear on her neck.

> *'It's because I'm different isn't it?*
> *Why can't I just be*
> *like everyone else?'*
>
> KEVIN KRYDER
>
> *Revelations*

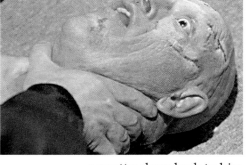

The murder of Owen Jarvis raises as many questions as it answers in Revelations

So if we accept that our stigmatics are psychologically fragile, suggestible people, mentally re-enacting Christ's torments, rather than those perceived as part of their own past lives, what triggers them? And why were there no recorded stigmatics in the eleven hundred years of Christianity before St Francis?

The answer seems to lie in the radical shift in the way the Passion of Christ was portrayed in art. Until the medieval period Christ on the cross had a pretty clean look to him. There was little blood. He was clothed. There was no apparent pain.

The thirteenth century saw a new realism in religious art. Christ on the cross was torn, bleeding, suffering. The crucifix that inspired the young Francis to donate his wealth to restore the old church was particularly gruesome, as was the one he was praying in front of when his stigmata first materialised.

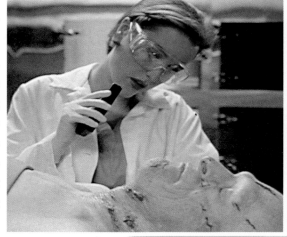

*'The sun shall be turned to darkness,
and the moon into blood'*
THE 'MILLENNIUM MAN'
(THE INDIVIDUAL RESPONSIBLE FOR THE MURDERS)
Revelations

At a time when self-flagellation and self-mutilation were not uncommon means of penance, meditating at length on all this divine agony may have been just the trigger needed. And St Francis was by no means the only stigmatic of the thirteenth century. He may not even have been the first. When a wall fell on the Blessed Dodo of Hascha in 1231, killing him, it was discovered that he had open wounds in his hands, feet and sides. How long he had had them, no one knew. He had simply been too humble to draw attention to them while he was alive.

The link between art and stigmata is reinforced by the fact that stigmatics tend to emulate the wounds of their favourite crucifix. If it shows Christ lanced on the left side, they have a wound on the left, and vice versa. And in spite of all the punctured palms and feet both in Christian art and on stigmatics, the truth is that the Romans would have driven the nails through Christ's wrists and ankles. Interestingly, as contemporary religious art starts to incorporate this historical detail, new stigmatics are showing wounds on their wrists and ankles.

This may also explain why other religions have no comparable phenomenon to stigmata. If a suitably suggestible person becomes a Buddhist, their spiritual energies are not devoted to contemplating and, more importantly, identifying with images of pain and violent death.

Stigmatic types will always exist, waiting for something to engage their imagination and their passion. But in our increasingly secular world, where visits from angels are being supplanted by visits from aliens, perhaps a new generation, inspired instead by our ever-increasing abduction lore, will be showing miraculous wounds in the shape of microchip implants.

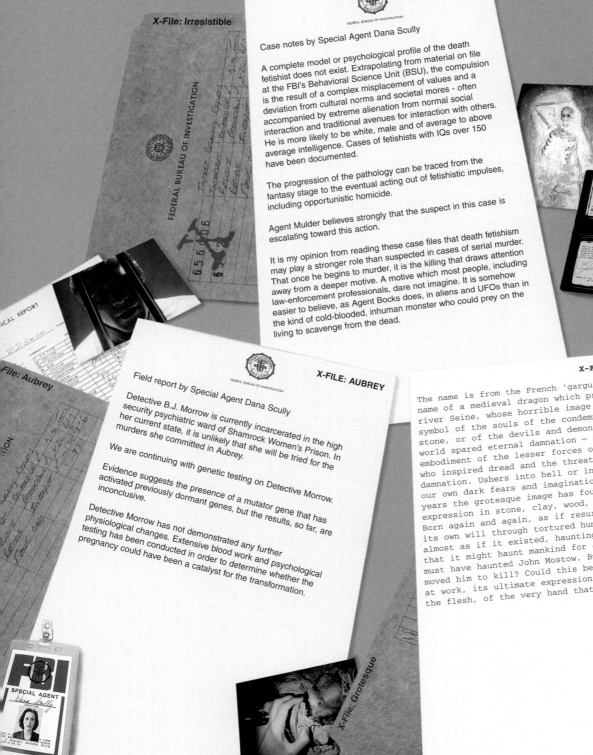

FEDERAL BUREAU OF INVESTIGATION

656906

X-FILE: IRRESISTIBLE

FEDERAL BUREAU OF INVESTIGATION

Case notes by Special Agent Dana Scully

A complete model or psychological profile of the death fetishist does not exist. Extrapolating from material on file at the FBI's Behavioral Science Unit (BSU), the compulsion is the result of a complex misplacement of values and a deviation from cultural norms and societal mores - often accompanied by extreme alienation from normal social interaction and traditional avenues for interaction with others. He is more likely to be white, male and of average to above average intelligence. Cases of fetishists with IQs over 150 have been documented.

The progression of the pathology can be traced from the fantasy stage to the eventual acting out of fetishistic impulses, including opportunistic homicide.

Agent Mulder believes strongly that the suspect in this case is escalating toward this action.

It is my opinion from reading these case files that death fetishism may play a stronger role than suspected in cases of serial murder. That once he begins to murder, it is the killing that draws attention away from a deeper motive. A motive which most people, including law-enforcement professionals, dare not imagine. It is somehow easier to believe, as Agent Bocks does, in aliens and UFOs than in the kind of cold-blooded, inhuman monster who could prey on the living to scavenge from the dead.

DEPARTMENT of INVESTIGATION

FBI

SPECIAL AGENT

MEDICAL REPORT

File: Aubrey

X-FILE: AUBREY

FEDERAL BUREAU OF INVESTIGATION

Field report by Special Agent Dana Scully

Detective B.J. Morrow is currently incarcerated in the high security psychiatric ward of Shamrock Women's Prison. In her current state, it is unlikely that she will be tried for the murders she committed in Aubrey.

We are continuing with genetic testing on Detective Morrow.

Evidence suggests the presence of a mutator gene that has activated previously dormant genes, but the results, so far, are inconclusive.

Detective Morrow has not demonstrated any further physiological changes. Extensive blood work and psychological testing has been conducted in order to determine whether the pregnancy could have been a catalyst for the transformation.

X-FILE: GROTESQUE

The name is from the French 'garguille' - the name of a medieval dragon which prowled the river Seine, whose horrible image became the symbol of the souls of the condemned turned to stone, or of the devils and demons of the under world spared eternal damnation — the embodiment of the lesser forces of the universe who inspired dread and the threat of our own damnation. Ushers into hell or into the realm of our own dark fears and imagination. For over 1200 years the grotesque image has found its expression in stone, clay, wood, oil and charcoal. Born again and again, as if resurrecting itself by its own will through tortured human expression; almost as if it existed, haunting men inwardly so that it might haunt mankind for eternity, as it must have haunted John Mostow. But what impulses moved him to kill? Could this be the same dark fo[r] at work, its ultimate expression the destruction [of] the flesh, of the very hand that creates it?

FBI

SPECIAL AGENT

X-File: Grotesque

LOOKING INTO THE ABYSS

Ask any *X-Files* fan which episodes they have found the most unsettling, and they're likely to mention those which see the Agents pitting their wits not against aliens, mutants or spirits, but against the sheer force of evil which can exist in human beings.

Think about *Aubrey*'s disturbed police officer, B.J. Morrow, her dreams haunted by flashes of the word 'sister' slashed deep into women's chests, unaware that she is perpetrating the crimes herself. Think about *Irresistible*'s Donnie Pfaster, a mild-mannered loner whose secret vice and driving passion is necrophilia. Or *Grotesque*'s John Mostow, who carves his victim's faces after the image of the gargoyles which obsess him; and Bill Patterson, the equally obsessive senior FBI profiler, dizzy from years of dancing with evil, who unconsciously takes up where Mostow left off. These villains are unassuming. But beneath their surface normality lies evil so palpable that it is almost alive, autonomous, charging the episodes with a powerful undercurrent of malevolence and horror.

Aubrey's B.J. Morrow - victim or villain?

'I wanted to do an episode that dealt with what really scared Scully,' says Chris Carter, speaking of his motivation for writing the unspeakably disturbing *Irresistible*. 'And I thought that what really scares Scully is not the paranormal, but something that is actually quite banal and normal, tangible: the idea that the man standing next to you in the supermarket line or at the post office is as frightening as anything. There's a line in *Irresistible* that I think is quite telling: that people would rather believe in aliens than in the idea that these things really exist. That was interesting to me, too.'

The monsters among us are all too real. In the chillingly succinct words of multiple murderer Ted Bundy: 'We serial killers are your sons, we are your husbands, we are everywhere. And there will be more of your children dead tomorrow.'

The label 'serial killer' is a recent invention (coined by FBI veteran Robert Ressler, of whom more later). The phenomenon itself is not. The first recorded case of serial murder dates back to the fifth century, when, over a period of several years, a well-bred man named Zu Shenatir lured an unspecified number of young boys from the streets of Aden into his home. Shenatir raped his victims and killed them by throwing them from a high upstairs window. His reign of terror ended only when he was stabbed to death by an intended victim.

Scully finds herself at the mercy of the despicable Donny Pfaster in Irresistible

Not enough data exists to allow fair comparison between previous eras and this one. But in the last few years of this century, in America at least, it seems that the instance of serial murder has escalated dramatically. The United States, with around 6% of the world's population, spawns more than three quarters of all serial killers, and records confirm a staggering increase. Between 1900 and 1959, each year would produce, on average, 1.7 new cases. Through the 1960s, the figure grew to five a year, and by 1980 it had tripled. By 1990, it was 36 per year – which averages out to three a month, and represents a rise of 940% in the space of just three decades. The FBI have estimated that, by the millennium, serial murders could be claiming an average of 11 lives *a day*.

The Federal Bureau of Investigation has not waged war on this epidemic unarmed. But for all its sophisticated forensic technologies, its most effective weapon may well be its human resources, in the form of the Behavioral Science Unit.

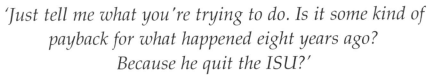

'Just tell me what you're trying to do. Is it some kind of payback for what happened eight years ago? Because he quit the ISU?'

SCULLY

'My motivations aren't that petty . . . I asked for Mulder because I want to close the book on this godforsaken case once and for all'

BEHAVIORAL SCIENCE VETERAN BILL PATTERSON

Grotesque

The Behavioral Science Investigative Support Unit plays an important role in *The X-Files* universe. It was here that Mulder began his career with the Bureau, putting his acute instincts and Oxford University psychology degree to good use as a criminal profiler. Many episodes have referred back to this successful period in Mulder's life, but *Grotesque* goes deeper still when it introduces Bill Patterson, Mulder's rather abrasive mentor.

Howard Gordon reveals that he based the character of Patterson on FBI profiler John Douglas, after reading Douglas's book *Mindhunter'*. The guy who ghost-wrote it, Mark Alshaker, is the cousin of a friend of mine. I had a preview copy, and that was the inspiration. My biggest insight was what a regular guy (Douglas) is. He's a family man, married, with kids: but he *is* haunted, he has nightmares, and he did have a breakdown . . .'

Gordon's interest in psychological profiling and serial murder was established some years before *The X-Files* when he read *Whoever Fights Monsters*, by pioneering FBI profiler Robert Ressler.

Ressler's book takes its title from Friedrich Nietzsche's *Thus Spake Zarathustra* – the same quote that inspired Gordon to write Mulder's concluding speech in *Grotesque*:

'Whoever fights monsters should see to it that in the process he does not become a monster. And when you look into an abyss, the abyss also looks into you.'

Criminal profiling is the art of studying a murder in order to build up a psychological profile of the murderer. With the right data a skilled 'mindhunter' (as the profilers are often called) can take a highly-educated guess at the personal history, even the attitude and appearance, of the most likely suspect. As Robert Ressler puts it, 'What plus why equals who'. The 'hits' are often preternaturally accurate – in one famous case, the profile even included an accurate prediction of what the suspect would be wearing.

FBI profilers also assist local authorities in assessing suspects who have been detained, and preparing evidence for pending court cases. Their work is so valuable that it is hard to imagine the FBI without them. But without the ingenuity and skill of a handful of men, the Behavioral Science Unit would not exist. One of those men is Robert Ressler.

'Scully, this is Bill Patterson. He runs the Investigative Support Unit out of Quantico'

MULDER

'Yes, I know. Behavioral Science – you wrote the book. It's an honour . . .'

SCULLY

Grotesque

Colonel Robert K. Ressler is one of the few renaissance men in modern crime fighting. Equally at ease in the think tanks of Quantico (he was in the FBI for 20 years, 16 of them with the Behavioral Science Unit),

Jeffrey Dahmer - the 'Milwaukee Cannibal' - in court

on an Army base (he served in the military for 35 years) or in the halls of academe (he is affiliated to over half-a-dozen universities, and has taught at many more), Ressler combines a practical understanding of the dynamics of crime with a theoretical methodology that enables him to transmit that knowledge.

While he was with the FBI, Ressler initiated a drive to interview as many incarcerated serial killers as possible. The idea was that a better understanding of their motivation could help catch other criminals still at large (as in *Silence of the Lambs*, for which Ressler acted as consultant to author Robert Harris).

Ressler himself has interviewed over a hundred serial killers and rapists including Richard Trenton Chase (the 'Vampire Killer'), Ted Bundy (the 'Co-ed Killer'), David Berkowitz (the 'Son of Sam'), John Wayne Gacy ('The Killer Clown'), Charles Manson and Jeffrey Dahmer (the 'Milwaukee Cannibal').

Since retiring from the FBI in 1990, Ressler travels constantly, acting as an expert witness in legal cases, lecturing at universities, and training police forces in criminal profiling.

'What my colleagues and I have done is design a little expertise . . . looking beyond what the conventional police investigator sees,' Ressler explains. 'That's where I become a prototype for Mulder and Scully. What they're doing is stepping beyond the traditional role of the investigator and looking at things from a perspective that very few people have.

'Theoretically they're into aliens and monsters and cannibals and vampires. But basically, that's what I'm into. Aliens I don't know, but I'm into vampires, and I'm into cannibals . . . I can see things at a crime scene that a traditional cop is going to miss by a million miles. If I can bring that to an investigation, they are better off for it.

'When I came in to the FBI in 1970, there was no criminal profiling program. No psychological services. By '72 they had opened the FBI Academy [at Quantico] and the Behavioral Science Unit under Howard Teten and Pat Mullany was formulated. I evolved and grew with it . . . I created, with about half-a-dozen other people, what the FBI has today.'

*'Patterson had this saying about tracking a killer: if you
want to know the artist, look at his art. What he was really
saying was, if you want to catch a monster,
you've got to become one yourself'*

MULDER

Grotesque

By some definitions, profiling is more an art than a science, a fact
reflected in the difficulty of teaching its techniques to new recruits.

'When we trained our 55 original agents,' says Ressler, 'many came in
saying, "OK, stop giving us all this crap, give us the secret handbook, the
one with the check list in it." I said: "There is no such thing." One guy stood
up and said, "Bullshit, Ressler! Don't give me that! You're holding back this
stuff because you want to be the expert, and we're going to be your flunkies!"
This is the kind of confrontation you have in the FBI . . . When you're dealing
with agents you have to be ready to put on the gloves almost anytime.
Basically, what they were saying was: "You've got the secret . . . if you give
it to us, we can do what you do." Well, I give it to everybody. Some can do
what I do. Some are better at what I do. Some will never be able to do what
I do. It's not a matter of ABC learning, it's more intuitive. It's something that
you really can't share with a lot of people.'

Colonel Robert K. Ressler

Grotesque's images of Mulder's apartment, crowded with John Mostow's
artwork, with crime photos and reports, provided an accurate – if somewhat
disturbing – portrait of a fertile working environment for successful profiling.

'When I work on one of these cases I've got papers all over the floor,'
says Ressler. 'I lay it all out and then I absorb it like a sponge. I sit and suck
it up. Having access to everything, looking at everything, and just getting
perceptions is the way you develop profiles.'

*'Extrapolating from material on file at the FBI's Behavioral
Science Unit . . . He is more likely to be white, male and of
average to above average intelligence . . . '*

SCULLY

Irresistible

You move through the paperwork and the crime scenes. It's like building
a house,' says Ressler. 'As you're looking at this stuff you build the
foundation. You feel: OK, we're dealing with a male, for sure, and he's

probably white, probably mid-twenties. Then you build the next level and the next. As you go, you're building this conceptual picture of this individual and when you're done, you've got your profile.

'When I deliver a profile, either I feel good about it or I feel iffy. If I feel iffy about it I say: "I don't think there's enough here for me to deal with." But when I feel good about it, I feel real good.

'It's based on factual data. It's based on knowledge. But it's not a science, it's more of a intuitive approach. You don't see Mulder and Scully going down a check list. The perceptions they get are based on their experience, and that's accurate.

'If I could put it all in a book, *How to Profile* by Bob Ressler, I'd have it made for life. I could start a university. I could charge a fortune.

'But I can't impart that to a person unless they have the qualities. And you have to want to do this stuff, you know. You have to want to do it.'

'I need you to help me go deeper, John. . .'
MULDER, INTERVIEWING JOHN MOSTOW

Grotesque

Once a suspect is caught and detained, the long and gruelling interview process begins. Its primary function is to extract a confession for use in court, and to assist further investigation. Did the killer have an accomplice? Did he commit other murders than those which have led to his arrest?

But each interview also hones the profiler's skills, giving him or her the opportunity to plunge into the mind of a killer – a journey for which emotional detachment and mental clarity are essential.

'When I go in to do an interview I leave emotional baggage outside the

A policeman picks through the junk-littered kitchen of serial murderer and fetishist Ed Gein in 1957

door,' says Ressler. 'I leave all my prejudices, my biases, my hates, my likes, my dislikes, outside. I go in without the knowledge of the crime scenes, the murders, the devastation to the families. I go in clean.

'Then I build a rapport one-on-one with the individual. I admire their talents, their abilities, their intelligence. I am not turned off at them as a person for what they have done.

'If they're hostile so be it. I don't get along with them. But, more likely, I build a rapport. I build a relationship and we exchange information. I provide that which I want to control and I take that which I need. It becomes a seduction process. I'm courting these people and – I'll be the first to admit it – I'm manipulating these people.

'They know I'm not just there to visit with them. They know I'm there for information. It's up to me whether or not I can get it out of them.

'Then you bid good-bye, shake hands, walk out the door, pick up your emotional luggage and take it back into your personality. Then check and balance what you've just gone through in the room.'

'IT killed them! How many times do I have to tell you?!'

JOHN MOSTOW

' "Its" fingerprints weren't found on the murder weapon – yours were. And "it" won't be tried for seven murders under the death penalty'

SCULLY

Grotesque

'W hen I went and talked to David Berkowitz, the Son of Sam killer, he told me he killed women because The Talking Dog, a three-thousand-year-old demon, was telling him to.

'I slammed down my note book. "David, I guess our interview is over already, isn't it?"

'He said: " What do you mean, Mr Ressler? Hey, we're getting along fine here."

'I said: "Now you're just loading me full of bullshit about the Talking Dog and the demons. Where is that dog now? I want to interview the dog. Where does he live? I'll get more out of the dog than I'll get out of you."

'He laughed. I caught him. And he got back down to business.

'A lot of traditional psychiatrists would say: "Oh, the talking demon, David, what did he say to you and when does he come to you? In the daytime or at night?" If you're going to play that silly game with him, he's just going to lead you all over the place.'

'The man is clearly delusional. But I get a sense even he doesn't really believe his claims. For now, we have to go along with his . . . beliefs'

MULDER, AFTER INTERVIEWING SELF-PROCLAIMED
VAMPIRE 'THE SON'

Three

Mulder's experience with the suspect in *Three*'s vampiric murders was not dissimilar to Ressler's real-life interviews with Richard Trenton Chase, known as 'The Vampire Killer'. Chase was convinced that his blood was turning to powder and killed both humans and animals to replenish his own supply. He claimed to be suffering from a little-known ailment called 'soap-dish poisoning'(he knew this, he said, because the underside of his soap was slimy, not dry), and believed that UFOs (operated in connection with a Nazi syndicate) had sent him telepathic signals telling him to drink blood. Mulder's deft treading of the line between playing along with his suspect's beliefs and dismissing them outright mirrors Ressler's own technique.

'Richard Trenton Chase was mentally ill,' Ressler explains. 'What you had to do was play it as you believed he believed it. He told me he had a Star of David emblazoned on his forehead. I was unsure of what he was doing.

B.J. Morrow finds the impulse to kill impossible to resist in Aubrey

Was he testing me?

'So I said: "Richard, I don't see the Star of David. But I didn't bring my reading glasses and the light's kind of dim." You don't want to challenge his illusion if he's having a delusion, but neither do you want to agree with something you don't really see. If they're creating a fantasy, don't jump into their fantasy. Once they figure you're buying their line, you've lost them. It really takes a little bit of moxy to go in and deal with these people.'

'What were their names, the younger Agents?'
DONNIE PFASTER
'I don't remember his name. She was Scully'
SUSPECT INTERVIEWED IN PRISON BY MULDER AND SCULLY
Irresistible

Amongst the many scenes in *Irresistible* guaranteed to make the flesh crawl is the one in which it becomes apparent that fetishist Donnie Pfaster is planning to make Scully his next victim. Pfaster seeks to extract information from a fellow offender – who, in his own unsavoury way, has also clearly clocked our favourite female agent.

The implication of exposing a female agent to the attentions of a dangerous sex offender is one which does not go ignored at the FBI.

'There are certain types of offender that a woman would be better off interviewing than a male,' explains Col. Ressler. 'Others, a woman is the last one you'd want to bring in there.

'I used to take one woman on some of these interviews in prisons. When we would walk into the room with one of these violent sexual offenders, (it was as if) I was gone, I wasn't even in the room. They focused right in on her, interacting with her because they were getting their jollies. The only thing that prevented anything from happening was me being there and them being in a prison.'

A strikingly unpleasant thought. 'Yeah, it's not for everybody. Women or men.'

'You think you can find a way to deal with these things . . . In your FBI training you are confronted with cases, the most terrible and violent cases. You think you can look into the face of pure evil. And then you find yourself paralysed by it'
SCULLY
Irresistible

'Son of Sam' killer David Berkowitz appears unsettlingly calm and collected in this 1977 picture

*I*rresistible sees Scully disturbed to a degree where she is driven to seek help from an FBI counsellor, and begins to question her ability to deal with the distressing nature of her work. In real life, such doubt is not unusual.

'There were several that were in the program when it developed who just bailed out because they couldn't handle it,' Ressler recalls. 'There was one woman who was getting herself crazy. She was internalising all this stuff. She was putting fifteen locks on her doors and barring her windows. She was really coming apart at the seams with nightmares. She just said: "I'm out of here, I can't take this on a daily basis." I give her credit for having the guts to say, "I don't want to do this".'

The demonic image fleetingly glimpsed in Irresistible *(above) was strictly metaphorical - Donny Pfaster (below) was spine-chillingly evil enough without needing to be anything other than human*

'I've seen agents with twenty years in the field fall apart on cases like this'

MULDER

Irresistible

Even long-standing agents are not immune to the stress and distress inherent in the job. Ressler cites the case of his colleague Ken Lanning who, for no apparent reason, suddenly lost 40 lbs in weight. 'He looked like some kind of a World War II death camp guy. He thought he had AIDS. He thought he was dying. He thought he had tuberculosis. He just thought the worst things. He went and got totally worked over and they said there was nothing wrong with him. One doctor asked "What do you do for a living?" He told him and the doctor said: "Maybe you ought to consider a career change."

'Lanning underwent some shifts and changes. He got his weight back. But there was never anything wrong with him. That's happened to a number of people.'

*'We work in the dark. We do what we can to battle the
monsters that would otherwise destroy us . . . Yet sometimes
the weight of this burden causes us to bend and falter,
allowing evil to breach the fragile fortress of our mind.
Allowing the monsters without to turn within.
And we are left alone, staring into the abyss . . .
into the laughing face of madness'*

MULDER

Grotesque

Nietzche's quote . . . pertains to me, and people like me, who are fighting the monsters that are among us,' says Ressler. Fortunately, *Grotesque's* Bill Patterson – he who fought monsters but was unable to see to it that he did not become one – is the product of Howard Gordon's fertile imagination. In real life the BSU has not spawned any murderous agents. But according to Colonel Ressler, not all have safely negotiated the abyss.

*'Every day and every night for three years, you lived and
dreamed the horror show in his head . . . Imagining
everything he imagined, sinking yourself
deeper into the mire – just like you taught us to
do. But when you finally caught up
with him, it didn't go away'*

MULDER

Grotesque

Ressler recalls: 'One FBI guy who was interviewing Ted Bundy got caught up to the point where he became emotionally unbalanced about the whole thing, exchanging secret mail with Bundy, paying him an inordinate number of visits, and giving more information to Bundy than he was getting. He was converted. Totally devastated, personality-wise, by a very skilled con-man.

'When Bundy was in his last 72 hours of life, he was supposed to be meeting with police officers and providing information. The room was glass partitioned. Bundy was on one side and this FBI agent was on the other. The FBI guy walked up to the divider, looked at Bundy, and put his hand up on the glass. Bundy did the same. They looked at each other like two lovers who had been separated.

'I think Bundy was playing the guy like a fiddle. The FBI guy was caught up so bad. After the execution he came back looking like he had lost his best friend. Really traumatised. Then he went through a series of lectures where he just talked about Bundy and referred to him lovingly as "Ted", "my friend Ted". It was pretty spooky. This guy fell into the abyss in my opinion.'

Grotesque's Bill Patterson, *whose metamorphosis from investigator to perpetrator warns of the danger of looking into an abyss*

'If this guy looks regular-like and if he doesn't have a record, he's gonna be near-impossible to find'

AGENT MOE BOCKS

'Until he kills again. Or until we can determine what's driving him'

MULDER

Irresistible

The mind of a murderer may be a dangerous place to be, but getting into it is often as essential and effective a part of crime-solving as collecting forensic evidence. Grasping a murderer's motivation is often the only way his next move can be anticipated.

In *Irresistible*, it is Donnie Pfaster's 'death fetish' which provides the spur. Although Pfaster's activities seem to be limited to collecting his victim's nails and hair, escalating to post-mortem mutilation, Chris Carter's true intentions for the character were far more gruesome.

'I couldn't call him a necrophiliac,' Carter reveals. 'I couldn't say "necrophiliac" and I couldn't talk about him having sex with the dead or anything sexual involving the dead, because it was *verboten* here on network television to make those connections. When I originally wrote the script, I received a letter back saying this script is not approved or suitable for our broadcast standards: change it. So I had to change him from a necrophiliac to a death fetishist, but I think everyone who's got a little bit of sophistication understood that I was calling it one thing but I meant another . . . It was all semantics.'

Carter found his research understandably disturbing, and yet compelling. 'It's fascinating, the idea that somebody would want to have sexual contact with the dead. It is so stomach-turning . . . that there is a fascination, as there is about anything where we can't imagine what could make someone have such a repulsive motivation.

'There are all sorts of suggestions about why these things happen, but I think no one can quite fathom these kind of fetishistic, ritualistic behaviours, so it's mysterious, and that's another reason why it's interesting.'

'Why do they do it?'

SCULLY

'Some people collect salt and pepper shakers.
The fetishist collects dead things. Hair,
fingernails . . . no one quite knows why.
Though I've never understood salt
and pepper shakers myself'

MULDER

Irresistible

'Fetishists are a dime a dozen,' says Colonel Ressler, somewhat alarmingly. Many fetishists – people with unusual sexual fixations – are harmless. But if a fetishist is also disturbed, he may, for a number of reasons, go on to kill.

'Back in 1945 William Heirens was a fetish burglar who ended up killing a number of women,' says Ressler, by way of example. For Heirens, it was the act of burglary which excited him; the women he killed had merely interrupted his fantasy. Ressler also mentions the case of Jerome Brudos, a man from Oregon who had a fetish for women's high-heeled shoes. Brudos's career in crime, which was spurred by his desire to add to his collection of shoes, began with non-violent theft of items he sold to support his habit. He escalated to assaulting women on the street in order to steal their footwear, before discovering new ways of getting his kicks and graduating to rape, murder and mutilation.

For others killing is simply a means to an end. 'Ed Gein had a fetish for human flesh,' Ressler explains, referring to the murderer whose singularly unpleasant career has inspired several works of fiction, including *Psycho*, *The Texas Chain-Saw Massacre* and, in some part, *The Silence of the Lambs*. On his arrest, Gein's home in Wisconsin was found to contain furniture upholstered with human skin and decorated with skulls, faces hanging on the walls like decorative masks (Gein admitted that he wore these on occasion), female genitalia stored in shoe-boxes (including his mother's, painted silver), and ornaments and clothing that Gein had fashioned from body parts, such as a

Ted Bundy, a charismatic and articulate killer who was the catalyst for a formerly well-balanced FBI agent's descent into psychological chaos

belt made from human nipples.

Other fetishists, for whom the act of killing is simply a necessary step in the pursuit of their goal include 'vampires', cannibals – and necrophiliacs. These fetishes are sometimes acquired later by a 'normal' murderer as his career progresses. Ressler cites Ted Bundy as an example. 'The more Bundy killed . . . the more vicious he became. It's not common knowledge that towards the end of his crimes he was involved in necrophilia and in flesh-eating. He was really becoming very brutal and primitive.

'The origin of vampirism and cannibalism is the basic perversity of man: man's ability to revert to the caveman. Their instincts are: "Want food: take food." "Want woman: take woman." "Want woman *and* food: kill woman and then eat her." It's almost like the guy with the club blasting through the woods. In a normal, civilised state, we wouldn't think of drinking blood or eating human flesh, cooked or otherwise.

'With a serial killer, the first couple of homicides, these people are scared silly. They are paranoid because they have been conditioned to believe that to take a human life is the ultimate crime and they will be caught. When they're not caught after two, three, four victims, they start feeling more powerful. By five or six victims they think they're up there on Mount Vesuvius, they're walking with the gods. They've stepped away from the common rules of man and they can get away with anything. Once they get into that, they become more and more perverse, they experiment.

'You don't drink blood or eat flesh the first time you kill unless you're totally psychotic. It's an evolutionary process, like giving in to the dark side of man's potential. The further you go, the deeper you fall into the abyss.'

'Listen to this Scully . . . "One must wonder how these monsters are created. Did their homelife mold them into creatures that must main and kill? Or are they demons from birth?" '

MULDER, READING THE WORDS OF A DECEASED FBI PROFILER

Aubrey

In *Aubrey* the reason for Detective Morrow's homicidal tendencies seems to lie in her genes – specifically those passed on by her grandfather, a convicted murderer. He in turn is found to have had a tormented childhood, dominated by his mother and older sisters – a plight hinted at, too, for *Irresistible*'s Donnie Pfaster. *Grotesque*'s John Mostow is clearly the victim of some acute psychosis, and, as discussed, the same episode's Bill Patterson has simply stared too long into the abyss.

In real life, it is still not known exactly what makes a killer. Statistically, neglect and maltreatment in childhood appear to play an important part. But it may not be so much that monsters are created, as that we are *all* potential demons from birth.

'We want to believe that we're superior beings, that we've got it all together,' says Ressler. 'I try to bring people down to their basics. They aren't a lot different from one culture to another. As complex as people are, they all come from a very simple origin. They come from civilization, training, education, learning. All these are what make people complex beings. At the beginning, they're all coming from the same primitive instinct that is present in everybody. It just becomes a matter of putting a lid on that.

'Normal behaviour is an escape, a removal from aberrant behaviour. I think everybody is basically aberrant. At birth everybody's just a raw throbbing id, non-socialized, no ego control. Kids are screaming. They want food. If you don't feed them they'll keep screaming . . . Infants are small and weak for a reason. If you had a two-hundred-pound infant, it'd kill you if you didn't feed it. Along with growth and development comes socialisation, making these infants civilised. The ones that become the predators and the abusers are the ones that have not been socialised.

'When I sit across the table from Ted Bundy or John Gacy or Bob Berdella or any of these guys, I recognise immediately that we started the same way. Gacy and I grew up in the same neighbourhood, for God's sake. He said: "Bob, I could be sitting there and you could be sitting here. We could be on the other sides of the coin." I agree.'

Child-murderer John Wayne Gacy. His nickname the 'Killer Clown' refers to the costume he wore for his part-time job as a children's entertainer

> *'Every generation, like the ones before it must defend itself against a demon spawn. The names make our skin crawl: Manson, Dahmer, Speck. That their crimes differ is irrelevant. They are the embodiment of pure evil. Interchangeable as eggs in a carton'*
>
> MULDER
> *Irresistible*

Ed Gein, whose unspeakably hideous deeds inspired a number of movies, including The Texas Chainsaw Massacre *(opposite, top). Hannibal Lecter is the most memorable character in Thomas Harris's astounding novel* The Silence of the Lambs *and its subsequent movie adaptation (opposite, below), but the depraved acts of Jame Gumb - the murderer into whom the FBI hope that Lecter will provide insight - are a resonant echo of Gein's revolting MO*

Irresistible was a landmark episode for *The X-Files*, the first to present the Agents with a case utterly devoid of any supernatural, paranormal or science-fiction element. 'It shows some early desire on my part to do a show like *Millennium*, which is really about psychological terror and about real psychological illnesses and their manifestations and how we come into contact with these people and we can't quite see the world as they do,' reflects Chris Carter, referring to the new, non-paranormal series he has created.

One season later, *Grotesque* also remained firmly in the realm of real-life horror. The fleeting glimpses of demonic figures in both episodes were intended not to infer a paranormal element but as metaphorical representations of evil.

'Is this evil something born in each of us, crouching in the shadow of every human soul, waiting to emerge . . . a monster that violates our bodies, and twists our will to do its bidding? Is this the monster called madness?'

MULDER

Grotesque

'Initially I'd written a draft [of *Grotesque*] where in fact it was a spirit,' says Howard Gordon. 'It was a much more literal interpretation of what was going on, and it didn't work at all. So we had to completely abandon it.' Gordon still wanted an image to represent the spirit that the murderer claimed to be possessed by, and hit upon the idea of the gargoyle when he looked up to see a pair of them staring malevolently down at him from the front of a building. 'I made the idea of madness more metaphorical, and the gargoyle became the governing image, the archetype of madness.'

Gordon confirms that the resemblance between the 'visual archetypes' in the two episodes was intentional. 'I knew at some level that it would be referenced, and even when we art-directed the gargoyle, I said, let's look at (the demon figure from *Irresistible*). We thought it was a good thing ultimately that there is a repetition of these images.'

It is possible to interpret the images as an inference that there exists a spirit of evil: a dark force which can 'possess' mankind. It is an idea which interests Howard Gordon. 'I'm of the mind that a person is responsible for his or her own actions regardless of where they came from . . . But I'm interested in that grey area, the evil that we're all capable of committing . . . that's why I like *Grotesque*, because it was Mulder stepping over that line. I hope it showed how fragile his own construct was. But do I believe in evil as absolute? I think the point is that in the right context, we're all capable of evil.'

Chris Carter also confirms that the demonic imagery of these episodes was intended to represent an embodiment of the spirit of evil. Asked whether he believes that such a thing exists, he answers without hesitation.'Yes. I know it: I've seen it.'

The Texas Chainsaw Massacre

His blue eyes are sincere yet inscrutable. 'I've looked it right in the face: I've looked at the face of evil and I've seen it in its pure, unadulterated form . . . I've seen it in the eyes of human beings.'

A long time ago, something happened to Chris Carter, something he has not spoken about publicly thus far and intends to keep private. Something that enables him to say with disquieting conviction: 'I know evil exists and I know that it's soul-shaking.'

One can't help but wonder whether creating the demon-haunted worlds of *The X-Files* and *Millennium* is part of a cathartic process for him. 'Yes,' he replies simply. 'That's why I'm a writer.'

'The conquest of fear lies in the moment of its acceptance; in understanding what scares us most is that which is most familiar, most commonplace.

That the boy next door . . . could grow up to be the devil in a button-down shirt. It's been said that the fear of the unknown

Antony Hopkins as Hanibal Lecter in The Silence of The Lambs

is an irrational response to the excesses of the imagination, but our fear of the everyday,of the lurking stranger and the sound of footfalls on stairs, the fear of violent death and the primitive impulse to survive are as frightening as any X-File . . . and as real as the acceptance that it could happen to you'
MULDER
Irresistible

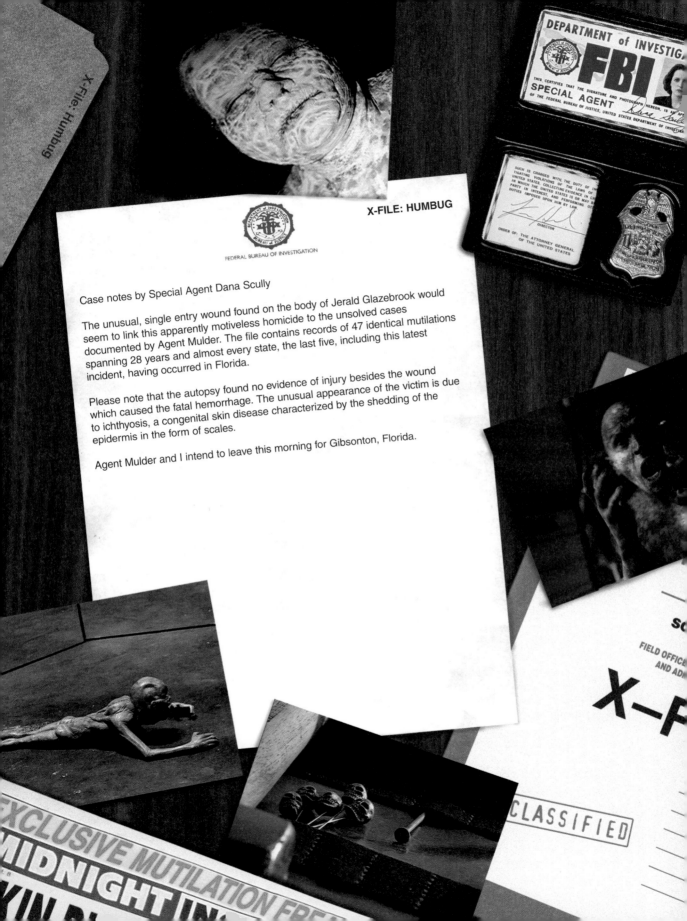

X-FILE: HUMBUG

FEDERAL BUREAU OF INVESTIGATION

Case notes by Special Agent Dana Scully

The unusual, single entry wound found on the body of Jerald Glazebrook would seem to link this apparently motiveless homicide to the unsolved cases documented by Agent Mulder. The file contains records of 47 identical mutilations spanning 28 years and almost every state, the last five, including this latest incident, having occurred in Florida.

Please note that the autopsy found no evidence of injury besides the wound which caused the fatal hemorrhage. The unusual appearance of the victim is due to ichthyosis, a congenital skin disease characterized by the shedding of the epidermis in the form of scales.

Agent Mulder and I intend to leave this morning for Gibsonton, Florida.

PHYSICAL ANOMALIES

Frequently in interviews Chris Carter has impishly warned *X-Files* viewers not to get complacent. The murder of Deep Throat at the close of season one proved that this was not an idle threat. In complete contrast to the shadowy, edgy note of the episodes that preceded it, season two produced *Humbug*, with its gloriously skewed high-comedy dialogue, quirky slapstick and outrageous storyline. In the hands of Darin Morgan (whose initiation into *The X-Files* team was marked by an on-screen stint as the fluke-man in *The Host*) *The X-Files* took a trip down a new and decidedly off-beat alley.

Following the murder of Jerald Glazebrook, known professionally as The Alligator Man, Mulder and Scully arrive in Gibsonton, Florida, a community of retired and resting side-show performers, to embark on their weirdest investigation yet, complete with a suspect list that reads like the playbill for a Barnum spectacular.

The idea for *Humbug* came during a chat between Darin and his brother, former *X-Files* writer and producer Glen Morgan. 'Glen just said: You should do something about freaks,' Morgan recalls. The two of them later watched a tape of Jim Rose in performance, and although they did not know whether Rose would be available or interested in a guest appearance, Morgan kept him and his tattooed colleague, The Enigma, in mind and began research in earnest.

Gibsonton provided him with the perfect setting. For many years the abode of choice for members of the side-show profession, in real life the town even boasts a rest-home for retired human oddities.

Morgan, though fascinated by his subject, has never been to a side-show. 'I don't know if I would want to. But my parents went to one when my mom was pregnant with me. That explains a lot!' he quips.

Mulder and Scully in Gibsonton for the funeral of murder victim Jerald Glazebrook. In 1992, Gibsonton was the real-life setting of a bizarre murder: carnival worker Mary Stiles and her 'Human Blockhead' stepson, Harry Glenn Newman, ordered the contract slaying of her husband, Grady Styles Jr. - known as 'Lobster Boy' due to his claw-shaped lower arms

'Jo-Jo the dog-faced boy'
(centre)

'Mulder . . . imagine going through your whole life looking like this'
SCULLY,
CONSIDERING THE PLIGHT OF THE ALLIGATOR MAN
Humbug

Whether the sight of someone who deviates from our concept of 'normality' evokes revulsion or pity, fear or fascination, there is something about it which simply compels us to look, even if we try our best to disguise or resist this urge. But for the best part of a century, this drive was out in the open, displayed with little shame and exploited with none. Freak shows were much more than simple exhibitions of people. Such creativity and imagination in the marketing of acts has rarely been seen since, and it was this which appealed to Darin Morgan. 'It was that idea of showmanship . . . of exactly how you show off your deformity. It's one thing to stand there and say: Look at me, I'm deformed. It's another to think of that extra something.'

Usually, that extra something took the form of an exotic life-story. A fine example is that of Jo-Jo the Dogfaced Boy (the inspiration for *Humbug*'s Sheriff Hamilton, who took up law enforcement when encroaching hair loss ruined his career as Jim-Jim the Dogfaced Boy). Jo-Jo – real name Fedor Jeftichew – was said to have been found running wild in a Russian forest and captured after a fierce struggle. Jeftichew was Russian by birth, but had left Russia in 1884, spending time in London before joining Barnum in the US. He was multilingual, genteel, well-educated and did not like to bark and snarl on stage because he thought it rude.

Most billings did away with truth altogether, and if one story ceased to pull the crowds, another would replace it. Willie and George, albino African-Americans from Louisiana, started their career as 'Eko and Iko the sheep-headed men', members of an exotic 'sheep-headed' cannibal tribe, before becoming Eko and Iko the Martian Ambassadors, whose billing proclaimed that they had been found in the Mojave desert near the remains of their spaceship.

Typically, a freak-show had its own tent, known as the 'ten-in-one' – supposedly because the entrance fee bought the chance to see ten exhibits or acts. But the most impressive human oddity was usually hidden behind a curtain, an extra fee required for a peek. This was known as 'the blow off'.

Between 1840 and 1940, the sheer number of ten-in-ones on the road – not to mention the museums and shows with permanent sites – meant that the demand for side-show acts far outstripped the supply of human oddities. This gave rise to plenty of self-made freaks, including Darin Morgan's personal favourite, 'The Great Omi', also known as 'The Zebra Man'. Omi was a cultured British major who, having fallen on hard times, elected to undergo 150 hours of tattooing to cover his entire body in zebra stripes. 'I love the idea of a person thinking, "Okay, I know, I'm going to tattoo myself to look like a zebra!"' says Morgan with a laugh. 'It's such an enormous decision. It's either going to work or it's not and if it doesn't you're screwed. I just got a kick out of that. That and the fact that during World War II he tried to re-enlist and they wouldn't let him because he was a tattooed zebra man.'

But perhaps the strangest purpose-made side-show oddity was the remarkably imaginative scheme devised in 1890 by Dr Martin Couney, who invented the incubator. When medical institutions refused to fund his work, he ingeniously joined Coney Island's freak show, exhibiting his 'incubator babies' at the ten-in-one. The babies (who would otherwise have died) were saved and the crowds applauded the exhibit as marvellously freakish. In addition to the two-headed beasts, fat people and dwarves that populate the imaginary Isle of Phreex in *Wizard of Oz* author L. Frank Baum's 1906 story *John Dough and the Cherub*, the hero also encounters an incubator baby.

'In the classical sense, the Conundrum is a "geek"'

DR BLOCKHEAD

'He eats live animals?'

MULDER

'He eats anything. Live animals, dead animals, rocks, light-bulbs, corkscrews, battery cables, cranberries . . .'

DR BLOCKHEAD

Humbug

In addition to purpose-made freaks, most showmen bulked out their roster with 'gaffs' and 'working acts'. Gaffs were outrageous fake freaks created by special effects – the headless person and the giant spider with the head of a woman were perennially popular. Working acts, being people with genuine unusual abilities, were much less disappointing. These included contortionists and 'India-Rubber Men' who could slip through a coat-hanger or suck in the abdomen until the backbone was visible. The most common acts, however, were the 'geek' and the 'human blockhead'.

The 'geek' traditionally sat in a pit eating live animals. Side-show legend had it that geeks were generally alcoholic or feeble-minded, but this was not strictly true. Many took pride in their art and looked down upon the kind of geek who, instead of catching his quarry and ripping it apart, had to have it thrust into his drooling maw by an assistant. (Although *Humbug*'s Conundrum is a geek, Paul Lawrence – stage name The Enigma – who played him, is not. True, he started his career as 'The Slug', devouring insects, roadkill and other unsavoury items supplied by his audience, but his skills include sword-swallowing, fire-eating, lifting weights using his eye sockets, playing the keyboard and composing music.)

The 'human blockhead' – exemplified in *Humbug* by Jim Rose as Dr Blockhead – would stun the crowds with pain-defying feats (although, as Rose has explained, the popular nail-into-nose trick takes advantage of the public's ignorance of anatomy, utilising the little-known secondary nasal cavity, which goes straight back into the head).

'What's the feejee mermaid?'

SCULLY

'It's a bit of humbug Barnum pulled in the last century'

SHERIFF

Humbug

Another popular 'filler' exhibit was what were affectionately known in the trade as 'pickled punks' – the preserved bodies of deformed animals, the occasional deformed baby and other oddities. But here too supply failed to meet demand – and it was this that gave P.T. Barnum the opportunity for one of his most successful and notorious scams.

In 1842, unprecedented crowds flocked to Barnum's New York museum to glimpse a real mermaid whose discovery had been announced in the Press. In fact, Barnum had cunningly sent reports to the newspapers from different locations around the US, purportedly written by parties unconnected

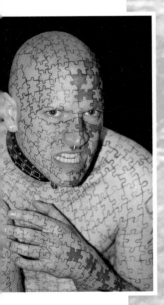

Darin Morgan describes The Enigma as 'A very, very sweet man, extremely shy ... It was my theory that he tattooed his whole body to make people just look at the tattoos – you find that you never look him in the eye – it's almost another way of being shy, another step within'

with the museum, about a remarkable artifact found in the Feejee (sic) Islands. Months later, he announced that he had succeeded in acquiring it at great cost. The ploy worked perfectly.

The 'mermaid' itself was an extremely unattractive item fashioned from the top half of a monkey and the tail end of a large fish. Nevertheless, it was hugely popular and spawned dozens of imitations.

'But see, that's why Barnum was a genius. You never know where the truth ends and where the humbug begins'

HEPCAT HELM

Humbug

Darin Morgan has a particular fondness for P.T. Barnum. 'As a kid I'd heard the legend about his museum becoming too crowded, so he had a sign made saying: "This way to the egress". No one knew what "egress" meant, so they followed the sign and found that they were outside. I'd always loved that story. That sense of showmanship is a lost art, in a way. The idea of someone going: Now look, I'm going to try to fool you and you've got to try to catch me.'

Uber-showman Phineas Taylor Barnum (1810 – 1891)

Morgan worked the 'egress' gag into his script for *Humbug,* along with another of his favourite Barnum anecdotes. Barnum used to charge an entrance fee to a train box-car to glimpse 'the great unknown'. The box-car was empty. In *Humbug,* the box-car became a large empty box in the backroom of a museum which the hapless Scully shells out five bucks for the privilege of viewing.

Most victims took Barnum's bluffs in good humour, perhaps regarding themselves less as having been hoaxed than as being 'in on the joke'. Crowds could always be found clustered by the museum's 'egress' and the entrance to 'the great unknown', enjoying the spectacle of the uninitiated taking the walk to suckerhood.

'People were just so happy with how well they'd been swindled. They appreciated it.' Morgan remarks. 'That would never happen nowadays. Now you'd have lawsuits.'

'Occasionally, I'd say, "Ladies and gentlemen, I'd like you to meet my brother Leonard . . . Excuse him – he's shy" Big laughs, I tell you. Big laughs'

LANNY

Humbug

If there was one human side-show exhibit guaranteed to bring in the crowds it was the man or woman with a conjoined or 'parasitic' twin.

It is not uncommon for the foetus of a twin which has not developed properly to be absorbed without trace by its sibling during gestation, and parasitic twins are the rare result of incomplete absorption. It was this syndrome which provided Darin Morgan with the inspiration for Humbug's storyline.

'Just having a twin attached to you looks weird enough,' he says, 'and some of the guys claimed that their twins could move a little bit – one had a third leg and his act was kicking a soccer ball. So I thought: well, what if you take it one step further and say, if it can move . . . what if it could somehow come out? There's your killer!'

Morgan's three-legged muse was Franscisco 'Frank' Lentini, often referred to as 'King of the Freaks', as much for his charm and business acumen as for his appearance.

Born in Sicily in 1889, Lentini had two sets of genitals as well as the three legs for which he was famed. Arriving in the USA in 1898 he found immediate success, touring with many different circus side-shows, including Barnum and Bailey. Besides kicking a soccer ball, he would thrill the crowds with other displays of athletic prowess, amongst them cycling and roller-skating. It wasn't long before his popularity and his bank-account permitted him to launch his own touring ten-in-one.

The young Francisco 'Frank' Lentini, a primary inspiration for the Humbug *story*

Although Lentini had not had the most pleasant start in life – the midwife who delivered him had thrown him under the bed and run away, and his parents refused to admit that he existed – he was a well-adjusted, good-humoured man who considered himself fortunate. Besides the success it brought him, he found his extra leg, which grew from the base of his spine, to be most useful. He proudly employed it as a sort of built-in 'shooting-stick' for sitting on whilst fishing, and attributed his talent for swimming to his use of the extra leg as a rudder.

Bizarrely, however, although Lentini was proud of his third leg, he was extremely sensitive about an extra thumb which grew from his knee.

It was easy to forget that Lentini's extra appendages belonged to a partially absorbed sibling, since they did not function independently. Although there is no record of anyone cursed with a totally autonomous malformed twin like *Humbug*'s tragic Lanny, some of the side-show circuit stars had parasitic siblings who were eerily active.

Pasqual Pinon and his not-entirely-convincing conjoined twin

'Laloo' was born in Oudh, India in 1874, and his small parasitic twin, who was perfectly formed apart from being headless, was able to urinate and get erections. There are at least two claims of parasitic twins who have given birth. Myrtle Corbin, billed as 'The Woman from Texas with Four Legs' had the small but fully-functioning lower half of a twin growing from between her legs. Myrtle's publicity claimed that of her five children, three had come from her own body and two from her twin's. This could easily be dismissed as side-show humbug if not for an 1889 British medical journal containing a doctor's discussion of a 20-year-old patient with a partly-formed parasitic twin (in this case, growing above her waist) which was found to be pregnant. The woman explained that her husband generally had intercourse with the twin. The baby had to be aborted, however, since the twin was judged unable to deliver it.

More sinister was the case of Pasqual Pinon, who had an active extra head growing from his forehead. Fortunately, it was fake – a notorious gaff. But the case of Edward Mordake, who suffered a similar condition, seems horribly genuine, since he did not profit from exhibition, but was attended by doctors who recorded his sad and disturbing story in a number of medical journals. Mordake was a young, attractive, scholarly aristocrat whose second face grew from the back of his head. Its eyes followed people, giving the clear impression that it could see; its mouth and facial muscles were fully functional, and its lips would gibber as if it was trying to talk. It could laugh soundlessly, and cry real tears. More alarming still, it was reported to laugh and sneer when Mordake cried, which, not surprisingly, he did often. Mordake begged the medical profession to remove what he called his 'devil twin', and claimed that it kept him awake, whispering terrible things to him through the night. No doctor would operate on him, and at the age of 23, he ended his misery by committing suicide.

'I was just reading about the "fascinating"
true life of Chang and Eng . . .'

SCULLY

Humbug

Chang and Eng, the united twins whose story intrigued Scully in the museum, were the first to find fame and to bring the syndrome to public attention. It was these brothers, born in Siam (now Thailand) in 1811, who gave modern language the term 'Siamese Twins'.

United twins occur when a single fertilised egg, dividing to create identical twins, fails to divide completely. The nature of the attachment varies, and in Chang and Eng's case, it was by way of a slim, five-inch long band of cartilaginous tissue.

The debonair and talented Chang and Eng

Chang and Eng's appeal extended far beyond curiosity value. They were talented performers whose act included impressive acrobatics, tricks and humorous repartee. Entrance fees to their shows were often astronomical, but the public judged it worth every last cent.

Chang and Eng frequently made the news, usually for good-humoured if bizarre japes, like boarding a train wearing a cape and refusing to buy more than one ticket. A more serious incident – a court case in which Chang was accused of assaulting a man, but was let off when the judge ruled that it would be unfair to send the innocent Eng to prison – inspired Mark Twain to write *Those Extraordinary Twins!* (Although Twain also drew his inspiration from the Tocci brothers – boys born in Italy in 1877 representing a rare case of dicephalus twins: both perfectly normal from the head down to the waist, where they joined to share only one pelvis and one pair of legs).

Chang and Eng were clever and financially astute, and by their mid-twenties had amassed enough cash to buy a large tract of land in North Carolina. Over the years, they consulted many doctors about the possibility of separation, pursuing the matter with renewed vigour after becoming engaged to Sarah and Adelaide Yates, two local sisters.

Without X-Ray technology to establish the internal physiology of the connection, dividing it was a chancy proposition, and finding a willing doctor was difficult. Eventually it was the Yates sisters who dissuaded Chang and Eng from risking their lives. This was fortunate: their post-mortem many years

later revealed that the brothers shared a circulatory system, and the operation would likely have proved fatal for one or both of them.

Chang and Eng married regardless, and had 21 children between them. When their house became too crowded, they built two separate family homes a mile apart, living three days at a time in each. An agreement that each called the shots in his own home made co-existence as harmonious as possible in the circumstances, especially considering that Chang and Eng did not get along with one another particularly well.

'. . . and I was wondering if their death was just as fascinating'
SCULLY
'Oh, very much so'
CURATOR
Humbug

Unfortunately the twins' rule meant that Eng was unable to stop Chang from drinking in his own house, which he did with gusto. Chang's health declined until he suffered a stroke – which did not affect Eng – and became gradually weaker until, in January 1874, at the age of 63, he developed bronchitis which gave way to pneumonia. Eng awoke suddenly one night to find that his brother was not breathing. Pinned down by the lifeless Chang, Eng screamed for help in the darkness. His call was answered by one of his older sons, who examined Chang and pronounced his uncle dead. Eng burst into tears, sobbing: 'Then I am going too.' By the time a doctor arrived, Eng was dead. As the museum curator ominously informed Scully, the post-mortem at the College of Physicians and Surgeons in Philadelphia recorded that Chang had died of a cerebral clot, Eng of fright.

'Did it not bother you to have people stare at you?'
SCULLY
'Best job I ever had. All I had to do was stand there'
LANNY
Humbug

Today the concept of exhibiting human beings makes people uneasy, conjuring up images of exploitation and degradation. But many freak-show performers regarded their work as well paid and enjoyable, and appreciated the companionship provided by life on the road. Numerous marriages were forged on the circuit, bringing not just personal happiness but added revenue. 'Percilla The Monkey Girl' and her husband 'Emmett The Alligator-Skinned Man' (who, like *Humbug*'s Jerald Glazebrook, suffered from Ichthyosis) were one of many pairs whose billing as 'the world's oddest married couple' greatly upped their pulling power.

But there is no doubt that others lived in abject misery. Robert Wadlow, born in 1918 in Alton, Illinois, was just under nine feet tall and could not hold a pencil or sit on an ordinary chair. He dreamed of a career in law, but had little financial alternative but to exhibit himself. He joined the Ringling Brothers troupe, where he spent a great deal of time in tears and had to wear a leg brace to help him stand up during shows. He died in 1940 as a result of an infected sore caused by the brace.

Sadder still were those exploited by cruel and mercenary individuals. Some, like united twins Daisy and Violet Hilton, were the virtual slaves of 'managers' who adopted deformed children rejected by their parents, with the sole intent of exhibiting them. The manager of the severely deformed Julia Pastrana sensitively billed her as 'the ugliest woman in the world', forbade her to go out in public lest her novelty-value wore off, and married her, allegedly in order to prevent her joining another showman. When Julia became pregnant in 1860, he sold tickets to the delivery. The baby, who had similar deformities to his mother, lived only a few hours, and Julia died soon afterwards from complications arising from the birth. Reluctant to bid his cash-cow farewell, Julia's husband had both bodies embalmed and displayed in a glass case (an observer recalled that the baby was perched on a bar 'like a parrot') which he took on a lengthy and lucrative world tour.

Julia Pastrana, whose life-story is one of the side-show era's most tragic

One aspect of the side-show which is particularly offensive to modern sensibilities was the exhibition of the mentally handicapped, the most common example being people with microcephaly – delicately referred to as 'pin-heads', although more for the pointed appearance of their skulls than for the childlike personality and low IQ that generally accompanies the condition. (There are cases of microcephalics of normal intelligence – the most famous being Triboulet, court jester of Francis I of France in the early sixteenth century, who inspired Victor Hugo's *Le Roi S'Amuse* and Verdi's *Rigoletto*, and was famed for wearing half an orange peel as a hat.)

Although microcephalics were dependent on their employers in every sense, showmen fought accusations of exploitation with the insistence that they seemed contented and relished the attention and applause. And there are indeed at least two cases of microcephalics becoming wildly despondent after being 'rescued' from showbusiness and put into institutions by well-meaning protesters. One concerned Schlitzie, who appeared in Tod Browning's extraordinary movie *Freaks*. Placed in an insititution when his manager died, Schlitzie's health declined and he lost the will to live. After a Montreal showman secured his release and took him on the road again, Schlitzie recovered and lived, reportedly in great contentment, to be 80 years old.

> *'You thought because I am of small stature, the only career I could procure would be confined to the so-called big top. You took one quick look at me, and presumed to deduce my entire life'*
>
> MR NUTT, DIMINUTIVE HOTEL MANAGER

HUMBUG

Another argument in defence of the freak-show is that it created lucrative job opportunities for people otherwise shunned by society and therefore without hope of employment. While essentially true, this is countered by the accusation that the freak-show, by marginalising its performers, in fact helped to deprive them of the right to the same jobs as everyone else. Moreover the popularity of the freak-show perpetuated the division between the 'normal' and the 'different' – an attitude which, at the height of side-show mania, affected anyone who was different. Violinist Frank Delphino, a small man whose musical talents were easily impressive enough to carry his career on their own merit, was justly enraged by persistently being billed as 'the world's smallest violinist'.

The medical and scientific communities were by no means without blame. Doctors and scientists attended freak-shows in droves, recording their observations without a word of objection to the displays. Dr Hunter, a famous British anatomist, collected and displayed the skeletons of human oddities as a hobby and even the kindly Dr Treves, celebrated for rescuing John Merrick from a life of maltreatment and exhibition, was quite happy to allow curious members of London high society to take tea with The Elephant Man in exchange for cash. Admittedly, these quiet, polite visits contributed to Merrick's gradual acquisition of dignity and confidence, and the 'donations' left discreetly by the door of Treves' apartment helped pay for Merrick's medical care. Nevertheless, the suggestion by author Daniel P. Mannix in his classic *Freaks: We Who are Not As Others*, that Treves was running a 'high class blow-off' is as thought-provoking as it is amusing.

> *'I didn't even know side-shows were still in existence. . .'*
>
> MULDER
>
> *Humbug*

While American 'roadside' museums and the few remaining side-shows still feature some classic exhibits, the inclusion of human oddities is a rarity and the traditional side-show all but a memory. The change in social climate that brought about the decline of the freak-show in the 1940s was set in motion around the turn of the century by discoveries that led to the demystification of physical anomaly. Medical advances in human physiology explained the cause of many conditions. Travel and exploration exploded the myths and the ignorance that sustained credence and interest in exhibits where people of different races were billed as oddities and oddities billed as members of exotic tribes.

A crowd who would clamour to see a dog-faced boy or an 'Aztec', may balk at ogling a child with hypertrichosis and a microcephalic wearing a loin-cloth. The scientific and medical communities began to object to the public display of human exhibits, not so much in defence of human dignity, but because, having now labelled the range of conditions, doctors felt that this should be their exclusive province. They regarded freak-shows as the unacceptable display of 'sick' people – despite the fact that the overwhelming majority of performers were not in need of any medical attention.

Protests against freak-shows became more frequent, until the dramatic decrease in attendance meant that the side-show ceased to be the sure-fire business proposition it once was. Although the tradition struggled weakly on for a few decades more, it was effectively finished.

> *'The kindhearted manager here convinced me that to make my living by publicly displaying my deformity lacked dignity, and so now . . . I carry other people's luggage'*
>
> LANNY
>
> *Humbug*

Humbug's Lanny certainly had a point to make – there are a hundred degrees of degradation. The human rights movement of the sixties, with its fight for freedom of personal choice, somehow excluded side-show performers from its manifesto. In 1969, when protesters banned a Florida side-show, a performer known as 'Sealo' argued in the Supreme Court that he and his fellow performers were being unfairly denied the chance to make a living. The ban was lifted.

Misplaced concern may still infringe on the rights of the very people it is intended to help. In 1990 Gabriel and Victor Gomez left school and found work at the Mexican Circus Nationale,

The cast of Freaks, *horror-master Tod Browning's astounding 1932 tale of camaraderie and cruelty on the side-show circuit*

Gabriel with a clowning troupe and Victor on the sound-crew. When the circus came to England a year later for a season at Blackpool, a ban was placed on the boys having any involvement in the show. The reason? The Gomez brothers have hypertrichosis, a hereditary condition which causes hair to grow all over the face and body. The media largely supported the brothers, but apparently saw no contradiction in dubbing them 'The Mexican Wolf Boys' or reporting the flurry of outrage. At its height, an Animal Welfare Alliance spokesman (who for some reason thought it appropriate to pass comment) suggested that the boys should be 'in a hospital or in a home', although both are in full physical and mental health. Again, the ban was lifted, this time after public protest at the violation of the brothers' rights.

'It's up to self-made freaks like me and the Conundrum to go out and remind people . . . Nature abhors normality'

DR BLOCKHEAD

Humbug

Whilst few would argue for the resurrection of the freak-show, many lament the art of showmanship that seemed to die with it. One of the handful keeping that tradition alive is *Humbug* guest-star Jim Rose, who, with his Circus Side Show, serves up a feast of astounding acts that is not for the weak of stomach.

'Today I play a freak on TV,' writes Rose in his hugely entertaining autobiography *Freak Like Me*, referring not just to *The X-Files* but to his soaring career in general, 'but not long ago I really was one.'

Born cross-eyed, Rose was tormented by other children, unhappy and alienated. At the age of six, with a failed corrective operation behind him, he spent most of a miserable summer tied to a telephone pole by local children playing Cowboys and Indians. 'Every night,' he writes, 'as I stood . . . waiting for my parents to retrieve me, I cursed the universe for making me such an easy target.' Rose found a magic book and taught himself escapology – a skill which not only put a stop to his daily miseries, but gave him a taste for performance. And with the notoriety gained from tricks like allowing dogs to lap milk from his mouth came profound change. 'I was no longer a victim, I was a force to be reckoned with . . . I knew how to amuse peers and transform hostile energy and I hadn't even read a self-help book.' Despite a degree in political science, Rose found the lure of the stage irresistible.

'You must be one of those rare individuals whose nerve endings don't register pain'
SCULLY
'That's right - just keep telling yourself that'
DR BLOCKHEAD
Humbug

Jim Rose and some of his Circus Side Show co-performers. Darin Morgan describes Rose as 'Just a really nice guy'

Rose honed his art in street performance, but, encountering the blasé crowds at California's Venice Beach in 1990, he decided that merely performing his act (which included escapology, pounding a screwdriver up his nose and burying his face in a pile of broken lightbulbs while his wife, Bebe, stood on his head) was not enough. 'I figured out a fundamental rule of performing,' he recalls. 'Being able to market what you do is more important than what you actually do.'

Moving to Seattle, Rose assembled his own troupe, including a car-insurance salesman who lifted weights with his pierced body parts, a pharmacist who used a length of rubber tubing to get beer and other fluids into his stomach via his nose (and out again), a sword swallower, a human pin-cushion and a guy who put his hand in a raccoon trap. Early successes led to national press coverage and the spot on the Lollapalooza '92 tour which catapulted the Jim Rose Circus Side-Show to international notoriety.

Jim Rose has not so much resurrected the side-show as

captured its spirit – the showmanship, the shock-value, the thrill of the forbidden. There was one element of his act that Morgan regretted being unable to include in his script for *Humbug*. 'Jim does this thing, Organ Origami,' he explains. 'He takes his genitalia and shapes it in weird forms.' Morgan was, however, able to secure a private viewing. 'When he first starts doing it, you're thinking: I'm looking at a naked guy. Help. But then as he keeps doing it, you kind of forget about that and you just go: Wow, how does he do that one? So that's what Jim, who has no deformities himself, has managed do, to say: Look what I can do with my body. You could, if you wanted to, take that into weird philosophical implications . . . I'd rather not do that, and just laugh at his penis, I guess. It's quite remarkable.'

Humbug's Lenny – Lanny's not-so-conjoined twin whose deadly antics turn out merely to be misguided attempts to find, and attach himself to, a new brother

'Modern science is wiping out any deviant strain of the human form. In the 21st century, genetic engineering will not only eradicate Siamese twins and alligator skinned people, but you'll be hard pressed to find a person with a slight overbite or not-so high cheekbones. I've seen the future, and the future looks . . . just like him!'

DR BLOCKHEAD,

POINTING ACCUSINGLY AT AGENT MULDER

Humbug

The closing speech that Morgan wrote for Jim Rose is a thought-provoking comment on humanity's drive to create a world without physical imperfection.

'The truth of the matter is that it is going to happen,' muses Morgan, 'and who is to say whether that's a good or a bad thing?' He admits, however, that this is not the point he was trying to make. 'Thinking back on it, I was actually just trying to make fun of Duchovny! Is that my nightmare – a world full of people who look like David Duchovny? Very much so! I guess I'm not the most handsome man in the world, so I'm sure that there is a bit of jealousy in there. But everyone's different and you just accept that, and I think it's more important than everyone being fanatical about their looks.'

'Imagine going through your whole life looking like that'

DR BLOCKHEAD, REGARDING MULDER WITH PITY

Humbug

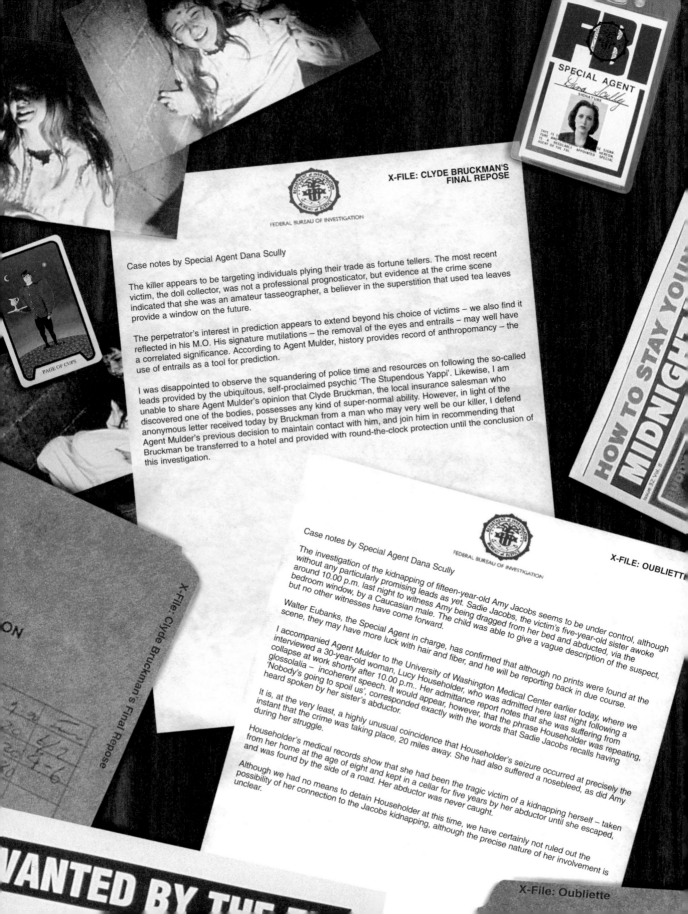

SPECIAL AGENT

X-FILE: CLYDE BRUCKMAN'S FINAL REPOSE

FEDERAL BUREAU OF INVESTIGATION

Case notes by Special Agent Dana Scully

The killer appears to be targeting individuals plying their trade as fortune tellers. The most recent victim, the doll collector, was not a professional prognosticator, a believer in the superstition that used tea leaves indicated that she was an amateur tasseographer, a believer in the superstition that used tea leaves provide a window on the future.

The perpetrator's interest in prediction appears to extend beyond his choice of victims – we also find it reflected in his M.O. His signature mutilations – the removal of the eyes and entrails – may well have a correlated significance. According to Agent Mulder, history provides record of anthropomancy – the use of entrails as a tool for prediction.

I was disappointed to observe the squandering of police time and resources on following the so-called leads provided by the ubiquitous, self-proclaimed psychic 'The Stupendous Yappi'. Likewise, I am unable to share Agent Mulder's opinion that Clyde Bruckman, the local insurance salesman who discovered one of the bodies, possesses any kind of super-normal ability. However, in light of the anonymous letter received today by Bruckman from a man who may very well be our killer, I defend Agent Mulder's previous decision to maintain contact with him, and join him in recommending that Bruckman be transferred to a hotel and provided with round-the-clock protection until the conclusion of this investigation.

PAGE OF CUPS

HOW TO STAY YOU... MIDNIGHT Issue 32, Vol 8

X-File: Clyde Bruckman's Final Repose

X-FILE: OUBLIETTE

FEDERAL BUREAU OF INVESTIGATION

Case notes by Special Agent Dana Scully

The investigation of the kidnapping of fifteen-year-old Amy Jacobs seems to be under control, although without any particularly promising leads as yet. Sadie Jacobs, the victim's five-year-old sister awoke around 10.00 p.m. last night to witness Amy being dragged from her bed and abducted, via the bedroom window, by a Caucasian male. The child was able to give a vague description of the suspect, but no other witnesses have come forward.

Walter Eubanks, the Special Agent in charge, has confirmed that although no prints were found at the scene, they may have more luck with hair and fiber, and he will be reporting back in due course.

I accompanied Agent Mulder to the University of Washington Medical Center earlier today, where we interviewed a 30-year-old woman, Lucy Householder, who was admitted here last night following a collapse at work shortly after 10.00 p.m.. Her admittance report notes that she was suffering from glossolalia – incoherent speech. It would appear, however, that the phrase Householder was repeating, 'Nobody's going to spoil us', corresponded exactly with the words that Sadie Jacobs recalls having heard spoken by her sister's abductor.

It is, at the very least, a highly unusual coincidence that the crime was taking place, 20 miles away. She had also suffered a nosebleed, as did Amy during her struggle.

Householder's medical records show that she had been the tragic victim of a kidnapping herself – taken from her home at the age of eight and kept in a cellar for five years by her abductor until she escaped, and was found by the side of a road. Her abductor was never caught.

Although we had no means to detain Householder at this time, we have certainly not ruled out the possibility of her connection to the Jacobs kidnapping, although the precise nature of her involvement is unclear.

X-File: Oubliette

ANTED BY THE

PSYCHIC DETECTIVES

Information garnered by anomalous means has helped Mulder and Scully in their investigations several times. In season one's outstanding *Beyond the Sea*, a death row inmate's channelling abilities help lead the Agents to a homicidal kidnapper. Two seasons later, in *Oubliette*, a former kidnap victim finds herself inexplicably re-living the traumas of her abductor's latest victim. With Mulder's sympathy and trust, her nightmarish visions result in the successful apprehension of the perpetrator.

And in the exceptional *Clyde Bruckman's Final Repose*, Mulder and Scully find themselves hunting a killer who is targeting fortune tellers with the help of reluctant psychic Clyde Bruckman, a depressive insurance salesman. Local law enforcement, meanwhile, enlist the help of The Stupendous Yappi, a flamboyant 'psychic detective'.

Mulder and Scully meet Clyde Bruckman

The episode was the second to be written by Darin Morgan, following *Humbug*.

'*Humbug* was a terrible experience for me,' says Morgan. 'I was very happy with the script, but then everyone freaked out like it was going to destroy the show. The network were terrified, saying it was a comedy and *The X-Files* is not a comedy, and the director was petrified.

'I didn't think I would ever come back to the show, but I survived, and it was very popular with the fans and then it was: "we want you back"...

'I looked at *Humbug* again... Then I watched *Beyond the Sea*, which my brother [ex-staffer Glen Morgan] wrote, and which is still my favourite episode. And I thought: if we could do an episode of that quality every week, this would be one of the greatest shows of all time. So I planned something much more serious. I said: *I'm going to show everyone. I'm not going to have* any *jokes, it's going to be very serious, very depressing. I want this episode to be the most depressing thing ever.*

'In our research library we have this book with actual crime scene photos from homicide investigations ... It used to be on my desk and people would come in and they'd surf through it, and I'd warn them not to: I'd say, "This is going to bother you for days" and they'd ignore me, and then they'd come back afterwards and say, "Man, I couldn't sleep, this was really disturbing". And so I figured that if a psychic could know the future, theoretically he would be able to see everybody's eventual future, which is their deaths. You wouldn't be able to live with that. You'd go insane and you'd kill yourself.'

'You know, I'm sure there are worse ways to go,
but I can't think of a more undignified one
than autoerotic asphyxiation'
CLYDE BRUCKMAN
'Why are you telling me this?'
MULDER
'Look, forget I mentioned it. It's none of my business'
CLYDE BRUCKMAN

Clyde Bruckman's Final Repose

For all his plans to write a sombre tale, Morgan was (to the delight of his fans) unable to suppress his unique humour. 'Unfortunately, the gruesomeness of the idea was sort of lost along the way,' he admits. 'But I think it was clear enough that the character had seen so many deaths that he was depressed all of his life.'

The idea of psychic ability as a curse also influenced Morgan's creation of the killer. 'I gave him some psychic ability but not enough to really figure anything out. In the script I called that character The Puppet because I just wanted the idea that this guy *felt* like a puppet. He could see his future and he wasn't in control of it.'

Bruckman suffers from a disturbing reoccuring dream in which he watches his body decompose

It's a haunting notion, and one to which Morgan gave much thought. 'I don't personally feel that things are pre-determined, and yet, if I were to find out that they *were*, I wouldn't be that shocked. I think it basically comes down to the feeling of: *who am I to say?*

'It's kind of creepy, isn't it ? The Stupendous Yappi said the first victim's body has been dumped somewhere, and then we find it in a dumpster'

DETECTIVE CLINE

'I just got a chill down my spine'

MULDER

Clyde Bruckman's Final Repose

As a writer, Morgan managed skilfully to stalk the middle ground by contrasting Bruckman, with his genuine gift/curse, with The Stupendous Yappi, a shameless charlatan. A voracious researcher, Morgan read dozens of books on psychics, and particularly 'psychic detectives' – people who claim to put their extra sense to good use by helping the police solve crimes.

His main source was a book called *Psychic Sleuths*, for which eleven researchers spent a year investigating well-known psychics. Reading it left Morgan's opinion on the subject profoundly changed. 'You think maybe it's possible, or you don't really think about it. You go: *they borrowed a psychic and he found a body . . . wow, that's weird.* Then if you start to look closer, look at specific examples, you go: *oh it's so* obvious *that it's not.'*

'Let me impress you with my own psychic abilities. Yappi proclaimed the victim's body would be found near water.A church or school would be in the vicinity. He got a flash of the letter "S" and/or the number "7"'

MULDER

'So what's your point?'

DETECTIVE CLINE

'His leads are so vague as to be useless practically, yet easily interpreted as being correct after the fact'

MULDER

Clyde Bruckman's Final Repose

'They are wrong so much of the time, and they say things that are very general. I did so much research on that angle, and all it came down to was those few lines of Mulder's . . . Still, I really like that scene. 'Charlatans don't irritate me, but I believe it's wrong. There's a difference between what Barnum did, which was a sense of: *I'm fooling you and you've got*

PAGE OF CUPS

to try to guess how, as opposed to the psychic detectives who go "I can help you find your missing boy" when people are emotionally distraught. Getting people's hopes up can be very harmful, I should think.'

*'Do you want to know what lies ahead? Then call me – The Stupendous Yappi. For years I have entertained audiences with my psychic abilities.
I have been consulted by Hollywood stars, police departments, even presidents'*
YAPPI'S TV ADVERTISEMENT
Clyde Bruckman's Final Repose

Many psychic sleuths are inveterate self-promoters. After all, it isn't the lawmen who leak their uncanny insights to the media. How many police agencies are eager to spread the word that a psychic with a mystic vision was able to crack a case they couldn't solve?

And only successful psychic input gets reported. For every miraculous, spot-on psychic deduction, there are perhaps thousands of useless paranormally generated clues – placing the correct ones well into the realm of random chance.

Nonetheless there *have* been cases through the years in which a psychic has provided such detailed and accurate information that even the most determined sceptic would have to reconsider. Arthur Lyons and Marcello Truzzi

The Stupendous Yappi was named after the actor who played him, Jaap [pronounced yap] Broeker. 'Jaap is David Duchovny's stand-in,' explains Darin Morgan. 'He's this Dutch guy, and I met him when I did Humbug. *He's one of the most interesting people I've ever met. He's got a weird face and an accent, and the way he talks ... well he's not really acting too much when he plays Yappi! I just thought, I've got to get this guy in here somehow!'*

claim to have begun researching their book on psychic detectives, *The Blue Sense,* with a healthy dose of cynicism. Truzzi was even a member of a prominent sceptics' association. Yet both authors ended up championing some of the people detailed therein.

So let's meet some of the men and women of the Paranormal Patrol.

GERARD CROISET

The reputation of Gerard Croiset, whose speciality was locating missing persons – dead and alive – rests on his good fortune in attracting a supporter with impeccable academic credentials: Professor Willem Tenhaeff, a lecturer in parapsychology at Utrecht University. Croiset submitted himself to Tenhaeff in 1956 for long-term study, and when he died in 1980 it was with the sobriquet 'world's most tested psychic'.

For this reason, it is hard to contest Croiset's record. In several instances, he was able either to find the missing person or predict when and where the person – or the body – would be discovered (he himself claimed an 80% success rate in accidental disappearances).

Croiset began his career – and made his fortune – as a psychic healer. He also claimed precognition as one of his gifts, and would perform a stunt devised by Tenhaeff in which he would 'project into the future', predicting details about an apparently random person who would be sitting in a specific chair a week or so hence.

Commendations: Besides being one of the few psychics to submit to 'scientific' testing, Croiset would accept no money for his body-locating services (although his fame in this field certainly boosted his considerable income from psychic healing). His 'hit ratio' of located persons appears to exceed chance.

Complaints: Collusion? Professor Tenhaeff had as much to gain from supporting Croiset as Croiset had from Tenhaeff's endorsement. And the 'chair test' with its flamboyant showmanship and many opportunities for cheating seems more like a magic trick than a demonstration of genuine clairvoyance.

PETER HURKOS

Hurkos, a Dutchman like Croiset, craved and cultivated fame, along with an ecccentric mystique. He tried to insinuate himself into many notorious cases, including that of the Boston Strangler (for which he fingered the wrong man yet still claimed credit for helping with the investigation) and the Tate–LaBianca murders, for which he came nowhere close to describing the Manson Family and even misidentified the victims. He was also under the delusion that he had solved the murder of a priest in Amsterdam and had received a letter of commendation from the Pope – neither of which ever happened. Nonetheless, his claims were rarely disputed, and, self-propelled, he rode to fame on the airwaves of Europe and the USA.

Hurkos, born Pieter van der Hurk in 1911, supposedly gained his powers after a fall from a ladder whilst painting a Nazi barracks in The Hague during World War II. Although he claimed many powers his speciality was psychometry: divining details through touching appropriate objects. Regardless of his dubious gifts, Hurkos knew instinctively that the media would gladly report a clever hoax as true in order to feed the public appetite for such stories, and he clearly had a masterful grasp of publicity.

Commendations: He clearly had what the Yiddish call 'chutzpah', or what the Spanish call 'los cojones grandes'. . .

Complaints: He was undoubtedly a fake.

The attempt on President Reagan's life – as foreseen, apparently, by Noreen Renier

NOREEN RENIER

Noreen Renier stakes her fame on two 'forecasts' she issued in 1981. According to her PR machine, she successfully predicted both John 'Hey, Jodie, Lookit Me!' Hinckley's shooting of Ronald Reagan, and the assassination of Egyptian president Anwar Sadat. On the heels of those triumphs, Robert Ressler invited her to speak about psychic detection at the FBI academy at Quantico. In her profession, it doesn't get any better than this.

So why quibble and point out that she had earlier predicted that Jimmy Carter would be re-elected in 1980 and then assassinated on the White House lawn, and that his vice president, Walter Mondale, would commit suicide? Or that in fact she had indicated that Reagan, not Sadat, would be killed by machine-gun fire in the autumn of 1981. ('See, I knew it would be a president,' she reportedly said.)

Renier claims that she relives crimes psychometrically, suffering as the victim suffered, by holding objects associated with the deed. Robert Ressler confirms that she *has* worked on cases for the FBI. 'I invited her to the Academy. I work with her off and on. I had her at the Academy as a lecturer to my classes, but I used her in a couple of cases and the Bureau went bonkers because they said *"You're using psychics and that's voodoo and witchcraft."'*

Ressler describes the first time he watched Renier's technique. 'I met Noreen back in the '70s at a conference on parapsychology down in Southern Virginia,' he says. 'She came up and did her little routine. People put these metal objects in envelopes and sent them down front and put an identifying initial on it, then she'd pick it up and say *"Ohhh, let's see, this guy is a big tall guy, and he's young, robust, well built."* That described most of the cops in the room. *"And he likes speed and excitement."* I thought, most cops do. Now she says *he had an operation, he has a scar on the back of his left leg, he's single,* then she says *he's got black hair, no, he's got white hair, no, he's got black hair, no, white hair. . . I don't understand this.*

'Pretty soon a guy gets up. He's a young guy, tall, muscular, big chest and shoulders. He says, I have a motorcycle, I have a Corvette, I like speed, and I drive like a maniac even though I'm a cop. He fits the general pattern. . .

'He has a baseball cap on. He had jet black hair. She says, "Well, I said you had black hair. I guess I was right." He takes his hat off: he's got a white lock right up the centre of his hair.'

Commendations: Has impressed many people in the media and law enforcement. Speaking at Quantico and working with the FBI was a considerable coup.

Complaints: Has exaggerated or misrepresented cases she has predicted or solved. Makes numerous appearances on vacuous daytime TV shows.

NELLA JONES

Probably no case ever thrust psychic detection into the spotlight as intensely as that of the Yorkshire Ripper. July 1979 saw a tabloid frenzy of psychic predictions and sketches. Frustrated police brought in a stream of psychics and followed up on countless dead-end clues. Weighing in with her own vision of the killer – by far the closest that anyone came to describing Peter Sutcliffe, who was arrested in 1981 – was Nella Jones.

Nella told a tabloid journalist that the Ripper was a transvestite who also donned priestly vestments now and then. This was incorrect. But she said that his name was Peter, and that he lived in a large house, number six on the street, on an elevated site in Bradford, Yorkshire. She said he was a lorry driver, and that the cab of his truck was emblazoned with the company's name, which began with the letter C. She also said he would kill again on 17 November. And all of this was true.

Until recently she was called upon regularly by Scotland Yard. And although it is difficult to confirm whether her information has ever conclusively solved a crime, she has made a large number of accurate declarations. She says she has worked on 150 cases and 'I've never been wrong yet, love, not yet.'

'It started in 1970 or 1971,' recalls Nella, 'with the big Vermeer robbery from Kenwood House [on Hampstead Heath, North London]. I was watching the television news, and they were on about this painting . . . I thought: They won't find it, because they are looking in the wrong place. I sat down and drew a map, and put a cross there and a cross there, and I rang up.

'I tried to explain that I was clairvoyant. Ten minutes later the phone went again: "Mrs Jones, can you come up and help us?" So I took them to Kenwood House.'

There, at the crosses on Nella's map, the police found the frame and the alarm system from the painting. 'I was taken to Superintendant Arthur Pike. His first words – I shall never forget them as long as I live – were, "Well done, Nella. When did you put them there?" I said, "Typical copper – I go out of me way to help you, and this is all you can say."'

Nella went on to describe a cemetery where she said the painting was hidden. The police thought it sounded like nearby Highgate, but the ensuing search proved fruitless. 'They still thought I'd done it. Arthur Pike said afterwards that he was on the point of arresting me twice . . . Where did they find the picture? In the cemetery – the next one down to Highgate.

'I would have liked some of the reward money I was entitled to. They had a reward up for the painting. I didn't get a penny.'

(In fact, the painting had been stolen by the IRA, who threatened to burn it on St Patrick's Day. The cemetery they had hidden it in was in the City of London – more than ten miles from Highgate – and it was found by a policeman from another force.)

Nella once submitted to a test conducted by James Randi in which she examined several items, one of which had been used in a gruesome crime. 'Nella failed miserably,' says Randi. 'She gave totally wrong histories and then made all kinds of excuses: "Well, if you want to test it, this isn't the correct way." The correct way is to make her look good.'

'They'll never get it to work under scientific conditions,' says Nella.'It's got to be absolutely free, absolutely natural. The minute you start putting labels on it, it doesn't happen.'

Randi is unimpressed. 'She gave all kinds of horrendous histories for objects that had been taken directly off the assembly line with plastic gloves and had never been touched by anybody who even had an evil thought. And when she came upon the fireman's axe that had actually been used not only to murder two people in bed, but also to chop their bodies into little pieces, she said this was used to force entry into a room. I think you'd call that missing the point somewhat. It was a totally miserable failure. But the audience was very much on her side.

'There are so many people who believe her, and media people dote on her because she's a good story. Nella Jones fails? Well, that's a non-story . . .'

Commendations: Good calls on numerous cases. Great call on the Ripper case, but it did not contribute to his capture. Scotland Yard once sent Nella an official letter of commendation.

Complaints: Failed Randi's test. Openly bitter about the lack of financial reward in psychic detection.

> *'Look, all I know is that so far, Yappi has provided more solid, concrete leads on this case than you have. Now if you don't mind, I have to get an APB out on a* — (checks notebook) *white male, age 17 - 34, with or without a beard and maybe a tattoo, who's impotent'*
> DETECTIVE CLINE
> *'Might as well go home Mulder. This case is as good as solved'*
> SCULLY
> *Clyde Bruckman's Final Repose*

Authors Jane Ayers Sweat and Mark W. Durm polled police departments of the 50 largest cities in the US on the subject of psychic detection and published their results in the *Skeptical Inquirer*. Of those that responded, 65% said they never used psychic information, and none admitted taking much stock of it at all. Several complained that it actually hampered an investigation. At best, the chief of detectives for the Chicago PD, Edward Wodnicki, told of two occasions on which psychic information had proved accurate.

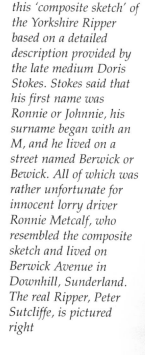

The authors were criticised for confining their survey to cities. Rural PDs, it was argued, with looser bureaucracies and fewer resources, were more likely to employ psychics. So Sweat and Durm did a second survey, this time of small-town police – and found that they were actually even *less* disposed toward employing psychics. No less than 81% said they had never used psychics, and not one related an instance in which a psychic had been of any use.

In 1979 Martin Reiser, director of the Behavioral Sciences Services Section of the Los Angeles Police Department asked 12 psychics to provide clues for two solved crimes and two unsolved crimes. Little or nothing useful came as a result. In 1980 he matched 12 psychics, 11 college students, and 12 homicide detectives. The psychics provided ten times the information of the other groups, but fared no better than they did in terms of solving crime.

Across the board the problem seems to be that everyone is so concerned with debating whether or not psychic detectives really are psychic that they have forgotten the more important question of whether they really are detectives. And the answer, for now, seems to be negative.

The researchers on the book *Psychic Sleuths* were unable to find a single example of a case which could not have been solved without the 'assistance' provided by a psychic. So we shouldn't plan to give up on straightforward police work just yet.

In July 1979 the Sunday People *printed this 'composite sketch' of the Yorkshire Ripper based on a detailed description provided by the late medium Doris Stokes. Stokes said that his first name was Ronnie or Johnnie, his surname began with an M, and he lived on a street named Berwick or Bewick. All of which was rather unfortunate for innocent lorry driver Ronnie Metcalf, who resembled the composite sketch and lived on Berwick Avenue in Downhill, Sunderland. The real Ripper, Peter Sutcliffe, is pictured right*

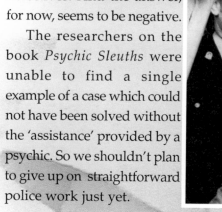

*'Yeah, this is more like it. No more psychics
and their vague visions and predictions. Hell, we
don't even need our own hunches. This case is now just
about good ol' fashioned forensic police work'*
DETECTIVE CLINE

*'Mulder – it's the bellhop! He's the killer.
The bellhop at the hotel'*
SCULLY

'How the hell does she know that?'
DETECTIVE CLINE

'Woman's intuition'
MULDER

Clyde Bruckman's Final Repose

There again, maybe police work is not always so straightforward. Robert Ressler remarks that after observing the FBI Behavioral Science Unit at work, Noreen Renier informed him that the most talented criminal profilers were those who had some psychic ability.

'I don't disagree, you know. I don't particularly agree. I have never questioned myself as to how I profile. I'm open minded.'

*'I've worked with many psychic detectives,
Scully. They're all more pathetic than prophetic.
And yet . . . I know there's someone out there. Someone who
possesses the ability to "see". Who can be
used in a way that'll change the
nature of criminal investigations for . . .
Well, I can dream, can't I?'*
MULDER

Clyde Bruckman's Final Repose

I WANT TO BELIEVE

TOP SECRET
CLASSIFIED

CLASSIFIED

X-FILE: QUAGMIRE

FEDERAL BUREAU OF INVESTIGATION

Preliminary case notes by Special Agent Fox Mulder

U.S. Forestry Service employee Dr. William Bailey is not the first person to be reported missing from the environs of Heuvelmans Lake. According to the police report, a scout troop leader last seen leaving his troop to answer the call of nature has not been seen or heard from for over a week.

The legend of 'Big Blue' the unknown creature reputed to inhabit the lake may or may not be relevant. But given our jurisdiction to investigate the disappearance of Dr. Bailey, I am keen to take the case on. Providing Agent Scully is amenable, I intend to depart for Georgia early tomorrow morning (Saturday).

LAKE MONSTERS

Investigating a spate of lakeside disappearances, the Agents ponder a local legend. But *Quagmire's* Big Blue is hard to pin down. First it's a huge, prehistoric beast. Then it's a hoax to lure tourists. Then it's an errant alligator, and finally . . . it's a huge prehistoric beast.

This air of perplexity mirrors the real-life hunt for lake-dwelling leviathans.

'Like most kids, I was fascinated by the idea. And the theory that during the glacial thaw 10,000 years ago, lakes were formed as land levels rose, trapping certain marine species. Some becoming extinct, but others adapting over the centuries to the desalinizing water . . . But then I grew up and became a scientist'

SCULLY

'Some cryptozoologists speculate that it may be an evolutionary throwback. Possibly prehistoric'

MULDER

Quagmire

Cryptozoology is the study of undocumented, out-of-place or otherwise enigmatic creatures, and *Quagmire* was the first time the field had been mentioned by name in a TV drama. This delighted cryptozoologists almost as much as the fact that *Quagmire's* lake was named after Dr Bernard Heuvelmans, father of the discipline.

The concept of prehistoric creatures existing underwater is not entirely far-fetched. A thriving colony of Coelacanth, a fish presumed extinct for the last 65 million years, was discovered this century off the south east coast of Africa. As for the alligator, *Quagmire's* 'red herring'; we may take this familiar species for granted, but it is nothing if not a prehistoric monster. (And according to veteran cryptozoologist Loren Coleman, 'crocs and 'gators seem to like to teleport' – that is, they've been known to turn up in the unlikeliest places.)

Background picture - Loren Coleman - Fortean and cryptozoologist extraordinaire

*'On the old mariner maps, the cartographers would designate
unexplored territories by simply writing: Here Be Monsters'*
SCULLY
'I've seen the same thing on maps of New York City'
MULDER

Quagmire

Reports of strange aquatic beasts date back to the 'sea serpents' of timeless sailors' lore. Many were no doubt the products of misidentification, superstition, or the rapture of the sea. But sightings continue today, usually in concentrated bursts not unlike UFO 'flaps'.

Descriptions tempt comparison with the plesiosaur, an aquatic reptile with a broad, flat body, short tail, long, flexible neck, and large, paddle-like limbs, believed to have become extinct 65 million years ago. In 1977, a Japanese fishing vessel, the *Zuiyo-maru*, caught a rotting carcass in its nets off Christchurch, New Zealand. Before they threw it back, the crew snapped

several photographs, the evidence of which is clearly suggestive of a plesiosaur-type creature.

Others believe them to be zeuglodons – snake-like whales presumed extinct for the last 20 million years. But at least one 'sea monster' belongs to a recognised species, grown gargantuan. The Kraken, legendary terror of the North Seas, was in fact a form of squid, *Architeuthis*.

A dredged carcass found 30 miles east of Christchurch, New Zealand on 25 April 1977. Unfortunately, it smelt so unpleasant that the crew of the Zuiyo-Maru had to toss it back

There are unconfirmed reports of squid exceeding 100 feet in length, although the largest documented specimen was a 65-footer beached in New Zealand in 1880. Could some lake monsters fall into this category? Loren Coleman is doubtful. 'There are several reports of sharks, seals and octopus found out-of-place in fresh water. However, there have been no reports as far as I know of giant squid found in lakes or lochs.'

'Lake creatures have been reported for centuries, in dozens of countries. From the monsters in Loch Ness and Shiel to the Ogopogo in Lake Okanagan'

MULDER

'And Lake Champlain; Lagerflot, Iceland; and a number of other places in the Northern Hemisphere'

SCULLY

Quagmire

Although lake monsters seem to lurk most often in the inland waters of Celtic and Scandanavian countries – whose folkloric traditions are redolent with aquatic assailants – denizens of the deep have been affectionately documented throughout the world. Lake Ikeda in southeast Satsuma, Japan, has long been reputed to be haunted by dinosaur-like beasts. A curious creature which appeared to be over 10 metres long was captured on video there in 1991. Ikeda is home to a thriving population of two-metre eels, so that a mutated eel – promising enough anago sushi to feed an army of sumo wrestlers – is one possibile explanation. Lake Nahuel Huapi, Argentina, has a monster tradition older than that of Loch Ness. One recent sighting describes 'Nahuelito' as 10 metres long and greyish-green in colour, having several humps and breathing in loud snorts.

A lake monster legend – as the locals appreciated in *Quagmire* – is a guaranteed tourist draw. Port Henry, New York, and Drumnadrochit, Scotland, base major tourist industries on monsters Champ and Nessie respectively. One of the more unlikely tourist booms is currently enriching remote Tianchitianchi Lake on Changbai Mountain in China's Jilin Province, where crowds hoping to glimpse the 'Changbai Queer Animal' –

An artist's impression from 'eye witness' accounts of a giant squid discovered off the coast of Tenerife on 30 November 1861. The crew were able to retrieve only the tail, which was 20-24 feet long

described as either golden or black, one- or two-headed, with horns and a long neck – usually have to settle for a teeshirt or keyring instead.

Has anyone resorted to overt trickery to draw the crowds, like *Quagmire*'s unfortunate shop-keeper? Perhaps. In August 1972, Thetis Lake, near Colwood, British Columbia, was invaded by a five-foot-tall amphibious monster resembling the Creature From The Black Lagoon. For three days it rampaged around the shore alarming vacationers . . . then disappeared for ever.

> *'They're fictional creatures, Mulder. Folktales born out of some collective fear of the unknown'*
>
> SCULLY
>
> *'A folktale that quite possibly ate a biologist and a Boy Scout leader'*
>
> MULDER
>
> *Quagmire*

In *Quagmire* it is ambiguous whether the mayhem wrought upon the victims (and on Scully's poor little pup, Queequeg) is the work of a giant alligator or of Big Blue.

Fortunately, there is no authenticated instance of a lake-monster lunching on a local. But could they perhaps be the secret behind the lakes that do not surrender their drowned?

'There is a long tradition of temperate-zone lakes not giving up their dead,' says Loren Coleman. 'Several lakes throughout Maine and Quebec are well known "death traps", where bodies are never found.' Lake Superior and Switzerland's Walensee also have reputations for retaining corpses. In 1975, when three campers who drowned in Lake Pohenegamook, Quebec were never found, many blamed a monster named Ponik which is rumoured to inhabit the lake's underwater caverns. Similarly, Nessie has been accused of devouring missing bathers – and in reality, some bodies *are* never recovered from Loch Ness.

A rather friendly-looking model of Issie the beast reputed to inhabit Japan's Lake Ikeda. But could the sightings be mis-identifications of one of the Lake's enormous eels?

'We're talking about a prehistoric creature that's gone unnoticed for thousands of years'

MULDER

Quagmire

As Mulder noted elsewhere, reports of lake monsters have surfaced sporadically for centuries. But these are very different from the broadly consistent plesiosaur-type animals reported today. To a folklorist it is clear that the factual elements of such tales are inextricably bound up with popular mythic motifs, so that any attempt to separate the literal from the fantastic and compare historic and contemporary accounts is foolish.

Lake Traun in Austria, once home to a monster traditionally described as an aquatic 'lady' is a prime example. As the

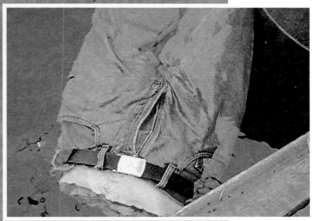

Quagmire's *Big Blue* seems to exist . . . but is she really snacking on the locals?

eighteenth-century writer, Otto Graber zu Stein, reported, 'People say that this lady of the lake often appeared mounted on a water-dragon resembling a skinned horse . . . The shore dwellers of Lake Traun assure us with unanimity that, within human memory, more than one hundred people have drowned there . . . Likewise, the fishermen say that certain of their colleagues, on different occasions, had been caught by this woman and dragged into the abyss, without any trace returning to the surface.'

So are our modern lake monsters no more than myths made palatable for the age of reason? Or are they flesh and blood ? Let us consider the big three.

NESSIE

Loch Ness, Scotland

Legend has it that the first sighting was made in the year 560 by St Columba. Reports continued periodically over the years, but the mystery didn't really take hold – and the reports gain consistency in their details – until the age of mass communications.

Interest in Nessie boomed in 1933–34. Sightings abounded, and newspapers all over the world carried the latest reports, amongst them the 'Surgeon's Photo' – one of the best-known images in the history of cryptozoology. Gynacologist Robert Wilson enjoyed 60 years of notoriety for his lucky snapshot, until researchers Alastair Boyd and David Martin finally debunked its authenticity. Wilson, approaching the end of his life, confessed to the hoax.

In 1960, using a small Bolex movie camera, Tim Dinsdale shot the first

The infamous 'surgeon's photo' of a small model glued to a toy submarine. Gynaecologist Robert Wilson inisted for six decades that his snap was a bona fide image of Nessie

and most famous moving image of the monster. His film was analysed by the RAF Reconnaissance Intelligence Centre, who concluded that it showed 'probably an animate object 12–16 feet long, 3 feet high and 6 feet wide, travelling at 12 m.p.h.'

Other credible witnesses followed. Ian Cameron, former head of the Highlands Criminal Investigations Department, reported a sighting lasting for over an hour in June 1965. His claim was corroborated by his fishing companion and by seven strangers on the other side of the loch.

In 1969 the submarine *Pisces* headed the first underwater investigation, followed soon after by *Yellow Submarine* from the United States. In 1972, researchers from the Academy of Applied Sciences in Massachusetts and the Loch Ness Investigation Bureau picked up two 20- to 30-foot objects on sonar near Urquhart Bay. Although they failed to obtain a decent photograph their sonar recording was widely accepted as genuine. A decade later a massive 1500-hour sonar hunt by a team of 150 shed no further light on the mystery. But interest – and the hunt – continued.

The sonar room aboard MV SIMRAD, part of 1992's Project Urquhart - yet another in a long line of technologically advanced searches for anomalous beasts in Loch Ness

The sheer persistence of the Nessie phenomenon begs many questions. Some believe that Nessie is able to commute between the loch and the open sea. Submarine film of undersea caverns has prompted the idea that perhaps the loch is linked to the sea or other bodies of water by tunnels through which Nessie is able to come and go at will. Or perhaps she follows a land route. 'There are enough reports of the larger loch creatures being sighted on land,' says Loren Coleman, 'for us to assume they can cross from the sea to rivers to lochs.' In fact, the 1920s and 30s brought a number of land-based sightings, and in 1933 a couple driving along the eastern shore of Loch Ness reported a 25- to 30-foot, elephant-gray, serpent-like creature with an arched body jerking its way across the road.

Convincing video footage made by a visitor to Urquhart Castle in August 1992 so impressed the respected zoologist Peter Meadows that he concluded it could well depict a living object, and in 1994, science joined forces with tourism when a 34-foot submarine deployed to study the lochbed took on six tourists at a time to help finance the project. In July 1995 mysterious grunts were heard 450 feet below the surface, but as yet the longed-for sighting remains elusive.

OGOPOGO

Lake Okanagan, British Columbia

Unlike Nessie and her possibly plesiosauric kin, Ogopogo and other major North American monsters – including Manipogo in Lake Manitoba and Winnipogo in Lake Winnepegosis – are said to resemble zeuglodons.

In 1974 a teenage girl swimming in Lake Okanagan felt a large creature brush against her. Clambering aboard a raft, she saw 'a hump or coil which was eight feet long and four feet above the water, moving in a forward motion. Five to ten feet behind the hump, about five to eight feet below the surface, I could see its tail. It was forked and horizontal like a whale's, and it was four to six feet wide.'

Although there has never been a convincing photograph or sonar reading taken of the beast, eyewitness testimony is extensive and credible. The local populace, however, has undermined Ogopogo's authenticity by exploiting the monster heavily as a source of tourism, erecting a cartoonish public statue and staging an annual Ogopogo Day festival.

CHAMP

Lake Champlain, USA

One of the most impressive – and, so far, not effectively discounted – monster photographs was taken on Lake Champlain in July 1977 by Sandra Mansi, a tourist from Connecticut. A deep, cold, lake stretching 109 miles along the New York–Vermont border, Champlain is the location of more than 300 recorded sightings of America's pre-eminent lake monster.

The Mansis claimed that for between two and four minutes they had observed a prehistoric-looking creature gambolling in the lake. For three years the bright colour snapshot, distinctly showing a large, unknown object estimated at between 24 and 78 feet long, was just another entry in the Mansi family album, until a social studies teacher heard about it from a colleague of Sandra Mansi's. He persuaded the family to release the photograph for study, and it was found to be untampered with. Considering that the Mansis gained nothing from it, and made no attempts to sell or promote it, a deliberate hoax is unlikely. Strangely, the object resembles a plesiosaur rather than the zeuglodon-like Champ of most reports, although, under close examination, what is presumed to be the head and neck of the beast might also be interpreted as the flipper of a small whale swimming on its side.

Sandra Mansi gazes at Lake Champlain. The jury is still out on her picture of Champ

Champ is one monster which has never been diffident. On 9 July 1873 the *Whitehall* (New York) *Times* reported that a railway construction crew working by the lake saw the head of 'an enormous serpent sticking out of the water and approaching them'. The beast was allegedly covered in glistening silver scales, with two rows of teeth and an unusual head that was broad and flat, 'with a hood spreading out from the lower part of it like a rubber cap often worn by mariners with a cape to keep the rain from running down the neck'. As it approached, it would occasionally spurt a 20-foot stream of water from its nostrils.

Within a few days, local farmers began to report missing livestock and tracks suggestive of animal carcasses being dragged to the water. In August, the *WB Eddy*, a small steamship, reported that it had nearly overturned when it struck the serpent, and a few days later the *Whitehall Times* reported that another ship, the *Molyneaux*, had trapped the beast in a thickly weeded bay, where its crew had shot and killed it. Oddly enough, the carcass of the serpent was never recovered, despite a $50,000 reward offered by showman P.T. Barnum.

On 21 July 1883 the *Plattsburgh Morning Telegram* published an account of a sighting by the local county sheriff of 'an enormous snake or water serpent', and by 1886 Champ was being sighted almost daily. In the ensuing years the beast terrorised a group of lakeside picnickers in Vermont, surprised a duck hunter on the Mississquoi River (which flows from Lake Champlain) who found an 'enormous serpent coiled up on the swampy shore and asleep' and glided along a road near Lake George, where it was spotted by a farmer who described it as being somewhere between 25 and 75 feet long.

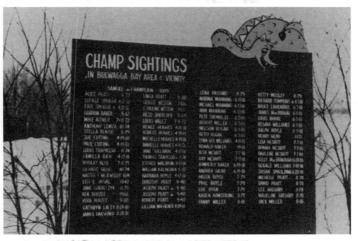

Reports of a snakelike creature in Lake Champlain continued into the 1970s, when they began to be joined by reports of a dinosaur-like creature with humps, much like those from Loch Ness.

How do these creatures manage to survive the centuries, changing their shape and behaviour, wriggling across dry land or diving through subterranean tunnels?

Cryptozoologists point out that, although pet names like Nessie and Champ suggest a single individual, such creatures, if they really exist, would be part of a breeding colony – which may at least explain their apparent longevity.

Many, however, remain convinced that the unexplored and shadowy depths from which these monsters spring are those of the human mind.

MORE WEIRD NATURE

Mulder and Scully find their lives in mortal danger in *Firewalker*, the story of Daniel Trepkos, a brilliant scientist driven to the brink of insanity when he discovers a new life-form dwelling in a volcano, and of Trepkos's doomed team of fellow researchers who become infected by it.

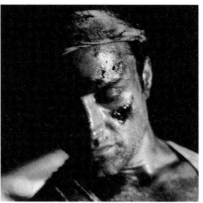

Doomed scientist Daniel Trepkos

The story behind *Firewalker* provides a fascinating insight into the conception of an *X-Files* episode. Writer Howard Gordon wanted to weave a dark and foreboding tale styled after *Heart of Darkness*, Joseph Conrad's classic journey into madness and obsession. 'This guy, Trepkos, was Mulder's counterpart,' Gordon explains. 'He had so maniacally wanted to pursue what was inside. . . at the cost of his relationship and his team, and finally his own sanity. But, ultimately, I wasn't Joseph Conrad, and the thing fell short thematically.' Gordon notes that having less than an hour of screen time to fill and only three weeks in which to write an episode can sometimes be difficult, but he concludes: 'It came out okay. I didn't love it, but I was happy with it.'

In terms of the storyline itself Gordon describes *Firewalker* as 'essentially the marriage of two different ideas'. A habitual reader of the scientific press, Gordon came upon the seeds of inspiration for *Firewalker* among his stack of journals. The first was the news of volcanic explorations carried out by the NASA-funded robotic probe Dante II (for more, see *The Search for Extraterrestrial Intelligence*), which inspired the episode's titular robot. The other, explains Gordon, 'was an article on the stink ant'.

> *'It's a parasite. It lives to find a host,*
> *to perpetuate its genetic material'*
>
> DANIEL TREPKOS
>
> *Firewalker*

The stink ant, *Megaloponera foetens*, is a large, floor-dwelling ant native to the ancient rain forests of Cameroon, in west central Africa. And frequently, it stars as the victim in one of nature's grisliest horror stories.

Among the undergrowth through which the stink ant forages daily for food lurk the spores of an arboreal fungus known as *Tomentella*. The spores are so minute (invisible, in fact, to the human eye) that one can easily be absorbed by an unfortunate ant, after which it heads directly for its victim's brain and lodges itself there. As the spore begins to grow, the ant's behaviour patterns change and it appears to lose its grip on sanity, emitting cries loud enough to be heard by the human ear (the stink ant is the only member of the ant family capable of this) and displaying signs of anxiety and confusion. The next stage, however, is one of nature's most awe-inspiring examples of a parasitic organism manipulating its host's behaviour for its own purposes: a sudden injection of method into the infected ant's madness. The ant, who would otherwise remain on the forest floor from birth to death, chooses a plant or tree and begins to climb for the first – and last – time in his life.

The ant's ascent is arduous, but the ever-growing fungus in his brain compels him to continue. All his energy spent, he finally stops – at a height ideal for the fungus's purpose – and affixes himself to the plant with his mandibles. He stays motionless, as if aware that there is nothing left for him to do but give himself up to death and the fungus that is consuming him. After two weeks of feasting on its host, the maturing fungus develops a spike, about an inch and a half long with a bright orange tip, which bursts through the ant's head and eventually explodes, showering spores down onto the ground, where the cycle can begin again.

Howard Gordon was captivated by this macabre image. 'I thought: wow, how cool: just the image of a spike, literally an inch-and-a-half-long spike, coming out of a little ant head. So I said: what if that happened to a person?'

'Mulder, the fundamental building block of every organism known to man is carbon. From the smallest bacterium to the largest redwood tree'

SCULLY

'But silicon is the closest element to carbon. They react almost identically with other elements, the way they bind into complex molecules. A silicon life form in the deep biosphere is one of the Holy Grails of science . . . and maybe Trepkos found it'

MULDER

Firewalker

To make his fictional fungus's background more arcane, Gordon hit upon the idea of making it a silicon-based life-form. 'It had been done a couple hundred times on various things, but it *is* the alternate life-system approach.'

Perhaps the concept of a silicon-based life form has endured in fiction because it appears so tantalisingly close to the realm of possibility. On the periodic table of elements, silicon sits next to carbon (which forms the basis for all earthly life-forms). They share a number of fundamental properties, including the way they react with other elements. What has stirred the imagination of many a science fiction writer is the notion that just as human respiration combines carbon and oxygen to produce the compound CO_2 (carbon dioxide), silicon dioxide (SiO_2) – the compound made by silicon and oxygen – actually exists. Working backwards, creatively, it is tempting to propose that a silicon-based life-form could respirate also, and therefore survive on this planet. SiO_2 is better known as silica. Or sand. And in *Firewalker*, Mulder and Scully discover that the lungs and respiratory tracts of the fungus victims are full of it.

Firewalker's tragic, doomed genius Daniel Trepkos cradles his lost love, the victim of a silicon-based fungus

What makes the existence of silicon-based life-forms unlikely is the fact that silicon doesn't share the ability of carbon to build strands of molecules long enough to create a complex organism. But there again, proving beyond doubt that something *does not* exist is a scientific impossibility, and, who knows, a silicon-based life-system may yet be discovered. Let's just hope that whatever form it takes, it knows to cover its nose when it sneezes.

'It appears to be some kind of fungus . . . I'm not a botanist, but I think it's fair to guess that it's an unknown genus'

SCULLY

Firewalker

As sinister as *Firewalker*'s organism was, fungi do not need to be silicon-based in order to be alien, scary and downright weird. Few organisms on our planet are quite as strange as fungus. Even relatively straightforward types of fungi have seemingly incredible properties – such as having no apparent limit on their life-span. Although fungi *can* die, they have a remarkable ability to survive with very little nourishment by 'shutting down' all but a small section. When further nourishment becomes available, the ostensibly dead sections spring back to life. A 1992 article in *New Scientist* tells of a single fungus organism (a box-huckleberry clone more than 2000 metres in diameter) which, if fungi celebrated their birthdays, would require more than 13,000 candles on its cake.

Odder still are the slime-moulds, which are close relatives of fungi in their spore-amoeba-stalk-spore life-cycles but are just as easily compared to the absurd 'blobs' so beloved by the 1950s B-movie genre.

Fortean researcher Mark Chorvinsky authored a definitive article on blobs in the inaugural issue of his well-respected journal *Strange*, revealing that slime moulds fall somewhere between the realm of plant and animal. Although they are formed by vast quantities of amoebas, these are joined together to act as a single organism known as pseudoplasmodium, which is, as Chorvinsky puts it 'scientific jargon for blob'. As one might expect, blobs eat bacteria, grow, and develop a thin stalk topped with a ball full of spores, released when the ball breaks. What one might not expect, however, is that blobs migrate, moving around freely; sometimes climb, and seem to be attracted by sources of light as well as potential blob-chow. The sight of a marauding blob causes an understandable stir. In 1985 a four-foot-long specimen alarmed golfers as it wended its way past the sixteenth hole on a golf course in Orlando, Florida. And in 1973, blob-mania gripped Texas after reports of multiple sightings, including

A blob of slime-mold found recently in Norfolk

one by a woman in Seagoville who spotted a pulsating mass climbing a telephone pole. Another prominent Texas blob settled down in a garden belonging to Marie Harris, a resident of Garland, and grew sixteen-fold in size within two weeks. A sample of it was sent to a Colorado laboratory for tests, where befuddled scientists were unable to identify its genus, and posited that it may have been some kind of mutation. Dr Constantine Alexopoulus, a professor of botany at the University of Texas and a leading expert on slime moulds concluded, after more than three decades studying them, that 'they are sort of weird'.

Blobs may be weird, but, unlike *Firewalker*'s volcanic peril, they are not dangerous. Popular belief holds, in fact, that all fungi are essentially harmless unless they happen to be poisonous and are ingested. However, a letter sent to Mark Chorvinsky by a woman living near Palm Springs, California, details a nasty experience that, whilst not as horrific as the fate of *Firewalker*'s hapless researchers, certainly throws an eerie shadow of doubt onto the matter.

Whilst gardening one day, she spotted a cluster of *Podaxis Pistillaris*, a desert mushroom which, like *Firewalker*'s fictional species, thrives on heat, and which she describes as looking like 'a puffball on a stalk'. She was shocked when one released a cloud of black spores, most of which alighted on her left arm, and some of which remained even when she turned a hose on herself and scrubbed vigorously. A month later, small black growths began to emerge from her arm, also resistant to removal. They dried up and fell off, but her arm was left numb, cold, painfully itchy and bearing sores which oozed fluid. Even four years after the event, some sores remained and the rest of the arm was striated by white scars.

Podaxis Pistilaris *sprouting from a termite hill in Calahari Gensbok National Park, South Africa – perhaps not as harmless an organism as mycologists would have us believe?*

Local doctors denied that the fungus, held as safe to eat and touch, could be capable of invading the human body, but the victim found three other people who had had the same experience, and heard the testimonies of hunting enthusiasts who claimed they had found rabbits and ducks teeming with it. Despite this, she encountered denial and ridicule by the local authorities and newspapers, and felt a creeping suspicion that this was not unrelated to the fact that tourism accounts for a great deal of local revenue.

Following publication of the letter in *Strange* magazine, researcher Alexander Melbane took up the case. The North American Mycological Society informed him that they had received details of a similar case, and would be keeping their files open.

Firewalker is not the only *X-Files* episode to have turned a spotlight onto the weirdness of nature. *D.P.O.* saw Mulder and Scully pondering the enigma of lightning (see *Electric Skies*), and biological mysteries from *The X-Files'* first season included the lethal bugs awoken from their primal slumber in *Darkness Falls*, the other-worldly parasitic worms from *Ice*, and the Bigfoot-like creature which became a suspect in *The Jersey Devil* (for further reading on all of the above, see *The X-Files Book of the Unexplained*, Volume One).

In season two, *Die Hand Die Verletzt* featured yet another aspect of mother nature at her kookiest and most unpredictable.

'Mulder . . . toads just fell from the sky!'

SCULLY

'I guess their parachutes didn't open'

MULDER

Die Hand Die Verletzt

In the light of the sheer volume of strange goings-on in *Die Hand Die Verletzt*, Agent Mulder's nonchalance at getting caught in a shower of toads is hardly surprising.

What is intriguing, however, is just how common strange rains are in real life: there are thousands of occurrences on record around the globe. Showers of toads or other amphibians, like the one the Agents were caught in, are among the most common kinds of anomalous fall – and the real life events are often even more dramatic than those in *Die Hand Die Verletzt*. A fall of toads in Chalon-sur-Saone, France, in September 1922 went on for two days, and a frog-fall on 29 June 1979 in Comotini, Greece, was so heavy that the roads were carpeted by thousands and thousands of the creatures, bringing traffic to a standstill.

The phenomenon was first brought to public attention by Charles Fort, philosopher, visionary and great-granddaddy of anomalistic study. Fort whimsically dubbed these odd events 'Fafrotskies' – as in FAlls-FROm-The-SKIES – and collated almost 300 accounts from scientific journals, newspapers and other publications. And although he suggested, in his characteristically tongue-in-cheek fashion, that perhaps there was a land in the sky which housed all this debris, his purpose in gathering accounts of this and other phenomena was a serious one: a plea to the dogmatic men of science whose reaction to events which defied explanation was to ignore them.

But it would be unfair to tar the entire scientific community with the same brush. E.W. Gudger, a naturalist based at the American Museum of Natural History, also collected reports, mainly concentrating on fish falls, and wrote in a 1946 edition of *Science* magazine: 'The mass of evidence is as prodigious in volume as it is widespread in time and space. To disregard all this evidence, ranging from hearsay to scientifically attested, and to brand as "credulous" all those who, from personal observation or after much study of published accounts, accept much of it as credible seems . . . to indicate a refusal to consider the evidence offered or an inability to evaluate it.'

Falls of animals were first recorded in AD 77, in Pliny's *Natural History*, which scoffed at the idea that they could rain from the skies, suggesting instead that they *grew* from the ground after heavy rains. Modern science has come a little closer to reasonable consideration of the phenomenon, but still has a very long way to go, since no serious study has taken place.

One interesting new development is the observation made by scientific anomalist William Corliss that some falls occur in a pattern – a relatively small ellipse – which would correspond, by the laws of physics and aerodynamics, with objects journeying through the lower atmosphere having originated in the high atmosphere or outer space. We must assume, however (providing that Charles Fort was not inadvertently correct in his assessment of their origins) that what comes down must once have gone up. And the big question is *how?*

'The national weather service said there were tornadoes in northern Massachusetts. The winds probably picked the animals up into a storm'

SCULLY

Die Hand Die Verletzt

In *Die Hand Die Verletzt*, Scully gives voice to one of the most popular explanations for anomalous falls. Certainly the most powerful wind-related phenomena can and do pick up objects and deposit them elsewhere, and there are cases in which this hypothesis is convincing. In February 1988, The Gloucester Trust for Nature Conservation investigated a shower in Cirencester, England which had brought with it hundreds of tiny pink frogs. It was concluded that they were native to the Sahara, and had been 'air-lifted' across the continents by a freak wind. The sheets of red sand which

Just three of the small, dried fish that rained from the sky during a storm in East Ham in 1984

covered cars in the area at the same time seemed to back up the claim.

Some falls of fish – another remarkably common occurrence – can be explained by waterspouts, aquatic cousins of the tornado and the whirlwind. A powerful waterspout can completely empty a small pond, and in Holland in 1889 onlookers gaped as a waterspout formed over a pond, spiralled upwards and entirely lost contact with the ground, actually becoming a cloud before it exploded, dumping water, fish and pond debris nearby. Waterspouts can skim the surface of bodies of water too – a rain of sardines over Ipswich, Australia in February 1989 was traced to a Brisbane waterspout which had sucked up the fish from shallow waters and carried them into the atmosphere where they had travelled some distance before falling to earth.

The problem with the 'freak winds' hypothesis is that while it fits some cases, it leaves others with too many unanswered questions.

Tornadoes and waterspouts suck up just about everything in their path, yet anomalous falls are almost never accompanied by any other debris – the Cirencester frog fall, with its accompanying sand, was an anomaly in itself. Moreover, nearly all falls of living creatures involve only a single species. How could wind be so selective? Some have suggested that gravity would naturally separate items of similar weights, but it is faintly ridiculous to suggest that it could do so with such efficiency - one would expect to find at least *one* creature of the same weight but different genus slipping in, and yet this is virtually unheard of. Besides, there are falls that include more than one species, differing in size and aerodynamic detail, which do not even share the same habitat – such as an 1890 fall which consisted exclusively of frogs and sunfish.

There are other hurdles in providing a rational explanation for Fafrotskies, like explaining where the falling matter came from in the first place (one might expect the odd report of disappearing frog colonies and pond stock, but they are not forthcoming) and accounting for some of the distances travelled. We know, for instance, that powerful winds from terrains like the Sahara sometimes blow into far-flung continents. But how do we account for the September 1936 fall in Guam which consisted of tench, a fish exclusively indigenous to Europe?

To complicate matters further, the condition of falling creatures varies so widely that more than one hypothesis may be required in order to fit every fall. Fish, for instance, have fallen alive and in good health on countless occasions: ice-cold and apparently fresh-frozen from clear skies in Marksville Lousiana in October 1947; mutilated and rotting in India in 1830 (the *American Journal of Science* noted that the fish 'were seen at first in the sky like a flock of birds descending rapidly to the ground. There was rain drizzling at the time but no storm'); dead and dry in India in mid-May, 1831 and also in England on 24 August 1918, when a ten minute shower of completely stiff, dead eels fell just outside Sunderland.

And what of the showers of creatures whose habitats should be inaccessible to high winds or waterspouts? The falls of deep-sea fish, mussels, worms and reclusive lizards? The turtle encased in a large hailstone which plummeted to earth during a storm in Virginia? Or the eight live baby alligators which a doctor witnessed plopping to the ground from clear skies in a high, wide-open field in South Carolina?

Then there are the falls of inanimate matter. The summer of 1990 brought showers of straw and hay to both Switzerland and England, and there are numerous records of falling seeds, nuts, berries and grain. Falls of substances which cannot be identified are, of course, even harder to explain. Vast, billowing swathes of what appears to be cobweb have been spotted floating to earth, and equally common are blobs of unidentifiable

After meeting townsfolk who worship Satan, a demonic substitute teacher and a teenager claiming to have witnessed human sacrifices, Mulder and Scully aren't too surprised at being caught in a rain of toads, in Die Hand Die Verletzt

gelatinous material, which is sometimes classified as *pwdre ser* – Welsh for 'star rot' – which has been posited as extra-terrestrial in origin, a kind of squishy meteorite. But just because something can't be identified, it doesn't mean that science won't try, in a pretence of

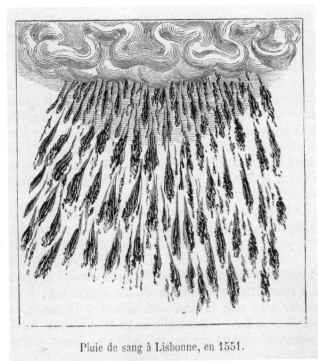

Pluie de sang à Lisbonne, en 1551.

An enthusiastic artist's depiction of a shower of blood that fell over Lisbon in 1551

maintaining control over this unruly planet of ours. When tiny, pea-sized balls of an earth-like substance fell near Muttenz, Switzerland on 9 August 1990, it was duly analysed and triumphantly labelled as 'animal mould'. What exactly this might be, or how it came to pelt down from the sky, remains unanswered.

The massive pieces of ice which regularly crash to earth are usually blamed on passing aeroplanes, shedding sheets of it which have gathered on the fuselage or accidentally jettisoning the contents of their toilets at high altitude. Anomalists argue that this explanation cannot account for the many ice falls recorded before the invention of the aeroplane (one early Indian incident claimed a block 'the size of an elephant'). Moreover, they point out, aeroplane toilets do not work like the toilets on trains. Having said this, aeroplane toilets *can* accidentally jettison their contents. The huge, mysterious piece of green ice which fell on a house in Hampshire, England in June 1990, and was described by the home owner as 'evil smelling', turned out to have just such an origin.

Other unpleasant falls have included a shower of fresh human excrement which fell from the sky in September 1995, pelting spectators at an Edinburgh tennis tournament. Edinburgh District Council's Department of Environmental Health duly launched an investigation, which conclusively absolved the airline operating the Birmingham to Edinburgh shuttle flight (which had been passing overhead at the time), but offered no alternative explanation. And since biblical times, there have been reports of rains of blood. Most of these have been blamed on finely powdered red sands blowing in from far-flung deserts and mingling with moisture in the atmosphere. But there *are* exceptions. Charles Fort recorded a fall of what appeared to be fresh blood in Messignadi, Italy which, on examination at laboratories in Rome, proved to be exactly that. He noted wearily that the scientists suggested it was the result of migratory birds being 'torn in a violent wind' – despite the fact that there had been no reports of wind, no feathers or flesh accompanying the shower, and no bird carcasses found anywhere in the surrounding area. Fort also published details of a July 1869 case in which blood, flesh and pieces of internal organ had rained down for three minutes near Los Angeles, covering a two-acre expanse which ominously centred on a farm where a funeral was about to begin.

Fortunately, nasty falls are counterbalanced by distinctly more welcome ones, such as the shower of £10 notes which fell on Kidlington, Oxfordshire in February 1995; a cloudburst in Bourges, France in April 1957 which brought thousands of 1000-Franc notes and another during which $7,070 worth of bills fluttered down on to a freeway in Boston, Massachusetts. What makes these and other accounts of 'pennies from heaven' so bizarre is that all occurred in wide open spaces with no tall buildings nearby, and none of the cash was ever claimed as lost or stolen.

Fortuitous falls go back to biblical times, when the 'manna' that fell on the Sinai desert fed the Israelites during their exodus from Egypt. It is quite possible that this story was based upon a genuine event. All manner of manna – edible substances – has been recorded as falling to earth, although most agree that it has a prosaic explanation in the form of lichen torn from rocks by the wind, sugary granules produced by arboreal insects, or edible sap and other substances from trees and vegetation – in particular the tamarisk tree. For all this, it is often no less miraculous – in March 1900 during a famine in Chanda, India, bamboo trees exuded edible manna which blew onto the grateful villagers.

Other falls of edible matter have been less poetic. The August 1993 edition of *Sky and Telescope* magazine records a plain, thin crust pizza which plummeted onto the bonnet of a car belonging to federal employee Peter W. Becker of White Mills, Pennsylvania. He was parked well out of the firing range of any high buildings and could see no birds or planes overhead. He also noted that the pizza was 'solid as a rock and stone cold' and added that personally, he preferred pepperoni.

X-FILE: D.P.O

FEDERAL BUREAU OF INVESTIGATION

NOBODY COOKS LIKE AUNT B
A B PIZZA

Report by Special Agent Dana Scully

Having now had the opportunity to examine the body of Jack Hammond, 21, who was discovered dead in his car, I could find no alternative explanation to challenge the County Coroner's attribution of this fatality to lightning.

Certainly Hammond's injuries were consistent with electrocution or exposure to high voltage direct current. Both eardrums were ruptured, heat-induced cataracts were present in both eyes, there was unusually severe localized tissue damage and extensive charring along the sternum, with concomitant rib fractures. However, I was unable to find a point of contact.

A number of elements contribute to my unease in declaring the case closed, primarily the statistical improbability of a fatal lightning strike occurring in the locality at this time. Hammond is the fifth resident of Connerville to apparently fall victim. A sixth individual suffered a direct strike, but survived. The annual number of fatal lightning strikes across the United States averages at around 60. Despite the close proximity of the Astadourian Lightning Observatory, which artificially stimulates lightning, it is difficult to reconcile the statistics with claims of six strikes occurring in the same small town in a relatively brief period.

DEPARTMENT of INVESTIGATION
FBI
THIS CERTIFIES THAT THE SIGNATURE AND PHOTOGRAPH HEREON, IS
SPECIAL AGENT
OF THE FEDERAL BUREAU OF JUSTICE, UNITED STATES DEPARTMENT OF INVES

SUCH IS CHARGED WITH THE DUTY OF IN
TIGATING VIOLATIONS OF THE LAWS OF
UNITED STATES, COLLECTING EVIDENCE IN CA
IN WHICH THE UNITED STATES IS OR MAY B
PARTY IN INTEREST, AND PERFORMING O
DUTIES IMPOSED UPON HIM BY LAW.

IGHTNING STRIKES

ELECTRIC SKIES

D.P.O., the story of a disaffected teenager who could manipulate lightning, was an episode brimming with both humour and pathos. Howard Gordon's acutely observed dialogue and the compelling performance turned in by young actor Giovanni Ribisi made the painfully confused and misguided Darin Oswald one of season three's most memorable characters. 'The inspiration came from, believe it or not, Beavis and Butthead!' Gordon laughs. 'What if Beavis could actually conduct lightning? That was the germ of the idea, but it really represented a kind of adolescent angst. In a way these kids were emblematic of a whole generation of disenfranchised youth who have no ability to bring any kind of concentration or focussed thought to bear on anything. If they ever *were* given this kind of power, how awful it would be. And again, how tragic ultimately: their misplaced aggression and love, their inability to understand what's going on in their lives.'

Beavis and Butthead – an unlikely pair of muses

EXPEARMiNT ONE
RUB YOUR BUTT BACK AND FORTH ON THE COUCH FOR, LiKE, THREE HOURS. YOU CAN MAKE LiGHTNiNG BOLTS FLY OUT OF YOUR FINGERS OR SOMETHiNG.

Besides the desire to explore teenage angst, Gordon had been keen to write an episode about lightning. ' "Lightning boy" is something we had up on our board for years,' he says, referring to the ideas board at *The X-Files* production office, which is home to dozens of file cards bearing neatly inscribed fragments of inspiration.

In researching *D.P.O.*, Gordon learned a great deal about lightning and man's curious relationship with it. He emerged from the experience with a sense of awe. 'It's incredible,' he muses. 'The instant power. The fact that some people don't die, and yet 50,000 volts course through them in a millisecond.'

'Do you know anything about lightning, Agent Scully. . . ?
Did you know lightning kills several people a year at home in
their showers or talking on the phone. . . ?'

SHERIFF JOHN TELLER

D.P.O.

Lightning has always posed a threat to man, but modern man is more vulnerable than ever. Not only does lightning have the power to zap the electronic and electrical systems on which we depend for so many things, but, through these systems, it puts our lives at ever greater risk. Aeroplanes average two strikes each per year, and although most of these have no effect, other strikes have set fire to fuel tanks, damaged fuselages and scrambled electronic signals in the cockpit. One has even burned the nose off a jet.

In the United States alone, lightning kills more than 200 people yearly.

A lightning bolt strikes a tele-communications tower in Finland

Some are victims of direct strikes; others are killed more insidiously. Death by telephone could be a greater hazard than anyone realises. Official figures place lightning-and-phone related deaths in the US at around three a year. But a 1984 study by the Consumer Product Safety Commission in Washington revealed that 100 people died that year and a further 1100 were injured in incidents related to telephones. The likelihood is that a great many of these were lightning related. It's not always easy to tell. The charge from a bolt can travel undetected along phone wires, leaving the wires undamaged, but delivering a fatal shock to someone using the line. A single strike in France on 18 August 1984 killed a fireman calling his colleagues to alert them to storm damage, and, further down the street, a teenage girl telephoning her boyfriend. The boyfriend, although even further away, was knocked to the floor by the charge.

'Did you know . . . that people have seen it dancing on the ground in balls?'

SHERIFF JOHN TELLER

D.P.O.

No natural phenomenon is weirder or more engimatic than ball lightning. Its mysteries are so stubbornly impenetrable, its traits so gleefully disobedient to the laws of science, that until very recently it was relegated to the domain of ghosts and UFOs, with many scientists insisting that reports of it must be mispeceptions, illusory experiences or just plain fibs.

Part of the inherent problem of understanding ball lightning is the difficulty in defining it. A typical report concerns a single, yellow, basketball-sized sphere which appears 'out of nowhere', either indoors (in aircraft or buildings) or outdoors, floats swiftly for up to ten seconds and vanishes with a bang. But few manifestations fit this description in every way, and the huge variation in detail complicates things further.

Ball lightning gives some farm folk in strange clogs a nasty surprise during a storm in France, 1845

Ball lightning has been known to manifest itself outdoors and then enter houses by passing through a window (usually without damaging it). It sometimes fades noiselessly instead of exploding, often moves slowly instead of fast and occasionally spins wildly instead of floating. There are well-established claims of balls lasting up to ten minutes, and they have appeared in a dozen different colours and varying degrees of definition – from sharply defined and compact, to 'fuzzy' or surrounded by a halo. More rarely, they have been recorded as being transparent or smoky instead of fiery. There have been sightings of pairs and trios of ball lightning as well as large balls which fragment into smaller ones on contact. Some people have reported ball lightning accompanied by the smell of ozone or of burning, and others by strange noises – including purring, rattling, crackling, humming, hissing, whistling and crunching. And despite the name, ball lightning has appeared in a variety of different shapes, including spikey spheres, 'dumbbells', 'rugby-balls' and rods; one case involved a rod of light which entered a room through a keyhole and formed itself into a ball on the other side. It comes in a vast range of dimensions, too. In 1936 a meterologist recorded a 'small oblong fireball the size of a pecan' which appeared indoors during a storm and attached itself to a woman's finger. Although most fall somewhere in the range between one inch and five feet, on 8 June 1977 a giant ball lightning 'about the size of a bus' was observed over Dyfed, Wales, by a coastguard. Fortunately, the big guys seem only to manifest themselves outdoors. And finally, ball lightning can be harmless and gentle or terrifyingly destructive – one moment tearing enormous holes in the sides of houses, the next gently pushing doors open without leaving so much as a mark.

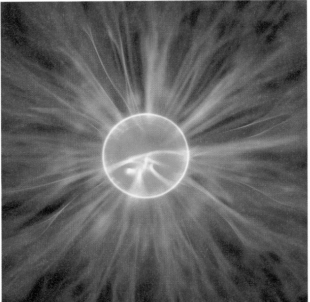

Light streamers inside a plasma globe demonstrate the discharge of static electricity

What baffles scientists most of all is the reported behaviour of ball lightning. Unlike regular lightning and other electrical phenomena, it ignores conductors, metals and water; instead moving in paths that could be described as arbitrary if not for the frequent claims of behaviour patterns that seem almost to be driven by an animal-like intelligence and curiosity: circling and following humans, 'exploring' rooms and stopping mid-glide to hover near objects as if to take a closer look.

In 1928, Reverend John Henry Lehn was in the bathroom at his home in Jim Thorpe, Pennsylvania during an electrical storm when he saw a grapefruit-sized ball of yellow fire outside his screen window. It passed silently through the screen without damaging it and 'rolled around' at the Reverend's feet for a while, then daintily bounded up into his basin and melted the steel chain on the plug before disappearing down into the drain. Bizarrely, the Reverend had the same experience some weeks later, but this time the ball's journey concluded in his bath, again melting the plug-chain and causing him to comment that it was almost as if the ball had visited on a melting-mission and ignored the already-melted basin chain!

In his book *Mysterious Fires and Lights*, veteran anomalist Vincent H. Gaddis listed some curious cases collected by French astronomer Camille Flammarion in the late 1800s. His files highlighted another bizarre aspect of ball lightning: that although balls are capable of causing damage and death, they are strangely benevolent in their treatment of humans. In one case a ball moved slowly across a farmyard towards a stable where two children were sheltering, finally exploding when one of the children kicked it. The resulting explosion killed 11 cows in the barn, but left the children unscathed. In another incident a little girl was left unhurt when a ball, which had been circling her, homed in on the kitten sitting on her lap, killing it instantly. Altogether, numerous animals have been killed by ball lightning, but human fatalities are rare.

No theory based on current scientific knowledge seems to fit. Indoor manifestations could *almost* be explained by the electrical forces generated by a thunderstorm ionizing the air in a closed environment, and creating a ball of plasma which disappears when the force dissipates – i.e. when the thunder discharges. But even supposing that outdoor manifestations were a completely separate phenomenon, this would still fail to account for the balls' habit of ignoring conductors, not to mention their animal-hunting antics.

And as science writer Gordon Stein points out: 'explanations that will work for a ball of one second's duration, for example, cannot account for a 10-second ball', which, he notes, 'requires an energy content so high that there is no known way for it to be formed.'

But with the relatively new field of plasma physics advancing all the time, we are getting closer to the answer.

> '*Scientists will tell you, push comes to shove, they don't really know how lightning works at all . . .*'
> SHERIFF JOHN TELLER
> *D.P.O.*

Besides the mystery of how it is made, lightning holds a trove of other secrets. One enduring enigma is the claimed ability of lightning to imprint a temporary silhouette of one object onto another, sometimes called a lightning shadowgraph or lightning figure.

The distinct image of tree branches that occasionally appears on the bodies of people struck by lightning is believed by some to be a shadowgraph of the victim's surroundings at the time of the strike. Most scientists prefer the prosaic explanation that the dendritic (branching) patterns left by electrical current passing through the body could be mistaken for 'pictures' of real trees and branches. This sounds reasonable. But what of the cases where the shadowgraphs have been of different images altogether? A sailor struck in Zante, Greece had the distinctly non-dendritic image of the number 44 imprinted on his body. Investigation revealed that a metallic number 44 was attached to the rigging nearby. Another sailor hit by a bolt bore the impression – ironically – of the horseshoe that had been nailed to the mast for luck.

These cases were documented in *Popular Science Monthly* in 1893 by a Professor Poey, who had amassed a file of 24 such incidents. The images in his collection included four crosses, some coins, a comb, the back of an armchair and a cow. *Scientific American* reported another bizarre case: eye-witnesses had seen a triple-pronged fork of lightning strike a tree, a robin sitting in it, and a sheep standing under it, killing both the robin and the sheep. Picking up the bird, which had fallen onto the sheep, the observers marvelled at the silhouette it had left on the sheep's body, perfect and detailed right down to the tiniest feathers. Cutting the sheep open, they found that the imprint was also visible on the inside of the skin.

Even harder to fathom are the cases of shadowgraphs where no living being is struck. In 1904, *Scientific American* wrote of a second officer standing on the bridge of his vessel who noticed, after a bright flash of lightning, that a perfect shadow imprint of his hand remained for five minutes on the steel cabinet he'd been leaning against. And during a storm in 1923, workers at a London office discovered, imprinted onto the wooden floorboards, a shadowgraph image of their wastepaper basket.

'Are you aware that something like 60 people die from lightning strikes across the country each year? And five of those happened right here in Connerville?'
SCULLY
'I know it's statistically improbable . . .'
COUNTY CORONER STAN BUXTON

D.P.O.

Lightning seems to take a gleeful pride in bucking probability, statistical and otherwise. Sometimes it seems to be playing pranks. In 1890 in County Mayo, Ireland, lightning struck a basket of eggs, shattering the shells but leaving the inner membranes intact, and in 1902 in Iowa, lightning broke every other dinner plate in a stack of a dozen. Other bolts have unclogged drains, popped bags of popcorn, and drilled neat circles of glass from window panes (once in 1972 at – most appropriately

– the University of Edinburgh's Department of Meteorology).

'Strange though lightning's pranks may be,' writes William Corliss, today's foremost cataloguer of scientific anomalies, 'careful studies of electrical conductivities, moisture contents, presence of metal, air currents, etc. should lead to a good understanding of each event.' This may be true of some of the 'pranks' played on humans by lightning; but then again, it may not. How can we account for cases like the golfer struck in Lancashire in 1991, who was left standing, completely unharmed, although his umbrella had been knocked from his hand and his false teeth had shattered in his mouth? Other strikes have fused zips and metal jewellery and torn off clothing, without causing injury to the person wearing them. In one incident, a baby lying in a pram escaped a strike unharmed although three sides had been ripped from the pram. And in 1991, 23-year-old Jennifer Roberts was reading under a tree in South Stradbroke Island, Australia, when a storm broke. Lightning struck the wristband of her watch, leaving her momentarily paralysed, but uninjured. Her book, however, was fried to a cinder. It was a copy of Stephen King's *The Dead Zone* – whose cover depicts a man being struck by lightning.

Darin Oswald recharges his batteries in D.P.O.

Anyone with a head for statistical probability will insist that with so many strikes occurring every year, the chances are that a few should take place under circumstances that seem strangely apt.

Even so, it is hard not to marvel at cases like that of Alan Wheatson of Kensham near Bristol who, in 1984, was thrown across his kitchen during a thunderstorm just seconds after shouting, 'May God strike me down if I'm wrong!' He had been arguing with his wife Debbie about how to carve a joint of meat. A similar event occurred the same year in Boston, when City Councillor Dapper O' Neill assured an angry caller on a radio phone-in that he would investigate her complaints about a hospital, adding, 'May lightning strike me dead if I don't.' Lightning struck the building that instant, sparing Dapper, but zapping the transmission off the air and leaving listeners worried.

> *'This local lightning is a lot more predictable than Teller realises. It seems to have a definite preference for who it strikes'*
>
> MULDER
>
> *D.P.O.*

Whoever coined the phrase 'lightning never strikes twice' must have lived on some other planet. Most tall structures, such as New York's Empire State building, have notched up *hundreds* of strikes, since they act as lightning rods. But harder to explain are the cases of unfortunate individuals and families plagued by lightning.

Australian farmer Jack McPherson, 55, was struck on 13 February 1983, whilst feeding a calf – at the exact same spot where he had been knocked unconscious 20 years earlier when lightning had struck a cow he was milking. But his experience pales beside that of Roy Cleveland Sullivan, a forest ranger

Multiple cloud-to-ground lightning over Tucson, Arizona

from Waynesboro, Virginia, who survived seven strikes over a period of 36 years. Some were more violent than others: lightning ripped off his toenail in 1942, singed his eyebrows in 1969, burned his shoulder in 1970, set his hair alight in 1972, and the following year burnt through his hat, threw him ten feet and blew his shoe off.

Even less fortunate were the Primardo family of Tanato, Italy. Twenty-seven-year-old Rolla Primardo was killed by lightning in his garden, at the spot where his father had suffered the same fate 20 years previously, just like his grandfather 30 years before that. And in the running for most unfortunate individual is Major R. Sumerford of Vancouver, British Columbia, who was first struck in 1918 whilst on patrol in Flanders, leaving him temporarily paralysed from the waist down. In 1924 he was hit again whilst on a fishing trip with three friends (who got off scot-free) and was paralysed again and put in hospital. The final hit came in 1930 during a walk in the park, this time leaving him permanently confined to a wheelchair. Two years after his death, a bolt reportedly struck and destroyed his tombstone.

One case of lightning striking twice has a positive spin, however. A boy leading a plough-team of oxen in Ermelo, South Africa in 1953 was left unconcious by a lightning strike. He would have been crushed by the oxen pulling the plough over him – had all eight of them not been killed by a second bolt.

'I'd say you're pretty lucky. All those people who've been hit by lightning . . . and you're the only one who's still alive'

MULDER

'Yeah. I never thought of it that way. I guess maybe you're right. Maybe I am lucky'

DARIN OSWALD

D.P.O.

Many survivors of lightning strikes have found the experience to be profoundly life-changing. Multiple strike victim Roy Cleveland Sullivan's experiences forged him a strange relationship with the elements (he once claimed that he 'could see lightning coming') but also left him prone to depression. He comitted suicide in 1983, at the age of seventy-one. It is not uncommon for lightning victims to undergo psychological changes, but they are just as likely to be positive as negative. During his research for *D.P.O.*, Howard Gordon was captivated by *Match to the Heart*, Gretyl Erlich's affecting account of her recovery from a strike and the spiritual awakening and newfound clarity of thought it brought her. There have been many recorded accounts of neurotic conditions and psychosomatic illnesses vanishing after the sufferer is struck by lightning, and a few of schizophrenia being alleviated – perhaps on a similar principle to electro-convulsive therapy. There are reports of certain kinds of blindness, deafness and paralysis being cured by lightning strikes, and one of America's best known self-proclaimed psychics, Greta Alexander, even claims that being struck by lightning caused the emergence of her psychic abilities.

'Let me get this straight . . . You're saying this kid's throwing lightning bolts?'

SHERIFF JOHN TELLER

D.P.O.

Throughout history, many cultures have believed that it is possible for an individual – usually a shaman or a witch – to control lightning. Although no contemporary account contains such provocative evidence as that seen in *D.P.O.*, reports proliferate in modern day South Africa, which has an especially high rate of lightning activity.

Fortean Times co-editor Bob Rickard, who has come across many such accounts, doubts whether such an ability exists. 'Witchdoctor types like to promote themselves,' he points out, 'and claiming responsibility for the death of some local idiot – who probably sheltered under a tree during a thunderstorm – is good for their business and intimidates the customers.'

The downside of this apparently popular promotional trick is that the notoriety it brings is as liable to invite persecution and murder as it is to boost business. 'Witch-hunting is a local pastime,' says Rickard, 'so we hear a lot about people accused of controlling lightning being burned as witches for their troubles.' Early in 1984, a man accused of manipulating lightning for malevolent purposes was stoned to death by 34 villagers in Pietersburg, South Africa. Local beliefs were further reinforced some weeks later, when, on 16 February, a female member of the lynch mob was herself struck and killed by a bolt.

'You said so yourself Sheriff: even science can't explain how lightning works'

SCULLY

D.P.O.

From the beginning of civilisation it was generally accepted that lightning was something the gods threw down when they were in a bad mood. Aristotle was the first to question this, but, unfortunately, the best alternative he could come up with – given the dearth of scientific resources available in 4 BC – was that lightning was burning wind. Surprisingly, we haven't come such a very long way since. Benjamin Franklin's kite-flying epiphany in 1752 taught us that lightning is an electrical phenomenon, but it wasn't until the early 1900s that anyone even ventured a guess at how it is triggered. After decades of research, the front-runner theory – that a cloud becomes positively charged on the top and negatively charged underneath – has finally been pronounced correct. But scientists and meteorologists are still arguing over exactly how this happens in the first place.

Studies have revealed the anatomy of a lightning bolt, thanks to photographic equipment which could see what the human eye could not. A 'single' bolt from the heavens actually consists of a near-invisible downward stroke which creates a channel of ionized air, through which a glowing burst of high-voltage current (almost five times hotter than the surface of the sun) zips up from the ground to the cloud at between a quarter and third of the speed of light. This is followed by more downward strokes – usually two or three, but sometimes as many as thirty.

The anguished Darin Oswald, memorably portrayed by young actor Giovanni Ribisi

The US Airforce launched a study of lightning in 1962, but serious funding – and with it, serious results – was not forthcoming until NASA waded in following the launch of Apollo 12 on 14 November 1969. Shortly after lift-off, the rocket was hit twice by lightning, disabling several of its vital systems. An investigation trashed the popular belief that airborne craft struck by lightning were simply in the wrong place at the wrong time. The investigators found that the bolts that hit Apollo 12 had been triggered by the rocket itself.

The NASA projects which followed this incident marked the beginning of modern lightning research, and further incidents provided the impetus for their work to continue. In March 1987 a lightning strike at Kennedy Space centre in Florida destroyed an unmanned Atlas Centaur rocket carrying a $160-million communications satellite. Three months later, bolts struck three unmanned rockets on the launch pad at Wallops Island, Virginia, causing two to take off by themselves and the third to fall over and shoot horizontally into the sea.

NASA's studies provided them with a reliable system of prediction which enables them to time launches for maximum safety. A shortage of funds in 1992 brought much of the research to a close, but work continues elsewhere.

'Do you know what we manufacture here in Connerville? What one of our local commodities is? We make lightning. At the Astadourian Lightning Observatory out on route 4. A hundred ionized rods pointing at the sky, designed to stimulate lightning'

SHERIFF JOHN TELLER

D.P.O.

D.P.O.'s Astadourian lightning observatory is fictional (aptly named, incidentally, after Mary Astadourian, Chris Carter's executive assistant, who is as captivating and feisty as lightning itself). But many facilities exist today, across America and the world, where lightning is studied. Howard Gordon drew his inspiration from one particular observatory in Soccorro, New Mexico. 'They actually generate lightning there,' he marvels. 'They send probes, rockets, up into the clouds trailing metal wires. It's amazing.'

At Soccorro and elsewhere, lighting is captured on film and video, its radio signals are examined, its magnetic and electrical fields scrutinised. At last some plausible hypotheses have been put forward to explain how clouds become electrified – although scientists are not in agreement about which, if any, is correct. The popular model is based on friction between ice particles moving around in the upper atmosphere. And collaboration between the University of Arizona and the University of Florida (America's most lightning-prone state) has produced a system that can detect upcoming lightning strikes anywhere in the continent – a service utilised by airlines, meteorological bureaus and power companies.

But lightning research is still in its infancy, and many questions remain unanswered: among them how lightning is triggered in a charged cloud; why planes and rockets should provide a trigger; how the first stroke of a bolt reaches the ground and how it 'connects' there; and why some bolts should be more sustained and destructive than others. Nor has science yet found satisfactory explanations for the rarer types of bolt: tubular, ribbon, bead and horizontal lightning. The last is the especially puzzling occurrence of lightning that does not take the path of least resistance to the highest point nearby, as it should, but streaks horizontally through the sky on a mad detour to strike elsewhere, often many miles away. A new theory proposes that horizontal lightning may actually be travelling through ionized paths created by cosmic rays, and that these rays may also create the reservoirs of charged particles needed to trigger a bolt. But proof is still a long way off.

Vladimir Rakov, a lightning expert at the University of Florida's Lightning Laboratory, sums up the situation succinctly. 'Actually,' he says, 'we know very little about lightning.'

I WANT TO
BELIEVE

X-FILE: FEARFUL SYMMETRY

FEDERAL BUREAU OF INVESTIGATION

Case notes by Special Agent Fox Mulder

The crimes committed in Fairfield were the acts of desperate individuals fighting not just one another, but against a force none of them could have anticipated — silent visitors whose purpose and plans can only be imagined.

Could this be an act of alien conservation? Of protecting the animals that man is driving hard towards extinction? Or possibly a judgment on our ability to protect them ourselves, on a global rate of extinction in this century that, at the hand of man, has risen to 1000 times its natural rate?

Could we one day find ourselves driven to this brink — desperate individuals fighting one another to annihilation? Might our fate and existence be finally dependent on the conservatorship of an extraterrestrial race? Or, in the simple words of a creature whose own future is uncertain, will man save man?

IS THERE INTELLIGENT LIFE ON EARTH

Fearful Symmetry sees Mulder and Scully puzzled by the strange nocturnal disappearances of animals from a small Idaho zoo, and their equally inexplicable reappearances elsewhere. By the close of their investigation, they have stumbled upon evidence of a captive breeding programme undertaken by unseen visitors who are not of this Earth (and apparently none too good at map-reading).

As seems fitting in such an unorthodox case, the Agents' primary source of information is an unusual one: a gorilla called Sophie, who can communicate with zoo supervisor Willa Ambrose in sign language.

While mankind continues to ponder the existence of an intelligent, non-human race like the extra-terrestrial naturalists of *Fearful Symmetry*, the facts behind the sub-plot of the episode are a stark reminder that, sometimes, the truth is as close as your own back yard.

How can an elephant disappear from a zoo and appear elsewhere? Mulder and Scully find out in Fearful Symmetry, *with a little help from an articulate gorilla*

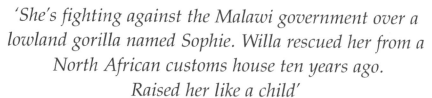

'She's fighting against the Malawi government over a lowland gorilla named Sophie. Willa rescued her from a North African customs house ten years ago. Raised her like a child'

ANIMAL RIGHTS ACTIVIST KYLE LANG

Fearful Symmetry

On 21 June 1966 two University of Nevada scientists, Allen and Beatrix Gardner, took delivery of an eight- to 14-month old chimpanzee called Washoe. Washoe was kept in a fully equipped trailer in a spacious fenced yard behind the Gardner's house. She was well fed, had toys to play with, trees to climb and constant companionship while awake. In return, she destroyed the myth of man's uniqueness.

There had been a few attempts to teach language to the great apes before, but they had concentrated on oral language, a skill which apes, lacking vocal cords, are not physically able to master. The Gardners' first innovation was to capitalise on chimpanzees' natural propensity to gesture by trying to teach Washoe American Sign Language. Research team members only used ASL in front of her and there were active teaching sessions that used a variety of techniques pioneered with deaf children.

The Gardners knew that their results would be closely scrutinised by the scientific community and they designed extremely strict parameters for assessing Washoe's development. Detailed daily records were kept. In order for a word to be considered 'mastered' an observer had to see Washoe use it spontaneously and appropriately at least once a day for fifteen days.

'She speaks to you?'

SCULLY

'Over 600 words, using American Sign Language. She understands over a thousand'

WILLA

Fearful Symmetry

Washoe signed her first word, 'more', after seven months. At 22 months, she had mastered 34 signs. At 40 months, she knew 92 signs. Her rate of learning just kept increasing.

By the time she had mastered 8 signs, Washoe was inventing combinations. Eventually, she even invented combinations for words she had no sign for; for example, 'open-eat-drink' for 'refrigerator'. She also invented new signs. She used her finger to trace the outline of a bib on her chest for the word 'bib'. It turned out to be a valid ASL sign. She asked a visitor his name and when he said he didn't have a sign for his name, she made one up for him.

Washoe

She could also extrapolate a class of referents from a single example; she would use the sign for 'dog' when looking at a picture of a dog and when hearing a dog bark.

Washoe became so good at signing that double-blind testers unfamiliar with the project but proficient in ASL could almost always understand what she was saying. This in spite of the fact that Washoe learned ASL relatively late in life and from teachers who were not themselves initially proficient in ASL.

This was not a dog sitting when told, 'sit'; this was making contact with intelligent life, on Earth.

One would tend to think that a breakthrough of such magnitude would rock the scientific world. But the scientific world didn't want to be rocked. Acknowledging that chimps - and, by association, other great apes - were feeling, sentient beings who had favourite colours, who teased, and who grieved, robbed science of its right to treat them as 'hairy test tubes'. And that wouldn't do. Ironic, given that chimpanzees are considered to be of particular value in scientific research precisely because they have so much in common with humans.

'They've cut off all funding. The animals are being shipped out to other zoos starting Monday'

WILLA

Fearful Symmetry

Getting research funding for language projects was always a problem. In 1970, the money finally ran out. To the vast majority of the scientific community, Washoe, who at this point had a vocabulary of at least 130 signs was just another 'clean chimp' (that is, not yet infected with a deadly disease or injected with toxins) potentially available for biomedical research.

The Gardners desperately tried to find Washoe a safe home and, after a great deal of uncertainty, (during which time she nearly ended up in a zoo), she finally went to the Institute for Primate Studies at the University of Oklahoma to be watched over by two of the Gardners' ex-graduate students, Roger and Debbie Fouts.

Introduced into a colony of 15 chimps, Washoe immediately tried to communicate through signing. Try as she might, her attempts were invariably frustrated. Once, she was on a island with some other chimps when a snake appeared and scared all but one into running away. Washoe signed 'come-hurry-up dear' to the solitary chimp before she gave up on communicating and ran off.

Washoe also showed her disgust (and all too human condescension) with non-signing rhesus monkeys by calling them 'dirty monkey'. 'Dirty' had previously only been used for faeces and soiled things. Now she was using it in a variety of situations, including when people weren't doing what she wanted.

The next stage of development of the chimp language project capitalised on Washoe's seeming need not only to communicate, but to teach others to communicate with her.

'Sophie desperately wanted a baby'

WILLA

Fearful Symmetry

While with the Gardners, Washoe had enjoyed playing with dolls, washing, kissing and even signing to them. After leaving the University of Nevada, she twice had a child which died soon after birth. The second time, the baby was taken from her for emergency medical intervention and died out of her sight. It was up to project director Roger Fouts to deliver the sad news. 'I had to go back the next morning and she was very depressed, of course, and quite, quite alone. Not signing with anybody. And so, I went in and she came up to me. Her eyes lit up. She came up to me and she said, "baby holding holding". And it was a question. She was saying, basically, "Where's my baby?" And I had to tell her, I said "he dead, he finished". And with that, the "baby" sign literally dropped into her lap, her head dropped, and she moved away into the corner and stopped signing.

'So we searched and searched and searched and, 10 days after [Washoe's baby's] death, we finally found a replacement. It was Loulis. He was 10 months old.

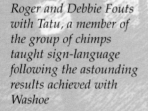

Roger and Debbie Fouts with Tatu, a member of the group of chimps taught sign-language following the astounding results achieved with Washoe

'The next morning I went in and I signed, "have baby". And she immediately started signing, "baby baby", getting very excited. "baby baby baby baby". Slapping her hands, bipedal, hair up, extreme excitement.

'And then, when she signed "my baby", I knew we were in trouble. I knew she misunderstood me. So I went out and got him – 10-months-old; he was on my chest – came in, and then went in the enclosure with her. And when I got about maybe two or three feet away, she got a good look at him. And all this time she's signing "baby baby baby baby". And she gets a good look at him and she just sits down. And then she looks back up. And then she signs: "baby". Obviously, she'd realized it wasn't her baby any longer, it was a strange baby.

'That night she tried to sleep with him like her own baby. He would have nothing to do with it. . . He laid down on his own end of the bench, and when she'd come, he'd move. And then, at four in the morning, she woke up, went into a bipedal swagger, banged the enclosure and signed, "come hug", slapping her hands, making a loud noise. And with that, he jumped up out of a sound sleep and leapt into the nearest hairy arms that were available, which were hers, and she literally engulfed him and lay back down. And from that moment on, they were inseparable.'

Washoe's adoptive son, Loulis, narrowly escaped life as a lab animal. His birth mother, like the tragic primate pictured below, was not so fortunate

'They want to know about Sophie's baby'
WILLA

Fearful Symmetry

Loulis had spent the beginning of his life in a cage at the Yerkes Regional Primate Center in Georgia, one of the places that breed chimps for laboratory use. His birth mother had been subject to brain implant experiments and had bolts in her head. She was so damaged that she couldn't raise him.

In spite of his deprived childhood – sadly typical of lab-raised chimps – Loulis blossomed under the care of Washoe. In order to evaluate if chimps would themselves teach sign language to their young, the humans involved in the project didn't sign in front of Loulis for the first five years. By the eighth day of his time with Washoe, he had used his first sign. Soon, he was chattering away like his adoptive mum.

*'They're putting her in an iron cage as we speak, without
bars or windows. It'll kill her'*

WILLA

Fearful Symmetry

Funding and housing continued to be a problem. Some of the sign
language chimps were lost to medical research. When AIDS first became
a major concern, there was a concerted drive to breed chimps for
research. It was only after hundreds were infected with HIV but never
developed AIDS that it was realized they were inappropriate for AIDS testing.
What to do with all the infected chimps is an ongoing problem.

*'Freedom to what – be killed by poachers?
Who'll cut her hands off as souvenirs?'*

WILLA

Fearful Symmetry

Releasing chimps into the wild is another problematic area. Captive-
bred chimps are simply not trained to survive on their own. It is, indeed,
a jungle out there. At least one sign language chimp was released by
well-intentioned but misguided animal rights activists. She died.

'Don't worry, Sophie. I'll be with you'
WILLA
Fearful Symmetry

Concern over the future of Washoe and Loulis led the Fouts to move again, in 1980, to the Chimpanzee and Human Communications Institute at the Central Washington University in Ellensberg, Washington.

A total of five adult signing chimps live in the specially-designed 7000 square foot facility, hard won after years of fund-raising. The chimps, around five foot tall and weighing approximately 150 pounds, are themselves now owned outright by the Friends of Washoe foundation, a non-profit organisation meant to keep the chimps safe for life. With luck, they will never have to join their 1400 relatives scattered around laboratories across the United States, most in tiny cages, waiting to die in the name of science.

There are other Great Ape language experiments going on in the United States and Japan, some using ASL, others using a variety of language codes including talking computers and lexigrams. Some linguists try to squirm out of the obvious by continuing to move the goalposts in their definition of language, but Washoe and her family have made one thing very clear. . . We are not alone.

Man has no pre-eminence above a beast:
for all his vanity ECCL 3:19
BIBLICAL QUOTATION ON A CHURCH MARQUIS,
SEEN BY MULDER AND SCULLY AS THEY LEAVE TOWN
Fearful Symmetry

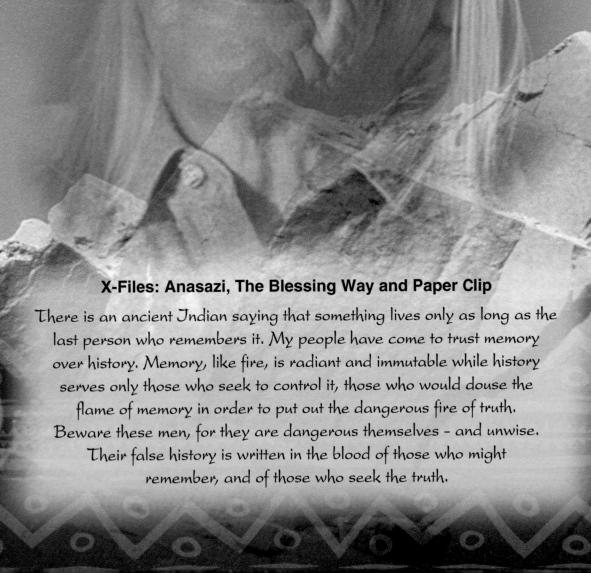

X-Files: Anasazi, The Blessing Way and Paper Clip

There is an ancient Indian saying that something lives only as long as the last person who remembers it. My people have come to trust memory over history. Memory, like fire, is radiant and immutable while history serves only those who seek to control it, those who would douse the flame of memory in order to put out the dangerous fire of truth. Beware these men, for they are dangerous themselves - and unwise. Their false history is written in the blood of those who might remember, and of those who seek the truth.

NATIVE AMERICAN WONDERS

hapes, season one's tale of lycanthropy with a Native American flavour, marked the first time that *The X-Files* had taken its inspiration from Native American culture. It was not to be the last. *Anasazi*, *The Blessing Way* and *Paper Clip*, the trilogy of episodes which straddled the close of season two and the beginning of season three, drew even deeper on this ancient and mystical source.

The trilogy formed an important part of what is referred to as 'The *X-Files* Mythology': the show's ongoing and ever-thickening web of intrigue (for more details, see *Conspiracy*). In *Anasazi*, the finale of season two, 'The Thinker' (the fourth, previously unseen, member of the Lone Gunmen, Mulder's conspiracy-theorist allies) hacks into the government's most closely guarded files, bringing Mulder closer to the truth than ever before. Mulder's quest leads him to the deserts of New Mexico, where he makes an earth-shattering discovery that almost costs him his life.

So near and yet so far . . . Mulder expresses his disappointment that the crucial files are filled with what appears to be incomprehensible nonsense

> *'Mulder, this may not be gibberish . . . I think it's just encrypted, and I think I recognise it: it looks like Navajo. It was used during World War II. My father told me it was the only code the Japanese couldn't break . . .'*

SCULLY

Anasazi

s a result of Scully's quest to make sense of stolen government files which have been encrypted in Navajo code, the Agents meet Albert Hosteen, a wise and benevolent tribal elder (played with radiant warmth by Native American actor Floyd 'Redcrow' Westerman). Hosteen is introduced as a surviving member of the original team of 'Navajo Codetalkers' from World War II. This is one of several elements woven into *The X-Files* mythology that are entirely factual.

'You're going to laugh at me . . .' warns Chris Carter, when asked how the subject of the Navajo Codetalkers had come to his attention. 'I had travelled across country with my wife about a year before I came up with

Bill Mulder dies from a fatal gunshot wound before he can divulge the dark secrets of his past which would shed light upon the cryptic contents of the files (above)

Getting too close to the truth has cost Mulder dearly, as Scully discovers when her partner shows up reeling from the shock of bereavement and desperately sick as a result of drugs covertly filtered into his water supply. (below)

the idea of *The X-Files*, and when we were in the Southwest we stopped in a McDonalds. And they had a little memorial to the Navajo Codetalkers inside the McDonalds. I read the literature that was there, and I parked it in the back of my brain somewhere. I always thought it was a very interesting thing: that here were these people who were once warriors who became something other than warriors and helped us to win the war through their oral traditions.'

'Only a handful of people can decipher it'

SCULLY

Anasazi

Navajo is an abstruse language: the kind in which one word, given four different inflections, has four different meanings. The syntax is Byzantine at best; the vocabulary is rich and full and torture to memorize.

Not many non-Navajo can speak it. In the early days of Navajo–European contact, white settlers tried to force the Native Americans to learn Spanish or English (depending on who was trying to steal their land). During the early part of this century, Navajo children were literally kidnapped and forced to attend government boarding schools where they were not allowed to speak their own tongue. Native languages remained unpopular with the powers that declared themselves in charge – until World War II.

Axis powers were breaking codes faster than the Allied cryptographers could devise them. The Japanese even had soldiers who would issue instructions to US troops on US Army frequencies in perfect idiomatic English. The situation was so desperate that there was an alleged Allied attempt to use Yiddish on the Italian front, knowing that any German who admitted to speaking Yiddish would be sent to a concentration camp.

The American need – and failure – to create an unbreakable code was no secret. Even Philip Johnston, a mild-mannered civil engineer in Los Angeles, California knew about it. Fortunately for the Free World, he also knew Navajo.

The son of a missionary, Johnston had been raised on a Navajo reserve. He spoke Navajo so fluently that, at the age of nine, he accompanied his father and Navajo representatives on a visit to Washington to plead for better conditions on the reservation, acting as translator during their meeting with President Roosevelt.

Johnston became convinced that Navajo, then an unwritten language which was known by only a handful of non-Natives, would make the perfect basis for a code. He persuaded a nearby Marine base to take up the idea, and training began with 29 Navajo boys (some as young as 15) recruited from a government boarding school.

'There are words there I recognise but you will need an actual code-talker to make any sense of this . . . This word means "goods", "merchandise". This word means "vaccination". They are modern words, that's why they stand out'

JOSEPHINE DOAN

Anasazi

Although Navajo does include some modern words, most of those used in the Navajo code were made up from existing Navajo terms. The Capitol became *tkah-chae*, the 'sweat house'. The Army was *lei-cha-ih-yil-knee-ih* – 'dog faces'. The order 'submarine, fire torpedo' became *besh-lo, coh lobe-ca* – 'iron fish, fire fish shell'.

The final version contained over 411 words, and to spell out place names, or words that hadn't been coded, several code words for each letter of the alphabet were devised ('I' was 'ice', 'itch' or 'intestines'). The code was so complete that Navajos not trained in it could not understand it.

Navajo Codetalkers were expected not only to learn the code, Morse, and the use of communications equipment, but also to carry out all the duties of a normal marine. Quite a task, especially considering that most of the men had never been off the reservation before. 'When we got to the [Marine] camp, we thought we were in a penitentiary,' recalled one Navajo recruit. Another, Teddy Draper, commented on the irony of this call to duty. 'When I was going to boarding school, the US government told us not to speak Navajo, but during the war, they *wanted* us to speak it.'

When the first Codetalkers were finally shipped out, they were not met with the enthusiasm one would hope for. The first Navajo broadcast created a panic among the ranks because the soldiers heard the unfamiliar language and thought the Japanese had taken over the airwaves. The secrecy of the venture caused even worse problems later on, with soldiers capturing and sometimes shooting at the Navajos, thinking that they were Japanese. By the end of the war, a number of the Codetalkers were given white bodyguards to keep them safe from 'friendly fire'.

Regardless, the Codetalkers were involved in every Marine assault in the Pacific. The entire attack on Iwo Jima was directed in code, and in the first furious 48 hours, Codetalkers sent and received over 800 messages without error. Afterwards, Major Howard Conner acknowledged, 'Were it not for the Navajo, the Marines would never have taken Iwo Jima.'

By the end of World War II there were over 400 Codetalkers and a total of 3,600 Navajo men and women in the armed services. But despite its distinction as one of the few unbroken codes in the history of warfare, the Codetalker programme ended with the war.

'Officialdom seemed to think there would be no more war,' reflected Philip Johnston. 'The code was allowed to die.' However, many of the Codetalkers went on to important positions in the Navajo community, and one, Peter MacDonald, even became Tribal Chairman.

> *'What is this?'*
> THE CIGARETTE SMOKING MAN

> *'This is where you pucker up and kiss my ass . . .*
> *This man's name is Albert Hosteen — you should remember*
> *that, because if Agents Mulder or Scully come down with so*
> *much as a case of the flu, Albert is prepared to recite chapter*
> *and verse, file for file, everything that is on your precious*
> *tape. I'm sure you're thinking that Albert's an old man and*
> *that there are plenty of ways you might kill him too. Which is*
> *why in the ancient oral tradition of his people, he's told*
> *twenty other men the information in those files. So unless*
> *you kill every Navajo living in four states, that information*
> *is available with a simple phone call. Welcome to the*
> *wonderful world of high technology'*
> FBI A.D. WALTER SKINNER

> *Paper Clip*

Hosteen's grandson takes Mulder to the quarry where he has discovered a box-car buried beneath the earth

Like the original Codetalkers, *The X-Files* reminds us that no matter how sophisticated a new invention may be – whether a laboriously constructed code or a computer filing system – sometimes you just can't beat the old-fashioned way.

'I thought that the oral tradition was a wonderful ironic contrast to the new *electronic* traditions,' says Chris Carter. 'I think that all comes through: that nice switch and reversal. The ironies were easy to see.'

Ironic humour is something that the Navajo themselves appreciate. In 1966, NASA were testing equipment for the upcoming moon launch in a barren corner of the Navajo Reservation near Tuba City. As two men in full spacesuits waddled around while being monitored by scientists, a Navajo shepherd and his son ambled over to find out what was going on. The father

The US marines at Iwo Jima's Mount Suribachi, 1945

spoke no English, but the son asked about the odd encased beings, and one of the scientists explained that they were men preparing to go to the moon. When the father heard his son's translation, he became very excited and asked if the astronauts would carry a message to the moon.

The NASA boys thought it a great joke and produced a tape recorder so that he could record his message. The son refused to translate what his father had said. After some difficulty, the NASA representatives found a Navajo prepared to tell them, and heard that the message ran: 'Watch out for these guys, they come to take your land.'

'There was a tribe of Indians who lived here more than 600 years ago. Their name was Anasazi. It means Ancient Aliens'

ALBERT HOSTEEN

Anasazi

Anasazi, the first episode in the trilogy, took its name from a people who lived in the American Southwest from around AD 1 to AD 1300. Skilful architects and potters, they built multi-storey houses and cliff dwellings, and widely traded ceramics.

Their name is cause for much debate, as Chris Carter found out. 'According to our research, there are many translations, and that is one. So I didn't make that up,' he asserts. 'But I think

The weird and wonderful Anasazi cliff dwellings at the Bandelier National Monument in New Mexico

it's not one of the three or four most popular.'

The reason for the abundance of translations is the complexity of the Navajo language. Finding an exact interpretation is, in this case, impossible. 'Ancient Aliens', as Chris Carter noted, is not one of the more usual choices. The most common include 'The Ancient Ones' and 'Ancient Ancestors'. But many Navajo admit that 'Ancient Enemies' is closest.

If the Anasazi are related to any present-day Native Americans, they are among the ancestors of the modern Puebloans, including the Hopi and the Zuni. Many Puebloans want the world at large to accept the Hopi names for the disappeared culture, replacing the Navajo word Anasazi with *Moqui* ('The Dead'), or *Hisatsinom* ('Those Who Came Before').

For the moment, both the Navajo (who prefer to call themselves *Dineh*, as opposed to the name the Spanish gave them) and the Hopi are losing the name game. Academics and archaeologists have settled on the wildly unromantic 'Ancestral Pueblan People' – decidedly *not* an evocative title for an *X-Files* episode.

Unsure of whom to trust, Scully holds Assistant Director Skinner at gunpoint; she learns later that he is a brave and resourceful ally indeed (above)

Albert Hosteen and his people prove to be the perfect low-tech weapon in the fight for the truth (below)

'Historians say that they disappeared without a trace . . .'
ALBERT HOSTEEN
'Do you think they were abducted?'
MULDER

Anasazi

The Anasazi originally inhabited the area of the Grand Canyon before migrating East – probably because of prolonged drought – around AD. 1100 Some two hundred years later, they disappeared.

Vanishing without a trace is not a fate exclusive to the Anasazi – several tribes, especially in the Southwest, have done so. And outside of *The X-Files*, the theories put forward for the disappearance of the Anasazi are not particularly sinister. Changing climatic conditions are usually given precedence over suggestions of extraterrestrial intervention.

But it is not simply the translation 'Ancient Aliens' which has given rise to such notions. The Anasazi are known to have had a powerful understanding of all things celestial. Many of their petroglyphs (rock paintings) depict moon phases, eclipses and comets. An Anasazi *kiva* (subterranean ceremonial chamber) discovered in Chaco Canyon, New Mexico, has a main door which opens at night to reveal the point known as Celestial North, which appears to remain static as the heavens revolve around it. The Anasazi also left behind tall stone towers, purpose of which is unknown.

'The FBI man would have surely died had he not stayed underground, protected like the jackrabbit or the fox'

ALBERT HOSTEEN

The Blessing Way

Anasazi aired in the US in spring, leaving Chris Carter the summer ahead of him to work on the concluding episodes of the three-part story in which Mulder's narrow escape from death would be explained. It was during this break that a serendipitous opportunity for further inspiration came his way.

Carter and his executive assistant Mary Astadourian had carried out a great deal of research in preparation for writing *Anasazi*, but had been unable to secure the help of a native consultant. 'I had made some factual errors about the Navajo culture,' Carter admits, 'and that was pointed out to me subsequent to the airing of *Anasazi*. Tribal elders never wear their long hair down – it's not a sign of their position. They would never touch something dead; they would not touch a snake. Just little things like that. So I said: fine. We tried our best. We tried to ask people and got little to no help in conducting this research. But I said I would be interested to meet the Navajo and to learn more about the culture in order to write about it accurately. And they, in turn, invited me to this Native American Church Peyote ceremony.'

Carter travelled to Window Rock, Arizona to attend the eight-hour ceremony, which was held in a teepee. 'It was like a birthday ceremony for the son of what they call the Road Man – the equivalent of the Medicine Man for this area. We sat there, all these Navajo and I, and we did the peyote ceremony. They chanted all night long, took the peyote – the peyote tea and the peyote paste – and it was one of those experiences that you can't buy.'

The ceremony left Carter with many vivid memories, some more pleasant than others. 'I'm not used to sitting on the ground, so it was excruciatingly painful, sitting there on that hard floor all night long; that really is my main memory . . . That and the taste of the peyote. It's bitter, very earthy tasting.

Ancient Navajo paintings found at Canyon de Chelly, Arizona. Pronounced 'de-shay', the canyon also boasts cliff dwellings dating back to AD 4 and the Spider Rock monument which, according to Navajo legend, is the home of Spider Woman, the creator of the Navajo, and Talking God, her assistant (above)

The tea's not bad, but it has nothing flavourful about it . . . You also take what they call mountian smoke: it's tobacco, which is not nicotine tobacco, rolled in a corn husk. You smoke that, and that's part of the ritual. So I remember that part too, because I'm not a smoker – I've never smoked a cigarette in my life.

'I remember the tending of the fire. The fire has a spirit of its own. During a bathroom break – I think we took two during the night – one of the women commented on the quality of the fire. She said: "The fire is very calm and gentle tonight, not angry or violent." And I thought that was a very interesting thing: that they see meaning in all the elements. And they see life in them, too: that's very much a part of the way they think. They're very much of the land.

'The peyote did have an effect on me. It was kind of enlightening, in a way, but I don't think I ate enough peyote to find myself transcending. I was afraid of getting sick: everyone says that if you have never done it before you can very easily get sick, and I was a little concerned about spending the whole time on my hands and knees.

'I'm glad I had the experience, but I can't say that I was transported to the place where they hope to be transported, which is to make contact with their ancestors. My father had died just prior to that, so I was hoping it would have something of a spirtual quality, but ultimately, I think it was more just a very interesting experience.'

On his return to Los Angeles, Carter wrote *The Blessing Way* and *Paperclip*, using much of what he had learned in Arizona . 'I have to say that it was very helpful for me to have gone down there. They're very proud people, and I think that comes through in the rest of the trilogy.'

'In accordance with our ancient traditions, we put four oak twigs on the beams of the hogan to summon the holy people and tell them that a ceremony will be held. It is called the Blessing Way chant'

ALBERT HOSTEEN

The Blessing Way

Ritual ceremonies are a fundamental part of everyday life for the Navajo. The Blessing Way ceremony that we see in the episode of the same name forms the core of the Navajo social and religious structure and is not reserved solely for rare, extreme situations like the one in which the Navajo found Mulder.

In Navajo belief, there are all sorts of dangers lurking, waiting to pounce on unsuspecting and unprotected souls. Their belief system encompasses witches, sorcerers, wizards and other sundry malevolent beings, and an astounding array of taboos relating to animals, natural phenomena and even healing ceremonies. Be careful not to pee on coyote tracks, lest the Coyote spirits become enraged. Don't build your hogan facing anything but East. Don't touch the recently dead.

The Well Manicured Man, a senior member of the shadowy secret consortium, approaches Scully at Bill Mulder's funeral, eager to find out why she is so confident that her missing partner is still alive. She doesn't mention the dream she had - which may even have been an anomalous communication from Mulder whilst in limbo between life and death, under the mystical care of the Navajo

Ensuring spiritual safety is paramount. And on the assumption that two nights of prevention is worth nine nights of cure, the Navajo perform the Blessing Way on a regular basis.

'The Blessing Way has been passed down by our ancient ancestors. Its songs and prayers must be followed just as they have been for centuries or the holy people will not be summoned'

ALBERT HOSTEEN

The Blessing Way

The Navajo believe that their creators, their ancestors, the Holy People, came up from the inner earth. When First Man, First Woman, First Boy, First Girl, Wind, The Cardinal Lights and all the rest of them emerged, they immediately held a Blessing Way ritual at the edge of Emergence Lake. As a result, mountains, plants, and everything else were created and given inner life.

The Blessing Way is frequently performed just to ensure that everything is, and will remain, in harmony. But what if something bad does happen? Suppose some evil, smoking member of a shadowy governmental organisation tries

The Blessingway ritual saved Mulder from death at the hands of the consortium, but many, including this unidentified victim and the others found by Mulder in the box-car (left), were not so fortunate

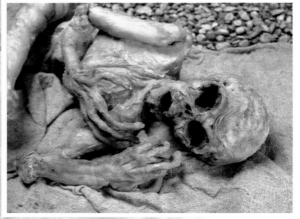

to blow you up in a railway car full of vaccinated alien-like corpses. What then? Fortunately, there is a full range of 'curative' ceremonies, based on the Blessing Way, and designed to target a specific problem.

'When the FBI man Mulder was cured by the holy people, we were reminded of the story of the gila monster, who symbolises the healing powers of the medicine man. In this myth the gila monster restores a man by taking all his parts and putting them back together. His blood is gathered by the ants, his eyes and ears by the sun, his mind by talking god and pollen boy. Then lightning and thunder bring the man back to life'

ALBERT HOSTEEN

The Blessing Way

Mulder awakes in New Mexico, his health much improved thanks to the tender care of Scully and kindly Navajo elder Albert Hosteen, played by Floyd 'Red Crow' Westerman (above)

Hosteen tells Mulder of the secrets buried in the deserts of New Mexico (centre)

In the case of a physical or spiritual ailment, the first step is diagnosis. The Navajo classify disease not by the symptoms but by the cause. This is sometimes hard to determine, so you need to call in either a 'listener', a 'stargazer' or a 'handtrembler'. The first two have learned their craft over years of study; the third relies more on 'divine inspiration' and on being possessed by the Gila Monster. All three go into a trance-like state while diagnosing. Once they figure out what you have (or more to the point, what has you), the appropriate ritual or chant is performed.

Singers (also called chanters) are extremely skilled and usually limit themselves to learning no more than one or two ceremonies. These can last up to nine days and include singing, sandpainting and sometimes ritual bathing. The goal is to attract the Holy People and exhibit such attentive devotion to them that they decide to help you.

Navajo faith in ritual is absolute, and many former Codetalkers credit their safe return from the war to the fact that their families at home performed Blessing Way ceremonies for them. Once home, many were also given Enemyway ceremonies, designed to protect them from the ghosts of those people for whose deaths they had been responsible during the war.

The Navajo themselves have suffered at the hands of the US government. So while they may not actually have a Conspiracyway, they would certainly have the means to help Mulder's soul survive his encounter with its officials.

X-Files viewers may rest assured that the Agents will cross the path of Hosteen and the Navajo again. Chris Carter says that his fascination with Native American culture endures, and adds: 'I loved working with Floyd "Redcrow" Westerman, and so I'd like to bring him back.'

Mulder lies unconscious during the three-day Navajo ritual that is to save his life

FEDERAL BUREAU OF INVESTIGATION

Case notes by Special Agent Fox Mulder.

In the past year, the perpetrators have claimed six lives in two States. I feel confident in my conviction that they have now arrived in California. The Hollywood Hills homicide fits the M.O. in every detail.

To recapitulate: the murders take place at night. The victim is drained of blood; bite marks are found on the exterior jugular and median cubital veins, however, the majority of the blood extraction is expedited by the use of hypodermic needles. Every mirror at the crime scene is smashed. Using the victim's blood, a passage from John 52:54 is daubed on a wall: 'He who eats my flesh and drinks my blood has eternal life, and I will raise him up the last day.'

I believe that the gang perceive themselves as an 'unholy trinity'. Certainly the homicides, in clusters of three, appear to follow a biblically styled pattern. The first victim in each cycle is a father: in the Memphis murders, James Ellis, the 'father' of Ellis and Sons Clothiers; in Portland, Father Wallace, a priest. The second Memphis victim was named Linda Sun; the second Portland victim was the only son in a family of six children. The third victims in each cycle were, respectively, a Jesuit Theologian and the owner of The Holy Spirit, a new-age book shop.

Garrett Lorre, the California victim, was a father of three. Unless we are able to locate the perpetrators with some speed, we can almost certainly expect a further two homicides before the week is out.

SPECIAL AGENT
Dana Scully
SIGNATURE

FEDERAL BUREAU OF INVESTIGATION

Case notes by Special Agent Dana Scully

Although Cleveland PD had warned us about the anomalous nature of the case, I had certainly not expected to be at quite such a loss in recording my first impressions in regard to the cause of Lauren Mackalvey's death, or possible explanations for the condition of the victim's body, which was without any trace of epidermis, and covered entirely with some kind of viscous substance.

I had intended to perform an autopsy, but this was not possible, since in the short period of time that elapsed following the transfer of the cadaver to the Cuyahoga County Morgue, it had undergone an unnatural, and unnaturally speedy, process of disintegration. Indeed, I found only a corroded skeleton and a substantial pool of fluid.

Analysis of the fluid found quantities of pepsin – a digestive enzyme – and large concentrations of hydrochloric acid, almost identical in chemical structure to that naturally secreted by the gastric mucosa, but with at least twice the acidic strength of natural stomach acid. This would seem to account for the accelerated autolysis of the body. The rest of the fluid contained the expected liquefied body tissues of the victim, although only trace amounts of adipose were recorded. Agent Mulder has noted that this missing fatty tissue would account for the discrepancy in the victim's weight as recorded by the medical examiner post-mortem – 122 lbs – and the weight recorded on her driving license – 165 lbs. I concede, but am unable to explain either how or why the murderer might have endeavored to remove his victim's fatty tissue.

According to the victim's room mate, Jennifer Workman, Lauren had agreed to meet with a man she had become acquainted with through a computer on-line service. Workman was able to provide the screen-name used by the man. Thanks to this information, Agent Mulder subsequently discovered that his account had been established using a credit card stolen from a female resident of Aberdeen, Mississippi, who had disappeared two months previously – confirming the link between her disappearance, that of three other Aberdeen women who had answered 'lonely hearts' adverts, and our current case.

THE NIGHT STALKERS

3 finds Agent Mulder in Los Angeles on a murder investigation – alone. Agent Scully, kidnapped by unstable ex-FBI agent Duane Barry and taken to a mountain top from which she has been abducted by who knows whom, is still missing.

(3 is the only episode of *The X-Files* in which Scully does not appear. In real life, this was because actress Gillian Anderson had a rather pressing appointment – delivering her first baby, Piper, by Caesarean section.)

Shattered by the disappearance of his friend and colleague, Mulder gathers his wits as best he can to tackle a trio of blood-guzzling killers who call themselves The Father, The Son and The Unholy Spirit. This unholy trinity believe themselves to be genuine vampires, and, although wildly sceptical at first, Mulder finds their assertion increasingly difficult to dismiss.

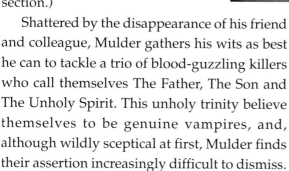

Mulder finds solace in the arms of suspect Kristen Kilar, a recreational vampire who is as lost and in pain as he is. And although she turns out to be all-too mortal, we are left in little doubt that in *The X-Files* universe at least, vampires really do walk amongst us.

> *'I take the life of others inside me. Into my blood.'*
> KRISTEN
> 3

T he vampire seems so at home in late twentieth-century tales like *Three* that it is hard to remember how ancient an entity it is. Like so many elements of traditional folklore, the vampire legend was functional as

well as frightening. As Dr J. Gordon Melton, widely considered to be one of the foremost experts on the subject explains: 'In the very earliest layers of folklore tradition we have vampires who attacked babies, and it was a way of dealing with infant death in very early society. It explained things that nature could not.' Vampires like the *lamiai* of ancient Greek mythology preyed upon babies *and* on pregnant women, providing a pre-medicinal explanation for miscarriage and still-birth as well.

Mulder finds himself on the trail of a vampiric triumvirate in Three

In some cultures, including Russia, Romania and parts of Africa and China, it was thought that those who committed suicide might return as vampires. Perversely, this belief could be a healthy one, emotionally, for the bereaved. Our ancestors generally coped well with death, since most people died some time after falling ill, giving their loved ones time to prepare for the impending loss and reconcile themselves to their sorrow. Suicide, on the other hand, abruptly throws those left behind into the depths of grief, haunted by questions and unresolved issues.

According the deceased the curse of vampirism gave the mourners a legitimate opportunity to come to terms with their loss. Measures taken against the corpse – whether staking, dismemberment or cremation – in order to destroy the 'vampire' effectively ended the dead person's psychological presence among the living, allowing the living to move on.

Vampire lore also played a significant role in reinforcing mores about burial. 'Two, three hundred years ago, death was very much a family matter,' explains Dr Melton. 'There were very set routines for burial – how you prepared the body, how you wrapped it, where you buried it and what you did in terms of a wake or funeral. And if you didn't follow the rules, then your loved one, whom you were putting in the ground, would come back to you as a vampire. So the vampire was an important social reinforcement to make sure that you followed the proper procedures.

'One of the things that we found in our studies is that where the burial process is taken out of the hands of the family and put in the hands of a social functionary – i.e. an undertaker – then vampire beliefs begin to fade away. They no longer function.

'In part, they survive in Eastern Europe because in much of Eastern Europe you're still having to deal with the dead yourself. You don't have undertakers to assist you. Undertakers destroy vampire beliefs much more than campaigns against superstition do.'

But how did these beliefs come about in the first place? Dr Melton has a number of plausible answers.

'Our belief in vampirism seems to come from the fact that when you buried a body, you expected it to decay over a period of time. Once again, in Eastern Europe, the burial process even includes a part where you go back to the burial site four to six months later. You exhume the body, you clean the bones, and you rebury it. That's when they finish off the process [of grieving].'

In Three, *the vampire joint at which Mulder meets Kristen is named Club Tepes, after Romania's fierce warrior king, Vlad Tepes (pronounced T'se-pesh, meaning 'impaler'). Tepes was the son of Vlad Dracul, and since Dracula means Son of Dracul, he was the rightful holder of the legendary name. However, there is nothing to suggest vampiric tendencies: his legendary barbarism was simply contrived to afford him a terrifying reputation and psychological advantage over his enemies.*

Tepes is a respected historical figure in Romania, where this vampire business has come as a bit of a surprise – Dracula was not published in Romania until 1993, having previously been banned under communist rule.

Sometimes the body may not have decomposed as expected. 'There would be times when you would go back to dig up the body and the flesh was still all there. If there's not enough moisture for decay, or for example in the winter-time when the body might get frozen, it would stay in the ground as fresh and as wholesome as the day it was laid down there.'

Even under normal circumstances, a relatively recent corpse is likely to

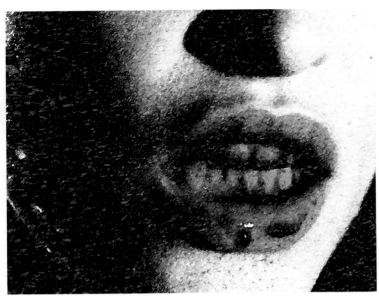

look healthier than one might suppose. Decomposition is slower after burial, skin can flake away exposing a fresh-looking layer beneath, and since rigor mortis is only a temporary condition, a body can be quite limp and pliable, more like a sleeping mortal than a stiff, newly-dead person.

Other anomalous but not uncommon occurrences make it easier still to project the condition of vampirism onto a corpse. Gas can cause a body to bloat, which could give the deceased a deceptively sleek and well-fed appearance, as if he or she had put on flesh after months of gorging. Most suggestive of all, gas pressure can also force blood that has pooled in the lungs up into the mouth, staining the gullet, gums and teeth, and sometimes even dribbling from the lips.

And if the 'vampire' was dispatched by the time-honoured method, there would often be yet more evidence to confirm suspicions. Finding fresh blood in a corpse is not unusual, since not all blood coagulates. And driving a stake through a bloated body will release the gas with a noise that sounds not unlike an ungodly wail.

'I have researched, and believed, the theory that ignorance of porphyria, as a disease, may have been the basis for the creation of the vampire legend in Asia at the onset of the medieval period'

MULDER

3

As Mulder pointed out in *Three*, 'evidence' for the existence of vampires may also have been provided by the unfortunate sufferers of a rare medical affliction.

'Porphyria is a condition caused by an inborn error of metabolism, where you cannot make the adequate amount of blood,' explains Dr Arthur Lurvey, a Los Angeles-based specialist in metabolic diseases. 'Two forms of porphyria are very light sensitive, so people with these forms develop severe blistering in sunlight.'

Consequently, sufferers – like the mythical vampire – do their best to avoid it. Those who do not or cannot, suffer from severe scarring. 'In fact, these people can be somewhat hideous looking,' says Lurvey, 'And a lot of scarring around the mouth and gums might also make the gums pull back so the teeth would become somewhat prominent. This would be grotesque or unusual, and would feed the legend.'

But the similarity between the porphyriac and the vampire stops beyond physical appearance and the need to avoid sunlight. Or does it?

'One treatment of porphyria is actually to give heme [blood] or heme components,' says Lurvey. This is done by injection, not by ingestion; and besides, it is not always effective. But unfortunately, this occasional method of treatment was seized upon in 1985 in a paper presented to the American Association for the Advancement of Sciences, which proposed an even stronger connection between the vampire legend and porphyria: that early sufferers may have attempted to relieve their symptoms by drinking blood.

The medical profession ferociously demolished this claim, citing both the lack of evidence and the fact that *drinking* blood would have no effect. The media, however, had already seized on the story, and accepted it without question. This brought misery to a great many porphyriacs, who, as a result, found themselves ostracised by those who believed them to be blood-drinkers.

'Are you dead?'

MULDER

'I never will be'

THE SON

3

Although vampire lore no longer serves a social function in Western societies, and we no longer dig up and scrutinise our dead, the vampire is still one of the best-known denizens of the netherworld. Why?

Dr Gordon Melton puts it down to the advent of the literary vampire. Writers have always plundered folklore for inspiration, and at the close of the eighteenth century the vampire made its first notable appearance in print – albeit without a name-check – in Samuel Taylor Coleridge's unfinished poem, *Christabel*. Soon afterwards, Robert Southey published his poem

Lord Byron

Thalaba, in which he specifically mentions vampirism.

The vampire's next appearance was in Lord Byron's 1813 epic *The Giaour*. The legend, however, was still so unfamiliar in Western literature that Byron included a reference note explaining it.

Three years later, whilst summering at the Villa Diodati beside Lake Geneva, Byron inadvertently changed the course of vampire history in one night. On the rainy evening of 15 June, the poet suggested to his companions that they have a ghost story competition. The winner was Mary Wollstonecraft Godwin, the 19-year-old lover of Percy Bysshe Shelley. Two years later, her creation was published under the title of *Frankenstein*. Mary in fact met little challenge from the two renowned wordsmiths present. Shelley was so unnerved by the atmosphere that he ran out of the room, shrieking something about a woman with eyes where her nipples should be; and Byron offered only a small fragment of a story.

Also present that night was Byron's physician and travelling companion, Dr John Polidori. Back in England, Polidori appropriated Byron's fragment, expanded and completed it, and published it as *The Vampyre*, paving the way

Bram Stoker

for scores of fictional vampires. And then in 1897 came the most influential of them all: Bram Stoker's Count Dracula.

Dracula set the agenda for a very simple reason – it is a masterpiece. But beyond the grace with which the plot, the sub-plots and the wide cast of elegantly-constructed characters interplay, Stoker's strongest card, whether he was aware of it or not, was the powerful erotic undertone that suffuses the novel. The unavoidable intimacy and the irrefutably sexual nature of one person biting through the skin and tasting the fluids of another served the book – and the vampire mythos – in good stead.

Although *Dracula* failed to achieve much popularity during Stoker's lifetime, it went on to enormous success as a stage play and later as a series of films. As we approach the book's centenary it is remarkable to consider that it has never been out of print, and has sold untold millions of copies worldwide.

Moreover, *Dracula* was responsible for many of the elements we commonly associate with vampires. The cape, for example, is a modern addition, donned in the 1920s, says Dr Melton, 'when the vampire appeared on stage and had to be properly dressed to enter a British drawing room of the period.'

Tom Cruise plays Lestat de Lioncourt, the latest in a long line of romantic literary vampires, in the movie adaptation of Anne Rice's Interview with the Vampire

The literary vampire continues to flourish. In recent years Anne Rice's series of Vampire Chronicles, beginning with the hugely popular *Interview with the Vampire*, has helped to pump fresh blood into the genre and turn its erotic undertones into overt celebration. Elsewhere, the field has broadened to include psychic vampires, vampires from outer space, and even, in *The X-Files*, a fat-sucking vampire.

In *2Shy*, Mulder and Scully encounter Virgil Incanto, a quiet, scholarly man who seduces overweight women via lonely hearts groups on the internet to fuel his medical need for fat-cells. Despite this unconventional twist, Incanto is, in many ways, the archetypal vampire – romantic, erudite, charming and deadly.

'He tasted my blood and I tasted his. Somehow the feelings . . . changed. From then on, we were into "blood sports"'

KRISTEN

3

Perversely, it is thanks to the enduring and growing appeal of the vampire in fiction that it is today comparatively easy to find people who drink the blood of others on a regular basis. All over the world, vampire wannabes like 3's Kristen ape the lifestyle of the mythical undead.

Dr Melton has encountered 'vampire' groups in most of the larger Western cities. 'There are some people who have gotten into blood drinking, who have integrated vampirism into their lives. They live totally in the evening; they find jobs as night-watchmen or chauffeuring cars – anything so they can work at night and sleep during the day. And there are brands of kinky sex that have adopted vampirism as an element – cutting a little bit, sharing some blood. That's all part of the scene. You see it more in Europe – there are large communities in London and Paris – but certainly in the US and in Canada you have no problem in finding vampire clubs – places where blood drinking and kinky sex are mixed together. The largest community in North America seems to be in New York. And in Los Angeles, we're talking about a couple of hundred people who are heavily into vampirism.'

A victim of 2Shy's *fat-sucking vampire, Virgil Incanto*

These people can be described as vampires in the most basic sense – they drink human blood. But their activities are consensual and they do not kill their 'victims': in other words, they're harmless (though it's doubtful that anyone would want them to babysit). The greatest risk the trend poses is to those who indulge in it – the obvious danger being that of contracting AIDS and other blood-borne diseases. Less gravely, blood is also extremely fattening. Dr Arthur Lurvey estimates that a litre provides approximately a thousand calories of high-fat, high-protein nutrition. After a few such feasts, a visit from Mr Incanto might seem a welcome prospect.

'Eternal life. Smashed Mirrors. Blood drinking. Should I be issuing my men stakes and cloves of garlic?'

COMMANDER CARVER, LAPD

'Only if they're hungry'

MULDER

3

There is also some very non-consensual blood-drinking going on. US law-enforcement agencies have seen cases that disturbingly mirror 3 and 2Shy.

John Brennan Crutchley, a 39-year-old computer engineer for the Harris Corporation, a NASA contractor, was one of them. The FBI were called in to profile Crutchley after a naked, hand-cuffed teenager was found crawling by the roadside near Malabar, Florida in November 1985. She pointed out Crutchley's home, where she had been held prisoner, before being taken to hospital, where she was found to have lost between 40 and 45% of her blood supply.

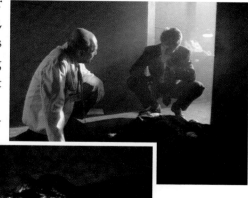

The police learned that she had been abducted by Crutchley whilst hitchhiking. At his home, he raped her several times and drank her blood, carefully extracting it from her arms and wrists with hypodermic needles (like the killers in 3). He told her that he was a vampire.

During his trial, Crutchley said that he had been introduced to blood-drinking as a consensual sexual ritual by a nurse fifteen years earlier, adding that in this case, he had not actually drunk the blood, since it had coagulated and he could not stomach it.

The FBI found clear evidence that Crutchley was into 'unlimited sexual experimentation'. After the trial, his wife insisted that he was not guilty of brutality and was just 'a kinky sort of guy'. However, the authorities had good reason – but no hard evidence – to suspect that he may have been responsible for a number of murders. Although he was sentenced to 25 years – life in prison, Crutchley's release on parole is imminent.

'It's still just a theory, but what if the killer isn't acting out of some psychotic impulse, but out of a more physical hunger?'

MULDER

2Shy

Are there now, or have there ever been, real vampires? Despite a lack of evidence – at least of the kind that might convince the sceptics – literal belief in the vampire has by no means disappeared.

In May 1992 the Philippines was abuzz with news of a *manananggal* – the Filipino version of the vampire – said to be marauding in the Tondo district of Manila. On the night of 6 May the home of an elderly woman named Teresita Beronqui was stormed by a dozen men and a television news crew who had it on good authority that she was the *manananggal*. TV reporter Cesar Soriano invited her to prove her innocence by touching the tail of a dried stingray, which a *manananggal* would be neither willing nor able to do. A dried

A fine array of vampire-hunting accoutrements. This collection is owned by Sean Manchester, president of the Vampire Research Society

stingray was produced and touched and Beronqui's name was cleared before the nation. The true identity of the vampire remained a mystery.

In 1993 the citizens of Pisco, Peru were greatly disturbed by an imported vampire. Sarah Ellen Roberts, said to be the third bride of Dracula, was interred in a small Pisco cemetery on 7 June 1913. It was widely believed that she had been buried alive in a lead-lined coffin, from which she had bitterly vowed to rise 80 years hence.

Sean Manchester in 1970, entering the tomb of the Highgate vampire, armed with all known vampire antidotes

As the anniversary of her burial approached, few doorways in Pisco were free of garlic and crucifixes, and vampire kits (£1.60 for a mallet, a stake and a head of garlic) had sold out completely. A large crack which appeared mysteriously in her headstone further fanned the flames of anxiety.

On the night of 7 June more than 1000 people congregated at the graveyard. Protective spells were cast; dances designed to ward off spirits were performed; garlic and crucifixes wielded. One can only assume that all these measures were effective, since not a peep came from the grave.

Vampire belief persists in urban Europe, too. In the late 1960s, the newspapers of north London were filled with reports of a hideous entity seen prowling Highgate cemetery by night, and several dead animals were found there, drained of blood.

Sean Manchester, head of the UK-based Vampire Research Society, investigated these claims, which he firmly believed to be paranormal in nature, and in March of 1970 he was permitted to perform a ritual in a vault which had been found to contain three empty coffins.

The police became rather less permissive that August when amateur vampire hunters exhumed and decapitated the body of a woman buried at the cemetery. However, Manchester, convinced he was on the vampire's trail, sealed up another vault with garlic-impregnated bricks, to the approval of the assembled crowds.

3 years later Manchester found what he believed to be the body of the Highgate vampire in a casket beneath a derelict house. According to his report, he staked the corpse, which then rapidly decomposed as he photographed it.

Sean Manchester, who in recent years has been ordained as the Bishop of an ancient Catholic sect, shown here reading an exorcism rite to someone believed to be under vampiric attack

'Don't you want to live forever?'

THE SON

'Not if drawstring pants come back in style'

MULDER

3

Today, while creations like the werewolf, the succubus and the fairy have become rather quaint, vampires are, if anything, more popular than ever before.

Some things – such as drawstring pants – may go in and out of style; but it seems that our fascination with immortality – and the provocative question of what price we would be willing to pay for it – is as eternal as death itself.

SPECIAL AGENT

Dana Scully

SIGNATURE

FBI

X-File: Die Hand Die Verlezcht

X-FILE: DIE
DIE VERLE

FEDERAL BUREAU OF INVESTIGATION

Case notes by Special Agent Dana Scully

The murder of high school student Jerry Stevens, whose body was discovered early this mornir the woods of Milford Haven, New Hampshire, has provided an unfortunate boost to local rumour, already rife, of a covert group of witches or Satanists operating in the area.

The body had been mutilated in a fashion suggestive of, but not limited to, ritual murder. It was discovered in close proximity to a tree stump believed by the residents of Milford Haven to be habitually used as an altar in occult ceremonies. However, no evidence was discovered to support the notion that any kind of ceremony had taken place.

It is my suspicion, at this stage in the investigation, that the perpetrator is knowingly taking advantage of local folklore.

X-FILE: THE CALUSARI

FEDERAL BUREAU OF INVESTIGATION

Case notes by Special Agent Dana Scully

At this preliminary stage in the investigation, I am still unconvinced that the death of two-year-old Teddy Holvey, who ran in front of a miniature train at a state fair, is anything other than a tragic accident.

I share Agent Mulder's concern regarding the boy's grandmother, an elderly and superstitious Romanian, who, according to her daughter, is convinced that the Holvey family and their home are being threatened by evil spirits, and that Teddy's eight-year-old brother, Charlie, is himself evil.

X-File: The Calusari

X-FILE: OUR TOWN

FEDERAL BUREAU OF INVESTIGATION

Case notes by Special Agent Dana Scully

Pending a thorough review, the Chaco chicken processing plant has been closed by the USDA.

Ozark legends attribute sudden disappearances to balls of fire and evil spirits. But the true cause of the vanishings in Dudley is even more frightening – a people willing to purchase health and prosperity with the slaughter of others.

It remains unknown how many citizens participated in ritual activity and cannibalism.

What is known is that a transport plane carrying Walter Chaco was shot down in 1944 over New Guinea. Chaco was the only survivor of that crash. According to Naval records, he spent six months with the Jale, a tribe whose cannibalistic practices have been long-suspected by anthropologists, though never proven.

Naval records also show that Walter 'Chic' Chaco was born in 1902 – making him 93 years old at the time of his death. As of this date, his remains have still not been found.

X-File: Our Town

A DARK COLLUSION

Investigating the disappearance of a federal health-inspector sent to assess a food processing company in a small Arkansas community, Mulder and Scully discover that the citizens of Dudley are united in an ungodly doctrine: one in which cannibalism promises access to the fountain of youth. This is the basis of *Our Town*, a gruesome and gripping tale from the pen of Frank Spotnitz.

A vital member of *The X-Files* team, Spotnitz took up the post of writer and story editor towards the close of season two. His first episode was *End Game*, the compelling conclusion to *Colony* – the pivotal *X-Files* mythology episode created by Chris Carter and David Duchovny, in which Mulder meets a cloned version of his long-lost sister.

Our Town represented Spotnitz's first opportunity to create a story from scratch, and he knew exactly what he wanted it to be about.

'I knew I wanted to do something about cannibalism because it's such a great taboo. I've always been morbidly fascinated with it and I think many other people are, too. I just knew it would be inherently interesting as a subject.'

At first, however, Spotnitz could not decide what form his cannibalism story should take. Then he came upon a *New Scientist* article about some salamanders which had contracted diseases from eating sick members of their own population. 'And I realised: that's the story that I can do about cannibalism: what if somebody got food poisoning!'

Spotnitz already knew that cannibals in New Guinea reputedly caught a disease called Kuru from eating infected human brains. 'I thought about Kuru, but then I realised that that would immediately tip it off, because a lot of other people have heard of that too. So I picked a related disease, Creutzfeldt-Jacob Disease, which was less well known.'

Spotnitz had learned about CJD from a *Scientific American* article on Britain's early concerns over 'Mad Cow' Disease. Scully even mentions the

A 1963 shot of an Asmat tribesman, allegedly displaying the head of a victim. In actuality, the existence of ritual cannibalistic practice has not conclusively been proven (centre)

British predicament in *Our Town*. Not long after the episode's first airing in the UK, the Mad Cow situation escalated to fever pitch, with the ironic result that the disease Spotnitz had chosen for its relative obscurity became one of the most talked about in Europe.

> *'What is known is that a transport plane carrying Walter Chaco was shot down in 1944 over New Guinea. Chaco was the only survivor of that crash. According to Naval records, he spent six months with the Jale, a tribe whose cannibalistic practices have been long-suspected by anthropologists, though never proven'*
>
> SCULLY
>
> *Our Town*

Walter Chaco, founder of the successful Chaco Chicken company, is the ring-leader of *Our Town*'s grisly conspiracy and the man responsible for introducing the citizens of Dudley to ritual cannibalism.

'I tried to do a lot of research on cannibalistic practices,' says Spotnitz, 'but most of it is very unreliable. There is a big debate about whether (tribal) cannibalism ever existed at all. What I did take, though, was the principle that cannibalistic tribes supposedly don't feed on themselves; they would feed on a warring tribe. And so that's what led me to come up with the idea that this is an outsider who comes to town, who is rejected by the tribe and must be sacrificed for the health of the community.'

Although the unfortunate inspector is murdered to prevent him from lodging damaging complaints against Chaco Chicken, the people of Dudley consume him and their other victims in the (successful) pursuit of longevity and a youthful appearance.

Cannibalistic tribes were said to believe that particular parts of the body bestowed powerful benefits. 'In some of the myths it was said that if you eat the heart you will get strength; if you eat the sex organs you get fertility; if you eat the eyes you improve your own vision. So I just sort of took that idea and extrapolated on it,' explains Spotnitz.

Although the rituals in *Our Town* differ from any found in New Guinea, the tribe mentioned – the Jale – is a real one. 'I made up a fictitious tribe that Mr Chaco had spent time with when he was shot down during World War II,' says Spotnitz, 'and then Standards and Practices (20th Century Fox Television's in-house moral watchdogs) insisted that I come up with a real tribe, which I thought was odd. You'd think it would be just the opposite!'

Fortunately, the rest of the script was approved – especially since Spotnitz decided to remove all the jokes he had originally included about human flesh tasting like chicken. And despite the contentious subject matter, there were no complaints from viewers. (Although Spotnitz comments that the episode must have cost the show one fan: a woman had written in two weeks earlier complaining specifically about live chickens being used in *The Calusari*, and threatening that she would cease to watch *The X-Files* if it ever featured another chicken.)

There was, however, a letter addressed to Spotnitz containing a recipe for human brain stew. 'I didn't know what to make of it; I couldn't tell whether it was tongue in cheek . . . The note really didn't tip off the intention of the person who sent in the recipe. It was a little disturbing.'

> *'I came to see hypocrisy in the others. In me. They'd say Christians only go to church on Easter and Christmas, but we only attended rituals on Walpurgisnacht'*
>
> AUSBURY, (CITIZEN OF MILFORD HAVEN)
>
> *Die Hand Die Verletzt*

The concept of a small town fostering a conspiracy of occult religious practice also provided the framework for *Die Hand Die Verletzt*, an episode which had Mulder and Scully investigating allegations of ritual murder in Milford Haven, New Hampshire. Although the town is home to a thriving population of Satanists, they turn out to be not only harmless but pretty lax in the observance of their faith. The havoc seems, in fact, to be visited on them by dark forces (embodied by a sinister substitute teacher from nowhere) as punishment for their neglect.

'If you detect a hint of skepticism or incredulity in Agent Scully's voice, it's due to the overwhelming evidence gathered by the FBI debunking virtually all claims of ritual abuse by satanic cults'

MULDER

Syzygy

Satanism recurs in Chris Carter's *Syzygy* (see *Written in the Stars*), in which a Satanic cult is once again implicated in a string of murders. But this time, no such cult exists. It is simply a rumour the townsfolk have seized on and perpetuated through a combination of unquestioning credulity and misinterpretation.

In this respect, *Syzygy* perfectly mirrors real life. Chris Carter firmly believes the notion of covert Satanic networks, sexually abusing children and indulging in human sacrifice, to be nothing more than an urban myth.

'The FBI feels this way,' says Carter, who has done a great deal of reading on the subject, 'and I tend to think that they're not hiding anything in this case.'

An image of 'The Evil One', from the Book of Psalms

Carter's desire to get at the truth behind claims of ritual abuse and murder was first aroused several years ago, on an occasion which proved to be highly significant for *The X-Files*. 'There's a show here called *Larry King Live*,' explains Carter, 'and in fact one of the early inspirations for *The X-Files* was that he had an FBI agent on, whose job was investigating these claims.'

In fact the FBI had two men in charge of so-called 'occult' crimes. Kenneth V. Lanning specialised in allegations of Satanic ritual abuse while his associate, behavioural science pioneer Robert Ressler (see *Looking Into the Abyss*), handled cases which appeared to involve ritual murder. 'They used to call Lanning and me the Satanic Duo . . .' recalls Ressler. 'Lanning ended up doing a paper on satanic and occult cases.'

'My religion, my family, Agent Mulder . . .
goes back in this town seven generations'

AUSBURY

Die Hand Die Verletzt

Medieval heretics may have perverted the Christian mass, but they did not worship the devil. And there is no reliable evidence that the so-called witches and sorcerers of any era did so either. The notion of Satanism as we recognise it today – the invocation of figures from Christian demonology, the Black Mass, the inverted crosses and immoral rituals – has existed only since the occult revival of the late nineteenth century. And allegations that children are systematically sexually and psychologically abused by large groups of adults in ritualistic ceremonies are more recent still.

Most people trace this phenomenon to the publication in 1980 of *Michelle Remembers*, by psychiatrist Dr Lawrence Pazder and his patient Michelle Smith. During the course of her unconventional therapy, Michelle was not only hypnotised, but was baptised by a priest. She recounted a horrific story of Satanic abuse: babies being sacrificed, snakes, surgically implanted horns; the whole nine yards.

Dr Pazder, a Catholic, divorced his wife and married Michelle. No evidence was ever found of the crimes she reported witnessing.

'The FBI recently concluded a seven year study
and found little or no evidence of the existence
of occult conspiracies'

SCULLY

Die Hand Die Verletzt

By the mid-1980s the 'Satanic panic' had reached such proportions that the FBI became involved, and in 1989 the Bureau published Kenneth Lanning's report, *Satanic, Occult, Ritualistic Crime: A Law Enforcement Perspective.*

The results of Lanning's study show that while sexual abuse of children happens more than we would like to admit, it is most often perpetrated by single individuals who know the child – a family member, a carer, a teacher. Even when there is more than one abuser, Lanning writes, 'the actual involvement of Satanism or the occult in these cases usually turns out to be secondary, insignificant or non-existent.'

'She's one of us now. Part of our town'
WALTER CHACO
*'If we don't do something about her, there
won't be any town left to speak of'*
JESS HAROLD, HIS SIDE-KICK
Our Town

*An 1890 depiction of a
Masonic gathering before an
effigy of Baphomet. The
Masons are amongst the
numerous factions accused,
throughout the years, of
worshipping the dark forces*

Any covert criminal sect like Walter Chaco's is liable to be destroyed by internal squabbles like the one which occurs in *Our Town*. According to Lanning, 'Many people do not understand how difficult it is to commit a conspiracy crime involving numerous co-conspirators. One clever and cunning individual has a good chance of getting away with a well-planned interpersonal crime. Bring one partner into the crime and the chances of getting away with it drop considerably. The more people involved in the crime, the harder it is to get away with it. Why? Human nature is the answer. People get angry and jealous. They come to resent the fact that another conspirator is getting "more" than they are. They get in trouble and want to make a deal for themselves by informing on others. If a group of individuals degenerate to the point of engaging in human sacrifice and cannibalism, that would most likely be the beginning of the end for such a group. The odds are that someone in the group would have a problem with such acts and be unable to maintain the secret.'

'If the number of murders attributed to occult conspiracies
were true, it would mean thousands of people killing tens of
thousands of people a year . . . without any evidence.
Without being exposed.
It would be the greatest criminal conspiracy
in the history of civilisation'

SCULLY

Die Hand Die Verletzt

'The mayor in any given town, the chief of police, the director of the FBI, the Attorney General, the President: they're all Satanists,' says Robert Ressler, outlining what he has found to be the popular perception of Satanic and occult behaviour. 'They've got this big network and everybody's secretly controlling things. This a myth. The concept of the Satanic conspiracy where everybody is linked together and 666 is going to come and lead everybody to hell . . . I don't believe any of that.'

'Modern witches, known as Wiccan, are a religion. They have
great reverence for nature and all life. They don't even cast
harmful spells. They do not worship
the devil. And even the church of Satan
renounces murder and torture'

MULDER

Die Hand Die Verletzt

Anton LeVey –
leader of San
Francisco's
notorious Satanic
sect. In the FBI's
experience, LeVey
and his ilk are
harmless

Ressler's conclusions on the subject of those who follow occult religions are the much the same as Mulder's. 'The traditional Satanist, the guy that has his robes in the closet, goes to the meetings and chants; these people are harmless. They do not sacrifice human beings. Every city, every state has a Satanic and occult-type group. The Church of Satan and the Temple of Set. In San Francisco, you've got Anton LeVey. All these different characters are visible. It's a secret society, but how different is it from the Elks and the Moose and the Shriners?

'People get a lot of recognition when they delve into this sort of thing because they become known as "the person who's the witch" . . . and it becomes kind of trendy to dabble in the occult. People are seeking out the abnormal and the bizarre and the dark side of life.

'You've got the witches and the warlocks and the Wiccans and all this sort of thing. They've got their little groups and they do what they do. They're just pursuing some sort of odd religion.'

'Listen to this . . . I found it on the internet . . . "The discovery yesterday of a mutilated teenage boy in the forest has police officials distressed about the possibility of a conspiratorial organization of Dark Forces . . ."'

SCULLY

'Where's that pulled from, local paper?'

MULDER

' ". . .The jew is known to remove organs and sacrifice teens in their religious ceremonies." . . . Volkischer Beobachter: *the Nazi newspaper in 1934. The rumours remain the same, only the blanks are filled in with whoever must be feared . . . or persecuted. In this case, Occultists'*

SCULLY

Die Hand Die Verletzt

Mulder and Scully find no shortage of nasty goings-on in Our Town

As culture and values shift and change, so do the concepts of evil and of Satan. During the Middle Ages in Europe, Satan took the guise of werewolves and vampires. In the United States during the 1830s and 1840s, it was the Catholics who were regarded as agents of the devil. Now, in the Middle East, it is the United States who is the 'Great Satan'.

Satan, from the Hebrew word for 'adversary', can mean anything the speaker is opposed to. At one point or another, according to Kenneth Lanning, everything from vegetarianism to judo to astrology to Buddhism has been called Satanism.

Unfortunately, the reputation of Satanism has suffered from the fact that crimes *are* committed in its name, albeit by those who are not genuinely involved in it.

'The dangerous ones are the dabblers,' says Colonel Ressler. 'The psychopaths that are using it to control other people, and the adolescents that get together and start conjuring up their own rituals when they have no knowledge of what they're doing. These are the people that really become dangerous because often one will lead others into sacrifices: human sacrifices and stuff like that which has no bearing on true Satanism.

'There was a guy in Chicago named Robin Gecht who was a psychopath. He had a gang . . . they were burglars and rapists and everything. He had an old house and up in the attic he had all these crosses upside down and pentagrams on the floor. He was following no traditional form of Satanism – except the Gecht version. Part of that was to rape women and kill them.

'When Richard Ramirez, the California Night Stalker, was brought to court, he had a pentagram drawn on his hand. He held it up and said, "Satan lives." Everybody went nuts: "Oh, a Satanist! See what he did! He's a Satanist!"'

But, says Ressler, '. . . traditional Satanists don't do that stuff. As an analogy, if some guy says "I'm a Catholic", but has no Catholic background, and he suddenly starts robbing banks and raping women in the name of Catholicism, are you going to say: that was a Catholic crime? To say that these are Satanic crimes is equally stupid.'

'Certain cannibal rituals are enacted with the belief that they can prolong life'
MULDER
Our Town

Adolpho de Jesus Constanzo committed a stomach-churning array of crimes in the name of Satan. But from the FBI's standpoint, his was 'no more a Satanic group than the man in the moon'

The 'dabblers' have been known to create their own outrageous belief systems. Ressler cites the example of Adolfo de Jesus Constanzo, the leader of a group who ritually killed and cannibalised 15 men and boys in the late 1980s as part of their drug-running operation at Matamoros, Mexico, near the US–Mexican border.

'Constanzo led these guys into killing kids, chopping them up and making their spinal cords into necklaces. All in the name of Satanism. But that was no more a Satanic group than the man in the moon. It was a psychopath using mumbo jumbo . . . basically getting them to run drugs for him and telling them: "you're wearing the spinal cord which will protect you from police bullets."'

Constanzo also preached the belief that his magic rituals would make the gang invisible. Fortunately for the FBI, he was mistaken.

'The evil here has always been. It has gone by different names through history . . . Cain, Lucifer, Hitler . . . It doesn't care if it kills one boy or a million men. If you try to stop us, the blood will be on your hands'

CALUSARI ELDER

The Calusari

The good folks of Dudley, Arkansas collude to perpetrate some spectacularly bad deeds in Our Town. *In real life, we may rest assured that, according to FBI expert Kenneth Lanning, a criminal conspiracy involving so many people would have its cover blown at a very early stage in the game*

In *The Calusari*, Mulder and Scully encounter a family beset by tragedy and the clan of Romanian priests who are trying to save them from the apparent cause: the powers of darkness. It is an episode which illustrates very well the ancient belief that evil is not something within us, but an autonomous force.

Whether dark forces exist or not, there can be no doubt about our own capacity for cruelty and destruction (see *Looking Into the Abyss*). The reluctance to accept this fact has, throughout history, led mankind to blame the devil – in any of his many guises – for misfortune, for the actions of others, and, sometimes, for the things we do ourselves.

'Satan made me do it' is one of the world's oldest excuses for crime. Robert Ressler, who has looked into the abyss for longer than most, doesn't buy it.

'You could kill people by the order of the Fire Plug, saying "that fire plug outside of my house is what tells me to kill."

'Richard Ramirez professed that the devil made him do it: in fact it was *himself* that made him do it.'

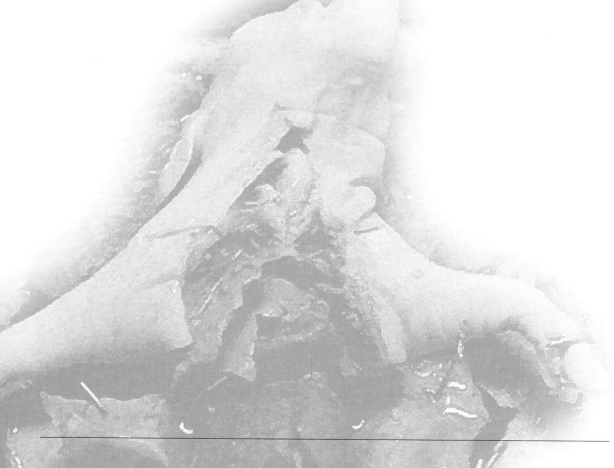

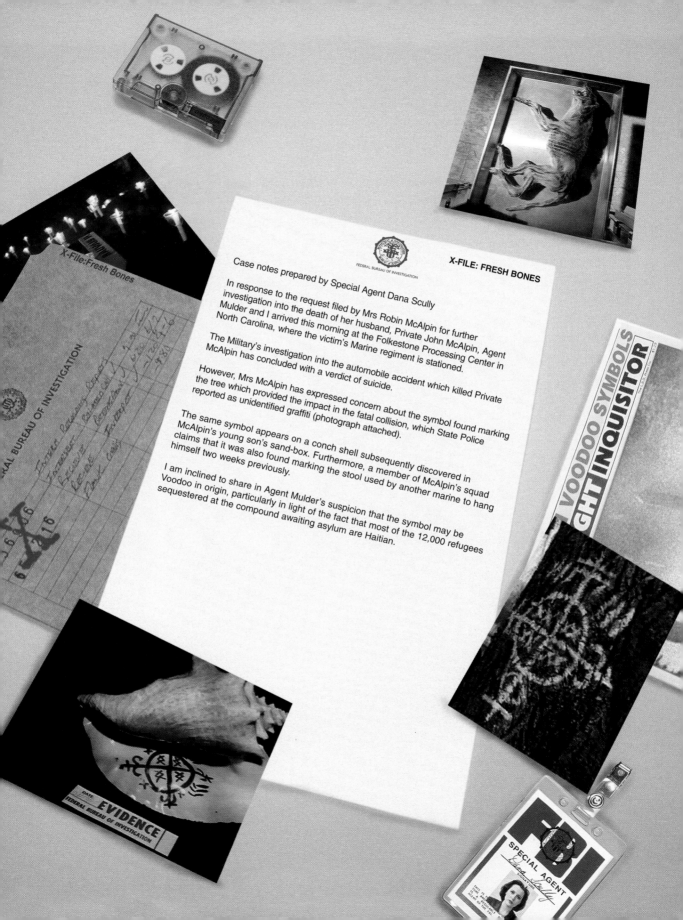

X-FILE: FRESH BONES

Case notes prepared by Special Agent Dana Scully

In response to the request filed by Mrs Robin McAlpin for further investigation into the death of her husband, Private John McAlpin, Agent Mulder and I arrived this morning at the Folkestone Processing Center in North Carolina, where the victim's Marine regiment is stationed.

The Military's investigation into the automobile accident which killed Private McAlpin has concluded with a verdict of suicide.

However, Mrs McAlpin has expressed concern about the symbol found marking the tree which provided the impact in the fatal collision, which State Police reported as unidentified graffiti (photograph attached).

The same symbol appears on a conch shell subsequently discovered in McAlpin's young son's sand-box. Furthermore, a member of McAlpin's squad claims that it was also found marking the stool used by another marine to hang himself two weeks previously.

I am inclined to share in Agent Mulder's suspicion that the symbol may be Voodoo in origin, particularly in light of the fact that most of the 12,000 refugees sequestered at the compound awaiting asylum are Haitian.

X-File:Fresh Bones

VOODOO SYMBOLS

GHT INQUISITOR

EVIDENCE
FEDERAL BUREAU OF INVESTIGATION

SPECIAL AGENT

VOODOO

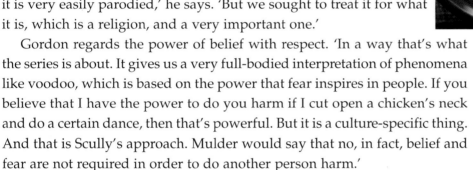

Fresh Bones takes Mulder and Scully to a Haitian refugee camp in North Carolina to investigate a series of apparent suicides amongst the Marine squad patrolling the camp. Needless to say, all is not what it seems, and the Agents soon uncover a battle raging between the commander of the camp and Pierre Bauvais, a voodoo practitioner amongst the refugees – both of whom may be drawing upon the power of magic.

In writing *Fresh Bones*, Howard Gordon was intent on treating Voodoo beliefs with reverence, acutely aware of the ease with which these aims can be forgotten in the quest for drama. 'The danger is that it is very easily parodied,' he says. 'But we sought to treat it for what it is, which is a religion, and a very important one.'

Gordon regards the power of belief with respect. 'In a way that's what the series is about. It gives us a very full-bodied interpretation of phenomena like voodoo, which is based on the power that fear inspires in people. If you believe that I have the power to do you harm if I cut open a chicken's neck and do a certain dance, then that's powerful. But it is a culture-specific thing. And that is Scully's approach. Mulder would say that no, in fact, belief and fear are not required in order to do another person harm.'

And Gordon himself? 'I sure hope that it's a culture specific thing!' he laughs, before adding: 'I believe it is a psychological phenomenon, that the Loa [Haitian deities] aren't really roaming around inducing people to do harm.'

He keeps his options open, however. 'You wouldn't want to upset the Loa!' he admits, only half joking. 'It did occur to me: what if I'm wrong? So I may as well cover my bets. I'm still young. I don't want to check out just yet!'

Gordon contends that keeping an open mind benefitted the episode. 'It's much more interesting to investigate something in a rounded way rather than a dismissive or a close-minded way. And it's Mulder's way. Even though we tell it from Scully's point of view, I think we treat it as Mulder would: with respect, with an eye toward appreciating its power and its beauty rather than as something to be parodied.'

The *X-Files* approach is – sadly – far from typical, and the clearest example of *Fresh Bones*' integrity is its handling of the element of voodoo lore which has been parodied and misrepresented in fiction more often than any other: the zombie.

Historically, the concept of the zombie originates from the turbulent Caribbean nation of Haiti, and the religion that we call voodoo. Many anthropologists use the term *Vodoun* when speaking of Haiti's rich religion, in order to draw a distinction between the fact and the Hollywood fantasy which has coloured our understanding of it. Likewise, the Haitian *zombi* bears very little resemblance to our western notions of the undead.

The Haitian zombi is not a monster preying on the living, but a victim. A person dies what is known as an 'unnatural death' and is buried. A priest exhumes him, ceremonially reanimates him, drugs him with *datura stramonium* (a hallucinogenic plant known in Haiti as *concombre zombi* – the zombi's cucumber), beats him into further submission, and then commonly puts him to work in the fields.

A voodoo symbol, the loco-miroir, has a life-shattering effect on Private Jack McAlpin and his family in Fresh Bones

'The neurologist suspects that he suffered a severe concussion during the crash, resulting in amnesia'
SCULLY
'Plausible diagnosis . . . only I'm more interested in how he came back to life'
MULDER
'Obviously, he never left. Dr Foyle made a gross error when he signed the death certificate'
SCULLY
Fresh Bones

In order for the priest, known as a bokor, to bring someone back to life, he must bring about the 'unnatural death' in the first place. The bokor poisons his subject with a *coup poudre*, which contains human bones and frogs and other magical objects. But the active ingredient is tetrodotoxin, which comes from a local breed of puffer fish. A precise dosage of tetrodotoxin will bring on all the signs of death. It has even fooled some western doctors. The victim remains conscious throughout – firing on all five senses – although completely paralysed. He is able to hear himself pronounced dead; he sees his relatives mourning, hears the nails banged into his coffin, and is buried alive. Fortunately, it is difficult to judge the dose exactly: too much tetrodotoxin kills instantly, but often the extract does nothing at all. Wrong fish, wrong time of year; too little poison . . .

> *'In 1982, a Harvard ethnobotanist named Wade Davis did extensive field work in Haiti on the zombification phenomenon . . .'*
>
> MULDER
>
> *Fresh Bones*

None of this would be widely known in the western world were it not for the work of one man: Wade Davis. An expert in anthropology as well as ethnobotany, Davis went to Haiti in 1982 to research the zombi phenomenon. His experiences amounted to a real-life detective story, straddling the realms of science and spirituality; a talented writer, he vividly committed them to paper in his absorbing and seductive 1988 book *The Serpent and the Rainbow* (later to become a lamentable Wes Craven film).

Long before *The X-Files*, this book sparked in Howard Gordon an intense interest in the Vodoun religion. It was the Haitian zombi tradition which inspired the plight of *Fresh Bones'* Private Jack McAlpin, and Gordon ensured that Wade Davis got a name-check in the episode.

Wade Davis, the intrepid Harvard ethnobotanist and author whose work profoundly inspired Howard Gordon

'We're not sure what happened. But there is a medical explanation for his condition'

SCULLY

Fresh Bones

In Haiti Wade Davis met Dr Lamarque Douyon, who was studying cases of zombification. 'Douyon was approaching this in a very clinical way,' says Davis, 'even though like all Haitians he was inspired by his own intuitions for the phantasmagoric. This notion of a zombi has lingered in the Haitian imagination for a long time. It ranges all the way from something like a bogeyman or ghost tale – the sort of folk tales that we ourselves have in our culture – to a set of cases that, at least collectively, demand investigation. Douyon was able to obtain some degree of documentation, particularly in the case of Narcisse.'

Clairvius Narcisse was declared dead on 2 May 1962 at the American-run Albert Schweitzer Hospital in Haiti. But in 1980, in a busy Artibonite Valley market, the same Narcisse walked up to his sister Angelina – who had attended his burial 18 years earlier – and whispered his childhood nickname. He was described as unsteady, vague, and dazed; and said that he had been labouring on a sugar plantation. He claimed that his brother had contracted out his zombification after a bitter land dispute.

Narcisse's was one of the first well-documented cases of zombification. 'Narcisse was perfectly lucid, and could tell his story. He seemed to be a reasonable guy,' recalls Davis. 'One zombi cracked the mirror of disbelief.'

Far from becoming a local celebrity, however, Narcisse found himself in limbo. 'He went back to his village to live, and nobody would have him,' explains Davis. 'Because everybody had no doubt that he was a zombi, he had entered a realm between the living and the dead. Even though he appeared to be fine, he was in some sense in a state of perpetual purgatory.

'I once asked Herard Simon (one-time head of a large faction of the Ton-Ton Macoute militia) whether a zombi can be made whole again, and he said, "Of course. I can return his soul to him. But on the other hand, if you were a woman, would you want an ex-zombi to dance with you?" It seems funny, but he was really pointing out something profound: this is a form of social death.'

Davis and Douyon searched for the drug used by the bokor to induce the 'unnatural death'. 'I knew nothing about Haiti and nothing about Vodoun and certainly nothing about zombis, but I did know something about folk

The deceptively
cute Puffer Fish

preparations,' says Davis, whose earlier research had found him working with shamans in tribal Latin America.

It wasn't long before Davis had the opportunity to observe a *coup poudre* being made – the essential first step in identifying the crucial active ingredient of the 'zombi poison', if indeed such a thing existed.

'I wasn't looking for a drug that could kill somebody. It had to make someone *appear* to be dead. I didn't know of a drug that could do that. So when I saw the thing made, I got all the plants and all the various animals and brought them back to Harvard.'

Amongst his haul, Davis found a number of toxic and irritant ingredients. But it wasn't until his Mulderesque quest led him to the department of ichthyotoxicology that he learned the significance of an ingredient that turned out to be the vital one: the puffer fish.

'This is strange: the lab detected trace levels of tetrodotoxin. It's a poison found in the liver and reproductive organs of puffer fish . . . A Japanese delicacy'

SCULLY

'Except I have a feeling Private McAlpin didn't frequent many sushi bars'

MULDER

Fresh Bones

I didn't know a puffer fish from a salmon,' Davis recalls. 'So I had this amusing experience where I went down to the labs and this young ichthyotoxicologist sort of bounces his head up from this big ugly fish he's looking at and pulls out a volume of the James Bond book, *From Russia With Love*. He shows me the last scene, which involves tetrodotoxin poisoning and says: "this is one of the greatest moments in ichthyotoxicology!"'

The more Davis learned about tetrodotoxin, the most powerful natural nerve poison known to man, the more certain he became that at least one part of the enigma had been solved. 'It showed without a doubt that the Haitian Vodounists had identified in their environment a natural product that they manipulated in folk preparations, which we knew if applied and consumed in the right way at the right time could make someone appear to be dead.'

But Davis felt there was more to the mystery than tetrodotoxin poisoning. 'This is where I diverged from the more strictly Descartian scientists,' he says. 'Suddenly, everybody wanted me to make zombi rats with this poison. I tried to suggest that the biogenesis of tetrodotoxin in the fish was not understood. We knew that 50% of the time in nature the fish were not toxic, we knew the levels of the toxin within the fish varied tremendously from individual to individual, season to season, within the gender of the fish and so on. So there was no way these bokors were going down to the seashore, getting a few fish and making a standard extract. This was clearly a serendipitous preparation in some sense, and that became problematic. How does a belief system insulate itself from falsification if the preparation itself can never be counted on?'

A participant at a ceremony in Haiti collapses in exhaustion after being possessed by the Loa - an experience typified by frenzied dancing

It took an anthropological mind like Davis's to find the answer. And it was watching a traditional Vodoun ceremony, in which a young woman was 'possessed' by the Loa, that provided a clue.

'You were living in a culture that was so surrealistic, so alive, where the power of belief was so strong, that by invoking some technique of ecstasy, in this case spirit possession, the people were able to propel themselves into states of trance that were so profound they could handle burning embers with impunity. I saw that with my own eyes. This was a tremendously provocative clue to the richness of the spiritual and psychological landscape of Haiti.

'You had to ask: What does a zombi really mean within this culture, and how could the mind of the individual mediate the belief?'

The answer, Davis realised, was that the belief system itself had a way of mediating the undependability of the drug. 'There are two types of death in Vodoun: natural death and unnatural death. Natural deaths are calls from god and beyond the reach of sorcery. Unnatural deaths are all others. The use of a poison is a very effective way of bringing on an unnatural death. But the critical act of making the zombi is not the use of the poison but the capturing of the soul, which is perceived as purely a magical act.

'Why this becomes important is that the bokor has an immediate out. If, for example, I get a preparation which is inert and doesn't do a damn thing, I can say that my death spell must have been broken by a benevolent priest hired by my enemy. If, on the other hand, I have a preparation which is excessively toxic and actually kills, I can say that the death was a natural death – a call from god and beyond the reach of my sorcery. And so the belief system that mediates the event has a wonderful way of rationalising failures, emphasising successes and insulating (itself) from falsification.'

Davis estimates that the creation of a physical zombi is an extremely rare event. And when it occurs, it succeeds not just because of the administration of a correct dosage of poison, but also because of what is known in hallucinogenic pharmacology as the 'set and setting' – the state of mind and expectations of the experiencer and the circumstances of the experience.

'I've learned in my study of shamanism and hallucinogenic plants in general that set and setting is paramount, a template through which cultural forces go to work. The Japanese victims of the poison (often accidentally ingested when eating raw puffer-fish) get out of the grave and say: "Well, that was awful, that was a bad scene, I was nailed in my coffin", but the Vodounist has a whole different set of expectations. In Narcisse's mind, he knows what it means to be a zombi, he knows why a zombi's made, he knows what's going on.'

Francois 'Papa Doc' Duvalier

But there was still a piece of the puzzle missing. 'Once you understood the psychological step and the spiritual thing, you had to ask: Who the hell's doing this and why? Who's controlling this belief system? And that's where you got into the sociology of the secret society.'

In Haiti, secret societies abound and always have done. (Dictator Francois 'Papa Doc' Duvalier, who ruled from 1957–71, quickly and efficiently formed his frightful private army, the Ton-Ton Macoute, by recruiting their members.) These societies are often involved in the policing of social transgressions, such as female adultery or land theft. The local society might get one of their bokors, for example, to turn a transgressor into a zombi. And in fact, Davis describes both Narcisse and a female zombi he encountered as pariahs in their communities.

'What do you know about zombies?'
MULDER
*'I hope you don't intend to tell Robin McAlpin that she
married one'*
SCULLY

Fresh Bones

Western culture with its various belief systems is simply not open to serious, unanimous acceptance of the fantastical. But Haiti is another story, and its profound depths of literal belief in the spiritual became evident to Davis very early on. 'Zombis by definition exist in Haiti because people believe in zombis. In the early stages of the research I tried to buy a zombi. I was so certain this phenomenon didn't occur that I was quite cavalier in calling people's bluffs.

'At one point I go, "Bring me a zombi!" We're bartering about price, and my contact says, "Well, bring the zombi, maybe it'll loosen his purse," and they suddenly brought this little fetish out of a bag. My contact exploded, "No you fools, he doesn't want a *zombi astral*! He wants a *zombi corps cadavre*!", of the flesh. They said: "That's ridiculous, with a *zombi astral* you can do anything you want, you can make it into a spirit, blah, blah, blah. A *zombi corps cadavre* is just a lump of flesh, a vegetable. And besides, how is he going to get it through customs?!" I realised I was in a Fellini movie.'

'Western scientists would have dismissed an encounter like that as droll, without seeing that it told you immense amounts about the intensity of this belief, the casual acceptance. This phenomenon doesn't dominate the religion; it's one small thread woven through it. But it exists.'

Davis was disappointed at the reception of his report, and feels that the media's obsession with his chemical findings 'missed to a great extent the point of the study. The real purpose of my work was to study the phenomenon of the zombi; what it means. The poison was only one aspect. What they wanted was this image of a Harvard scientist proving that in fact zombies do crawl out of the ground to attack people.

'This idea of voodoo being evil and nefarious is a twentieth-century phenomenon. To a great extent it came after the US Marine Corps occupied Haiti. Everybody above the rank of sergeant got a book contract. There were a dozen or more of these books, and all of them were filled with children fed to the cauldron . . . zombies . . . pins and dolls . . . In any other era they would have been forgotten as the pulp fiction they were, but at that time they said to the American people that any country where such abominations occur can only find redemption through military occupation. And those books gave rise to the Hollywood movies *Zombies of the Stratosphere*, *Zombies on Broadway* . . .

'There was a parallel track of serious anthropological research going on, scientific men and women promoting the legitimacy of Haitian peasant institutions and the legitimacy of the Vodoun faith. And for them these tales were anathema – they exemplified the way this religion had been denigrated in what they thought was an explicitly racist way. So because of that, the whole idea of the zombi became taboo for scholarly researchers. I benefitted from the fact that nobody had taken the zombi phenomenon seriously.'

'My country was born in the blood of slaves. Freedom is our most sacred legacy'

PIERRE BAUVAIS

Fresh Bones

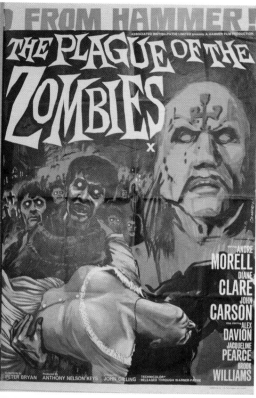

A typically Western rendition of the zombie mythos

Davis explains the spiritual context of zombification, and the fact that Haitians fear not so much zombis walking amongst them as themselves *becoming* zombis.

'The whole point of Vodoun is that there is no final death. Death is just a moment where the spiritual and the physical part of the body momentarily dissociate. The *ti bon ange*, the 'little good angel' – that part of the spirit which gives you your personality, your willpower, your identity – is particularly susceptible to death by sorcery. In a proper death the *ti bon ange* goes beneath the grave . . . and it is ritualistic to reclaim it a year and a day after death: it's put into a little jar.

'In time, that spirit, initially associated with a particular ancestor, becomes part of the vast ancestral pool of energy. But in this quintessentially democratic faith even the dead must be made to serve the living. They must become manifest, and out of that pool emerge the archetypes who are the spirits of the Vodoun pantheon.

'To serve the living they must return to earth, responding to the invocation of the drums to momentarily displace the soul of the living. And for the Vodoun, this is what spirit possession is. It's not a moment of pathology as people have suggested, but rather it is a moment of divine grace, a perfect affirmation of the power of the faith, and it is at that supreme, sublime moment when the people handle the burning embers. So the goal of life in some sense is to give birth to the spirits, and there is an active and dynamic dialogue between the living and the dead. They express it with an adage: "White people go to church and speak about god; we dance in the temple and *become* god."

'And so the fate of the *ti bon ange* is of critical interest to the Vodounist. If it's stolen by sorcery you break that cycle of life and death and rebirth. That moment of death, when the soul dissociates and can be stolen, is what a zombi is – someone who has had their soul stolen. That's why a zombi is so listless in folklore: because they have no personality, no will. And that's why the fear is not of zombis, but of becoming one.'

'When did you first think that your husband's death might involve something out of the ordinary?'
MULDER

'One of the boys in his squad told me what they found at the scene of the accident. He said it was some kind of voodoo curse. The same one they found on the stool that Puerto Rican boy used to hang himself'
ROBIN McALPIN (PRIVATE McALPIN'S WIDOW)

Fresh Bones

Wade Davis describes Vodoun society as a 'closed web of belief', within which there is no such thing as chance, coincidence or fate. And he observes that the whole social structure 'immediates and enhances the power of faith, the power of belief, because a closed set of beliefs is much more fertile in terms of the human imagination – and constantly reaffirmed.'

But how potent is the power of faith when an outsider wanders into the web? As far as most Haitians are concerned, it makes no difference. Such is their confidence in the power of ritual that when the US invaded Haiti in September of 1994, the Cédras junta warned that the invading troops would be met by members of the secret societies, who would hex them or turn them into zombis. Americans would shoot themselves and one another, their aircraft would plummet spontaneously from the sky and their vessels would sink.

All of these promises remained unfulfilled – except one. By mid-October, in an odd and tragic enigma echoed in *Fresh Bones*, three of the American troops had committed suicide. It was reported that one, Geraldo Luciano, had been playing cards with fellow GIs when he suddenly grabbed his M16 rifle and shot himself in the head.

Can hexes work? Or were the three suicides coincidental? The problem is that one man's coincidence is another man's proof. Belief systems – including the belief that there is nothing outside scientific causality except coincidence – survive because people subscribe to them, and make subjective judgments according to those beliefs, ensuring that their faith is confirmed.

Early in 1995, the land around the home of world record cricketer Brian Lara in Port-of-Spain, Trinidad, was found scattered with powders, black candles, chicken heads and entrails. This was deemed to be the work of an Obeah Man, a practitioner of voodoo-like rituals. Lara, a prolific run-scorer who has twice broken the world test record, followed his sensationally successful 1994 season with a distinctly mediocre one. On 5 June, during the West Indies' 1995 English tour, Lara was out second ball for a duck – a far cry from his record-breaking score of 501 not out. A sportsman's loss of form – or voodoo?

A Haitian Houngan (priest) presides over a ritual ceremony. Practitioners do not use the word 'voodoo' or any equivalent. They most often refer to their religion as Servi Loa - serving the gods

'Mulder, voodoo only works by instilling fear among its believers. You saw the way Bauvais tried to intimidate me. The power of suggestion is considerable, I'll admit . . . But this is no more magic than a pair of fuzzy dice'

SCULLY, PRODDING A VOODOO CHARM

Fresh Bones

Hexes which apparently result in death are not so simple to rationalise. And there are many such cases to be found. Researcher Walter B. Cannon studied the subject extensively through the forties and fifties and was the first to put forward a hypothesis. His idea was that the fear created by a hex triggers the primal fight-or-flight mechanisms within the victim's body, effectively preparing it for action. If the sympathico-adrenal system is stimulated, but no action taken, blood circulation would be reduced and blood pressure would drop – possibly to a fatal degree. Cannon noted a number of syndromes besides hex death which could be explained by his theory, including cases of Army personnel dying *before* going into battle, post-operative patients dying despite the fact that their operations had been successful and unexplained deaths occurring after minor injuries or ingestion of non-lethal doses of poison.

There are also records of people dying after being 'shot' with an unloaded gun, or narrowly escaping being hit by a car. In other words, the fear created by the conviction that death is imminent can itself be lethal. The reason, however, may not be the one originally proposed by Cannon. Under conditions of extreme stress, shock or fear, the body produces chemicals called catecholamines. In experiments on dogs, large doses of these have proved fatal. Death occurs due to severe damage to the heart.

Prolonged stress and fear, as opposed to a sudden burst of terror, while it would not trigger a lethal dose of catecholamines, could slow the metabolism to dangerous levels and eventually result in illness and death.

Current researchers feel that both theories could apply to apparent cases of hex death. Joan Halifax Grof, an anthropologist and parapsychologist, also draws attention to the possibility of auto-suggestion, noting that in controlled tests, subjects under hypnosis who believe that they are being burned have actually come up in blisters. A less dramatic but equally pertinent example of the power of auto-suggestion is the fact that in medical tests, placebos are frequently seen to work.

Few doubt the potency of the link between mind and body. As Wade Davis says, 'Nobody ever got a cold the day after they fell in love. We all know we get colds more often when we're depressed. Even doctors of the most traditional sort admit the role that psychology plays in health, and more and more thoughtful doctors recognise that that role is much higher than we acknowledge. Once you accept the possibility of the mind mediating the body in any way at all . . . it's very difficult to draw limits on the extent to which that mind can affect the body.'

This view is shared by *The X-Files'* Howard Gordon, both of whose brothers are doctors. 'I do believe that in much more marginal terms, people are capable of healing themselves, and I think the converse of that is that one can harm oneself. My brother – who is a sceptic, he's Scully all the way through – says there's no doubt that people with a positive frame of mind heal better, heal quicker. Clearly the mind does affect the body's recuperative abilities. And again, if you push that further,

The agents study the loco-miroir symbol on the tree into which Private McAlpin crashed his car

one could conceivably heal or hurt another person with the power of their own mind.'

Rationalist James Randi agrees that state of mind can affect health, but maintains that it need not trigger any mysterious physiological reaction in order to do so.

'It's been proven many times that people who have a positive attitude about their illness tend to recover more quickly, and some of the reasons are perfectly mundane. They don't just sit on the edge of the bed and say, "I'm gonna die". They take their medication, they tend to treat themselves better, they get better nutrition, they get more rest, more exercise, they have a better attitude . . . and all those things mean that they're much more likely to survive.'

Conversely, 'If someone believes that they have been cursed, and they believe in curses, they're just going to say "Hey I'm doomed, that's it, good-bye", and withdraw from life. They're going to not look after themselves. They know they're not going to survive, so why should they pay much attention to hygiene or safety or taking medicine? And often they do die. But that's no mystery.'

Outside the western world, social and cultural factors are also highly significant. In many cultures, the subject of a hex will die a 'social death' long before he actually ceases to live. His friends and family will first mourn openly in front of him, as if he were dead already, and then withdraw completely from him. Effectively ostracised, and entirely isolated, he is deprived of basic emotional needs: comfort, company, purpose in life, hope for the future.

Wade Davis notes that for the Aboriginal peoples, eventual physical death can be mediated by an even more straightforward factor: 'In Australia it's been well documented that someone who was declared to have received a hex was deemed to have died socially, and so, in certain cases, family members took away vital subsistence: food and water. In fact they were dying of thirst.'

So is there *anything* mysterious about hex deaths? Some researchers are still prepared to consider that there may be. Joan Halifax-Grof believes that there are 'aspects of certain cases of hex death and of the process of hexing reported in the literature for which . . . scientific interpretations would appear to be inadequate'. Amongst other things, she suggests that psychokinesis – mental control of another person's mind or body – could be a factor in some cases, as could premonition: foreknowledge of an impending death.

She cites a case recorded at the Johns Hopkins medical school in Baltimore, Maryland. On 29 July 1966, a 22-year-old African-American woman from the

The mortuary bay thought to contain the body of Private McAlpin is found to contain a chilling decoy

Deep South was admitted to hospital suffering from breathing difficulties and chest pains. She confided in her physician that she feared she would not live beyond her next birthday, which was imminent. She had been born on Friday the thirteenth, and the attending midwife had declared that all three of the children she had delivered that day were hexed. The midwife specified that the three would die before the ages of 16, 21 and 23 respectively, with the patient being the last to go. The patient reported that one of her fellow hex victims had died in a car accident on the day before her sixteenth birthday; the other, having made it to her twenty-first birthday, went to a bar to celebrate and was killed by a stray bullet fired during a brawl. The patient remained in hospital, where doctors observed that, although she seemed 'terrified', her physical condition was not a cause for concern. Nevertheless, two weeks after her admission and one day before her twenty-third birthday, she died of heart failure. Neither the doctors nor the resident pathologists could find a physical reason for her death or its timing.

Halifax-Grof wisely points out that while three deaths occurring on cue is a highly improbable coincidence, there is no proof that the two previous deaths really did take place as the patient had said.

What is notable about the case, however, is the acceptance of the hexing phenomenon by distinguished doctors. Professor Freisinger, Assistant Professor of medicine at Johns Hopkins stated in his summary of the case that the hex could not be ruled out as the cause of death. 'It is not a part of our society and hence we know little about it; I suspect many of us would prefer to think that it did not exist,' he wrote. 'Special circumstances and beliefs in a community must exist before an individual can die by hex, but once the proper background and individual conditioning exist, there is no reason why (the described physiological processes). . . cannot occur and lead to death, at the proper time.'

One aspect that almost every medically-documented account of hex death has in common is the failure of western doctors to save the victim. Indigenous doctors and priests have historically had better luck. Dr Mike Lampkin, a western doctor in South Carolina (where 'Hoodoo' – a hybrid of Vodoun and

Catholicism – is a common faith) took note of this fact and successfully applied it to his work. In one case he persuaded a hexed woman that he could draw evil spirits into a jar, which she could dispose of in the river, freeing herself from the hex.

All of these cases indicate that the victim's state of mind is a vital factor in hex deaths.

'*Did he believe in voodoo?*
MULDER
'*The Marines, his family, football . . . pretty much sums up everything Jack believed in*'
ROBIN McALPIN
Fresh Bones

So what happens when a non-believer receives a hex? J. Gatty Dowling, a South Carolina lawyer, found out when he discovered a 'symbolic root' – an artifact of Hoodoo hexing – in his house. He asserted that he was not concerned. Soon afterwards, however, Dowling suffered a ruptured appendix, his wife caught chicken-pox along with his baby (who also contracted measles), and his eldest son became seriously ill with respiratory problems. Drawing a legal analogy, Dowling agreed that if a court were to hear the evidence, the power of the root would be indicted.

Colonel Robert Heinl Jr. served as chief of the US Naval mission in Haiti from 1958 to 1963. On his return he began to write a book about Haiti entitled *Written in Blood*, together with his wife, who had spent those five years studying the Vodoun religion. In 1971, Simone Duvalier, the widow of Haitian dictator 'Papa Doc', got wind of the book, and placed a curse on it. The Heinls were amused and flattered at the notion that their book was worth cursing. Their nonchalance didn't last long. First the manuscript was lost on its way to the publishers, and attempts at preparing a second copy were hampered when a binding machine broke. Four months later, the first copy showed up in a disused room at the publishing house. A *Washington Post* reporter who was due to interview the Heinls was stuck down with acute appendicitis, the Colonel fell through a stage during a lecture and, shortly afterwards, was bitten by a dog. On 5 May 1979, whilst on holiday in St Barthelemy (an island not far from Haiti), he died of heart attack. Colonel Heinl's widow sadly recalled that she had heard that the closer one gets to Haiti, the more vulnerable one is to the power of magic.

The agents' investigations in Fresh Bones *prove to be both unsettling and dangerous*

What is interesting about both these cases is that although both J. Gatty Dowling and the Heinls claimed to be utterly sceptical about the power of magic, somewhere along the line they changed their minds. Belief in the hex is all-important – whether in mediating the magic, creating a vulnerable physical state, or merely in finding enough unfortunate coincidences to give the hex some credence. There do not appear to be any cases where misfortune has followed a hex when the victim felt no unease, no apprehension, no conviction of the hex's power, or, more important still, did not even *know* he had been hexed.

Thus the key factor in 'successful' hexing is the belief of the targeted victim, and no degree of belief on the part of the sorcerer can take its place.

In Miami, which has a large Haitian and Cuban population, the administrators of the main courthouse have had to appoint an official 'voodoo squad' to clean up the ritual artifacts which appear on its steps and in its courtrooms, placed there by defendants hoping to influence their trials. Lawyers' and judges' chairs often need to be dusted clean of ritual powders, and the daily haul has included charms, dead chickens and goats, two dead lizards with their mouths tied shut, black pepper, corn kernels (which are supposed to speed up a trial), eggs (to make a case collapse) and cakes (to sweeten a judge's attitude). Despite this, conviction rates in Dade County have not been affected.

Dr Brier, a parapsychologist who, in the 1970s, taught the subject at universities, was once joined by a student who claimed he had the ability to perform hex deaths. Brier and the student agreed that they would put it to the test, with Brier as the intended victim. The student would receive an 'A' for his term paper if Brier died within a year; an 'F' if he survived. The student received an 'F'. Brier was willing to submit to the experiment because he did not believe that he would lose his life. This again suggests that the *victim* is the important factor in hexing. If the student did have special powers we must assume that they could not work on a victim who did not believe in them.

> *'Superstition breeds fear . . . which is what voodoo*
> *is all about. But it's about as irrational as*
> *avoiding a crack in the sidewalk'*

SCULLY

Fresh Bones

Scully may, in her typically Descartian way, have a point. But it doesn't pay to underestimate the power of fear – or the power of belief. Says Davis: 'We don't want to dismiss other aspects of the human tradition, and I've never quite understood why science has a sort of reflexive need to put them down . . . you'd think its position would be secure enough.'

I WANT TO BELIEVE

TOP SECRET
CLASSIFIED

CLASSIFIED

X-FILE: SYZYGY

FEDERAL BUREAU OF INVESTIGATION

Case notes by Special Agent Fox Mulder

We are but visitors on this rock, hurtling through time and space at 66,000 miles an hour, tethered to a burning sphere by an invisible force in an unfathomable universe. This most of us take for granted, while refusing to believe these forces have any more effect on us than cheese on macaroni.

Or that two girls, born on the same date, at the same time, in the sam place might not find themselves the unseen focus of similar unseen forc converging like the planets themselves into burning pin-points of cos energy whose absolute gravity would threaten to swallow and consume everything in its path.

Or maybe the answer lies even further from our grasp.

WRITTEN IN THE STARS

On a glittering wave of black humour, *Syzygy* swept Mulder and Scully into a small town gripped by rumours of Satanic cult activity and a heavy dose of full-moon fever. A rare celestial conjunction, coupled with the town's location in a mysterious geographical vortex, is inciting the townsfolk to varying degrees of uncharacteristic behaviour. Worst affected are teenagers Terri Roberts and Margi Kleinjan, transformed overnight from clueless high-school bunnies to conniving homicidal vixens. But even the Agents are not immune to the pernicious influence of the heavens, and the sight of a boozing, lascivious Mulder and an acerbic, cigarette-puffing Scully getting increasingly tetchy with one another shakes up the viewer, pulling the rug of comfort from under our feet and giving us the uneasy but deliciously intoxicating sense that our world, too, has taken a crazy detour from normality.

Mulder visits an astrologer in the hope of getting a handle on the high-weirdness that is afoot in Syzygy

The episode's title – pronounced sizz-a-jee – is an astronomical term for a celestial conjunction or opposition, particularly of the moon with the sun.

'I'd wanted to do something about a lunar occurrence since the first year,' recalls Chris Carter, 'and then I found out there was an astrological event in January that only came round once every 86 years, and I thought: what a perfect opportunity to make people behave as they wouldn't usually behave, and give them a kind of lunacy . . .'

> *'Why do you always have to drive? Because you're the guy? Because you're the big macho man?'*
> SCULLY
> *'No. Because I was never sure if your little feet could touch the pedals'*
> MULDER
> *Syzygy*

Having an excuse for Mulder and Scully to behave out of character enabled Carter to address humorously the issues which obsess the show's most analytical fans. 'When we go to conventions, people constantly ask me: Why does Mulder always drive, why does Mulder never do this, why does Scully always do that?' he explains. But besides providing laughter, the Agents' bickering in *Syzygy* also humanises them – after all, what friendship doesn't have days like these?

Fortunately, the real-life lunar event which had inspired Carter passed without any *Syzygy*-type incidents on *The X-Files* set. But he admits that he himself has cautiously entertained the veracity of astrology. 'I think that there may be something to it, only because I know people who believe in it so thoroughly. I believe that we've now been desensitised to the elements, to our environment, to such a degree that we pooh-pooh these things, but the truth is that you can find all kinds of rhythms and patterns in nature and in our behaviour as well.'

'I feel weird'
COMITY POLICE DETECTIVE ANGELA WHITE,
STRADDLING AGENT MULDER

Syzygy

It is no coincidence that many languages derive their words for mental disturbance from the latin *luna*. That the moon affects human behaviour is an ancient and deep-seated belief. In an informal 1982 survey of American police chiefs and hospital admissions clerks, most believed that

Terri Roberts and Margi Kleinjan - victims of astrological mayhem, full-moon fever, or just really, really bad PMT ?

things took a turn for the weird during a full moon. But whether the facts back up this widespread belief is a matter of debate.

In 1972 psychiatrists Arnold Lieber and Carolyn Sherin studied 15 years of homicides in Dade County, Florida, and found a significant correlation between the killings and the cycles of the moon. But when other researchers looked at different sets of data – police records, psychiatric hospital admissions, suicide reports, maritime disasters and traffic accidents – nearly all of them found absolutely nothing of significance.

Interestingly, many of the positive results came from studies which included a large number of women. A 1975 study of incidents of self-inflicted injury found a significant lunar influence for women, but not for men. And in 1991, it was found that developmentally delayed women in institutions were more likely to misbehave during full moon than at any other time.

Syzygy may reflect real life: it is possible that women are more susceptible to the moon's effects than men. Most people have a vague notion that the female menstrual cycle has *something* to do with the moon, but this is probably because we are aware that it is roughly the same length as the lunar month. Of course, they are not actually synchronised with one another; but once upon a time it might have been a different story. History has left us a provocative trail, including ancient fertility rites timed in accordance with the moon, and an observation by Aristotle that menstruation begins when the moon is waning. Did moonlight once provide the monthly trigger for the hormones which bring on menstruation, before mankind invented curtains and women were no longer directly exposed to it?

In 1980, physicist Dr E.P. Dewan tested this theory with seventeen women, all of whom had long, short or irregular menstrual cycles. Dewan exposed the women to artificial 'moonlight' at night, mimicking the lunar cycle. All but two found their cycles returned to normal immediately.

The hormones associated with menstruation are medically recognised as affecting state of mind to varying degrees. If the moon is able to trigger their production, it is not unreasonable to consider whether this might account for disturbed behaviour in women which seems to follow the lunar cycle. Indeed, you could wonder whether *Syzygy*'s lunar conjunction simply saddled its teenage villainesses with a bout of super-intense PMT. Chris Carter cracks a devilish smile and nods vigorously when asked whether this had occurred to him when he wrote the episode. 'Yes! Yes! Of course!' he says, laughing. 'But these things you can't exactly *say*!'

'We are but visitors on this rock, hurtling through time and space at sixty-six thousand miles an hour, tethered to a burning sphere by an invisible force in an unfathomable universe. This most of us take for granted, while refusing to believe these forces have any more effect on us than cheese on macaroni'

MULDER

Syzygy

Most scientists insist that the moon cannot affect human behaviour; but psychologists point out that the link need not be a physical or a scientific one – belief that the moon can influence us is so deeply entrenched that merely seeing a full moon could trigger irrational behaviour in someone who was perhaps already unbalanced.

Astrology is another matter altogether. Rational thinkers have a mountain of bones to pick with the notion that the planets and constellations could influence human behaviour, personality or destiny. They argue:

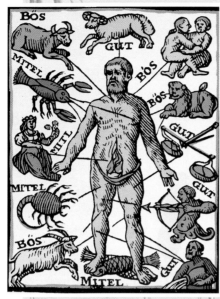

A 1665 depiction of the planetary influences on man. If there ever existed an accompanying explanation as to why this fellow's intestines are falling out, it has been lost in the mists of time

• Planets and stars have no gravitational effect on Earth, nor is there any other logical manner in which they could affect us.

• Even if they could, some of the stars are not in fact 'there' any more – what we are seeing is light they emitted thousands of years ago.

• Other stars *are* there – including one constellation firmly within the boundaries of the zodiac 'wheel' – but are ignored by astrology. Why?

• Why should the moment of birth be astrologically significant? Why not the moment of conception? Would our personalities really be different if our mother's obstetrician could have fitted her in for a Caesarian section on the Tuesday instead of the Thursday? And even the majority of professional astrologers deride the concept of 'sun sign' astrology, with its implication that all those born under the same sign – roughly one twelfth of the world's population – will share the same characteristics and destiny.

'I think this town's lost its marbles. You'd think I'd have seen it coming, but it's hard being a small business owner. You should see the paperwork'

MADAME ZIRINKA

In the United States alone more than 20,000 people, like *Syzygy's* Madame Zirinka, make a living as astrologers. Since it was first practised in Ancient Babylon around 1700 BC, astrology has never entirely lost its followers, despite attacks from the rational thinkers of every era. Here is a quick quiz. Who said, 'Astrology is not a science; it is a disease'? Ubersceptic James Randi perhaps? In fact it was written in the twelfth century by the philosopher and physician Maimonides (1135–1204), in his *Responsa I*.

But not all eminent thinkers have eschewed astrology entirely. The pioneering psychologist Carl Gustav Jung (1875–1961), while he did not believe that the movements of the stars 'caused' or even influenced matters on Earth, felt that there could be a connection of 'meaningful coincidence' – an example of what he termed Synchronicity. Jung thought of Synchronicity as a 'law' which could account not only for coincidence, but also for the application of astrology and other esoteric practices such as the I-Ching.

Astrologers frequently quote Jung (usually out of context) to lend credence to their beliefs, but his conclusions did no favours to the traditional notion of astrology. His experiments led him to believe that an astrologer searching for meaning in a chart was likely to find either exactly what he *wanted* to find, or else a mysterious reflection of his own psyche. Either way, a client visiting an astrologer is not getting what he believes he is paying for – an impartial translator who understands the language of celestial bodies and is able to relay its meaning.

'I'm just waiting for authorisation . . . Okay, you're good for up to three hundred bucks. How can I help you?'

MADAME ZIRINKA

Syzygy

As Mulder discovers, the services of an astrologer don't come cheap. But does astrology work? As Philip Levine, a practitioner based in Portland, Maine, points out, 'The more psychologically oriented astrologers tend to acknowledge that there does not seem to be any certainty in correlating planetary movements with specific events, because we have no way of knowing if a particular 'theme' will manifest in any one of many possibilities. For example, do planetary indicators of death experiences refer to a literal death, and if so at one's own hands or by the acts of others? Or do they refer to the loss of a cherished aspect of identity, a relationship, a professional role?'

Plenty of astrologers ply their trade regardless, confident of making successful forecasts. But in tests of all kinds – statistical and psychological, controlled and in-the-field – astrology has consistently failed to prove itself a reliable system.

A 1984 survey of 3011 astrological predictions published in magazines found only 338 correct, and the majority of these were either vague or the kind of educated guesses that could be made by anyone (some celebrity will marry his girlfriend; conflict will continue between warring factions, and so on).

In another test, statistician Geoffrey Dean had 1198 subjects sit a personality test, selected 60 each of the most stable, most unstable, most extroverted and most introverted people, and had their birth charts drawn up. He then asked 45 astrologers to look at the charts and separate them into four batches representing each of the four different traits. It took them nearly 20 hours of study. Then he asked another 45 astrologers to categorise the subjects by guesswork alone, without looking at the charts. The astrologers who had looked at the charts got just over half of their deductions right. Unfortunately, so did the ones who were guessing – in fact, they did fractionally better. Dean also noted that the first group's choices had disagreed with one another, and that no single astrologer had done significantly better than the others.

The 'Scorpio' constellation (above and below)

In 1982 D. Hamblin, later chairman of the British Astrological Association, summed up the astrologer's advantage with a shrewd assessment. 'If I find a very meek and unaggressive person with five planets in Aries, this does

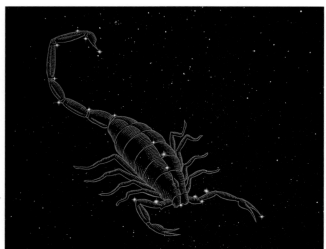

not cause me to doubt that Aries means aggression . . . I can simply say that he has not yet fulfilled his Aries potential. Or I can argue (as I have heard argued) that, if a person has an *excess* of planets in a particular sign, he will tend to suppress the characteristics of that sign because he is scared that, if he reveals them, he will carry them to excess. But if on the next day I meet a very aggressive person who also has five planets in Aries, I will change my tune: I will say that he *had* to be like that because of his planets in Aries.'

So is there anything more to astrology than creative interpretation? French statistician Michel Gauquelin studied a large sample of data consisting of the date, place and time of birth of thousands of eminent individuals and found what came to be known as the 'Mars Effect'. Intriguingly, 22% of famous sportsmen were born with Mars 'rising' or 'transiting'. While this represented only a 5% deviation from chance, in statistical terms the difference is considerable. In fact, the odds against the deviation *itself* happening by chance are several million to one.

But the Mars effect, if it truly exists, is fairly weak. It only shows up in surveys of the *very best* athletes and for some reason doesn't show up at all for basketball players! And, of course, the overwhelming majority of those born with Mars rising or transiting will *not* be famous sportspeople. It may be an odd phenomenon, but it does not help to prove that astrology works.

> *'What is going on here, Mulder?'*
>
> SCULLY
>
> *'Something cosmic'*
>
> MULDER
>
> *Syzygy*

Many psychologists have sought to find out why so many people continue to believe in astrology. Here are some of their conclusions.

THE 'BARNUM EFFECT'

Much of the information given in readings is so vague or general that it can be applied to anyone. The effect was discovered in 1949 by a psychology professor who succeeded in writing a lengthy personality description which every single one of his students believed referred to them.

FLATTERY WILL GET YOU EVERYWHERE

Readings are generally positive. If someone tells us that we are intuitive, imaginative, sociable, adventurous, intelligent, sensitive, easy-going or thoughtful, we're disinclined to question it.

WILL TO BELIEVE

No one visits an astrologer hoping that he or she will get it wrong, and our desire to believe manifests itself in all sorts of ways. We give clues about ourselves which help the astrologer to tell us things that seem pertinent. And if initially we disagree with something, we talk ourselves round. ('I'm extravagant with money? I always thought I was quite careful. There, again there *was* that expensive pair of shoes last year . . .')

'DR FOX SYNDROME'

If we feel we are in a 'learning situation' and we believe we are listening to someone who knows what they are talking about, we will be satisfied that we have learned something, regardless of what was actually said. This was the theory put forward and tested by three medical educators in 1974, when they employed an actor to play the part of 'Dr Myron L. Fox'. Fifty-five psychiatrists, psychologists, teachers, school administrators and social workers showed up for Dr Fox's talk on 'Mathematical Game Theory as Applied to Physical Education'. The lecture was deliberate gobbledygook, but when asked to fill in anonymous questionaires, 42 of the attendees agreed that Dr Fox's lecture was well organised, that he had used enough examples to clarify the material and that the lecture stimulated their thinking. Fourteen felt that he had dwelt too much upon the obvious and one felt that the presentation had been too intellectual, but most of those with complaints said that they would like to learn more about the subject. Not a single person guessed that the lecture was a hoax.

THE 'CLEVER HANS EFFECT'

Many astrologers rely on their clients' body language and facial expressions to gauge whether they are on the right track. The syndrome was named after a horse which appeared to be able to do sums and tell the time, tapping his answers with his hoof, but which was in fact responding to human reactions (nodding if Hans was doing well, frowning if it seemed he was going to count too high).

SELECTIVE MEMORY

Numerous studies have shown that we will leave a consultation with the memory of what was relevant, correct or useful in the forefront of our minds. Unless there was a really dreadful howler, the memory of what was mistaken is pushed into the background and eventually fades away. If we choose to visit an astrologer, the likelihood is that we will remember our visit as useful and accurate, and our belief in astrology is reinforced.

This potent collection of human foibles makes it hard for astrologers to put a foot wrong. But this is not to say that the majority of astrologers are con-artists. More than half of them practise 'humanistic' astrology, eschewing predictions and even precise character analysis altogether, regarding astrology more as a useful framework within which people can examine their personalities and their lives.

Indeed, in 1982, psychology professor D. Lester made a study of astrological practice in America and concluded that it offered precisely the same benefits as a visit to a therapist – a listening ear, empathy, advice, support, increased self-esteem and help in addressing possible future difficulties – at a fraction of the cost, and without the stigma attached.

F.Emasculata

0   20   40   60   80   100   120

Case notes by Special Agent Dana Scully

The demise of the two convicts who broke out of the Cumberland Correctional Facility in Virginia brings the death toll to 15, following the outbreak of an unnamed fatal contagion at the prison. This includes the 14 prisoners who were infected, and Doctor Osborne, an epidemiologist at Pinck Pharmaceuticals who had arrived as part of a team falsely claiming to represent the Center for Disease Control. It is not yet known whether any members of the public who came into contact with the escapees have been infected.

The contagion, a deadly parasite that attacks the immune system, causing death within 36 hours, is commonly carried by the Faciphaga Emasculata - an insect native to Costa Rica. I can confirm the strong likelihood that the insect was introduced into the prison via a package sent by Pinck Pharmaceuticals to an inmate, Robert Torrance, who was the first victim.

It is not inconceivable that this was done in a deliberate attempt to circumvent the years of FDA trials necessary before a new drug can be marketed. However, I have since learned that a scientist under the company's employ, who had gone missing during research in Costa Rica, was also named Robert Torrance. Since this could conceivably be dismissed as a postal error, and in light of the lack of any other evidence to support the case for foul play and cover-up, it is with some regret that I concur to close the file on this case.

Page 1*

E Mail

0   20   40   60   80   100   120

To: 001013 (Dana Scully)
From: 000517 (F. Mulder)

Scully,

When you get this message I'll be too far away for you to stop me, but where I'm going I cannot allow you to follow. I won't let you jeopardize your life and your personal career for reasons purely personal to me. You were right, Scully - you said a line has to be drawn somewhere. I'm drawing it for you here. I'll contact you when I can.

85%   Page 1*

Piper Maru

20   40   60   80   100   120   140   160   180   200

100%

D.Scully-Hard Di

Colony

Endgame

Nisei/731

Piper Maru

Alien Autopsy

Apochrypha

F.Emasculata

Talitha Cur

Bin

CONSPIRACY

Episodes of *The X-Files* essentially fall into two categories: those in which the Agents investigate an isolated case, and those which continue what Chris Carter and the writers call 'The X-Files Mythology' – the ongoing story of a corrupt cabal, controlling and covering up a conspiracy of colossal proportions. (For the story so far, see the Guide to *The X-Files* Mythology .)

In many ways, the conspiracy that Mulder and Scully learn of little by little is the conspiracy to end all conspiracies, encompassing as it does nearly every prevailing real-life paranoia.

Presidential conspiracies are among the few that Chris Carter says he does not think he will touch on. But even this popular element receives a nod: *The Lone Gunman* – the underground journal edited by Mulder's allies Byers, Langly and Frohike – is named for the much-contested conclusion of the Warren Commission into the assassination of John F. Kennedy. The Lone Gunmen themselves were invented by influential season one and two staffers Glen Morgan and Jim Wong.

'I recognised those characters immediately,' says Carter. 'When you go to UFO conventions you see these fringe-dwellers, paranoiacs and tech-heads. There was a guy with rabid political tracts at one convention. He had a conspiracy theory about everything. There was no particular thrust to it . . . Paranoia was its thrust.'

The assassination of President John F. Kennedy on 22 November 1963 - the subject of the most famous of all conspiracy theories, but one which The X-Files won't be touching upon

Story editor Frank Spotnitz has had similar encounters. 'A lot of people who watch the show assume we subscribe to all these things. I go to a convention and they are handing me information, volunteering military secrets they say they have. Very intense.'

The individuals on *The X-Files* team all share a similar point at which lines are drawn in their own beliefs. 'I'm of two minds,' says Carter. 'I believe that conspiracies do exist, but I also believe that there are no secrets . . . people have a great inability to keep a confidence, and there are too many self-interested people. That's why I believe with, say, the JFK conspiracy theory, that there aren't enough people with enough dedication to the keeping of that secret to really have kept it this long. Death and deathbeds have a wonderful way of coughing up truths . . .'

Spotnitz shares Carter's view. 'I think most conspiracies unravel very quickly. I honestly think we know about most of them. I think there are covert government policies and actions and programmes and experiments that we probably don't know about. But in terms of grand political conspiracies, working with aliens or anything like that, I just don't think we are that competent.'

None of *The X-Files* team is convinced by the 'Alien Autopsy' footage said to prove the infamous Roswell incident (for both, see *The X-Files Book of the Unexplained* Volume One), although it did provide the inspiration for the videotape viewed by Mulder in *Nisei* that turns out to be a vital clue. The footage was also humorously referenced in *Jose Chung's 'From Outer Space'*. Here we find Scully cringing as she watches herself performing an 'alien' autopsy on a show presented by flamboyant celebrity psychic the Stupendous Yappi (first seen in *Clyde Bruckman's Final Repose*).

The real-life US 'alien autopsy' broadcast warranted a little friendly mockery. 'A friend of mine actually produced that!' grins Howard Gordon.

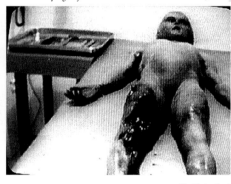

A still from the controversial 'alien autopsy' footage which surfaced in 1995. The film has not been proven a hoax, but very few remain who believe for a moment that it depicts the autopsy of an alien

'It was a tremendous hit. I couldn't believe it. So it was kind of a joke, and in a way we were parodying it.'

One can only guess, though, at how the members of the intelligence community react to the portrayal of *their* world on *The X-Files* – and at how closely the show mirrors reality. Carter has had some surprising, well-informed feedback. 'People from the intelligence community have come up and said to me, "Who's your contact? Because you don't know how right you have it."'

'I think it is pretty far-fetched that there would be a hit ordered on the assistant director of the FBI,' says Spotnitz, referring to the attempt on Skinner's life in *Apochrypha*, 'but the politics – I love all that stuff. I love doing all the conspiracy shows, I love the different parties that vie for power within government just as they do everywhere – in publishing houses, film studios, any business. Everywhere.'

'Just because you're paranoid it doesn't mean they're not out to get you, Scully'

MULDER

Soft Light

I s the world becoming more paranoid? Definitely. But whilst this cultural shift has been attributed to just about everything from millennial tension to *The X-Files* itself, there is a far more obvious reason for our diminishing trust and growing willingness to believe in the unthinkable. It's called learning from experience.

The X-Files stories are almost always inspired in some part by real-life incidents, phenomena or folklore. But *The X-Files* mythology is the area in which *The X-Files* universe most forcefully coincides with our own – for running through it are threads of unpalatable truth.

'We want to weave the fabric of history into the grand conspiracy that Chris has in mind for *The X-Files*,' says Spotnitz. 'Chris has this saying: *it's only as scary as it is real.*'

And Carter reveals an agenda beyond the desire to entertain. He would also like to educate. 'One of the most disturbing things in my life as an American is apathy towards the government and by the government. And I think one way to jolt people out of their complacency is to show them that in the absence of political or public mindedness, the people who wield the power will wield it in dangerous ways.

'There are factual accounts of horrendous experiments on the unwilling and the innocent, and they have happened in this century. The truth is still coming out and apologies are still being made, and this idea about apology being made policy is my expression of the sometimes amoral vacuum in which the government works.'

'Are you familiar with a post-World War II project known as Operation Paper Clip?'

LONE GUNMAN BYERS

Paper Clip

P *aper Clip* was the first *X-Files* episode to take its name, as well as elements of its story, from an historical event. 'I knew about the idea that [Werner Von] Braun and these people who had come to work on the space programme were German scientists and possibly war criminals,' says Carter. I don't know if it was ever proven, or that they were given special treatment, but I found it interesting, and certainly a shameful thing morally. But understandable, in the sense of the need to win in the global race for nuclear domination. It's kind of Hegelian, in that we've done whatever we have done to get to where we are.'

*'Our deal with the devil. The US government provided
safe haven for Nazi war criminals in exchange for
their scientific knowledge'*

MULDER

Paper Clip

With World War II over, the energies of the United States and the Soviet Union were redirected into the cold war. But Germany was far from forgotten. In 1946, as the US military was hunting down Nazi war criminals, a special intelligence office called the Joint Intelligence Objectives Agency (JIOA) instigated a plan to recruit German scientists into American research programs. These intellectual resources were valuable to the States – and securing them meant that the Soviets could not.

Operation Paper Clip was born – a code name said to have originated because an immigration form (holding the unspoken promise of problem-free naturalisation) was attached to the papers of each scientific recruit. Under the auspices of this and similar projects that succeeded it, lasting until the early 1970s, at least 1600 scientists and their families were quietly brought to the USA and given citizenship.

American government policy stated that 'ardent Nazis' and war criminals were not allowed to enter the country, and the project was, not surprisingly, the source of some controversy. Conveniently – according to files in the National Archives – most of the Paper Clip scientists had been affiliated to Nazi organisations as a mere formality, and were politically inactive.

In a letter to the State Department in April 1948, the director of JIOA, Captain Bosquet N. Wev, outlined the prevailing view of officialdom: 'In so far as German scientists are concerned, Nazism no longer should be a serious consideration from a viewpoint of national security when the far greater threat of Communism is now jeopardizing the entire world.'

*'The man standing next to your father is one of those
criminals, though not the most famous of the bunch. Werner
Von Braun, designer of the V2 rockets that leveled London,
may be the most notorious . . .'*

BYERS, STUDYING AN OLD PHOTO

Paper Clip

Paper Clip was considered a resounding success. The recruits were made welcome at a number of military research sites, including the Air Force's School of Aviation Medicine (SAM), at Brooks Air Force Base, Texas, where radiation experiments were conducted.

According to the government's own investigative body, the Advisory Committee on Human Radiation Experiments: 'Experiments at SAM included total-body irradiation, space-medicine and bed-rest studies, and flash-blindness studies . . . in connection with atomic weapons tests and data gathering for total-body irradiation studies conducted in Houston.'

Hubertus Strughold - today he is known in the USA as 'the father of space medicine'; once upon a time he had a laboratory at Dachau

Hubertus Strughold, who had had a laboratory at Dachau, began his US career at SAM, and is now known as 'the father of space medicine'. His chief subordinates at Dachau are widely believed to have been directly involved in 'aviation medicine' experiments – inhumanely conducted studies of high-altitude exposure, resistance to the cold, oxygen deprivation and the like – giving rise to repeated allegations that these medical atrocities were sanctioned by Strughold.

'. . . Victor Klemper certainly takes the prize for the most evil Nazi to escape the Nuremberg trials'

BYERS

'What did he do?'

SCULLY

'Experimented on the Jews. Drowned them, suffocated them, put them in pressure chambers. All in the name of "science"'

LONE GUNMAN LANGLY

Paper Clip

Although, like *The X-Files'* fictional Klemper, some Nazi war criminals managed to avoid prosecution for their crimes, many others were successfully tried at Nuremberg for experiments related to aviation research. The results of such experiments would be extremely useful in the protection of air crewmen.

In March 1951, General O.O. Benson Jr, the Commandant at SAM, wrote to the Surgeon General requesting another shipment of 'first-class scientists and highly qualified technologists from Germany,' since 'the first group of Paper Clip personnel contained a number of scientists that have proved to be of real value to the Air Force.'

The scientific community was not the only faction to benefit from the 'brain drain' at the close of World War II. Hitler's master spy Reinhard Gehlen became an important part of America's intelligence community and recruited others for a small overseas espionage group that helped nurse the CIA into existence. Although Gehlen promised not to recruit anyone who had been involved with the SS or the Gestapo, according to conspiracy experts Jonathan Vankin and John Whalen, 'he immediately broke his official word, hiring at least six SS and Sicherheitsdienst veterans. And America's intelligence elite looked the other way. Two of Gehlen's notorious postwar signings were Dr Franz Alfred Six and Emil Augsburg, SS intelligence veterans involved in the mass extermination of Jews. They were both fugitive war criminals.'

Numerous Nazi scientists were tried and convicted for their crimes at The Nuremberg Trials. Others were given sanctuary and high-level research posts in America under Project Paper Clip

'Do you know my work? Do you know what we achieved?'

KLEMPER

'As a Nazi? Or for the blood money we paid you?'

SCULLY

Paper Clip

The US Army's Counter Intelligence Corps later arrested Six. They caught up with Augsberg, too – and hired him. Klaus Barbie, the Butcher of Lyon, also assisted Gehlen for a while in his espionage work for the USA, and even spent some time living there. As Vankin and Whalen note, in an atmosphere of cold war paranoia US officials 'found expedient soul mates in the Nazi scientists and SS officers they recruited. After all, Nazi Germany's fascists were vehemently opposed to communism, too.'

'Science will save humanity or science will destroy it, Ms Scully. The ruler of the world is no longer the country with the bravest soldiers but the greatest scientists. Ishimaru . . . was one of those men'

FIRST ELDER

731

A few episodes later, *The X-Files* ventured even further into the realm of real-life conspiracy with the two-part story told in *Nisei* and *731*. In terms of horror, as Frank Spotnitz, writer of *731* and co-writer (with

Howard Gordon and Chris Carter) of *Nisei* notes: 'it's hard to rival the truth.'

In these episodes we meet Japanese war criminal Dr Ishimaru, who was involved with the unimaginable barbarity that took place at a covert research centre known as Unit 731. He was not punished for his war crimes, but was given sanctuary and invited to share his findings with the US authorities and continue his work in America. This is, essentially, a true story.

'Ishimaru is a butcher'

SCULLY

'In a world of madmen, knowledge supercedes morality'

FIRST ELDER

731

On 17 June 1925, still reeling from a senseless war that had decimated a generation, most of the earth's most powerful countries decided they no longer wanted to live in a world of madmen. They signed the Geneva Protocol, outlawing biological and chemical warfare.

The two most conspicuous abstentions were the ever-independent United States and imperial Japan. Japan, in fact, was so impressed by the fact that chemical and biological warfare was considered dangerous enough to ban that it immediately stepped up its research.

The guiding force behind the Japanese effort was a young doctor named Shiro Ishii. Ishii had graduated from the Department of Medicine at Kyoto University in 1920 and gone straight into the Japanese Imperial Army. In the late 1920s he was sent to Europe and the United States for two years to study the state of Western biological research. Soon after his return, Japan invaded and conquered Manchuria (in what is now China). Ishii and his team finally had a literal theatre of operations.

'His name is Dr Takeo Ishimaru . . . He was the commander of an elite section of the Japanese Medical Corps known as 731. A unit now known to have experimented on human subjects. They performed vivisections without anesthesia, tested frostbite tolerance levels on infants, exposed prisoners of war to diseases, to the Plague . . .'

MULDER

Nisei

The real-life Ishii did all that and more. In 1936 Emperor Hirohito's seal was affixed to a document that established Ishii's Manchuria-based 'Epidemic Prevention and Water Purification Department of the Kuantung Army' (changed to Unit 731 in 1941). The name was a masterpiece of hubris. In fact, the extremely well funded 'department' specialised in epidemic-causing toxins like anthrax, cholera, tetanus, botulism, meningitis, tuberculosis and bubonic plague. A constant supply of test victims was provided courtesy of the occupying Japanese Army. At first they were mostly Chinese and Russians, but once World War II began these were joined by specimens labelled 'American,' 'British' and 'Australian'. But the staff at Unit 731 had their own special name for the men, women and children they vivisected, almost invariably without anaesthetic. They called them *marutas*: logs.

'What was he exposing these people to?'
SCULLY
'Terrible things'
FIRST ELDER
731

Scully witnesses the horrific execution of an unusual-looking group of research subjects in 731. But no measure of fictional barbarity can compare to the unimaginable, inhuman acts that took place at the real Unit 731

The horrors of Unit 731 were unimaginable. Apart from the physical torture suffered by captives before they were killed, there were countless instances of emotional and mental cruelty. In one case, a Japanese doctor vivisected an unanaesthetised pregnant women whom he himself had impregnated.

One Unit 731 staffer recently tried to justify his actions: 'Of course there were experiments on children. But probably their fathers were spies.'

The extreme de-humanisation existed outside the army as well. Civilian Japanese doctors would regularly practise surgery techniques on healthy prisoners of war. In one case, eight American servicemen were killed in one day on the operating tables at the anatomy department of Kyushu University. They were taken apart bit by bit: first a lung, then a bit of liver, then part of a brain; until finally they died.

'Ask yourself, friend, what would be more valuable than Star Wars? What would be more valuable than the atomic bomb? Or the most advanced biological weapons?'
RED-HAIRED MAN
'A standing army immune to the effect of those weapons'
MULDER
731

Ishii's primary interest was not surgery but large-scale biological warfare. He was developing and testing diseases on his *marutas* with the goal of delivering a fatal dose to the enemy whilst learning to treat it in his own men. Throughout the war, Ishii had disease-infested animals (usually fleas) dropped on Chinese towns, where there were several outbreaks of bubonic plague as a result.

His plans extended to the United States. In December 1944, 200 balloon bombs were sent using prevailing air currents from Japan to the Western United States, killing seven people in Montana and Oregon. It is likely these balloons were testing the route for bacterial bombs.

As the war was drawing to a close, Ishii had one last bit of insanity up his sleeve. Operation Cherry Blossoms at Night would send plague-laden suicide bombers to San Diego, where the plague would be released and the entire Western seaboard infected. The date of attack was scheduled for 22 September 1945.

'They had been exposed'
FIRST ELDER
'Exposed to what?'
SCULLY
'The same thing all these people were exposed to – victims of an inhuman project. Run by a man named Zama'
FIRST ELDER
'You mean Ishimaru. This is where you hid him after the war – where he continued his experiments'
SCULLY
731

The war in the Pacific ended in August 1945. The cover-up began almost immediately. Ishii was declared dead and a mock funeral was held in his home town. Although he and his staff had destroyed some of the evidence against them before the end of the war, they had plenty of information left to barter. Under the advice of scientists from Fort Detrick, Maryland (the US Army's own bacteriological and chemical research unit), General Douglas MacArthur radioed Washington, recommending that Unit 731 scientists be granted immunity in exchange for their data.

The reply from the Committee for the Far East was: 'The value to the US of Japanese BW [Biological Warfare] data is of such importance to national security as to far outweigh the value accruing from war crimes prosecution.' To its credit, the State Department was against the plan, if only because it might later embarrass the United States.

Not a single member of Unit 731 was prosecuted for war crimes by the United States. The only ones to be prosecuted were twelve who were caught by the Soviets in China: their well-documented trial in 1949 was suppressed in the United States and regarded as Soviet propaganda.

'What am I on to here?'

MULDER

'Monsters begetting monsters'

SENATOR MATHESON

Nisei

In spite of articles in 1946 in both the *New York Times* and the *Pacific Stars and Stripes* (the official newspaper of the US Army) the government refused to admit that Americans had been the victims of Unit 731, let alone that Ishii was cooperating with the United States.

There were rumours throughout the 1950s that not only had Ishii lectured at Fort Detrick, he had also gone to Korea to help the American war effort. There was certainly some familiar-looking evidence. According to Jonathan Vankin and John Whalen: 'On an April night in 1952 an American F-82 fighter was spotted flying over a Chinese village near the Inner Mongolian border. With the break of day, residents were greeted by an infestation of more than seven hundred voles. Of the voles who survived both the night cold and ravaging cats, many "were sluggish or had fractured legs". A test on one dead vole showed that it was infected with the plague.'

The US government did its best to kill the rumours. In the 1950s, it even resorted to charges of treason against some American civilians who had dared to imply that the government might be using technology originating in Unit 731. The charges were thrown out for lack of evidence.

The cover-up continues. In 1987, US and British veterans of the Manchuria campaign were told there was 'no evidence' for claims that Unit 731 experimented on them. And as recently as 1989, a British book was published in the United States minus one chapter freely available in the British, Canadian, Australian and New Zealand editions. The chapter was called 'The Korean War'.

'Dr Zama isn't here anymore. None of the medical staff is.
ESCALANTE
'Where did they go?'
SCULLY
731

And what of the men of Unit 731? Ishii died of throat cancer at the age of 67 in 1959. Others went on to exalted positions in post-war Japan: Governor of Tokyo, president of the Japan Medical Association and head of the Japanese Olympic Committee. The leader of the team in charge of inflicting frostbite and vivisecting the victims went on to a lucrative career in the frozen fish industry.

In 1975, the United States finally signed the Geneva Protocol.

Frank Spotnitz admits to some trepidation in weaving the true story of Unit 731 into *The X-Files* mythology. 'There's a lot of sensitivity to this issue, in Japan especially. But I was born in Japan, and *I* had never heard of this, and I was just amazed . . . I am no expert, but I don't think the Japanese have had the national soul-searching which the Germans have certainly had . . .'

Spotnitz's main concern is for viewers to realise that 731 was a genuine historical event. 'I think we put in enough factual-sounding information so that they would recognise it. I hope so.'

'They've been doing tests since World War II. Tests on
innocent civilians. Experiments'
MULDER
731

Throughout *The X-Files* mythology, and even beyond it, in episodes like *F. Emasculata*, we find covert experiments on unwitting subjects, undertaken with official sanction. And once again *The X-Files* writers did not need to look far for inspiration.

Early in 1963 the Atomic Energy Commission held a conference in Fort Collins, Colorado, for scientists studying the effects of radiation on reproduction. It was the height of the cold war and there were questions that needed to be answered. Questions like the one asked by scientists at an AEC meeting in

Washington in 1955: 'How many bombs can we detonate without producing a race of monsters?' And questions like the one posed in 1949 by an Air Force colonel who enquired how safe nuclear-powered planes would be for his airmen's 'family jewels'. NASA wanted to know about the effects of solar radiation on astronauts. And the CIA wanted to know about everything.

Dr Carl G. Heller recalled what happened: 'A given group at Fort Collins was working on mice and another group was working on bulls, and then they extrapolated the data from bulls or mice to man. I commented one day to Dr [Paul] Henshaw, who was then . . . with the AEC, that if they were so interested in [what would happen to] man, why were they fussing around with mice and beagle dogs and canaries and so on? If they wanted to know about man, why not work on man?'

Nisei finds Mulder stalking a Japanese war criminal - a character based on Shiro Ishii, the unspeakably evil doctor responsible for the horrors of Unit 731

In October 1995, the US government's Advisory Committee on Human

Radiation Experiments published its final report. The committee had been assembled by President Clinton after dogged investigative journalist *Albuquerque Tribune* reporter Eileen Welsome uncovered evidence of government-sponsored radiation tests on civilians.

Whilst ground-breaking and laudable, the committee's mandate was limited to government-funded tests between 1944 and 1974. Another problem was that it relied on self-reporting from various government agencies. The CIA, for example, claim they did only one tiny, innocuous test whereas the Department of Energy admits to 435 studies involving 16,000 subjects. Regardless, the range of admitted tests was astounding.

'When was he exposed?'
DR OSBORNE
'Eighteen hours ago'
DR AUERBACH
'I've never heard of anything incubating so quickly'
DR OSBORNE
'Where's the prison doc? I want to see the prison doc'
BOBBY TORRANCE, INMATE
'We're specialists, Mr. Torrence . . .'
DR AUERBACH
F. Emasculata

In *F. Emasculata*, the Agents find themselves in the midst of a lethal viral outbreak in a prison. This is no accident, but part of a government-sanctioned experiment. Howard Gordon, co-writer (with Carter) of *F. Emasculata*, explains how the idea came about: 'Constant fodder for us are disenfranchised populations, whether illegal aliens, immigrants, etcetera, because they are controlled, containable. Chris had the idea of an experiment in a prison. Prisons are always interesting sets, and prisoners are interesting people.'

'What is this thing?!'
PAUL, FUGITIVE INMATE
'You were infected in prison'
MULDER
F. Emasculata

Prisons have long been a popular testing ground in America. Between 1963 and 1973 Dr Heller, an award-winning medical scientist, ran a series of experiments on inmates at the Oregon State Prison in order to assess the effect of radiation on sperm production. Another test involving radiation and reproduction was conducted in Washington State. Prisoners in Pennsylvania were used to test the effects of radiation on human skin. Inmates in Illinois drank water laced with radium. Prisoners in Utah had their blood removed, irradiated and re-injected. And the tests were not confined to radiation. Just one example: starting in 1944, hundreds of prisoners at Illinois Statesville Prison were given malaria in a project designed to develop a

President Bill Clinton, who assembled a committee to look into government-sanctioned experiments involving human subjects. Its final report was a catalogue of atrocities

prevention or cure for the disease that was disabling Allied forces in the Pacific.

According to the government's own report: 'It is difficult to overemphasize just how common the practice [of experimenting on prisoners] became in the United States during the postwar years. Researchers employed prisoners as subjects in a multitude of experiments that ranged in purpose from a desire to understand the cause of cancer to a need to test the effects of a new cosmetic. After the Food and Drug Administration's restructuring of drug-testing regulations in 1962, prisoners became almost the exclusive subjects in nonfederally funded Phase I pharmaceutical trials designed to test the toxicity of new drugs. By 1972, FDA officials estimated that more than 90% of all investigational drugs were first tested on prisoners.'

'What do you know about Pinck Pharmaceutical, Mulder?'

SCULLY

'One of, if not the biggest manufacturer of drugs in America. Why?'

MULDER

'They sent a package to a prisoner here who may have been the first victim of this contagion'

SCULLY

F. Emasculata

The Agents' discovery in *F. Emasculata* is a horrific one: a drug company has anonymously sent an inmate a contaminated pig's leg in order to research the contagion – all with the government's permission.

In reality, drug companies had no need to FedEx their infections; they often had direct access to prisoners. In at least one case, Upjohn and Parke-Davis built and maintained a large Phase I testing facility on the grounds of the State Prison of Southern Michigan.

Prison testing has more or less been abandoned since the late 1970s, not so much for humanitarian reasons but because the tests were coming under too much scrutiny. And it was becoming easier to employ two other sources of human experimental material: students and the poor.

'How're they doing?'

MULDER

'Not real good'

SEIZER

Piper Maru

The poor have a history of being subjected to government-run experiments. Amongst the most infamous was the Tuskegee Study of the early 1930s, in which 412 African-American sharecroppers suffering from syphilis were identified by the US Public Health Service but were not informed of their condition. For forty years – even after penicillin was discovered to treat syphilis – US PHS doctors observed the effects of the disease taking its course, from blindness and paralysis to dementia and death.

Not that treatment was any safer. Woe betide those who checked into a research hospital in the middle of this century. At various institutions across the United States, Canada and the United Kingdom, patients were injected with plutonium without their knowledge, given radioactive 'cocktails' or subjected to full body radiation. In one particularly appalling test, radioactive sodium was injected directly into the placentas of 270 pregnant women at Hammersmith Hospital in England. The adverse results of these experiments varied from amputation to birth defects to death.

'The madness we'd planned to unleash on the Japanese – we ended up setting it loose on ourselves'

JOHANSEN

Piper Maru

Given that much of this radiation testing was specifically intended to benefit the military, the average soldier did not fare much better than his civilian counterpart. Between 1946 and 1963 over 200,000 GIs were ordered to watch nuclear bomb tests either in the Pacific or in Nevada. One blast alone in the Marshall Islands was more than 1000 times the size of the Hiroshima bomb.

'Have the bodies destroyed'
THE CIGARETTE SMOKING MAN
'But . . . these men aren't dead yet'
DOCTOR
'Isn't that the prognosis?'
THE CIGARETTE SMOKING MAN
Apochrypha

E ven in death, citizens are not immune from government testing. Project Sunshine, which started in 1955, was an international bodysnatching program that secretly removed body parts from over 9000 corpses at 17 sites around the world and sent them to US laboratories for fallout testing. It was described by one sensitive American scientist as 'a delicate problem of public relations, obviously'.

Prisoners, rank-and-file military, the poor, pregnant women, the dead . . . Who had the government scientists left out (apart from white, middle-class males, of course)? How about children . . . ?

'I don't know what to say. You think Dr. Larson was doing some kind of tests on Gary?'
BETH
Red Museum

N ot surprisingly, scientists didn't run tests on their own children; they ran them on children in institutions and in reform schools. During the 1950s and 60s, Willowbrook State School in New York, an institution for the severely mentally retarded, was the site of hepatitis testing. Each newly arrived child was systematically infected. The rationale was that these places offered regulated environments that were perfect for replicating lab conditions. Oddly, even though private boarding schools also offered regulated environments, no one ever ran experiments there.

'What's he treating them for?'
SCULLY
'What's he treating them with?'
MULDER
Red Museum

The government's human radiation committee looked at 21 cases of experimentation on children involving over 800 subjects, a number that they themselves admit is just a small proportion of what went on. One of the cases they concentrated on was dietary research conducted by the Massachusetts Institute of Technology and the staff of Walter E. Fernald School, a residential institution for boys.

Former residents, some of whom ended up there simply because their families didn't want them any more, describe the school as being dirty and brutal. In 1946, researchers set up a 'science club' at the school, enticing boys to join with such perks as a quart of milk a day and the occasional chance to leave the building.

'Dr Larson gave him vitamin shots. He gave them to lots of kids. He said it was like treating their teeth with fluoride. As a preventative measure'

BETH

Red Museum

In return, the boys were to eat a special 'rich' diet (breakfast food 'enriched' with radioactive iron) and to submit to regular blood tests. Letters to the boys' parents implied that the testing would improve their health. The research, along with a later experiment at the school involving radioactive calcium, was funded by the National Institute of Health, the Atomic Energy Commission and the Quaker Oats Company.

The government report ends its section on 'non-therapeutic' tests on children with: 'Today, fifty years after the Fernald experiments, there are still no federal regulations protecting institutionalized children from unfair treatment in research involving human subjects.'

One ex-Fernald boy, Charlie Dyer, who has fathered two daughters with severe birth defects, said recently: 'Get to the truth fast before the government hides everything and you can't find nothing out. Because that's what the government does, putting it in boxes and crates and hiding everything from the public.'

Not all experiments are as carefully controlled as this French one, in which soil is being contaminated with radioactive material in a contained environment: 'I have a friend who is a virologist, a researcher,' says Chris Carter, 'and she told me that a lot of genetically-altered plant experiments take place on plots of fenced-in land, with a moat around them. Do you remember when there were big floods in the US? The Mississippi overflowed and all of middle America was under water? A lot of these genetically-altered plants, which had animal viruses put into them, were all washed downstream together . . . I've always wanted to do that in an

episode, but I've not figured out how to tell the story.'

'Two weeks ago the president made a public apology for secret radiation tests that had been conducted on innocent citizens up until 1974. Only, guess what?'

SCULLY

'Those tests never ended'

MULDER

731

In October 1995, President Clinton did indeed promise to 'make reparations to Americans whose lives were damaged or even cut short by these (human radiation) experiments'. Of course, it is up to the government (or government-appointed private contractors) to decide who has been 'damaged'. So far, the vast majority of claims have not been approved. And there are almost no follow-up studies for people irradiated without their knowledge; so they are unlikely even to know what it is that is killing them, let alone that they are eligible for compensation.

The case of 4500 Utah and Nevada sheep, grazing downwind of nuclear test sites, which died 'mysteriously' in 1953 shows how willingly reparations are handed out. It took 30 years, much of it spent in court, for the government to be forced into paying compensation. The presiding judge, A. Sherman Christensen, made a point of saying that the US Government had lied, pressured witnesses and manipulated the processes of the court.

And yes, the tests never ended.

'Scully – talk to me. I can see you're angry'

SKINNER

'Of course I'm angry. These people think justice is just a game'

SCULLY

Apochrypha

Howard Gordon sums up where decades of cold war zeal and governmental and scientific arrogance have left us: 'I'm not paranoid by nature, so I'm shocked by things like the Tuskegee Experiment, the confession of low-grade radiation released into the atmosphere, and population tests.

'Ultimately, nothing is inconceivable. All you have to do is look at Nazi Germany. Many machines have been built that have been engines for evil.

Institutionalized evil. Pure evil . . . You don't have to look too hard to imagine the horror that governments are capable of.

'In the end, it's the power of the individual that will overcome the inherent evil of a monolith like a government run amock. A little healthy paranoia is good, I suppose.'

'I've just been thinking about something a man said to me. He said that the dead speak to us from beyond the grave – that that's what conscience is . . . I think that the dead are speaking to us, Mulder – demanding justice. Maybe this man was right. Maybe we bury the dead alive'

SCULLY

Apochrypha

U.S DEPARTMENT OF JUSTICE

**FEDERAL BUREAU
OF
INVESTIGATION**

X-FILE: SLEEPLESS

SCULLY, D

OFFICE CRIM
AND ADMINIS

Report by Special Agent Dana Scully
Continued...

Also described in the report is a highly experimental neurosurgical procedure designed to induce a permanent waking state.

The procedure involved cutting part of the brain stem in the midpontile region – which would explain Henry Willig's scar. A similar scar should also be evident on Augustus Cole.

Post-op treatment included a regimen of synthetic supplements to replenish the organic deficits caused by prolonged lack of sleep. This is consistent with the anti-depressants Cole robbed from the pharmacy. These drugs maintain serotonin levels in the blood – serotonin being the primary substance product during sleep.

Although it seems certain that Augustus Cole is somehow responsible for the recent deaths, we are no closer to finding an explanation for their puzzling nature.

FEDERAL BUREAU OF INVESTIGATION

X-FILE: BLOOD

Case notes by Special Agent Fox Mulder

The sudden violent outburst in a public locale and the suspect's disregard for anonymity or survival define the Franklin incidents as spree killings.

The confounding element of these profiles is that, given their backgrounds, the perpetrators would be, statistically, more likely to be victims of violent crimes rather than the originators. The killers were all middle-income, responsible people, none with a history of violence.

Relatives and friends reported only minor displays of dysfunctional behavior: sleep disorders, headaches, eating difficulties. And witnesses *did* report that the last suspect displayed a claustrophobic reaction.

The single connecting trace evidence to the killings is the destruction of an electronic device at the crime scene; a pager, a fax machine, a cellular phone, the elevator's digital floor indicator.

I am convinced an outside factor is responsible ... but I must concede frustration to a determination of the cause.

TOP SE

FBI NATIONAL ACADEMY
QUANTICO, VIRGINIA

INVESTIGA

X-FILE: BLOOD

MULDER, FO

FIELD OFFICE CRIMINAL INVESTI
AND ADMINISTRATIVE FILE

X-FIL

X-FILE:

06

X-FILE: PUSHER

X-FILE: PUSHER

**Preliminary Hearing.
Defendant: Robert Patrick Modell**

Cont'd...

Judge: Agent Mulder, does the FBI believe that this defendant is responsible for fourteen murders?

Agent Fox Mulder: That is correct, your honor.

Judge: In each of these cases the coroner's office ruled for suicide.

Agent Fox Mulder: We believe they were indeed murders, your honor.

Judge: You believe. But do you have any actionable evidence?

Agent Fox Mulder: We have the defendant on audiotape confessing to the murders on several separate occasions. He clearly identifies them as such. Furthermore, the defendant knows crime scene details which are only available to the police.

Attorney for the Defense: Your honor, one of these so-called murder victims threw herself under a commuter train. This was on a crowded platform, a hundred witnesses ... Nobody pushed her. No one was within thirty feet of her.

Agent Fox Mulder: But your client was present.

Attorney for the Defense: Which is how he knew your crime scene details.

Judge: Make your point, Agent Mulder.

Agent Fox Mulder: I believe those people died because it was Mr. Modell's express will that they do so.

Judge: His will?

Agent Fox Mulder: This man admitted to being a killer for hire. I believe he has a unique suggestive ability which makes for the perfect M.O.: He talks his victims into injuring themselves. He overrides their wills with his own.

MIND CONTROL

In the outstanding *Pusher*, Mulder and Scully brush with Robert 'Pusher' Modell, a cunning killer-for-hire who commits his near-perfect crimes by insidiously persuading others to do his will.

It was an idea that newcomer Vince Gilligan had had in his mind for some time. 'I cannibalised an old science fiction movie script I had written,' he reveals. 'It was going have a really cool ending . . . the main bad guy is getting away. The good guy seems kinda calm; he whispers some code word to the bad guy and it turns out to be this top secret military brain-washing thing. Six months later, the bad guy's down in Costa Rica with a bimbo next to him in his convertible, and he's fat and happy . . . And he sees this blue truck coming down the highway. This code-word goes off in his head and he pulls in front of it, and: blammo!

'I figured it would be more interesting as an X-File if it was not military, but more paranormal. So I worked up the story based on that (Modell's preturnatural talents are the freak side-effect of brain tumour) and then I thought, what other cool things could someone make someone else do?

The character of Modell was the serendipitous result of a compromise between Gilligan and Chris Carter. 'I wanted the guy to be a loser who had never amounted to anything, and now he's really happy although he's dying,' Gilligan recalls. 'Chris was interested in making him a ninja, so I asked if we could split the difference, have him be one of these geeky characters who reads a lot of kung-fu magazines and talks like a ninja but doesn't really know any of it – and Chris agreed.'

Besides investigating the legends of ninja mind-control, Gilligan was also interested in methods tried out closer to home, such as subliminal techniques used in advertising, although he adds, 'I don't think any of those things have any power.'

In *The X-Files* universe, however, it seems that some shadowy faction has perfected the dubious art of subliminal persuasion. In *Blood*, a pesticide used for covert crop-dusting causes a chemical reaction in phobia-prone people, and a series of subliminal messages appears to instruct them on how to direct the violent urges induced by the resultant psychosis. And who knows, perhaps the same faction is behind the alarming goings-on in *Wetwired*, in which the agents discover that undetectable signals sent through the television sets of selected victims are inducing delusions, paranoia and homicide.

'Scully, are you familiar with subliminal messages?'

MULDER

Blood

In the late 1950s, a marketing researcher named James Vicary installed a device called a tachistoscope in the projection room of a cinema in Fort Lee, New Jersey: a gizmo capable of flashing a still image onto the screen so briefly that it would not be noticed by the conscious mind. Vicary's messages, which he ran every five seconds during movies, read 'Hungry? Eat Popcorn' and 'Drink Coca Cola'. In the six weeks that Vicary ran his experiment, more than 45,000 moviegoers were exposed to the messages, and he announced that sales of Coca Cola and popcorn had soared by 18% and 57.8% respectively.

Apparently, the minds of the masses could be manipulated without anyone knowing a thing about it. The media and the public were up in arms: if we could be induced to feel not only hungry and thirsty, but to crave a particular product, then, conceivably, any personal choice – what to buy, who to vote for, how to behave – could be tampered with. The *New York Times* spoke of minds being 'broken and entered' and *Newsday* called subliminal projection the most alarming invention since the atomic bomb.

However, when Vicary refused to release any written data, the president of a psychological research body insisted that he replicate the experiment under controlled conditions. This time, sales of Coke and popcorn did not budge. In 1962, Vicary admitted that he had fabricated his results in a bid to drum up custom for his flagging marketing business.

Other replications also failed. In 1948, the Canadian Broadcast Corporation warned viewers of an upcoming subliminal test and flashed up the message 'Phone Now!' 352 times during a popular Sunday night TV show. Nobody phoned the CBC, nor did general phone usage increase, but plenty of letters arrived afterwards from people helpfully reporting various impulses, including urges to drink beer, change the channel and go to the toilet.

But it was too late. The 'Eat popcorn/Drink Coca Cola' experiment was firmly entrenched in the realm of scientific mythology (alongside falsehoods like 'you only use 10% of your brain' and 'dreams happen in less than three seconds') and broadcast associations in the USA, Australia and Great Britain had already reacted with regulations that banned subliminal advertising.

Few flouted the new restrictions, with the exception of one US advertising agency who, at Christmas 1973, inserted split-second flashes of the words 'Get it!' into a commercial for a children's game, *Husker Du?*. When TV stations found out, they pulled the advertisement. They probably need not have bothered. While there is strong evidence for subliminal perception (the ability of the mind to subconsciously *register* images too quick or faint to be noticed, or sounds blended into other sounds) there is hardly any for subliminal *persuasion* – using such methods to influence behaviour.

Of course, something perceived subliminally might have *some* effect, and movie directors have tried these techniques to enhance feelings of tension or horror. *Exorcist* director William Friedkin twice superimposed fleeting shots of a ghastly face into the movie – during Father Karras's dream about his mother standing by a subway, and during his attempt to kill the possessed child, Regan. Alfred Hitchcock's 1945 black and white thriller *Spellbound* includes three single, hand-tinted, red frames (near the end, when Leo G. Carroll's gun fires at the camera), and his 1960 masterpiece *Psycho* includes a two-second, superimposed image of Bates's mother's cadaverous face as we fade from Anthony Perkins in his cell to Janet Leigh's car being

A scene from William Friedkin's 1973 horror classic The Exorcist. *Did hidden images enhance its terrifying impact?*

dredged from the mud. Tobe Hooper claimed enigmatically to have used subliminal techniques in his *Texas Chainsaw Massacre*, but refuses to reveal details of what they are.

One thing is certain, however: a scary subliminal can't increase the appeal of a bad film. A psychologist and an engineer who invented a tachistoscopic device produced two low-budget horror flicks in the late 1950s in which they flashed images of skulls, snakes and ominous words like 'Blood'. Both films sank without trace.

'You mean "sex" in ice-cubes on liquor ads?
Mulder, that's just paranoia'

SCULLY

Blood

Just who is behind the behaviour altering endeavours that take place in Blood?

According to prolific author Wilson Bryan Key, advertisers also latched on to the idea that a subliminal image could create a mood or emotion. Key's most famous declaration is the one discussed by Mulder and Scully: that the ice cubes in a magazine advert for Gilbeys Gin contained hidden images of the word 'sex'. Key's own experiment (which had no control group and was therefore scientifically meaningless) found that 62% of his subjects felt sexy when looking at the advert.

Key claims to have found thousands of advertisements containing 'embedded' words and pictures designed to arouse or to create a feeling of flirting with death and danger. Key also insists that the word 'sex' is subliminally baked into the surface of Ritz crackers.

A few of Key's sample photos, when enlarged, contain shadowy images that could be said to represent what he says that they do. Of course, pareidolic interpretation could be involved (see *Mass Hysteria And The Belief Engine*), but Key is not entirely alone in his beliefs. In the early 1980s, the *Journal of Advertising* ran an article by a DePaul University professor who agreed that 'embedding' was going on but reached no conclusion on whether the method affected sales.

Even so, most people's gut reaction to such claims is horror or anger at such insidious manipulation. Some might wonder why such reactions seem to be reserved for claims that advertisers are attempting to push products, manipulate our desires or play on our anxieties *covertly* – apparently *overt* advertisements with the same aims, the ones we see every day, are acceptable.

'It's a fact that some department stores use subliminal messages in ambient music to deter shoplifting'

MULDER

Blood

Today, two US companies provide subliminal communication services. Both say that they refuse to cater for advertisers or political clients, making their money instead from retailers, to whom they sell music tapes embedded with messages like 'Obey the law. Stay honest. Don't steal.' One company claims that their clients report 37%–65% drops in shoplifting.

But in controlled tests, other subliminal tapes – the 'self-help' kind, supposed to help people to quit smoking, lose weight, improve memory, increase self-esteem and so on – have been spectacularly ineffective. In one experiment, subjects completed memory and self-esteem tests and then listened daily to a subliminal tape – either for improved memory or self-esteem – for five weeks before completing both tests again. Nothing had changed. Interestingly, the subjects were first asked if *they* perceived an effect of any kind. Nearly all reported improvements of the type promised by the tape they had been listening to. But half of the group had received deliberately mislabelled tapes. No one who had listened to the memory tape reported improved memory if they *thought* they had the self-esteem tape, and vice versa.

Belief in subliminal persuasion, however, is notoriously hard to shake. In 1990 Judas Priest and their record company were taken to court by the families of Ray Belknap and James Vance, who had shot themselves after listening to one of the band's albums. The plaintiffs alleged that one song contained a subliminal implant of the phrase 'Do it', and many testified on their behalf, including Wilson Bryan Key. Judge Jerry Carr Whitehead ruled in favour of Judas Priest, noting that other factors present could explain the suicides (including drug and alcohol abuse, unemployment, learning disabilities and family violence). He also declared that 'The scientific research presented does not establish that subliminal stimuli, even if perceived, may precipitate conduct of this magnitude.'

The members of Judas Priest in court during the 1990 case which brought the subject of subliminal persuasion back into the public eye

That is not to say that the human mind is immune to outside influence.

'Suggestion is a powerful force. The science of hypnosis is predicated on it'

MULDER

Pusher

In the hypnotic state, external awareness and critical thinking are decreased and we become highly suggestible. Not everyone is equally susceptible: most people are moderately responsive, some highly so and others cannot be hypnotised at all.

This is why thousands of people spend money on hypnotherapy every year without the desired results, and is also the reason why stage hypnotists spend a great deal of time carefully scrutinising volunteers before selecting them. The first step is usually the suggestion to the entire audience that their arm has become leaden and cannot be raised, or is light as a feather and will float upwards. This weeds out the no-hopers; and trying out more advanced commands – like falling asleep or stroking an imaginary kitten – helps the hypnotist to select the best of the rest.

Self-hypnosis is also possible, as is spontaneous hypnosis. (Most of us have had experiences when we have driven somewhere 'on auto-pilot' arriving with little or no memory of the journey.) These undermine the popular notion that a hypnotist puts his subjects 'under a spell' – clearly the hypnotist simply coaxes the subject into accessing a natural capacity.

However, there are other techniques for increasing suggestibility or practising persuasion, and at a recent Las Vegas convention of the World Congress of Professional Hypnotists, hypnotist and researcher Dick Sutphen gave a lecture voicing his concern about their misuse.

> *'Pusher was rambling about cerulean blue . . . Talking about how it reminded him of a breeze or something. "Cerulean is a gentle breeze", over and over'*
>
> AGENT FRANK BURST
>
> *Pusher*

Pusher appeared to be using the 'Voice Roll', a technique Sutphen claims is used by revivalist preachers before requesting donations; and by lawyers 'when they desire to entrench a point firmly in the minds of the jurors'. It is 'a patterned, paced style used by hypnotists when inducing a trance . . . The words will usually be delivered at the rate of 45 to 60 beats per minute, maximising the hypnotic effect.'

Not all methods of persuasion are so subtle. Many animals have special ways of dealing with being trapped in unpleasant situations: rabbits freeze, for instance, and iguanas have a habit of shutting their eyes and 'zoning-out'. Humans have a similar safety mechanism – only we 'zone-out' mentally. In this state, says Sutphen, we are very suggestible; and certainly clinicians agree that 'narrowed perception' is one of the defining features of the hypnotic state. Tension and discomfort can induce such a condition, and Sutphen alleges that 'fire and brimstone' preachers, with their vivid and gory descriptions of hell and Armageddon, leave their congregations especially malleable.

The US Marine Corps talk about 'breaking' a man in order for him to be 'rebuilt' as an effective and dedicated soldier, and 'twelve-step' rehabilitation programmes operate on a similar de-programming/re-programming basis. Religious cults also rely on such methods to ensure loyalty and, in turn, financial gain. And many who think themselves too smart to get taken in by religious cults have succumbed to the expensive 'self improvement' courses known as 'Human Potential Trainings'. The 90s version of Est and Exegesis, these employ a wide range of tricks in their weekend 'seminars'.

Attendees are denied use of the telephone and kept for long hours in the lecture hall without breaks and with restricted access to the toilet. 'Trainers' make intimidating random verbal attacks to create tension and uncertainty, and the tasks they set induce fear, vulnerability and embarrassment – such as standing on stage and relaying one's innermost secrets, playing air guitar (for the women) or impersonating Shirley Temple (for the men). Towards the end of the seminar, the trainer in charge imparts the jargon-laden psychobabble that is supposed to make followers more confident, successful and fulfilled.

Some have been known to become besotted with the trainer in charge, a response not dissimilar to 'Stockholm Syndrome', occasionally seen in kidnap victims and hostages: the phenomenon of becoming enamoured of someone who controls you. It could also be that the commanding air and apparent power of many trainers makes them exceptionally charismatic – like *Pusher*'s Modell.

> *'You're saying he talked him into it?*
> *Somehow . . . willed him to do it?'*
>
> SCULLY
>
> *Pusher*

There are many linguistic tricks used with varying degrees of success in persuasion. One favoured especially by politicians and lawyers (said to refer to it as 'tightening the noose') runs as follows.

First there is what is called a 'yes set' – a clutch of statements with which the listeners will agree. Next come a brace of statements which are debatable but acceptable. Finally, the speaker slips in his suggestion, the idea being that since the listener has fallen into a pattern of agreeing without consideration, he will accept this final statement far more readily than he would have had he heard it in isolation. Sutphen uses a typical politician's speech as an example: 'Ladies and gentlemen: are you angry about high food prices? Are you tired of astronomical gas prices? Are you sick of out-of-control inflation?

Well, you know the Other Party allowed 18% inflation last year; you know crime has increased 50% nationwide in the last 12 months, and you know your paycheck hardly covers your expenses any more. Well, the answer to resolving these problems is to elect me, John Jones, to the US Senate.'

Another technique which Sutphen describes as 'unbelievably slippery' is known as Interspersal. 'The idea is to say one thing but to plant a subconscious impression of something else in the minds of listeners. Assume you are watching a television commentator make the following statement: "Senator Johnson is assisting local authorities to clear up the stupid mistakes of companies contributing to the nuclear waste problems." It sounds like a statement of fact, but if the speaker emphasises the right word, and especially if he makes the proper hand gestures on the key words, you could be left with the subconscious impression that Senator Johnson is stupid.'

Sutphen claims that there are even more subtle and powerful techniques which come under the banner of Neuro-Linguistics. These are 'so heavily protected that I found out the hard way that to even talk about them publicly or in print results in threatened legal action. Yet Neuro-Linguistic training is readily available to anyone willing to devote the time and pay the price . . . A good friend who recently attended a two-week seminar on Neuro-Linguistics found that many of those she talked to during the breaks were government people.'

'I'm guessing you shake on that salt like a maraca. You know what that's doing to your arteries? Terrible things. Waxy yellow chunks of plaque are tumbling through your bloodstream . . . Sticking like glue to your arterial walls . . . Squeezing shut your aorta . . .'

ROBERT MODELL

Pusher

'The basis of persuasion is always to access the right brain,' explains Sutphen. 'The left half of your brain is analytical and rational. The right side is creative and imaginative. So the idea is to distract the left brain.' For this reason, getting someone to visualise something – a task which occupies the right brain, subjugating the left – is a good way to increase the potency of a suggestion. Salesmen rely on this method a great deal ('I can just see you driving along in this car, roaring off at the lights, getting jealous looks . . .').

'Somebody is introducing a foreign signal into these people's homes – through their televisions'

MULDER

Wetwired

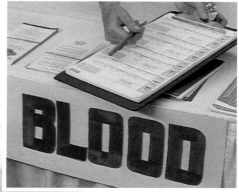

In Sutphen's view, the *Wetwired* scenario is not as far-fetched as it may seem. 'The more we find out about how human beings work through today's highly advanced technological research, the more we learn to control them. And what probably scares me the most is that the medium for takeover is already in place . . .

'Recent tests by researcher Herbert Krugman showed that, while viewers were watching TV, right-brain activity outnumbered left-brain activity by a ratio of two to one. To measure attention spans, psychophysiologist Thomas Mulholland of the Veterans Hospital in Bedford, Massachusetts, attached young viewers to an EEG machine that was wired to shut the TV set off whenever the children's brains produced a majority of alpha waves . . . only a few could keep the set on for more than 30 seconds.' The relaxed 'alpha' state is another which heightens suggestibility and Sutphen feels that it would be easy to 'deepen the trance' by adding imperceptible, rhythmic signals, leaving viewers open to suggestions and even commands, 'as long as those commands did not ask the viewer to do something contrary to his morals, religion, or self-preservation.'

If such a thing were possible, the medium would be ideal. In the average home, the TV set is on for more than six hours a day.

'Modell put the whammy on him'

MULDER

'Please explain to me the scientific nature of The Whammy'

SCULLY

Pusher

Experiments by neurologists support the theoretical effectiveness of many persuasion techniques. Dr Michael Persinger, Professor of Neuroscience at Canada's Laurentian University confirms: 'If we stimulate the right hemisphere only, we can get an increase in suggestibility:

the person becomes highly suggestible to what you say right afterwards.' He adds that such a technique can have positive uses, in psychotherapy, especially in dealing with depression.

Another technique involves what is known as the refutation process. Explains Persinger, 'In order for you to determine if something is true or not you first have to accept it as true and then you refute it . . . Social psychologists have found that if you tell somebody something that they know is false, and interfere with them at the point that they're making the refutation decision – which is about a half a second afterwards – people will say that it's true.'

Salesmen use this to their advantage, declaring the merit of their wares, then interfering with the refutation process by rapidly distracting the prospective customer's attention elsewhere. Sometimes this works; the scientific method is a lot less haphazard.

The subject is given a false piece of information: say, that a piece of green card is pink. A split second later, the refutation process is interfered with by electromagnetic stimulation of the brain. It is mind-bogglingly effective. Even though the subject obviously knows the difference between pink and green, they will say that the card is pink.

'I believe he has a unique suggestive ability which makes for the perfect MO: he talks his victims into injuring themselves. He overrides their wills with his own'

MULDER

Pusher

The Reverend Jim Jones

Could one person really persuade another to kill themselves? The Reverend Jim Jones reportedly did exactly that in 1978 when 913 of his followers comitted mass suicide at his compound in Guyana by drinking Kool-aid laced with cyanide.

Follow-up reports suggest that at least some of the victims had been persuaded not as a result of Jones's long-term indoctrination but by more prosaic means such as a gun to the head. Regardless, this sad story remains a potent testimony to the frailty of common sense and free-will.

'Willig and Cole were the lab rats'
MULDER
'Lab rats with the highest kill ratio in the
Marine Corps'
X

Sleepless

Just a few of the 913 victims who perished in the 1978 tragedy at Jonestown in Guyana

Government-sanctioned behaviour-control experiments have inspired several *X-Files* writers including Howard Gordon, whose *Sleepless* concerned an experiment to turn an army troop into cold-blooded killing machines who never sleep.

And according to Darin Morgan, *Jose Chung's 'From Outer Space'* is not so much about alien abduction as about mind-control and hypnosis. 'I'd done research on mind-control for a script I started before I took this job, and I found the CIA's experiments incredible. No one really knows about it. Even when I've said, "Well, when the CIA conducted their MK-ULTRA mind experiments back in the Fifties. . ." there have been people who just don't believe it, because it sounds so far-fetched. It does sound ridiculous, and yet they actually did it.'

The US government's exploration of mind and control began during World War II, when the Office of Strategic Services – the forerunner to the Central Intelligence Agency – set up a truth-drug committee. A young newspaper-executive-turned-OSS-recruit named Richard Helms took a special interest in this division. He would later head up the CIA.

One-time CIA head-honcho Richard Helms

The OSS soon began to explore other areas of psychological warfare, nurturing such creations as a putrid brown chemical called 'Who? Me?', designed to lower respect for Japanese officers by making civilians think they had soiled their pants. Children in occupied Chinese cities were enlisted to stalk officers on crowded streets and furtively squirt 'Who? Me?' at their backsides. 'Who? Me?' was viewed as a triumph. A plan to slip female hormones into Hitler's food so that his famous moustache would drop off was less successful.

Stanley Lovell, head of research and development, also wanted to hypnotise a German prisoner with a command to kill Hitler, then release him in Germany to accomplish the mission. Lovell dropped the idea on learning that hypnosis could not make a

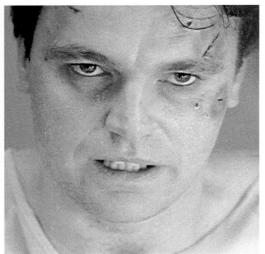

Pusher's Robert Modell may have had preternatual skills bestowed upon him as the freak result of a brain tumour. But it seems that alarming degrees of persuasion can be achieved without a hint of paranormal influence

person do anything that contravened his morals. But the concept would surface again in the cold war future.

The CIA proper set out its shingle in 1947. Its Project Bluebird was a look at mind control from a defensive standpoint: an attempt to weed out foreign agents under some sort of compelling influence. Testing included injecting Korean prisoners of war, a violation of the Nuremberg Code instituted to deter a repetition of Nazi atrocities. But in the climate of the times, communism was perceived as the greater threat, and 'gentlemen's agreements' were for show only.

In 1953, Helms helped usher in MK-ULTRA – a mind-control plan designed to create torture-proof couriers and programmed assassins. The project took a shine to LSD, discovered by Albert Hoffman a decade earlier whilst working for the Sandoz drug company in Switzerland. The CIA bought vast supplies from Sandoz amidst hopes that spies could be 'turned' under its influence; that it could be used as a 'truth drug' during interrogations; that it could be slipped to hostile leaders to publicly discredit them . . . or that maybe an entire hostile city could be incapacitated by dropping LSD in its water supply.

Under MK-ULTRA, the CIA dosed both witting and unwitting subjects, including inmates of California's Vacaville State Prison. In one study, seven unlucky subjects were kept on the drug in ever-increasing doses for 77 consecutive days. They set up houses in New York and San Francisco where random citizens were lured by prostitutes, then drugged with LSD and observed through a two-way mirror. (When auditors discovered this in 1963, MK-ULTRA was nominally shut down, though in fact it was just renamed MK-SEARCH.)

Most of the researchers themselves took LSD. Amazingly, MK-ULTRA staffers had an agreement that anyone could slip anyone else a Mickey Finn at any time. One CIA germ-warfare expert, Dr Frank Olson, threw himself out of a tenth-story window after an unplanned dose. (His family was told he had commited suicide because of psychological problems. When the truth came out 20 years later, they received an apology from President Ford and $750,000 compensation.)

Despite this and some other unpleasant trips, you can't help but smile at the image of steely, imperious government agents (think of Cigarette Smoking Man) suddenly marvelling at colours, stripping off their clothes and dancing to the vibrations of the universe. And from papers that have been released, the project seems to have been a complete failure. One conclusion was that LSD can make it easier to see through a façade, and is therefore unlikely to help an agent 'turn' an enemy or convince someone to do something he would not normally do.

> *'They were trying to manipulate behaviour. Alter people's decision making – what to buy, who to vote for—'*
> MULDER
> *'You think they'll stop at commerce or politics?'*
> X
> *Wetwired*

MK-ULTRA also took an interest in brainwashing and hypnosis, the ultimate goal being a 'Manchurian Candidate' assassin, a person programmed to kill without any memory of who sent him or why. Conspiracy theorists believe Robert Kennedy's assassin, Sirhan Sirhan, was the product of such an experiment; but, as far as we know, the CIA projects never bore fruit.

MK-ULTRA and its descendants lasted until 1973, when Helms quit the CIA and destroyed many of the files. But did behaviour-control experiments end? Darin Morgan doubts it: 'I can't imagine that they just went: *Right, stop working, let's forget about it* – especially if the Russians were also doing their own mind-control experiments. You can't have a mind-control gap, as I gather.'

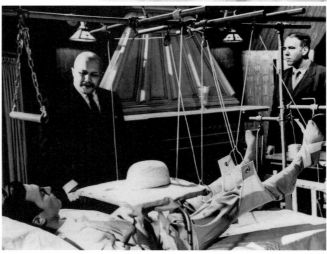

A scene from John Frankenheimer's harrowing 1962 movie adaptation of Richard Condon's The Manchurian Candidate

As the Advisory Committee on Human Radiation Experiments, formed under President Clinton to investigate government-sanctioned human experimentation, recently reported: 'The CIA indicated that it is currently performing classified human research projects. The agency informed the Advisory Committee that all human subjects are informed of the CIA's sponsorship and of the specific nature of the study in which they are participating, even if the general purposes of the research are classified.'

So if a be-suited stranger with a furtive air offers you a drink . . . just say no.

X-FILE: RED MUSEUM

FEDERAL BUREAU OF INVESTIGATION

Report by Special Agent Dana Scully

The identity of the man shot in the slaughterhouse has yet to be determined. His name, any record or artifact of his past, present or immigration status have not been found. His fingerprints are not on file in either the FBI or national system of records. At this time, it remains doubtful that anyone will come forward to claim the body.

Under further analysis, the inoculant found in the broken vials was isolated and determined to be an unstable antibody of no known biological origin. After three weeks of study, the components of the serum, probably synthetic, have broken down structurally and, in this retrograde state, cannot be analyzed further. This coincides with the development of a severe and undiagnosed flu-like ailment affecting the children who were believed to have been inoculated and some of the local families.

To date, none of the congregants or members of the Church of the Red Museum have contracted this illness.

The shipping manifests for what is believed to be beef and milk tainted by the unspecified inoculant do not provide enough information to track their destinations.

A local advisory and quarantine have been established. Further inquiry has been promised by the pertinent government health agencies.

The FBI's investigation into this case is currently at a standstill. The case remains open and unsolved.

X-File: The Red Museum

X-FILE: HELL MONEY

FEDERAL BUREAU OF INVESTIGATION

Case notes by Special Agent Dana Scully

Initial examination of the body discovered in the crematory oven by the watchman on duty at Bayside Funeral Home reveals that the victim was burned alive.

According to Lieutenant Neary of the San Francisco P.D., this murder matches the M.O. of two previous local incidents this year. Agent Mulder has record of a further eight nationally, occurring in Seattle, Los Angeles and Boston. In all cases, the victims were male, Chinese and between the ages of 20 and 40. All had recently emigrated.

In his statement, the night watchman at Bayside reported having seen three men, wearing traditional Chinese carnival masks, in the room where the oven was located. However, he entered the room to find them gone; it was then that he discovered the body.

There are no concrete leads on any of the murders at present. We have yet to discover the significance of a Chinese character discovered scratched by the victim into the inside door of the crematory oven, identified by SFPD detective Glen Chao as reading 'Gui' - Chinese for 'Ghost'. However, another discovery may prove more immediately useful: a piece of paper resembling a bill of currency which was found inside the crematorium. According to Chao, decorative bills of this kind, known as 'Hell Money', are used as an offering to the spirits during the Festival of the Hungry Ghosts, and batches are printed individually, to order. With any luck, this will provide us with the identity of our John Doe.

X-File: Hell Money

FEDERAL BUREAU OF INVESTIGATION

CLASSIFIED

FBI LAB REPORT X-FILE: THE HOST

Agent Scully -

Please find attached the biological analysis you ordered of sample PZF355723 (fluke larva).

Wanted to warn you that the findings are somewhat surprising. Certainly we have never seen anything previously which even approached similarity.

In short, dissection and analysis indicate reproductive and physiological cross-traiting, which appear to have resulted in some sort of quasi-vertebrate hominid.

You'll note the genetic mutations - extra chromosomes, abnormal cell fusion etc. This kind of suppression of natural genetic process, as you know, does not occur spontaneously. Off the record, my money is unquestionably on radiation.

Best wishes,

FBI
SPECIAL AGENT
Dana Scully

WORLD WE
INFOR
MARCH 25th 1996
DEADLY OUTBREA
UNNAMED CO

URBAN LEGENDS

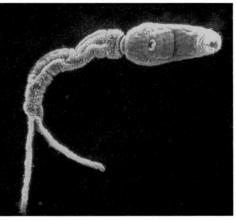

W oe betide any viewer who prepared a TV dinner before sitting down to enjoy *The Host*. Although the episode takes place during the suspension of *The X-Files* division, there is plenty of strangeness afoot. Not least some stomach-churning capers in the sewers of New Jersey, thanks to a genetic mutant in whom human DNA is revoltingly entertwined with the genetic material of a fluke-worm.

The initial idea came from what Chris Carter calls 'the most foul and disgusting inspiration'. Carter had found a parasitic worm, of the kind that infests dogs, on his lawn. To learn more about his unwelcome visitor, Carter plunged into worm-related literature, where he came upon the fluke. 'I found out what their biological process is, and I imagined what if, with the events at Chernobyl . . . biology and evolution had gotten confused by the addition of a radioactive substance . . . and one of these things had mutated and had come out of this tanker from a foreign place.

A fluke worm. You wouldn't want to meet a six-foot one in a dark sewer

'My father was a construction worker who put in sewers, so I was able to call him on the phone and ask about old sewers and how they were built. I found out that the New Jersey sewer system was actually quite old, and there I found my connection.'

The Host has a strong 'urban legend' theme running through it. The notion of something dangerous stalking the sewers, the idea of some creature laying its eggs in the body of an unwitting human being and the 'something nasty in the toilet' motif are all mainstays of modern oral tradition.

The scene in which the fluke-man lurks in a portable toilet is one of *The Host*'s most memorable moments. 'A lot of people have come to me and said they will never go into portable toilets again!' reports Carter. His own interest in this staple of contemporary folklore dates back to hearing just such a tale as a child.

'We were on vacation, and my parents told me the authorities had caught

a man who would go from campground to campground, dress himself in plastic garbage bags, crawl down into the women's portable toilets, hide down in there as the women campers would come in, and he would get a show! I always thought that was one of the most disgusting things I had ever heard in my life, and so I guess maybe that's part of my fascination . . .'

The Host is not the only *X-Files* episode that alludes to urban legends. 'Urban mythology is something that *The X-Files* plays with and touches on,' Carter confirms.

Even if you've never heard the expression 'urban mythology', you've almost certainly heard an urban myth. The lady who microwaved her poodle thinking it would get the dog dry after a walk in the rain . . . The woman who found a rat's skeleton in the box of southern-fried chicken she'd eaten in the dark at the cinema . . . The naked couple who find themselves in the middle of a surprise party . . . The choking dog taken to the vet, who dislodges two human fingers – belonging to the burglar still hiding in the owner's cupboard . . .

These are the modern oral tradition, the descendants of ancient legends, fairy tales and ballads. They are stories or rumours recounted in social situations – at sleepovers and around the campfire, at dinner parties and in pubs – and whether they are interesting, funny, terrifying, revolting, embarrassing or shocking, they all have the ring of truth, since it is part of the package that they include plenty of convincing detail. Most importantly, such stories tend to be about someone else's friends, relatives or acquaintances: there is always at least one link in the chain that divides the narrator from the source.

'They say a lot about who we are, what we believe and what we're afraid of,' says Chris Carter. 'Whether they're true or not, we tend to believe in them, and we tend to pass them on because they have a resonance that echoes on down though the ages.'

'I've been thinking it might have been a python . . . Or a boa constrictor. Somebody probably flushed their pet snake down the toilet. We found an alligator in the sewer a couple of years ago'

SEWERAGE WORKMAN

The Host

The *Host*'s horrific fluke-man made his home in the sewers of New Jersey. But real-life rumours of something living in the effluent below have abounded for centuries. The best-known contemporary version is the 'alligators in the sewers' story, which first surfaced in the early 1960s and concerns a thriving population of fearsome amphibians beneath the streets of New York City.

The alligators are said to be the progeny of unwanted pets which were flushed down the toilet when they lost their appeal or grew too big. Some versions pin the blame on a single (nameless) family who brought a pair of baby alligators home from a vacation in Florida. Others blame a fashion craze.

Thomas Pynchon recast the legend in his 1963 novel, *V*:

'Last year or maybe the year before, kids all over Nueva York bought these little alligators for pets. Macy's was selling them for fifty cents; every child, it seemed, had to have one. But soon the children grew bored with them . . .'

Pynchon included an embellishment that soon became part of the myth: *'. . . now they moved, big, blind and albino, all over the sewer system.'*

Nothing fortifies an urban legend like an appearance in print – even in a fictional context – so it's no surprise that the story still thrives today. More surprising, however, is the truth. Folklorist and cryptozoologist Loren Coleman reveals, 'There were real alligators in the New York sewers – in the 1930s. It was a well-known fact at the time. New York Sewer Commissioner Teddy May said most of them were in the two-foot range. His campaign of sending men with rifles down in the sewers to kill the 'gators was successful. While I was able to find records of a seven-and-a-half-foot alligator killed and pulled from a manhole in 1935, all the 'gators were apparently eradicated by 1937.'

Something about this story resonated sufficiently for it to pass into the realm of folklore, updated to whichever decade the story is told in, often accompanied by an explanation and a gruesome 'mutation' twist.

'No telling what's been breeding down there in the last hundred years'
SEWAGE-PLANT FOREMAN
The Host

A sewer patrol in Brighton, England, where tours of the sewers are a popular tourist attraction. Elsewhere, the murky depths beneath the streets remain an unknown quantity, and a fertile breeding ground for urban legends (amongst other things)

It is hardly surprising that sewers should feature in folklore. They are dark, fetid, and unseen by all but a few. They stimulate our primal fear and fascination with the hidden and unknown, with what lies beneath the civilized surface.

Another subterranean legend tells of 'New York White,' a strain of marijuana that supposedly proliferates in the New York sewers as a result of people flushing away their 'stash' during drug busts. No doubt it provides good roughage for all those albino 'gators.

A turn-of-the-century British forerunner of the alligator legend concerned a tribe of vicious wild pigs which thrived in the sewers of London's exclusive Hampstead district. The setting of this particular story may offer a clue to the popularity of both tales.

Demeaning those who are thought to give themselves airs is a common theme of legends ancient and modern. Scurrilous, unfounded rumours about celebrities – such as Jamie Lee Curtis being a hermaphrodite, Michael Jackson and his sister LaToya being the same person, Richard Gere rushing to hospital with a colonic obstruction of the gerbil kind – fall into this category.

The thought of unsavoury beasts swarming beneath the streets of an impoverished populace is rather unpleasant. But beneath the feet of the wealthy, erudite residents of an aspirational location? Cool! And better still if you can incorporate the notion that they brought it upon themselves, with their irresponsible and cruel discarding of impulsively-purchased exotic pets.

This element was blatantly obvious in the variation of the New York tale which spread among London schoolchildren in the 1970s (yes, it travelled that far). In this version the mass flushing was a result of a passing fad amongst socialites for wearing live baby alligators as brooches.

> *'Yeah, we're at a campsite approximately quarter of a mile from your position. Dogs tracked a scent to a chemical toilet here. Thought he might be hiding inside . . .'*
>
> MULDER
>
> *The Host*

The *Host* also touches on a genre not unrelated to sewer stories: toilet tales. After all, the toilet is the link between our civilized world and the underworld of the sewers. Unlike the majority of sewer stories, however, many tales of horrors in the loo are based on true incidents.

In February 1993, a woman in Gwinnet County, Georgia, was scratched on the shanks by a squirrel. That same month in Lancaster County, Pennsylvania, Mrs Virginia Bare discovered a two-foot lizard that had sneaked through the plumbing to emerge from her toilet. In August 1993, former Singaporian shot-put champion Fok Keng Choy was bitten on the testicles by a python lurking in the bowl.

There is one variation, however, which is almost certainly apocryphal: The Exploding Toilet. Sometimes the incident involves an unlikely confluence of events. A woman has sprayed the toilet with insect repellent, or accidentally doused it with hairspray: her husband sits down to use the toilet whilst smoking a cigarette, and BOOM!

In other versions, the explosion occurs in an old-fashioned outhouse or – Chris Carter's favourite – a portable toilet, which detonates because of a build-up of gas or chemicals. Sometimes the victim – despite the fact that he has reportedly been blown several feet into the air – humorously concludes that it must have been something he ate.

Aeroplane toilets have their very own folklore: namely, the rumour that if your bottom is expansive enough to cover the seat

The Host's Flukeman is only doing what comes naturally, but this is little consolation for the people he's doing it to

completely, you might create a vacuum and have your intestines sucked out. This has happened a number of times, as many people will readily inform you. Says an official from Boeing: 'I've heard of really heavy people getting stuck on the seat during descent, but I've never heard of the pressure seal being great enough to do any damage – other than to the ego, that is.'

When this story first emerged around 1992, it got a mention in a credible British broadsheet. The reporting of urban folklore as fact, whether orally, to one person or a group, or in print, reaching hundreds of thousands – is known by urban legend enthusiasts as vectoring. Vectoring is the life-blood of the legend, and when a story is vectored in the media it receives a massive infusion. Not only is there an increase in the number of new potential narrators, but the tale returns to oral circulation with added credibility. Never mind that the narrator can't name names or dates: he read it in the paper. It's obviously true.

The eggs of an embedded Chigger are squeezed from the skin of a victim's foot. The notion of playing host to a creepy crawly is a potent terror, and one that has inspired plenty of urban legends - not to mention The Host

'You're not going to like what I have to tell you . . . I think the fluke in the corpse – it was an incubating larva. The creature, or whatever it is, is transmitting eggs or larvae through its bite . . . it's looking for hosts. It attacks because the victim's body provides generative nourishment'

SCULLY

The Host

The idea of being used as a human incubator for the offspring of some grotesque creature evokes such a visceral reaction that it is no surprise to find it such a popular subject of urban legends.

The most famous example, which emerged in the 1960s, concerns a girl so proud of her massive, much-envied beehive hairdo that she ceases to wash it or take it down, instead simply re-spraying it with lacquer several times a day. After a few months she collapses, either at school or at work. Sometimes a trickle of blood is seen dribbling down her neck beforehand. All those present watch horrified as hundreds of baby spiders rush from the hairdo. A spider had laid its eggs there, and the hatchlings,

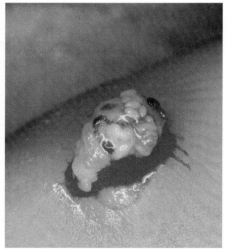

feasting on her scalp, had burrowed through to her brain.

Unfortunate people *have* returned from exotic travels with insect larvae beneath the skin (usually on the arm or leg), and in 1992, a British man had a spider removed from his ear canal, although it had not laid any eggs. But The Spider in the Hairdo is apocryphal (and impossible – spiders don't eat brains!).

Like many legends, it serves the function of a modern morality play, in this case, warning against excessive vanity. We clearly have a need to tell and hear such tales. The Spider in the Hairdo may have waned in popularity since the beehive went out of fashion, but in its place we have the story that Professor Jan Harold Brunvand, a leading expert on contemporary folklore, calls 'Curses, Broiled Again!' A girl foolishly goes for more than the recommended weekly amount of sun-bed sessions by signing up at four different tanning salons. After a few weeks she notices a peculiar smell, which a doctor solemnly informs her is her insides – cooked. This particular tale involves a confusion between ultraviolet rays and microwaves; but, as Brunvand says: 'The truth never stands in the way of a good story'.

'Victims? You mean there've been others?'

SCULLY

'One in eastern Wisconsin, one three towns away. Both with the same words written in black marker'

MULDER

Red Museum

Chris Carter cites the episode *Red Museum*, in which some youths are found wandering dazed and marked with the words: *s/he is one*, as another inspired by an urban legend.

'There was the idea that you could be drugged with scopolamine and wake up with something written on your back. Which is very similar to stories you hear about women being abducted on the street, given scopolamine, knocked out, gang raped, and then waking up with the words on their back or their chests or whatever: *welcome to the world of AIDS*. It was reported in *Time* magazine as news, and really it was a rumour. In fact, you never saw it anywhere else. *Time* magazine had been taken in by it.'

Many urban legends are born when one rumour or story gets inadvertently combined with another. The one mentioned by Carter, for example, is a composite of two different elements.

The first is an urban legend that folklorists call 'AIDS Mary'.

A man has a one-night stand with a beautiful woman he meets in a bar. When he wakes in the morning she is gone. On the bathroom mirror he sees, scrawled in red lipstick, her chilling message: *welcome to the world of AIDS*. (Or *welcome to the AIDS club*.) Embittered by having contracted the disease from a deceitful lover, she is on an avenging crusade against all men.

If AIDS Mary really exists, she must have been pretty busy. She seems to have played her hideous trick on friends of friends across the United States, Canada and Europe.

AIDS cases in the US are monitored by the Center for Disease Control in Atlanta, where spokesmen have heard the story of AIDS Mary, but consider it apocryphal. Jan Harold Brunvand, who has researched it in depth, found a number of cases in which infected people had knowingly continued to have unprotected sex; but virtually all of them were homosexual males, some were prostitutes, and none had left a message of any kind. (Brunvand also learned that the AIDS Mary rumour was particularly rife within the FBI: an agent in either California or Florida was said to have been a victim.)

The idea of an ominous message written in lipstick on a mirror may have orginated with a 1946 Chicago murder, widely reported at the time, in which the killer left, in just such a manner, a plea to be stopped before he killed again. Mary's mission itself may have been inspired by the real-life career of Mary Mallon, also known as Typhoid Mary, after whom folklorists named the new legend. A cook infected with typhoid, Mallon knowingly spread the disease to more than 50 people around the turn of the century. There again, Guy de Maupassant's 1884 tale *Le Lit 29* concerned a woman deliberately spreading syphilis throughout

the enemy forces during the Franco–Prussian war. And who knows, perhaps de Maupassant was inspired by an even older story. The birth of a legend is a slippery quarry indeed.

'Are you familiar with the substance scopolamine?'

SCULLY

Red Museum

The second element that inspired *Red Museum* is an interesting mutation in which the legend has become tangled with another horrific and bizarre story – a true one.

In 1993 New York City was struck by a series of crimes in which men – usually business travellers – reported that they had been seduced either in their hotel lounge or at a singles bar by an attractive woman who had accompanied them to their room, ostensibly for sex. The next thing they knew, morning had come and the woman was gone – along with their wallets, watches and other valuables. The men were dazed, incoherent, suffering from short-term memory loss and often hallucinating. (Weirdly, many of them reported visions of 'small people'.)

It was discovered that the victims had ingested scopolamine – a powerful tranquilizer that can easily be dropped unnoticed into a drink, since it is colourless, odorless and tasteless. An FBI report stated that some of the women (whom law-enforcement officers dubbed the Knockout Girls) instead applied a powdered form of the drug to their own lips and sedated their victims with a 'good night' kiss.

It is easy to see how the factual scopolomine story could get confused with the AIDS Mary legend. But, in the scopolomine legend encountered by Carter, how did the victim become female, the perpetrator a member of a gang, and the crime rape?

'Anything past point-two microgrammes and you've got a very powerful anaesthetic with hallucinogenic qualities. It's been in the news lately because Colombian gangs have been using it in kidnappings, to subdue their victims'

SCULLY

Red Museum

The answer lies with truly terrifying scopolamine-related crimes in Columbia, often reported alongside details of the New York assaults. There, a scopolamine-based drug called burundanga had been used

The sprawling cityscape of Bogota, Columbia, where the term 'lost weekend' is not used lightly

since the 1970s in offences similar to those of the Knockout Girls. But in 1985 a new and 'improved' version of the drug was created, the effects of which were a criminal's dream come true. The victim remains conscious and lucid, capable of performing tasks such as writing a cheque, opening a safe, handing over keys, and retrieving personal belongings. Moreover, he or she loses all willpower, and obediently follows any command. Once the drug wears off (in 6 to 36 hours), the victim recalls nothing and is unable to give a description of the criminal.

In Bogota today, burundanga is used in approximately four crimes a day. Dr Camilo Uribe, of the Bogota Toxicology Clinic, estimates that the drug is responsible for more than 80% of all poisoning cases handled in the emergency departments of Colombian hospitals. At Bogota's Kennedy Hospital, every weekend between 15 and 20 patients are admitted who have no idea where they have been or what has happened to them.

The answers, when they are found, can be astonishing. A senator and his wife learned that they had spent a night travelling with their abductors to the banks at which they held accounts, withdrawing and handing over vast quantities of cash, before letting the gang into their home and helping them to clear it out. On another occasion, a prominent diplomat was abducted from a fashionable bar in Bogota, kept drugged for four days and used as a courier for a delivery of cocaine to Chile.

But the most common crimes linked to burundunga are rape and sexual abuse. A young American tourist admitted to Kennedy Hospital on a Monday had absolutely no memory of the weekend – mercifully, since it transpired that she had been raped by at least seven different men.

'Mulder, do you know what the human body's worth?'
SCULLY

Hell Money

'Y**ou've heard, too, where a man will go with a prostitute somewhere, and he'll wake up and all of a sudden his kidney will be missing?'** asks Chris Carter, explaining that season three's *Hell Money* took this legend and 'put a twist on it'.

In *Hell Money*, poverty-stricken immigrants risk their lives playing a macabre lottery in the hopes of striking it rich. The coffers are swelled by the unfortunates who must forfeit their corneas, kidneys or, if they're really unlucky, their hearts, to be sold for transplant on the black market.

'You think this guy was selling his body parts?'
MULDER

'A kidney, a portion of the liver, bone marrow, a lobe of the lung. A cornea. A person can lose these things and live to cash their social security checks'
SCULLY

Hell Money

A**lthough – fortunately – such a lottery exists only in *The X-Files* universe, people *do* sell parts of themselves: legally, in India, and** illegally elsewhere through a small, covert private market. In his controversial manual *Sell Yourself to Science*, author Jim Hogshire reveals that you can hawk a cornea for $4,000 and a kidney for $10,000 plus. But in India, at least, this is the sum paid by the transplantee. Donors are usually given $500 to $1000, while the doctors get the remainder to cover the operation.

Mulder and Scully team up with the San Francisco police department and stumble upon a deadly game in Hell Money

'Let me ask you this: have you heard any word on the streets about the black market selling of body parts ? Anyone being kidnapped or abducted, waking up with a missing cornea or kidney?'

SCULLY

Hell Money

But the legend which really inspired *Hell Money* is organ theft – a recent myth whose variations span every corner of the globe. It is possible that the story had its genesis in the revelations of dissident Chinese journalist Harry Wu. Wu was jailed for exposing China's practice of keeping prisoners on Death Row until a 'spare part' is needed for a VIP, at which time the prisoner is executed and his organs cannibalised. But the version that swept Britain, the USA and Canada appeared to be a mutation of the familiar Scopolamine/AIDS Mary hybrid: boy meets girl; boy goes home with girl; boy loses kidney. This was alleged to have happened more than 80 times in Las Vegas, and dozens of times in the North of England. Not a single incident has ever been confirmed – yet the tale thrives. One hapless Hollywood producer even bought the 'exclusive rights' to the story of a young man who claimed to have been a Vegas victim.

Do visitors to Las Vegas risk losing more than their money?

In Guatemala, the Philippines and elsewhere, the yarn became even grislier: children were being adopted or even kidnapped by foreigners (usually Americans) and murdered for their organs. Unsurprisingly, the rumour caused mass panic, and a number of tourists were assaulted.

Since 1987, Todd Leventhal at the United States Information Agency in Washington, DC has tracked and investigated these rumours. In December 1994 he submitted a report to the United Nations in which he summarised his findings: 'No government, international body, non-governmental organisation, or investigative journalist has ever produced any credible evidence to substantiate this story . . . there is every reason to believe that the child organ trafficking rumor is a modern "urban legend", a false story that is commonly believed because it encapsulates, in story form, widespread anxieties about modern life.'

Leventhal detailed reasons why such clandestine traffic would be impossible and expressed concern about worldwide media coverage of the rumour, pointing out a plethora of inaccuracies. The media had in turn influenced a number of government and parliamentary reports. This is all the more disturbing for the fact that in 1994 in Guatemala, the rumours were accompanied by a detail which should have aroused suspicions about their veracity: some of the kidnappers, it was said, were dressed as clowns.

But nowhere has the situation been more disturbing than in India, where at first glance, it appears that urban legend has met horrific fact. In Bangalore, police inspector V.S. D'Souza heads an ongoing investigation into reports of kidney theft filed by more than 1000 individuals. 'The victims are poor ignorant villagers,' explains D'Souza. 'If these cases were brought in America, the doctors would be sued for billions of dollars. Here people don't know their rights.'

The truth is hard to find on the teeming streets of Bangalore

The first claimant was a man named Velu, an impoverished villager from Tamil Nadu who said that he was approached by two men and offered a well-paid job in Bangalore. Once in the city, the men suggested to Velu that he donate blood to earn some extra cash. They took him to the Yallama Desappa hospital where, according to the police report, he passed out whilst giving blood. He awoke to find a bandage on his side and said that he was told by a nephrologist, Dr Siddaraju, that he had become dizzy and fallen out of a first floor window. Velu was given 5000 rupees (£50) and sent home.

Three months later, Velu told the Press, 'I was in unbearable pain and went to a doctor who saw the mark and told me my kidney had been removed. I was amazed.' He returned to the hospital and demanded payment for the kidney, which was not forthcoming.

Dr Siddaraju, whom Inspector D'Souza called 'the architect of the whole racket', was suspended from his post as Professor of Nephrology at the Victoria public hospital and as kidney transplant supervisor at Yallama Desappa. It was suggested that he had stolen kidneys to sell to the rich, and to supply the charity he had set up for poor kidney patients. His trial is pending. Other surgeons indicted are accused of trafficking the stolen organs to wealthy patients in the Middle East.

But, as Jenny Barraclough, producer of the BBC TV documentary *The Great Organ Hunt* discovered, many aspects of Velu's tale did not quite gel.

For a start, the windows at the Yallama Desappa hospital are barred, so that Dr Siddaraju would hardly have told Velu that he had fallen out of one. But odder still is the fact that Velu (like many other claimants) needed a doctor to tell him what had happened. In most parts of India, including Bangalore, it is legal to sell one's own organs and more than 4000 people a year have a kidney removed. Local dress is such that kidney-donation scars are clearly visible, a common and familiar sight.

A Madras transplant surgeon, Dr Keshava Reddy, told Barraclough: 'It is quite impossible to steal someone's kidney without their knowledge. What's more there is not exactly a shortage of donors. It's a sad commentary on our poverty, but it's a fact of life. Of course, people can be cheated financially and perhaps that's what happened'. Reddy also dismissed as 'nonsense' claims that organs were transported to the Middle East, since they must be used swiftly after being removed from the donor. The police, he suggested, 'may have been a bit too gullible'.

Barraclough was the first member of the media to investigate all sides of the story, and she concluded with dismay in an article she wrote in May 1996 that 'the world's Press had carried a story that no one had bothered to check.'

Meanwhile, Dr Siddaraju's career is in ruins and the Indian medical profession in disrepute. More gravely still, the affair has led to Federal restrictions being placed on transplants and organ donation, depriving the needy of a viable way to earn money and placing a death sentence on many of the 80,000 people per year who require transplants. India has no organised programme to collect organs from the dead, nor does it have facilities for the storage and transport of donated organs.

Ironically, if, as is being suggested, a complete ban on voluntary donations is enforced, the urban legend could become, in part, a self-fulfilling prophesy. Warns Dr Reddy: 'If you ban them . . . an unsupervised black market will replace them.'

'This is called rumour panic. An antecedent event links with a popular satanic cult myth and increases tension in the community . . . There have been at least twenty incidents since 1983 – from upstate New York to Reno, Nevada. Not one of them turned up a shred of evidence to support the wild allegations'

SCULLY

Syzygy

The Organ theft frenzy reminds us that whilst for the most part urban legends are fun and fascinating, in certain circumstances they *can* cause panic, involve the authorities in costly investigations and damage people's lives. *Syzygy* addresses another such example – the myth of ritual satanic crimes (see *A Dark Collusion*).

Often in folklore the point of the story is to frighten. But whilst adults tend to vector only stories they can believe, children and teenagers also enjoy and vector stories that are more creative and fantastical. *Syzygy* features one of the most famous: the ancient legend known as 'Bloody Mary'.

'One, Bloody Mary, Two, Bloody Mary . . .'

TERRI ROBERTS AND MARGI KLEINJAN

'What are you doing?'

BRENDA

'You close your eyes and count to thirteen and Bloody Mary appears in the mirror . . .'

TERRI AND MARGI

Syzygy

The story goes that if you repeat the words 'Bloody Mary' a certain number of times whilst looking in a mirror, you will summon up the ghastly spirit of the said Mary. Alternative versions use different names, including Mary Worth, Mary Whales and Mary Lou, and detail various consequences. Sometimes Mary will simply appear in the mirror. In other versions she will claw at you, come at you with a knife, or 'tear your face off'. Mary can be given a local background, too – she is often a woman who was killed in a car accident nearby.

Needless to say, no one has ever seen Bloody Mary. But the legend – and the ritual itself – is still popular at sleepovers and has been for more than a century. Any urban legend provides a social bonding experience. Bloody Mary – with its implicit dare to try the ritual out – plays up this bonding effect.

> *'These South American Indians do it. Like, I saw it on the Discovery Channel. They've got this whole, you know, um, cult built up around this tree toad.*
> *The skin has this hallucinogenic property which allows them to see visions'*
>
> STONER

Quagmire

Another subgenre of urban folklore is the rumour – a mini-legend without an extended story structure. The antics of the stoner teens in *Quagmire* (the same kids, by the way, seen smoking manure in *War of the Coprophages*) referenced one of these: the belief that licking a toad will get you high.

This myth comes from a simple but extremely dangerous misconception. Both *Bufo Alvarius* and *Bufo Marinus* toads secrete a venom which, when dried and smoked in a pipe, gives a potent (though apparently rather

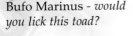

Bufo Marinus - *would you lick this toad?*

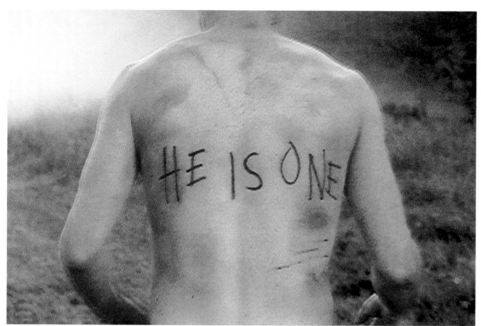

unpleasant) psychedelic experience. The raw venom, however, is a lethal poison: dogs which bite these toads usually wind up dead. Many human toad-licking excursions have resulted in seizures and heart attacks. Fortunately, the 'right' genus of toad is hard to find.

The toad-licking legend, like the Bloody Mary ritual, carries with it an element of the attraction of risk; a suggestion of something hazardous yet intriguing that the listener might want to try. This is unusual for an urban legend. Most serve quite the opposite function: to warn us about danger. Others warn about authority or injustice. Technically, many conspiracy theories are urban legends, from cover-ups of alien contact to the suppression of miracle products such as tyres that never wear down, or the low-cost Los Angeles monorail system that was quashed by a cartel of auto manufacturers and oil companies. Big Brother tales belong here too, like the Lone Gunmen's favourite theory about the metal strips in money, or the 'fact' that all US phone calls are electronically monitored by the intelligence services, and that if you say the acronyms 'FBI' or 'CIA' during a conversation, you might just hear the recording device that automatically clicks on.

The latest 'injustice' legend in the UK is 'Speed Snooker', in which the motorway police allegedly bust motorists in cars of certain colours. This has the owners of red cars worried (players need 15 per frame), not to mention those who own black (if a player wants to get that maximum 147 break, he'll be after 16 of these) and pink cars (only one required, but how many pink cars are there on the road?)

At the mass-panic end of the scare-mongering scale was the 'initiation ritual' of street gangs in various American cities. Supposedly, the initiate was made to drive at night with his headlights off, wait until a helpful motorist flashed him, and then pursue and murder the good Samaritan. This rumour was so widespread that in many cities even the police helped to propagate it. Despite this, there is no record of even one case matching this *modus operandi*.

'Nurse who?'
NURSE WILKINS
'Owens. Short, with straight, light brown hair?
She watched over me in intensive care.
And I'd like to thank her'
SCULLY
'Dana, I've worked here for ten years, and there's no Nurse
Owens at this hospital'
NURSE WILKINS

One Breath

The denouement of the episode *One Breath* incorporates a classic element of supernatural urban folklore: encountering someone only to discover that there is no logical possibility of the meeting ever having happened. The most famous tale in this category is 'The Vanishing Hitchhiker'. There are many variations but the typical one is this: A man gives a young girl a lift, and chats to her as she sits in the back seat of the car. When they arrive at the address she has requested, he finds that she has disappeared. Puzzled, he knocks on the door of the house and is greeted by the occupants, who tell him that their daughter fits the description of his passenger perfectly (sometimes there is even a handy picture on display) – except that she died ten years ago. Sometimes it is ten years 'to this very day'. Often this is imparted with bewilderment: 'But it couldn't have been our daughter!' In other versions, the parents nod knowingly and inform the driver that this kind of thing happens all the time.

In some modern versions the story is inverted, with a mortal hitchhiker and a ghostly driver – usually a truck driver who drops his passenger at a truck stop where the burly truckers turn white and reveal the sad story of the driver who died in an accident (sometimes, as in the original, 'this very night ten years ago'). This scenario features in Red Sovine's country-music gem *Phantom 409* and in the film *Pee-Wee's Big Adventure*, in which Pee-Wee Herman hitches a ride with the ghostly Large Marge.

Urban legends adapt to survive. If a story gets better in a particular retelling, the new element will stick. And sometimes, the people retelling it are professional writers. So don't be surprised if one day, someone tells you a story they heard from a friend of a friend about a woman who was about to be discharged from hospital, that ends: 'So anyway, she wanted to give the nurse this gold necklace of hers, to say thank you, you know? But the nurse wasn't around, so she asked this other nurse if she knew where she was, and this nurse said, "I've worked here for ten years . . . and there's no one here by that name . . ."'

Whilst Hell Money *and other episodes referenced urban legends, urban legends often evolve to incorporate elements of movies, books and TV shows. Far from being the threat to oral tradition that they once were perceived as, the printed word and the moving image exist happily alongside it, each simultaneously suckling from and nourishing the other*

File   Mode   Window   Select

F.Mulder: Hard D

X-File: War of
Coprophages

War of the Coprophages

20   40   60   80   100   120   140

The development of our cerebral cortex has been the greatest achievement of the evolutionary process. Big deal. While allowing us the thrills of intellect and the pangs of self-consciousness, it is all too often overruled by our inner, instinctive brain - the one that tells us to react, not reflect, to run rather than ruminate. Maybe we have gone as far as we can go, and the next advance - whatever that may be - will be made by beings we create ourselves using our own technology. Life forms we can design and program not to be ultimately governed and constricted by the rules of survival.

Or perhaps that step forward has already been achieved on another planet, by organisms that had a billion years head start on us. If these beings ever visited us, would we recognize what we were seeing? Upon catching sight of us, would they react in anything but horror at seeing such mindless, primitive creatures?

100%   Page 1*

War of the Coprophages

20   40   60   80   100   120   140   160   180   200

75%   PIC-3

Trash-Bir

MASS HYSTERIA AND THE BELIEF ENGINE

In *The War of the Coprophages* Agent Mulder's plans for a quiet weekend of UFO-spotting in Massachusetts are disrupted when he is drawn into investigating a series of curious deaths. It seems that a deadly colony of cockroaches – the eponymous coprophages, or excrement-eaters – is on a murderous rampage. Although something strange *is* going on (for more, see *The Search for Extraterrestrial Intelligence*), the roaches are proven innocent – but not in time to prevent a panic.

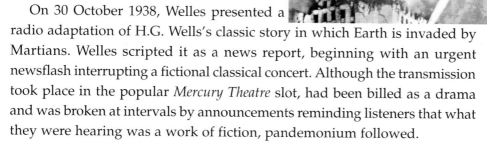

'The whole episode has to do with mass hysteria; how people, rather than thinking about things, just react right off,' explains writer Darin Morgan. The title itself refers to Orson Welles's radio broadcast of *The War of the Worlds*, one of the most notorious cases of mass hysteria on record.

On 30 October 1938, Welles presented a radio adaptation of H.G. Wells's classic story in which Earth is invaded by Martians. Welles scripted it as a news report, beginning with an urgent newsflash interrupting a fictional classical concert. Although the transmission took place in the popular *Mercury Theatre* slot, had been billed as a drama and was broken at intervals by announcements reminding listeners that what they were hearing was a work of fiction, pandemonium followed.

> *'Everything will be okay if everyone just calms down, and begins acting rationally. Now, where the hell are the road maps?!'*
>
> SCULLY
>
> *The War of the Coprophages*

Switchboards jammed as Americans flooded their local radio stations and police departments with frantic telephone calls. In New York City, the first location to be announced under attack in the play, Manhattan's

Numerous lawsuits were filed following the broadcast of The War of the Worlds, *adapted for radio by Orson Welles. All were unsuccessful, since the broadcast had been peppered with reminders that it was a work of fiction*

Dixie bus terminal overflowed with people scrambling to board any bus, not caring where it was headed.

San Franciscans flocked to local military headquarters, volunteering their services to combat the invasion, and in Indianapolis a woman sent a church congregation into a frenzy when she burst in and yelled: 'New York is destroyed! I just heard it on the radio! You may as well go home and wait to die!'

In college dormitories weeping students fought to use the telephone to bid their families farewell, and a man in Pittsburgh, Pennsylvania arrived home just in time to stop his wife from taking rat poison, as she shrieked, 'I'd rather die this way!'

'Everybody's getting the hell out of here!'
SUPERMARKET CUSTOMER
'Have you seen any cockroaches yourself?'
SCULLY
'No – but they're everywhere'
SUPERMARKET CUSTOMER

The War of the Coprophages

Much as we like to believe that we think for ourselves, we tend to rely on consensus – the opinions of the majority – to help us make judgements about what is true and what is not. Even if initially we find something difficult to believe, we find it harder – if not impossible – to dismiss it when people all around us are convinced. This is the principle religious cults employ to persuade apparently reasonable people to adopt their beliefs. Once they join, they are isolated from their families and friends, and deprived of any consensus but that of other cult members.

But in the case of *The War of the Worlds* – and *The War of the Coprophages* – how did anomalous beliefs spread so rapidly to so many people in the first place?

Research has found that perceptions of a situation – even inaccurate or outrageous ones – can be spread from one person to another, like a disease. It is not just that we pick up cues on how to react: our perceptions can actually be influenced by other people's responses to the point where our own faculties are overridden. Have you ever noticed how a comedy seems funnier in a cinema full of laughing people than it does when watched alone at home? A lone shopper who sees chocolate candies spilling onto the floor of a

Mulder investigates the cockroach 'problem' in War of the Coprophages

supermarket, as happens in *TWOTC*, will see them clearly for what they are. But bring in a crowd of people, screaming that the chocolates are cockroaches and reacting accordingly, and that same shopper's mind will play tricks on him or her. In a quick glance at the chocolates, he or she might even perceive movement, or the hint of a few little legs. This is sometimes called hysterical contagion. And if we are already feeling apprehensive – as the *TWOTC* shoppers were – our resistance is lowered, and we are even more vulnerable to 'catching' whatever perceptions are going around.

> *'Haven't you heard about the roaches? They're devouring people whole!'*
>
> SUPERMARKET CUSTOMER
>
> *The War of the Coprophages*

Epidemics of bizarre belief spring up far more often than one might imagine. In 1990, for instance, Nigeria was gripped by a rumour that evil sorcerers were stealing people's breasts and penises. The sorcerers were said to operate by casually touching the body part that they wanted to steal. Jostling in a crowded street or market would have everyone frantically checking that all their body parts were still where they should be, and, in the panic, at least one person would usually 'discover' something missing. Their cries of dismay would lead to further 'discoveries', and subsequent hunts for the guilty sorcerer often turned into full-blown riots.

In Egypt three years later thousands of teenage girls became caught up in a 'swooning' epidemic. The victims believed that some unknown infectious disease was causing them to faint. In fact, the only contagion was the belief itself. One of the most dramatic incidents took place in a station, where 150 girls passed out at once on hearing an erroneous report that a fainting victim had died in hospital.

'Mulder, this town is insane'

SCULLY

The War of the Coprophages

Most belief epidemics are contained within a relatively small area – this is partly what sustains them – and are short-lived. But occasionally one will be so exceptionally virulent that it travels vast distances and endures for years, maturing into a phenomenon somewhere between mass hysteria and urban legend.

Consider the Chupacabras. Pronounced Choo-pah-cahb-rahs, the name is Spanish for 'goat sucker', and was coined to describe the predations of a mysterious beast first reported in Puerto Rico in 1994. The Chupacabras is said to be grey-skinned, with fangs, red eyes and distinctive spinal quills. It stands upright, is between four and five feet tall, can fly, and roams around exsanguinating not only goats, but other livestock and household pets.

Early in 1996, by way of the Spanish-language media, the story travelled to the mainland United States; and so, it seems, did the Chupacabras itself – sightings of it have been reported in several cities, including Miami, New York, San Antonio, Cambridge (Massachusetts) and San Francisco. It has also been reported in New Jersey, where some confusion has arisen in separating tales of the Chupacabras from those of the Jersey Devil (see *The X-Files Book of the Unexplained,* Volume One).

Artist's impression of the Chupacabras

The stories themselves may have more in common with medieval tales of monsters than with modern folklore – but the reaction to them is pure late-twentieth century. In the cities where it has been 'sighted', there is a brisk trade in Chupacabras tee-shirts and other merchandise. A Princeton university student has set up a Chupacabras World Wide Web homepage on the internet; Spanish language radio stations play songs dedicated to it (such as 'Goat Busters'); and a number of local papers and news shows have reported on what they call 'Chupacabramania'. Sujayla Curras, a producer on Miami-based talk show *Cristina*, recently told *The Boston Globe*: 'Chupacabras is hot, it's happening . . . It's got it going on, like Brad Pitt . . .'

However, in Puerto Rico the Chupacabras is considered neither a joke nor a cultural icon but a very real threat. In Canovanas, where the first reports originated, public panic was such that an official search for the beast was led by the Mayor, Jose Soto, wielding a giant crucifix. Other towns in the area have been plagued by animal mutilations. In a typical report in November

1995, Angela Lajes from nearby Ponce found her dog and her sister's two cats dead, drained of blood, their guts missing. In the same month, the Chupacabras was said to have opened the window of a house in Caguas, where it destroyed a teddy bear and left a puddle of slime on the window-sill.

Jose 'Chemo' Soto, the mayor of Canovanas, checks the lock on a cage in which he later placed goats as bait for the Chupacabras. Schemes like this, and the weekly patrol in which he leads local volunteers in scouring the hills that skirt the town in search of the beast, have earned Soto the nickname 'Chemo Jones' – as in Indiana.
'Whatever it is, it's highly intelligent,' he recently told news reporters. 'Today it is attacking animals, but tomorrow it may attack people.'

In Puerto Rico, where government investigators have examined the evidence of dozens of animal carcasses, these events remain a mystery. The American reports, on the other hand, exhibit all the classic symptoms of mass hysteria.

'Police are asking that if you see any cockroaches, don't panic. Simply notify the local authorities and evacuate the area immediately!'

TV NEWS REPORTER

The War of the Coprophages

It is hard to ignore the influence of the media, who love to scare and titillate under the guise of informative reportage. The Chupacabras's first US appearance took place in Miami just three weeks after the first TV coverage, since when the Miami Police Department has been flooded with dozens of calls about Chupacabras sightings and animal deaths. By the end of March 1996, more than 50 animal victims had been reported. On 8 April a number of these were autopsied in front of a crowd of reporters. 'We had to conduct these autopsies to say, "Idiots, these are dog bites,"' says Detective Pat Brickman. He believes that hungry stray dogs are the culprits, and that panic and suggestibility have caused people to misinterpret perfectly commonplace deaths – not unlike the situation in *The War of the Coprophages*.

'Who died now?'

SCULLY

'The medical examiner. His body was found dead next to a toilet with roaches all over him. I really think you should come . . .'

MULDER

'A toilet? Mulder, check his eyes. Is one of them bloodshot with a dilated pupil . . . ? He probably had a brain aneurysm'

SCULLY

The War of the Coprophages

For most of *The War of the Coprophages*, we see Agent Mulder at the 'crime' scenes, increasingly convinced that something strange and cockroach-based is going on, and Agent Scully at home, cooly delivering over the telephone a prosaic – and correct – explanation for every death.

This entertaining structure was born out of a necessity to shoot actress Gillian Anderson's scenes all in one go, to enable her to take some time off from filming. But it led to a neat dramatic opportunity, as Darin Morgan elaborates. 'All those things that Scully says, those are legitimate things . . . People can die from allergies to cockroaches if they go into anaphylactic shock. There are certain forms of drug abusers who do hallucinate insects going under their skin – it's called Ekbom's syndrome – and they might cut themselves deliberately, trying to get the imaginary insects out. Many people do have brain aneurysms while on the toilet: it's the most common place. And one guy scares himself to death, has a heart attack. So they're all legitimate ways to die, but not necessarily with cockroaches.

'Mulder's natural thing is he sees a dead body, and hears about cockroaches, and he goes: "They're killer cockroaches." Whereas Scully is a bit more thoughtful and says, "No, it's probably this, it's probably this and it's probably that."'

So is Mulder more gullible than Scully? Not necessarily.

'The development of our cerebral cortex has been the greatest achievement of the evolutionary process. Big deal. While allowing us the thrills of intellect and the pangs of self-consciousness, it is all too often overruled by our inner, instinctive brain – the one that tells us to react, not reflect, to run rather than ruminate'

MULDER

The War of the Coprophages

Mulder was right on the money when, in his summing up of the investigation, he poured scorn on the workings of the human brain. The chances are that most people in his position would have jumped to the same conclusions as he did. Here's why:

PAREIDOLIA

To understand the world and make sense of the things we experience is one of the greatest human needs. Our brains serve that need by automatically finding sense in *anything*. Psychologists call this pareidolia, and once you've made a pareidolic interpretation of something, it's hard to see anything else. Pareidolia is what makes the Rorschach personality test work: you look at an abstract ink blot, and your brain finds a picture in it. Pareidolia also works with ideas. Mulder visits two separate death scenes and finds evidence of cockroaches at both, so he makes the pareidolic interpretation that the cockroaches must be responsible. The idea makes sense to him, and he finds it hard to let it go – even when Scully's alternative explanations seem to be correct.

Pareidolia works even better in helping us to find things that we believe we will find – even if those things are not really there. If, for instance, you were to listen to a song played backwards, you would be bound to find at least one vaguely coherent word or phrase, because your brain is actively seeking sense. The chances are, however, that everyone will find a different word or phrase, and it will be something like 'Ma, my chair's broken'. But if you have been forewarned that you'll hear the phrase 'All hail The Dark One and have sex with a sheep', you probably *will* hear it – again, because your brain is looking for it.

This is why people insist that there are secret messages deliberately hidden in certain songs when extensive objective research has found none. They believe that they have heard these things with their own ears, and, in a way, they have. The same goes for those who claim to have seen things like the burnt tortilla bearing the 'face of Christ' or the aubergine which looked like Richard Nixon. To the disinterested observer, both of these images could appear to be something else, or to resemble nothing at all. But to people who know what they 'should' be seeing, they are crystal clear.

Pareidolia is so common that even if we don't know the scientific name for it, we are all aware that it exists. Scully has twice accused Mulder of making a pareidolic interpretation: in *Syzygy*, when he insists he can see the shape of a 'horned beast' branded on the body of one of the murder victims, and in *Clyde Bruckman's Final Repose*. Remember the 'Fat Little White Nazi Stormtrooper'?

SENSATION SEEKING

According to Dr M. Zuckerman, the psychologist who devised a test to measure this trait, Sensation Seekers are usually creative, sexual and easily bored by routine; they are attracted by things that are exciting and unusual and are courageous, adventurous and unlikely to shy away from danger. They are open-minded, and positively drawn to ideas and beliefs that challenge the limits of scientific knowledge.

Sensation Seekers are not only open to believing that all manner of strange things are possible, but likely to pursue opportunities to learn more about strange subjects and anomalous events – first hand, if at all possible. They are also more likely to interpret confusing experiences as paranormal. Sound like anyone we know?

THE BELIEF ENGINE

We know that what we believe can influence what we experience, especially when it comes to the paranormal. But can we really trust our beliefs? Psychology professor James Alcock doubts it. His research has thrown much light on the way our beliefs are formed, and the results suggest that it is not as precise and discerning a process as we might like to think. He writes: 'Our brains and nervous systems constitute a belief-generating machine, an engine that produces beliefs without any particular respect for what is real or true and what is not. This belief engine selects information from the environment, shapes it, combines it with information from memory, and produces beliefs that are generally consistent with beliefs already held. This system is as capable of generating fallacious beliefs as it is of generating beliefs that are in line with truth . . . Nothing is fundamentally different about what we might think of as 'irrational' beliefs – they are generated in the same manner as are other beliefs. We may not have an evidential basis for belief in irrational concepts, but neither do we have such a basis for most of our beliefs.'

For example, we believe that brushing our teeth is good for us and that the solar system exists although (unless we are dentists or astronomers) we have not actually seen for ourselves the evidence to back up these beliefs. We've been told them, they seem to make sense to us, and we've never been led to question them.

Alcock describes the components of the belief engine in detail, but here are a few of the cogs which keep it running:

• The brain stores links, coincidences, conclusions about cause-and-effect and other positive thoughts more reliably than negative ones. Situations where there are no links to be made barely register at all. (We can all remember a time, for instance, when we thought of someone just before they telephoned. But do we remember the times we thought of someone and they didn't telephone, or they telephoned when we hadn't been thinking about them? Probably not.)

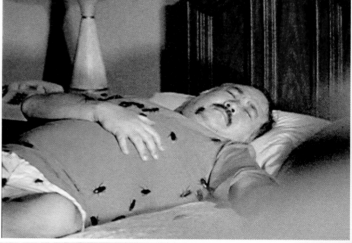

• Our rational mind is in constant conflict with our natural intuitions – and usually loses. For example, if we see a roulette wheel come up black ten times in a row, our intuition tells us that it must soon come up red. Our rational mind struggles to remind us that the wheel has no memory and that each spin is a fresh start for chance – the eleventh spin is just as likely to come up black again. And yet most of us will put our money on the red.

• We don't absorb information passively – we consciously organise what we see in order to construct a reality that makes sense to us and fits in with what we already believe.

A victim of killer cockroaches? As Mulder discovers, the human mind is particularly agile when jumping to conclusions

• If we have a strong emotional reaction at the same time as we evaluate an experience, it will fix that impression in our minds. (You're walking down the street and you think you see a relative who died recently. Your heart leaps

into your mouth: you may be shocked, alarmed or moved. When you look again, it is a stranger. But the feeling was so vivid . . . the chances are you will always wonder if maybe, just for a moment, you did see what you thought you saw.)

• Our memories are also vulnerable to bias and distortion, and we tend to ensure that they fit in with what we believe is possible. The problem is that we are not aware of this: we trust our memories and think of as them as perfect mental 'snap-shots' of the past. So we might argue that we believe

something because we remember evidence of it, but the truth is just as likely to be the other way around.

• We don't like to discard a belief, so if we read or learn something that challenges a belief we hold, we are naturally inclined to ignore it or debunk it.

• We tend to seek out people who believe the same things as we do, so our beliefs are not challenged. If we are close to someone who does not share our beliefs, we will constantly strive to convert them.

Our belief engines start to tick over from the moment we are born, and they have no off-switch. We can, however, override them by tossing in a spanner of logic and reason. But you can't tamper with a machine if you don't know where it is – and to find your belief engine, you have to accept that it exists, which means being prepared to accept the frightening thought that we can't always trust our own perceptions, our memories, *our minds*.

Some people are unable to do this. Others can and will. Scully, for example,

MASS HYSTERIA AND THE BELIEF ENGINE

has never leaped to conclusions even about her own anomalous experiences, and is amazingly adept at overriding her belief engine. Mulder's belief engine, on the other hand, is a finely-tuned machine, well-oiled by all those experiences which have confirmed his beliefs. It's not that he doesn't know it's there, it's just that, like a person who has worked in a factory all his life, he has become so used to the noise that an outsider, like Scully, is more aware of its machinations than he is. But at least Mulder is prepared to let her tinker with his belief engine. And let's hope he knows how lucky he is to have the services of such an able mechanic. For, as the episode's unfortunate Dr Eckerle proves, once your belief engine goes into overdrive, your next stop may be the junk-yard.

'How do I know you're not a cockroach?'
DR ECKERLE
'I assure you I'm just as human as you are, if not more so'
AGENT MULDER
(Mulder's mobile phone rings, the tone sounding similar to the cockroaches' chirp)
'You ARE one of them!'
DR ECKERLE
The War of the Coprophages

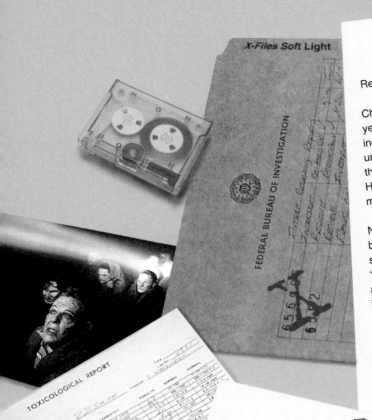

FEDERAL BUREAU OF INVESTIGATION

FEDERAL BUREAU OF INVESTIGATION

Report prepared by Special Agent Dana Scully

Chester Ray Banton, the physicist we arrested yesterday, has confessed to direct involvement in the incidents - which appear, at this time, to be extremely unconventional homicides. Certainly his connection to the victims and crime scenes has been proven. However, I strongly doubt that any official confession he makes will be admissible in a court of law.

Not only is Banton's mental health a matter for conjecture, but his claim that, as a result of an accident during scientific research, his shadow has been transformed into 'dark matter', capable of breaking down the components of any biological matter accidentally coming into contact with it, is without scientific precedent.

Nevertheless, the lack of caution displayed on the part of local law enforcement is cause for concern, and it is with some reluctance that Agent Mulder and myself have agreed to disengage ourselves from this investigation at the behest of Detective Barron, the primary on the case.

TOXICOLOGICAL REPORT

FEDERAL BUREAU OF INVESTIGATION

FEDERAL BUREAU OF INVESTIGATION

Case notes prepared by Special Agent Dana Scully

Further to Agent Mulder's initial report regarding the Navy destroyer, U.S.S. Ardent, which has been missing in the North Atlantic for the past two days, I can confirm my own commitment to investigating the case.

Eighteen crew members were found last night on a lifeboat intercepted by a Canadian trawler. Only one was alive. This man, identified as Lieutenant Richard Harper, was admitted to Bethesda Naval Hospital ICU under high security.

I was not permitted to examine the patient, who is on life support. However, my brief visit to his bedside this morning has convinced me that something is very gravely amiss.

Although ICU personnel confirmed that the fingerprints of the patient had been cross-checked at the time of admission, and matched those in Harper's military records, the man I saw appeared to be in his late 80s or early 90s.

Richard Harper's records note that he is 28 years old.

SPECIAL AGENT

Dana Scully

THE FRONTIERS OF REALITY

The episode *Soft Light* finds the Agents lending their expertise to an ex-student of Scully's, as a favour. But what begins as a set of baffling missing persons cases proves to be a chain of fatal accidents caused in all innocence by doomed scientist Chester Ray Banton. The victim of an experiment gone hideously awry, Banton's shadow has become 'dark matter', capable of obliterating all in its path, like a miniature black hole.

Soft Light was the first episode written by newcomer Vince Gilligan, who came up with the idea the night before his interview for a place on *The X-Files* writing team.

'I was sitting in my hotel room thinking: *Gee, I'd better come up with something to tell Chris Carter when I meet him for the first time tomorrow*. It was dark and I had the TV on, and I remember seeing my shadow on the wall next to me, and I was thinking how creepy it would be if it suddenly came to life.'

In the search for a suitable scientific premise for the creation of the unfortunate Banton's lethal shadow, Gilligan initially used the idea of a theoretical sub-atomic particle called the monopole, a building block of magnetism. 'Then in the rewrite, Chris said: I've heard of this stuff called Dark Matter. And it seemed to be more poetically precise – Dark Matter, the darkness of the shadow – so we changed it to that.'

Gilligan's love of science primarily embraces 'machinery, mechanisms, computers . . . all that kinda geeky guy-stuff,' but includes physics 'in an enthusiastic layman's sense.

'What interests me most are the beautiful moments in science, like when Archimedes yelled *Eureka* in the bathtub. The moments of a scientist using something other than science, using some spark of imagination. Creativity in science is a great thing . . . when someone takes the information they have and makes some sort of creative leap. Sometimes that almost feels paranormal.'

At the boundaries of science, however, there is a great deal else that sometimes almost feels paranormal, including the field from which the science fiction of *Soft Light* grew – quantum mechanics.

'[Chester was] researching dark matter. Quantum particles, neutrinos, gluons, mesons, quarks'

DR CHRISTOPHER DAVEY

'Subatomic particles'

SCULLY

'The mysteries of the universe. Theoretically, the very building blocks of reality'

DR DAVEY

Soft Light

When the atom was 'discovered', science threw a party. This was it. We had found the fundamental building blocks of the universe. Leaning back on its throne, a victorious science dubbed the newly quantified particle an 'atom', from the Greek word for 'indivisible'. And that was that.

Or that was *supposed* to be that. Pretty soon it became clear that not only was the atom divisible, it was a veritable box of lego. And the closer the scientists looked, the further they were from establishing what was going on. They did not make the same hubristic mistake twice. The new discoveries weren't given grave Greek names but whimsical ones like 'quark' – an invented word from James Joyce's *Finnegans Wake* – and 'gluon' (it 'glues' one quark to another – or so we think). Science, it seemed, had not only slipped off its throne; it was sitting in the corner mumbling to itself.

In the words of Vince Gilligan: 'It's sort of like peeling an onion, except you get to the last layer, and all of a sudden, you realise you've got a whole new onion.'

It was not the first time that physicists had had to wipe their slates clean. The theories of classical physics considered the world a predictable place, where every effect had a cause and time and space were absolute; where any system could be accurately understood and its past and future states determined; and where even something as complex as energy could be fathomed: neatly divided between the particle and the wave.

By the 1920s, studies had begun which would cast doubt on every one of these reassuring certainties. At the core of the new physics, known today as Quantum Theory, is a set of ideas unsurpassed in their usefulness, accuracy and reliability. Yet many aspects of quantum theory seem to defy common sense (some appear downright spooky), and the field is still surrounded by a dense fog of doubts and queries. Einstein, who played a major part in its birth, regarded certain aspects of it as sheer insanity, and spent much of his life in heated debate with fellow physicists.

Nor was he the only one concerned by the implications of some of the new discoveries. Erwin Schrodinger had formulated an equation pertaining to the quantum states of wave functions which some scientists took to mean that, under certain conditions, a particular wave function could be both decayed and not decayed at the same time. To illustrate what he considered the absurdity of this popular misinterpretation, Schrodinger visualised a cat trapped in a box in such a way that the cat would be killed by the resultant radioactivity if the wave function was decayed, and would survive if it was not. Hence, if the wave function could be at the same time decayed and undecayed, the cat must be at the same time both dead and alive.

However, this hypothetical scenario did not evoke the response that Schrodinger intended: ironically, the paradox of 'Schrodinger's Cat' is used today to help students understand quantum probability.

Of course the paradox is not a real paradox: if the box is opened and its contents observed, we would see only one of the two possible wave functions (and a cat that was either alive or dead). But the act of observation may play an even more significant – and weirder – role in the quantum jumps between atomic energy levels. In 1989 a group of scientists in Boulder, Colorado, were using radio waves to drive beryllium ions from one energy level to another when they discovered to their surprise that the more often they examined the ions, the less likely it was that a jump to a new energy state had taken place. It was almost scientific proof that a watched kettle never boils.

The first Solvay International Conference on Physics, 1911. In the next 16 years the tenets of 20th Century Physics were to evolve at a startling pace; By the time the fifth conference was held, in 1927 (attended by several of the original assembly, including Albert Einstein, second from the right, standing) quantum theory was the primary topic

'We've both seen the physical evidence, Scully'
MULDER
'I can't explain it, but then that's not our job'
SCULLY

Soft Light

Scientists often talk of 'missing variables' in quantum theory – unknown elements that somehow influence the behaviour of energy. Some believe that the very act of observation, or the presence of human consciousness, could be the crucial factor. Wolfgang Pauli – like Einstein, one of the early midwives of quantum physics – and Carl Jung were among the first to discuss this theoretical link between science and the human psyche. Today, researchers at Princeton University's Engineering Anomalies Research laboratory continue to explore this possibility. Perhaps, they say, this could be the key to understanding the effect of one mind on another, or on a machine, or on matter (see *In Search of the Truth*).

Others postulate that the missing variable is time. Richard Feynman, a physicist responsible for major advances in Quantum Electrodynamics, theorised that anti-matter was normal matter travelling backwards in time. And indeed there are many prepared to stick their necks out and say that some aspects of quantum theory allow the notion that it is possible for matter to move forwards and backwards in time. (Stephen Hawking, however, was not one of them, noting that 'we have not been invaded by hordes of tourists from the future.')

Given the mysterious nature of quantum theory, it is no surprise that it has been called upon to explain all manner of weirdness. One such is Bell's Theorem, a discovery to do with 'non-locality', the implications of which are still a matter of debate. Scientific anomalist and former physicist William Corliss explains: 'In the laboratory, Bell's Theorem is associated with an admittedly spooky effect: the measurements made on one particle affect the measurements on a second, far removed particle. In theory, the second particle could be on the other side of the galaxy, with absolutely no physical connection between the two – unless you admit to unexplained at-a-distance forces.'

Physicists not surprisingly object when Bell's Theorem is used to 'prove' such things as psychokinesis and ESP – a clear case, they say, of jumping the gun when we are still so far from understanding the fundamental behaviour of energy particles.

Richard Feynman, seen here addressing the Presidential Commission at Cape Canaveral in 1968 following the Challenger disaster

Some new-age doctrines have embraced quantum physics as if it were a branch of mysticism. Alas, most of these marriages between science and religion are severely wanting in the science department, thriving only because their followers are sufficiently blinded by jargon and equations they cannot grasp not to realise those who preach the message have failed to grasp them too.

Nevertheless there is much within quantum theory that genuinely penetrates the boundaries of philosophy. One fundamental question it addresses, for example, is whether an object which is not observed exists – a question which drags the old argument about a tree falling in an empty forest firmly into the realm of science.

Einstein, with his passion for order, did not like this possibility at all, and – like Schrodinger – tried to persuade others of the absurdity of a theory that could mean, for instance, that an object as vast and solid as the moon might not actually be there when no one was looking at it. Einstein's instincts told him that this could not be. But recent laboratory experiments have addressed the question again (not, of course, using the moon) and, amazingly, their results have shown that Einstein's instincts may have been incorrect.

William Corliss warns, however, against regarding quantum theory as paranormal. 'After all,' he notes, 'radioactivity was pretty mysterious not too many years ago. It still is, but we are accustomed to it now.'

'What else could it be?'
MULDER
'Whatever it is, Mulder, it's not a time warp'
SCULLY
Dod Kalm

Whilst the possibilities of quantum theory continue to provide writers the world over with inspiration, *The X-Files* has always tried to avoid straying too far into the realm of traditional, out-and-out science fiction. It is a rule that contributes significantly to the show's originality, but on one occasion, in Howard Gordon's opinion, it backfired.

In *Dod Kalm*, Mulder and Scully head for the open seas of Norway to discover what happened to the crew of the *USS Ardent* – young men apparently thrust into old age overnight following a bizarre incident at sea. The Agents, stranded aboard the doomed ship, appear to suffer the same fate . . . whatever its cause might be. And that was a question which caused *The X-Files* team no little consternation.

'We didn't want a time wrinkle, which we felt was too science-fiction-like for the series,' Howard Gordon recalls. 'We made it simply contaminated water and an ageing syndrome, which, ultimately, was anti-climactic. You *want* it to be a time wrinkle!

'*Dod Kalm* had an emotional power that I really liked, the idea of two people dying next to each other,' he adds. 'But it was a perfect example of the science being very flimsy. Flimsy to the point of *what the hell's going on?*'

'So far, I've tracked nine unexplained disappearances. Each of them passed through the sixty-fifth parallel, right here . . .'

MULDER

'Another Bermuda Triangle?'

SCULLY

Dod Kalm

Appropriately for an episode with a Scandinavian flavour, *Dod Kalm* is positively swimming with red herrings, the first of which is a classic mainstay of paranormal lore.

On 5 December 1945 five Grumman TBM Avenger bombers took off from the Naval Air Station in Fort Lauderdale, Florida. Their flight path took them into the heart of what is now called the Bermuda Triangle. The planes disappeared, as did one of the planes sent out to find them. No wreckage was found.

Charles Berlitz (grandson and heir of the phrasebook founder) wrote a sensational account entitled *The Bermuda Triangle*, in which the last transmission of the lead pilot, Lieutenant Charles C. Taylor was reported as: 'Don't come after me! They look like . . .'

The truth is, as usual, much more mundane. The planes became lost because of a faulty compass. The day that Berlitz reported as 'fine' was dangerously stormy. The 'highly experienced pilots' turned out to be mostly novices. The flight itself was a training exercise. And Lieutenant Taylor's chilling last message was in fact: 'We will have to ditch unless landfall . . . when the first plane drops to ten gallons we all go down together.'

And what of the 'missing' rescue plane? The crew of one ship, the *Gaines Mills*, saw it catch fire, hit the water and explode (it was a notoriously dangerous model), and the commander of the aircraft carrier *USS Solomons* watched it disappear from his radar at the exact same time.

As one Triangle researcher, Larry Kusche, concluded: 'If Berlitz were to report that a boat were red, the chance of it being some other colour is almost a certainty.'

But fiction is often more fun than truth. Berlitz sold millions of copies of his book, and the 'mystery' of the Bermuda Triangle remains firmly

The famous 'Bermuda triangle'. The term was coined by Veteran anomalist Vicent Gaddis who later expressed his regret at doing so.

Indeed, so many accidents and 'disappearances' have taken place outside the triangle as to render the notion of the 'damned trapezium' meaningless. Moreover, those that have occurred within it have not been anywhere near as mysterious as some would have us believe

entrenched and enduringly popular to this day.

According to venerable anomalist Ivan T. Sanderson, a leading proponent of deadly soul-sucking stretches of sea, there are in fact 12 evenly-spaced 'vile vortices' around the world. Others are not so precise. The original Triangle is located in the stretch of sea between Bermuda, Miami and Puerto Rico, but disappearances as far away as the Pacific Ocean have been attributed to its baneful forces. As Howard Gordon wryly observes, 'The triangle's getting bigger and bigger. They're widening it!'

Gordon admits that he himself 'always loved that stuff. Especially having grown up on the East coast . . . Wintering in Florida, it was right there. When I was a kid I was flying over that area once, in the Caribbean, and there was a really rough patch, and we dropped. I think it must have been a windshear of some kind. And I said, *Well, we're going down . . .*'

'*Scully, what do you know about the Philadelphia Experiment?*'

MULDER

'*It was a program during World War II, to render battleships invisible to radar*'

SCULLY

'*On July 8, 1944, the USS Eldridge did more than just hide from radar screens. It vanished from the Philadelphia Navy Yard . . . Only to reappear minutes later, hundreds of miles away in Norfolk, Virginia*'

MULDER

Dod Kalm

The inspiration for the plumpest of *Dod Kalm*'s red herrings was in fact the subject that gave Howard Gordon the idea for a ship-bound episode in the first place: The Philadelphia Experiment.

It began with a letter to astrophysicist and UFOlogist Morris Ketchum Jessup. In 1955, Jessup had published a book called *The Case for the UFO* in which he urged his readers to pressure their government representatives into funding research into the unified field theory, a murky bit of physics that Jessup thought could explain UFOs. On 13 January 1956, Jessup received a rambling missive which read, in part:

My dear Dr Jessup,
Your invocation to the Public that they move en Masse upon their Representatives and have thusly enough Pressure placed at the right & sufficient Number of Places where from a law demanding Research into Dr Albert Einstein's Unified Filed Theory May be enacted (1925–27) *is not* at all Necessary . . .

'Results' of My friend Dr Franklin Reno, *Were used* . . . The Results was & stands today as Proof that The Unified Field Theory to a certain extent is correct . . . The 'result' was complete invisibility of the ship, Destroyer type, *and all* of its crew. While at sea. (Oct. 1943) The Field Was effective in an oblate spheroidal shape, extending one Hundred yards (More or Less, due to Lunar position and latitude) *out* from each beam of the ship. Any Person Within that sphere became vague in form BUT He too observed those Persons aboard *that* ship as though they too were of the same state, yet, were walking on nothing. Any person without that sphere could see Nothing save the clearly *Defined shape of the Ships Hull in the Water* . . .

There are only a very few of the original Experimental D-E's Crew Left by Now, Sir. Most went insane, one just walked 'throo' His quarters Wall in sight of His Wife & Child & 2 other crew Members (WAS NEVER SEEN AGAIN), two 'went into 'The flame', i.e. They 'Froze' & caught fire, while carrying common Small-Boat compasses . . . THEY BURNED FOR 18 DAYS . . . The experiment was a complete success. The Men were Complete Failures.

The letter was signed 'Very Disrespectfully Yours, CARL M. ALLEN'. A legend was born.

'I'm no liar. I'm telling you, it happened. First to some of my men . . . Then to the rest . . .'
CAPTAIN BARCLAY
'What happened?'
SCULLY
'Time got lost . . .'
CAPTAIN BARCLAY
Dod Kalm

On 20 April 1959 Jessup was found dead in his car, a hose leading from the exhaust pipe into the passenger compartment, his apparent suicide adding fuel to the truth-consuming fires of conjecture.

Carl M. Allen (a man of many names, including Carlos Miguel Allende) had been in the merchant marines at the time of the alleged vanishing act and claimed to have seen the disappearance of the experimental vessel – identified as the *USS Eldridge* – from his own ship, the *SS Andrew Furuseth*. He also added that the *USS Eldridge* had teleported from Philadelphia to Virginia and back, although he himself had not seen that happen – he had read about it in the papers.

Later research confirmed that both the *Eldridge* and the *Andrew Furuseth* did exist and that Allen had served on the *Andrew Furuseth*. However, no one else on the *Andrew Furuseth* claims to have seen the *Eldridge*. The ships could have been in the same area during the war, but it seems unlikely. Almost as unlikely as the US Navy conducting top secret experiments in full view of a passing merchant marine vessel, and the experiment being reported in a Philadelphia newspaper – but only Allen remembering reading it.

And a scientist who might have been Allen's 'Dr Franklin Reno' *may* have been involved in Navy research into using electromagnetic fields to deflect torpedoes and mines; but that is a long way from teleportation and 'cloaking devices'.

The mythical feats of the *USS Eldridge* may not be *a priori* impossible, as Howard Gordon notes: 'In Newtonian physics, we think time and space are immutable – but maybe they're not. The physicists I have spoken to have posited that it is possible to have a wrinkle in the time-space continuum . . . so therefore it is *not* immutable.'

But it would be highly surprising if the Philadelphia Experiment ever took place. The simple fact is that even now, fifty years later, the only object that quantum physicists seem able to make disappear is . . . common sense.

From the 1984 sci-fi thriller The Philadelphia Experiment *- loosely based on a not-neccesarily-true story*

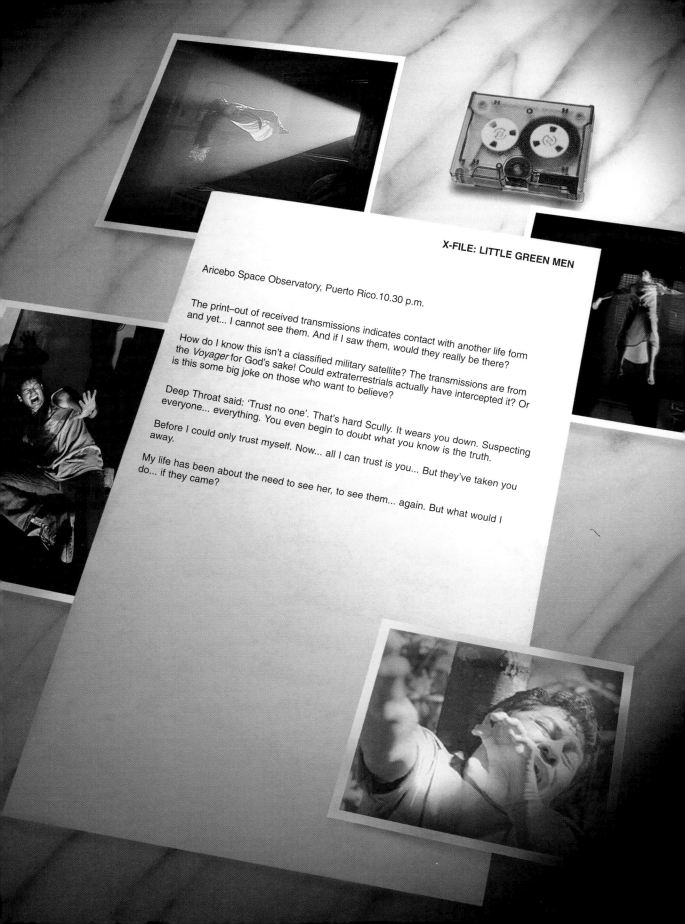

X-FILE: LITTLE GREEN MEN

Aricebo Space Observatory, Puerto Rico. 10.30 p.m.

The print–out of received transmissions indicates contact with another life form and yet... I cannot see them. And if I saw them, would they really be there?

How do I know this isn't a classified military satellite? The transmissions are from the *Voyager* for God's sake! Could extraterrestrials actually have intercepted it? Or is this some big joke on those who want to believe?

Deep Throat said: 'Trust no one'. That's hard Scully. It wears you down. Suspecting everyone... everything. You even begin to doubt what you know is the truth.

Before I could only trust myself. Now... all I can trust is you... But they've taken you away.

My life has been about the need to see her, to see them... again. But what would I do... if they came?

THE SEARCH FOR EXTRA-TERRESTRIAL INTELLIGENCE

Little Green Men, the first episode of *The X-Files'* second season, finds Special Agents Fox Mulder and Dana Scully at their lowest ebb. Mulder's trusted ally, Deep Throat, has been murdered. The X-Files division has been closed down. Scully has been transferred to a teaching post at the FBI's training facility and Mulder forced into the tedium of handling electronic surveillance on fraud cases.

But Mulder soon hangs up his headphones after receiving a tip-off from Senator Richard Matheson, his silent patron on Capitol Hill. Fleeing to the depths of Puerto Rico to find the remnants of NASA's defunct Search for Extraterrestrial Intelligence (SETI) project, he becomes embroiled in a terrifying adventure which stirs memories of his sister's abduction and causes him to doubt his own mind.

The episode was penned by Glen Morgan and Jim Wong before their much-lamented departure during the show's second season, and their extensive knowledge of the real-life search for extraterrestrial intelligence is evident throughout.

The question of whether mankind is alone in the universe is one of the most profound we can ask. And where investigations of UFO sightings and claimed alien abductions only raise more questions, looking to the heavens themselves may provide an answer.

For Morgan and Wong, the stars are a constant reminder of our quest. 'There are more in the heavens than all the humans who have ever lived on Earth,' they note. 'And, like each person, every star presents a possibility.'

'We wanted to believe'
MULDER
Little Green Men

Could there be life on other planets? Some, like Stephen Jay Gould, the eminent evolutionary biologist, are optimistic. 'The immensity of the universe, and the improbability of the absolute uniqueness of any part of it, leads to the immense probability that there is some kind of life all over.'

Others, like Dr Richard Dawkins, first holder of Oxford University's Charles Symoni chair in the public understanding of science, are not. 'The fact that life exists here tells us nothing about how likely life is to exist elsewhere . . . We animals and plants and fungi and bacteria all have DNA, and all share the same 64-word dictionary that translates DNA instructions into action. It would be too much of a coincidence for the same 64-word dictionary to spring up twice, independently.'

The truth is that we don't know. We can't guess at the probability, because we simply don't have the data we need to work it out.

We have a rough idea of the necessary ingredients for our kind of life: a watery planet just the right distance from a star, temperatures in the narrow band at which water is liquid, and an atmosphere hospitable to carbon-based life forms. But we have no idea how many planets might be out there that fit the bill.

In fact, until recently, we had no idea whether any planets were out there at all, since all we can actually see is stars. Then came the discovery that by studying a star's light waves over a long period of time, 'wobbles' could be detected that indicated the influence of a planet nearby.

In 1994, astronomer Aleksander Wolszczan of Pennsylvania State University found the first planets outside our solar system: at least three of them, orbiting a star more than 7,000 trillion miles away. But unlike our sun, the star was a pulsar: dead, spinning and spewing out radiation.

Astronomer Paul Butler tinkers with an Interplanetary Monitoring Platform (IMP) device in 1965. Just over three decades later, he and his colleague Geoffrey Marcy announced one of the most important discoveries ever made about our universe: that our sun is not the only star orbited by planets

On 6 October 1995 came a scientific breakthrough: two Swiss astronomers found a companion planet to the star known as 51 Pegasi. 51 Pegasi was pretty much like our sun. But the planet was so close to it that scientists wondered how it could survive the heat, estimated to be in the region of 1,800° F.

A second breakthrough occurred only three months later. San Francisco State University astronomers Geoffrey Marcy and Paul Butler, who had spent eight years monitoring over 120 stars using the best available technology in the world, announced the discovery of two more planets outside of our solar system: one each orbiting the stars 47 Ursae Majoris (in the 'Big Dipper') and 70 Virginis (in the 'Virgo' constellation). And once again, history was made: the stars resembled our sun, *and* the planets seemed 'livable' – at the right distance from their stars for water to be liquid. They might even have oceans, and rain.

The temperature on 70 Virginis is closer to that of earth than any other planet discovered so far – estimated to be 80° Celsius, 185° Fahrenheit, or about as hot as a cup of coffee. The planet would be stuffy, to say the least, but not prohibitive of life.

Through the rest of 1996, Marcy and Butler announced the discovery of several more. 'Planets aren't rare, after all,' Marcy told the press. The feeling within the planetary science community is that discovery of new planets, and entire solar systems, will become routine.

Probability suggests that someday soon, we'll find a planet the same size as ours, and the same distance from its star as we are from our sun. Can we assume that it will bear life? Unfortunately not. The problem is that we haven't a clue exactly how or why life started on *our* planet, so we can't deduce the likelihood of the same event taking place elsewhere. Speculation about other kinds of life is even more pointless. There could be Silicon-based life, for instance, swimming through oceans of lava (like the organism in *Firewalker*) or frolicking in ice and liquid ammonia (like *Ice*'s interplanetary hitch-hikers), but our knowledge in this area amounts to precisely zilch.

Even if a planet was to bear life, we have no way of knowing how far that life would evolve, since we still don't quite know why *we* began to leap the evolutionary hurdles that took us from being puddles of single-celled bacteria to intelligent life-forms capable of language and reasoning. The Summer 1996 announcement that what appear to be fossilised bacteria have been found in a Martian meteorite is potentially of mind-boggling importance. And to find

In a vivid flashback, Mulder recalls his sister's abduction. But is his mind playing tricks on him?

living bacteria on another planet would be epoch-making, one of the most important discoveries in the history of science. But – let's be honest – puddles of alien bacteria may be something of a disappointment to the rest of us, and unlikely to become the subject of a Steven Spielberg movie.

'On August 20 and September 5, 1977, two spacecraft were launched from the Kennedy Spaceflight Centre, Florida. They were called Voyager I and II. Each one carries a message; a gold-plated record depicting images, music and sounds of our planet, arranged so that it may be understood if ever intercepted by a technologically mature extraterrestrial civilisation'

MULDER

Little Green Men

Right now, somewhere out in space, a very, very long way beyond the orbit of Pluto and the influence of our sun, yet more than 40,000 years away from the neighbourhood of another star, the Voyager spacecraft are slicing through the darkness at speeds of over 35,000 m.p.h. Aboard each, a golden disk is sheathed in a protective aluminium jacket beside the tools needed to play it and symbolic instructions explaining how.

'Imagine Fox, if another civilisation out there were to hear this they would think, what a wonderful place the Earth must be'

SENATOR RICHARD MATHESON

Little Green Men

Carefully chosen by a committee chaired by eminent planetary scientist Carl Sagan, the sounds and images are a comprehensive introduction to planet earth and its inhabitants. They are also a moving celebration of our achievements and discoveries, the beauty of earth and the sheer marvel of life.

Among the 115 images are maps, photographs and diagrams of the planets, sun and solar system; of chemicals, DNA structure and cells. Diagrams explain human anatomy and reproduction, and how we grow and age. Family units, generations and life-span are explained in both diagrams and photographs: a mother breast-feeding her baby; a group of children; adults, elderly people, a family.

Other pictures of humans show the rich diversity of our cultures, and geographical and geological images show our diverse terrain. There is a sunset, a variety of plant life, and the creatures of land, sea and air.

Extraterrestrial strangers would learn about sport and music and books, and see that we educate our children; that we grow things to use and eat; and that we sell these things for others to buy so that they do not have to. There are pictures which show that we explore and farm our oceans, that we can travel across the land in cars and trains and fly through the air in planes, and that we build things: from simple dwellings to houses to magnificent structures like the Taj Mahal, the Golden Gate Bridge and the Great Wall of China.

And, if the recipients of the disk hadn't already guessed, shots of an Antarctic expedition, the Aricebo radio telescope, the Titan Centaur launch and an astronaut in space say that we are a race of intrepid explorers.

The many sounds on the Voyager disks include machines (a rocket, a car shifting gear); natural noises (surf, wind, thunder); birds, animals and whales; and human noises – a baby, laughter, a kiss. Additionally, there are spoken greetings in 55 different languages, from Akkadian (a language spoken 6000 years ago in Sumer) to Wu (a modern Chinese dialect).

Two men in silly outfits proudly display the golden discs that were shot into space aboard the Voyager spacecraft in 1977

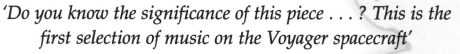

'Do you know the significance of this piece . . . ? This is the first selection of music on the Voyager spacecraft'

SENATOR MATHESON

Little Green Men

The musical portion of the disk begins with the first movement of Bach's Brandenburg Concerto No. 2 in F, performed by the Munich Bach Orchestra – the piece that Senator Matheson played to Mulder. The other tracks include a sampling of music from all over the world. Most are traditional, tribal, classical or opera, but there are also examples of jazz, the blues (Louis Armstrong performing *Melancholy Blues*) and rock and roll (Chuck Berry's *Johnny B. Goode*).

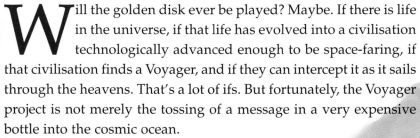

> *'Four and a half billion years from now, when the sun exhausts its fuel and swells to engulf the Earth, this expression will still be out there, travelling. Four and a half billion years. That is . . . if it's not intercepted first'*
>
> SENATOR MATHESON
>
> *Little Green Men*

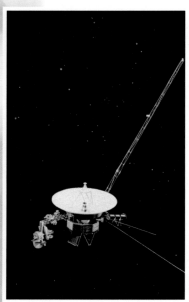

Will the golden disk ever be played? Maybe. If there is life in the universe, if that life has evolved into a civilisation technologically advanced enough to be space-faring, if that civilisation finds a Voyager, and if they can intercept it as it sails through the heavens. That's a lot of ifs. But fortunately, the Voyager project is not merely the tossing of a message in a very expensive bottle into the cosmic ocean.

Both craft continue to gather information and send it back to earth, and they won't stop until they run out of power, some time around 2020. In the course of their glorious careers so far, they have returned more than five trillion bits of scientific data and taught us more about the outer planets than had been garnered in the entire preceding history of astronomy and planetary science.

And no matter the fate of the golden disks, they have already imparted a powerful message, one addressed to ourselves: we are willing to open our minds to extreme possibilities.

A Voyager craft cruises through space with its precious cargo, gathering data all the while

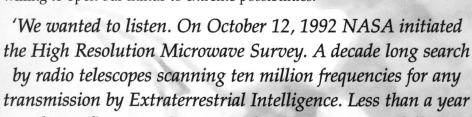

> *'We wanted to listen. On October 12, 1992 NASA initiated the High Resolution Microwave Survey. A decade long search by radio telescopes scanning ten million frequencies for any transmission by Extraterrestrial Intelligence. Less than a year later, first term Senator Richard Bryon successfully championed an amendment which terminated the project'*
>
> MULDER
>
> *Little Green Men*

Since the discovery of radio technology, earth has been sending a balloon of high-frequency microwave signals into space: the cacophonous song of satellites, televisions, radios, microwave ovens, mobile phones, garage-door openers and more.

If there is a technologically advanced civilisation out there, so popular scientific reasoning goes, then they too would emit such signals. Or they may be sending out a 'beacon' signal – one designed to alert other civilisations to their presence, perhaps bearing a message.

In the past three decades, many projects have looked for these signs of extraterrestrial life. But NASA's High Resolution Microwave Survey (HRMS) was to have been the most extensive search ever undertaken.

One group of researchers within the two-pronged project would scan the entire sky for signals coming from any direction. The other would use the most powerful radio telescopes in the world to perform targeted searches of 1000 selected stars: those which seemed to hold the greatest promise of being orbited by potentially inhabited planets.

With digital signal processing systems capable of simultaneously analysing tens of millions of the most promising radio frequency channels, the High Resolution Microwave Survey accomplished more in the first few minutes of operation than the combined effort of all the searches undertaken worldwide during the previous thirty years.

The project was scheduled to continue for a decade. If there was a signal out there, the chances looked good that the HRMS would find it. But almost exactly a year later, Congress directed NASA to discontinue its search for extraterrestrial intelligence, citing pressures on the Federal budget.

A large radio telescope twinkles pleasingly at twilight as it monitors signals from outer space

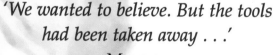

'We wanted to believe. But the tools had been taken away . . .'

MULDER

Little Green Men

Things certainly looked bleak – and absurd. Sixty million dollars had been spent on the project so far. The situation was best summed up by Seth Shostak of the California SETI Institute (a non-profit research body involved in the project), who went on record comparing the situation to 'Financing the Nina, Pinta, and Santa Maria; and then once the ships were built, telling Columbus that times were tight and they were going to mothball the fleet.'

But later that year, the project was partly rescued by funding from private sources, including Arthur C. Clarke. NASA's role has effectively been taken over by the SETI Institute, and the HRMS has been renamed Project Phoenix, having risen from the ashes.

Unfortunately, Phoenix's scope is slightly more limited than its predecessor – the multidirectional search isn't happening. The targeted search, fortunately, looks to be unaffected.

'You have to get to the radio telescope at Arecibo, Puerto Rico'

SENATOR MATHESON

Little Green Men

Just as in *Little Green Men*, the Aricebo observatory, deep in the jungles of Puerto Rico, was the site of the HRMS Targeted Search. It boasts the largest radio telescope of its kind in the world, as well as the most powerful radar system.

One NASA astronomer has compared it to an antenna for the human race to use as its interface with the rest of the universe, in the style of 'those little creatures that walk around using antennae as their primary interface with the rest of the world'.

Aricebo has not only listened: it has spoken. In October 1974, it sent out a 'beacon' signal which should reach some 300,000 stars in about 25,000 years time. The signal consists of a series of transmissions which, when decoded, make up a rather cute little strip of information – via binary data and pixellated pictures – about earth and mankind, looking oddly like graphics from a computer game *circa* the year of transmission. Still, it's the thought, as they say, that counts.

The gargantuan radio telescope dish at Aricebo, Puerto Rico: arguably the provider of our very best chance of picking signals from an unearthly intelligence

Although Mulder finds the Aricebo of *The X-Files* universe eerie and deserted, in our own, it remains a hive of research activity. It is currently being used for the University of California's SERENDIP III SETI project. Eventually, Project Phoenix will move in.

Ongoing upgrades at Aricebo have boosted capabilities, but so far, things have been fairly quiet. The same for Project Phoenix, currently using the giant telescope at Parkes Observatory in Australia, which is able to track 28 million radio frequencies at once. Not so much as a peep from outer space, just plenty of satellites, mobile phones and microwave ovens. 'We can tell when it's dinnertime . . .' offers Parkes astronomer Peter Backus.

'It looks like the "Wow Signal"'

ASTRONOMER DR KIP TROITSKY

'The Wow signal?'

SCULLY

'Ohio State has a radio telescope that conducts electronic searches for extraterrestrial intelligence. In August 1977 my buddy, Jerry Ehman, found a transmission on the printout like this. He was so excited, he wrote "wow" in the margins'

DR TROITSKY

Little Green Men

Ohio State University's telescope, nicknamed 'The Big Ear', is one of the largest in the world. But it is most famous for having picked up the anomalous signal that Dr Troitsky described to Scully.

At 10.16 p.m. on 15 August 1977 the Big Ear received a minute-long signal stronger than any it had heard before – or since. The next morning, astronomer Jerry Ehman studied the computer printout of the previous night's activity. Microwave signal strength is represented by numbers up to 9 and letters thereafter. The natural 'background noise' of space logs in at 1 or 2: anything over 5 is a strong signal. What Ehman saw was a signal that had registered as 6EQUJ5. His legendary scribble was entirely understandable.

The encoded message we sent into outer space in 1974. The upper portion contains various bits of scientific information. The giant vase with a stick in it squashing a headless pin-man on a trampoline is actually a representation of a DNA double-helix, a human and the dish at Aricebo. There may be some very confused aliens out there.

'It came through on the 21-centimeter frequency which no satellite transmitters are allowed to use. Its pattern of passage through the telescope's beam indicated it came from the stars. The signal was intermittent – like morse code. And most importantly, the signal seemed to turn itself on while in the telescope's beam. The "wow signal" is the best evidence of extraterrestrial intelligence . . .'

DR TROITSKY

Little Green Men

The amazing characteristics of the Wow Signal led Robert Dixon, Ohio State's SETI programme director, to confidently assert that it was 'unmistakeably of extraterrestrial origin and had all the hallmarks of coming from an intelligent civilisation'.

But any signal, no matter how exciting, has to be repeatable for science to be interested. A single signal, like the Wow, is considered a 'candidate signal' until picked up again and verified. If nothing else happens, the signal is deemed 'non-repeating data' – scientific jargon for being worth doodly-squat.

Several radio telescopes to date have picked up significant candidate signals. Those received at Harvard's META project occurred only once each, but remain unexplained. The majority, however, have had rather prosaic explanations. The microwave ovens operating in the kitchens of one observatory caused much excitement for a while, and more than once, astronomers have been duped by student pranks.

Still, research continues with enthusiasm – in most quarters, anyway. There is a school of thought which wonders whether we are barking up the right tree, since a technological civilisation may be detectable for only a limited amount of time. The more depressing of the hypotheses is that once a race becomes technologically advanced, it is capable of wiping itself out – and probably will. The cheerier view is that technical sophistication leads to the redundancy of the kind of technology we can hear. For instance, as cable television and fibre-optics become more widespread, our planet will be a great deal quieter. If we were also to become so peaceful that military radar was no longer used, we might appear almost silent from the depths of space.

But it is certainly not worth giving up yet – statistically, our search has barely begun. Of course, there are plenty of conspiracy theories suggesting that the search is already over, and the truth concealed.

One involves a series of signals picked up 30 years ago during Project Ozma, the very first SETI project, and dismissed by the National Science Foundation. Ozma's operations in Virginia were moved to Aricebo shortly afterwards, where, it is claimed, some of the data was classified.

The signals were said to have been backed up by the findings of international scientists, and to have come from the direction of the star Tau Ceti, near the Pisces constellation. Only 11.7 light years distant, Tau Ceti was recently described by David Latham of the Harvard-Smithsonian Centre for astrophysics as 'extraordinarily like our Sun' and 'a very good prospect' for having a planet capable of supporting life – an element which peppers the tale with added intrigue.

> *'The printouts of received transmissions indicate contact with another life form . . .'*
>
> MULDER

Little Green Men

What would happen if any of the SETI projects received a repeatable, artificial signal from outer space? In October 1988, the International Astronomical Congress meeting held in Bangalore, India, accepted a protocol called *The Declaration of Principles Concerning Activities Following the Detection of Extraterrestrial Intelligence.*

The first step would be to confirm beyond reasonable doubt that the signal was not from a natural or earthly source. Once the astronomers who had received it were certain, they would inform the relevant national authority (i.e. NASA in the US) and various independent research bodies who would double check their findings. During this process a heavy veil of secrecy would be drawn.

Once everyone agreed that the signal was what it seemed to be, and word had gone out to the United Nations, space-law organisations and the rest of the astronomical community, it would finally be the public's turn to hear the exciting news.

The protocol states that 'A confirmed detection of extraterrestrial intelligence should be disseminated promptly, openly, and widely through scientific channels and public media, observing the procedures in this declaration. The discoverer should have the privilege of making the first public announcement.'

The protocol states that 'No response to a signal or other

Mulder is determined to find out what is going on at the abandoned Aricebo observatory of the X-Files *universe*

evidence of extraterrestrial intelligence will be sent until appropriate international consultations have taken place.' By the rules stated in another treaty, any communication would have to:

1) be made on the behalf of humanity, 2) be peaceful, 3) be truthful and 4) declare that the people of earth are accepting of differences (which some might say slightly contravenes No. 3).

The protocol was the result of four years of discussion by an international group that included key representatives from the fields of astronomy and space law, as well as the director of the US State Department's Office of Advanced Technology. It aimed to ensure that 'false alarms' would not embarrass the scientific community or disappoint the public and, more importantly, it aimed to leave no room for the kind of political manoeuvring that could cut the scientists out of the picture or have even more frightening implications. A major concern in the SETI field has been that politicians might try to cover up news of significant signals and take the matter of responding into their own hands, for the potential advantages this might give them. And if one country brought in code-breakers to study a 'beacon' signal, earth's communication with the aliens could be snared in the domain of intelligence and counter-intelligence.

'My life has been about the need . . .
to see them again. But what would
I do if they came?'

MULDER

Little Green Men

T he protocol seems to conflict with the recommendations of a report
prepared in the early 1960s by the Brookings Institution think-tank.
This report drew NASA's attention to the possibility that the discovery
of an alien civilisation could have a devastating effect on human society,
destroying our political systems and scientific beliefs. Brookings noted that
the safest course would be to keep such a discovery secret.

But according to those behind Project Phoenix, more recent sociological
studies predict confusion, excitement and a desire for more information, but
little panic or hysteria.

Phoenix's appraisal concludes, 'Analogy is often made to Copernicus'
dramatic new cosmology, which deposed Earth from its throne at the center
of the universe. Another oft-cited historical analog is Charles Darwin's
celebrated hypothesis on biological evolution. To the extent that such analogies
are applicable, they suggest more of a gradual change in world view than a
dramatic upset in the day-to-day conduct of society.'

'The interplanetary explorers of alien civilisation will likely
be mechanical in nature. Yes, anyone who thinks alien
visitations will come not in the form of robots, but in living
beings with big eyes and grey skin has been brainwashed
by too much science fiction'

DR ALEXANDER IVANOV

War of the Coprophages

W hile scientists are excited about the possibilities presented by
SETI, few have time for UFO-related claims as proof of
extraterrestrial life. Most follow the reasoning outlined by Scully
way back in the very first episode of *The X-Files*: unless an alien civilisation
has discovered some way to travel vast distances at enormous speed, they're
not going to get much further in their explorations than we can.

It was this that gave Darin Morgan the idea for another episode that
touches on the hi-tech side of the alien issue. *War of the Coprophages* brings

the Agents to a town gripped by panic over an apparently deadly infestation of cockroaches (see *Mass Hysteria and the Belief Engine*). It turns out that the cockroaches – or some of them, at least – may be intricate space probes, sent to earth by an alien civilisation.

'I don't know how many people got it,' muses Darin Morgan. 'People just said, "Ooh, the cockroaches, they were creepy", and they never really commented on the idea, which I always thought was interesting myself. I guess that's why I wrote it.

'If people say "You know, I was visited by aliens" they don't think about the fact that in order for aliens to get here they would have to possess the technology to go faster than the speed of light, to have some technology that we cannot fathom.

'I'd done some research on artificial intelligence, and there is actually an artificial intelligence guy at MIT (the Massachusetts Institute of Technology) who does robots in the shape of insects. And he did have a kind of arrangement with NASA at one time, the idea being that the farther we try to go out into space, the more practical it is to have machines do it than humans. So you think: if that's true for us, then if there are aliens out there that are trying to get to our planet, they probably would not send live people, they would send robots.'

A Massachusetts Institute of Technology scientist proffers a robotic gnat – one of the smallest robot insects created so far in a project that inspired Darin Morgan to craft the intriguing twist in The War of the Coprophages' *tail*

'I've read about an Artificial Intelligence researcher who designs robots that resemble and behave like insects'
ENTOMOLOGIST DR BAMBI BERENBAUM
War of the Coprophages

Morgan's inspiration was a division at MIT called the Leg Lab, where robots based on insects and other creatures have been built for many years, with the goal of sending them to do things that humans cannot.

The Leg Lab robots had achieved a great deal. In a simulation, one even manoeuvred nicely in zero gravity. But no insect robot at *any* laboratory had managed to recreate the grace, speed and dexterity of its biological cousins. And with good reason: they just didn't move the same way.

The engineers had a good excuse for misjudgment in their early understanding of insect locomotion. Until the inception of Berkeley University's PolyPEDAL lab (PEDAL stands for *Performance, Enegetics and Dynamics of Animal Locomotion*), *nobody* really understood how insects moved.

Under the direction of physiologist Robert Full, the PolyPEDAL lab began to study the locomotive mysteries of arthropods – creatures that move on six legs or more and have external skeletons. 'We don't study arthropods because we like them,' Full points out. 'Many of them are actually disgusting. But they tell us secrets of nature.'

The laboratory's work with cockroaches required the development of special equipment sensitive enough to measure and trace the impact of a cockroach's steps. But the labour paid off. Full and his team amassed reams of data, including the fact that cockroaches are capable of running at five feet per second – a speed recognised by the *Guinness Book of Records* as the fastest of any insect on earth – and that they do so by rearing up and scampering along on their two back legs. They also discovered how roaches climb over huge obstacles so deftly, how they balance, and that they use their legs in pairs, for different purposes.

The PolyPEDAL lab handed their findings over to MIT, who are using them to develop a new generation of robots, with small front legs that act as brakes, longer middle legs capable of pushing in both directions, and even longer rear legs that push the robot roach forward. And who knows, perhaps one day on a far off planet, some extraterrestrial Mulder and Scully will be called in to investigate this strange visitor from outer space.

It is likely, however, that the first robot to explore another planet will be from the stable of an engineer called William 'Red' Whittaker.

Whittaker's first creation, Dante I, was designed with extraterrestrial exploration in mind, but was drafted into service here on earth to explore the interior of volcanoes – a job far too hazardous for humans. In 1994, its successor, Dante II, rappelled 700 ft down the interior wall of Alaska's active

Dante – he may look clunky but he's a dab hand at rappelling down the interior of volcanoes. Some day, one of his younger siblings will explore the surface of another planet

Mount Spurr volcano and crept across the crater floor, gathering samples for researchers monitoring the project in the safety of a trailer 80 miles away. (It was Dante II that inspired another episode of *The X-Files – Firewalker*.)

The Dante robots make it easy to imagine a robotic space-probe. Other robots created by Dante's parent company, the IM Group, include TROV, a remote-controlled submersible robot which has explored beneath the ice of Antarctica (very useful for icy planets) and Ranger, a robot currently under development in cooperation with the University of Maryland Space Systems Laboratory, designed to service satellites.

'Your contract is with NASA?'

MULDER

'The goal is to transport a fleet of robots to another planet, and allow them to explore the terrain, with more intricacy than any space probe has done before . . . this is the future of space exploration'

ROBOTICS EXPERT DR ALEXANDER IVANOV

War of the Coprophages

The first machine that Red Whittaker has proposed to develop for NASA is a big, bug-like, solar-powered planetary rover. 'They want a machine to cope with problems as they arise, traverse a thousand kilometers, and withstand Mars-like conditions,' says Whittaker.

'This machine will walk alone through the Dry Valleys of Antarctica. I'll put down 1000 miles of footprints and do whatever it takes to convince NASA that a robot can explore Mars. It has as much to do with machine decision-making and control as it does with hardware . . . Since the signal takes so long to get from Mars, by the time you see it, that bad step is something that happened 15 minutes ago. For planetary exploration, machine self-reliance and autonomy are critical. Humans can't be there to help.'

Whittaker points out that a robot can do anything a human can – from drilling for core samples to shooting video footage. It can also do much more: scale

At the close of Little Green Men, *a melancholy Mulder, still no closer to the truth, reluctantly returns to the bureaucratic nightmare of an assignment that he abandoned when he fled for Aricebo*

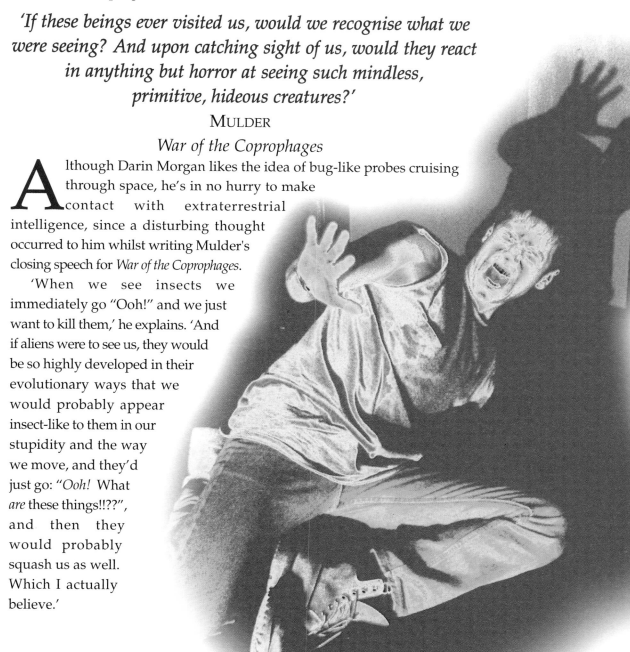

steep inclines, navigate ice and lava and, most importantly, roam a planet ceaselessly, for years at a stretch.

For now, Whittaker's dream is to send a robot to Mars or the Moon, equipped with high resolution stereo cameras and microphones 'to telecast the wonders of being on another world right into our living rooms – a space mission for the people.'

'If these beings ever visited us, would we recognise what we were seeing? And upon catching sight of us, would they react in anything but horror at seeing such mindless, primitive, hideous creatures?'

MULDER

War of the Coprophages

Although Darin Morgan likes the idea of bug-like probes cruising through space, he's in no hurry to make contact with extraterrestrial intelligence, since a disturbing thought occurred to him whilst writing Mulder's closing speech for *War of the Coprophages*.

'When we see insects we immediately go "Ooh!" and we just want to kill them,' he explains. 'And if aliens were to see us, they would be so highly developed in their evolutionary ways that we would probably appear insect-like to them in our stupidity and the way we move, and they'd just go: "*Ooh! What are these things!!??*", and then they would probably squash us as well. Which I actually believe.'

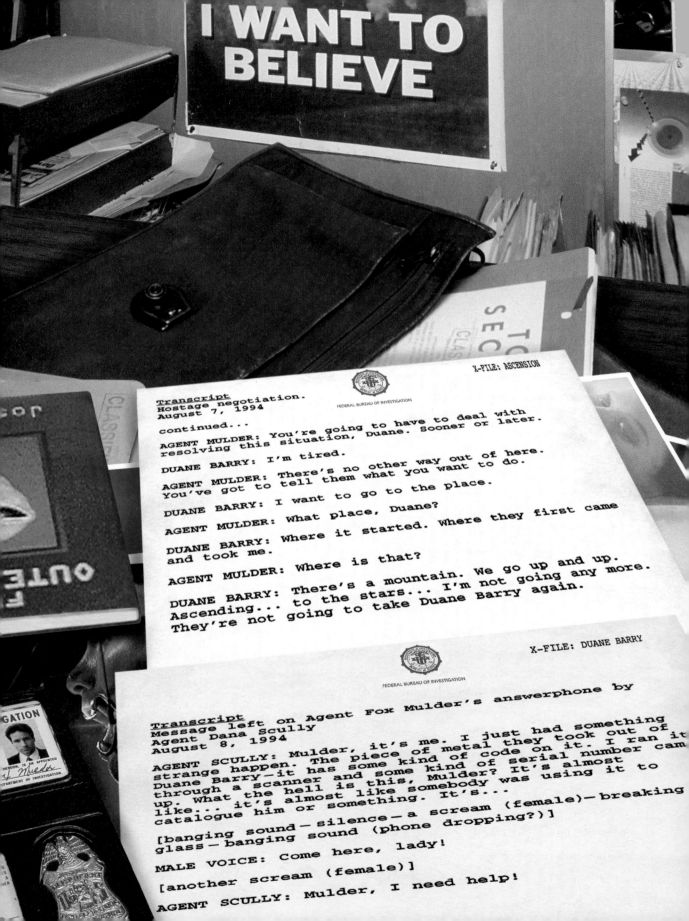

I WANT TO BELIEVE

X-FILE: ASCENSION

FEDERAL BUREAU OF INVESTIGATION

Transcript
Hostage negotiation.
August 7, 1994

continued...

AGENT MULDER: You're going to have to deal with resolving this situation, Duane. Sooner or later.

DUANE BARRY: I'm tired.

AGENT MULDER: There's no other way out of here. You've got to tell them what you want to do.

DUANE BARRY: I want to go to the place.

AGENT MULDER: What place, Duane?

DUANE BARRY: Where it started. Where they first came and took me.

AGENT MULDER: Where is that?

DUANE BARRY: There's a mountain. We go up and up. Ascending... to the stars... I'm not going any more. They're not going to take Duane Barry again.

X-FILE: DUANE BARRY

FEDERAL BUREAU OF INVESTIGATION

Transcript
Message left on Agent Fox Mulder's answerphone by
Agent Dana Scully
August 8, 1994

AGENT SCULLY: Mulder, it's me. I just had something strange happen. The piece of metal they took out of Duane Barry—it has some kind of code on it. I ran it through a scanner and some kind of serial number cam up. What the hell is this, Mulder? It's almost like... it's almost like somebody was using it to catalogue him or something. It's...

[banging sound — silence — a scream (female) — breaking glass — banging sound (phone dropping?)]

MALE VOICE: Come here, lady!

[another scream (female)]

AGENT SCULLY: Mulder, I need help!

ALIEN ABDUCTION

Season two's unforgettable *Duane Barry* begins when the eponymous Barry, a former FBI agent, escapes a psychiatric facility and holds four people hostage in a travel agency. Barry's conviction that he is a victim of alien abduction makes Mulder the ideal man to negotiate with him, and a chain of events is set into motion leading to the most significant and terrifying episode of Scully's life – her own abduction by forces unknown.

Written and directed by Chris Carter, *Duane Barry* is part one of three episodes (followed by *Ascension* and concluding with *One Breath*). 'Besides its significance to the ongoing *X-Files* mythology,' Carter explains, 'the story was very important in terms of practical aspects, since I had to get rid of Gillian [Anderson] so she could have her baby.

'I felt that we had never really done a good abduction story, and I had this idea of a man who believed he had been abducted, had been hospitalised in mental institutions for it, and had broken out.'

'They drilled my teeth! They drilled holes in my damn teeth!'
DUANE BARRY

'The idea of the holes drilled in Barry's teeth came from a story someone told me,' says Carter, 'about a guy who never quite fit into society, who was homeless and used to hang out, for some reason, under big electric power lines and sleep under them. One day he complained to his brother that he was being abducted and holes were being drilled in his teeth. His brother didn't pay any attention until they sent him to the dentist out of the kindness of their hearts, and the dentist called them and said: *Your brother has tiny holes in his teeth that couldn't have been drilled by any of the equipment of modern dentistry.*

John E. Mack

'I've met people who think they are followed by UFOs, and that they've been contacted and still have implants in them. They believe in it so completely, which erodes my scepticism. They seem like credible, normal folk. I have no reason to doubt *them*, it's only my own scepticism that causes me doubt. And I do believe the government's keeping secrets from us, but whether they are keeping *these* secrets from us or not is open to great debate. I read a lot about Dr John Mack – he was one of the guys who originally inspired me, because he was one of the first people to study the alien-abduction syndrome, as he calls it, scientifically. And he found that a lot of people had a kind of collective experience. Certain elements were running through all their experiences, and that's what caused

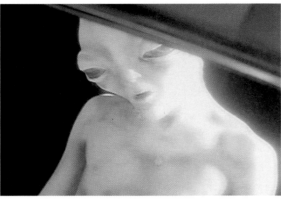

A being from outer space?

him to believe this syndrome was something valid and real. He has taken a lot of flack for it, too.'

Indeed, Mack, a tenured professor of psychiatry at Harvard Medical School and Pulitzer Prize-winning author, laid his prestigious career on the line when he wrote *Abduction: Human Encounters With Aliens*. In 1995 he was almost stripped of his tenure for alleged research improprieties in conjunction with the book. Clearly he was being censured not for his methodology but for his field of study – an outrageous violation of academic freedom. In the end, Mack's right to study whatever he wished was reaffirmed, but he was admonished to observe high standards of conduct in clinical investigations.

Mack, whose case studies include a woman who says she gave birth to a half-alien child and a man who talks of having an alien wife in a parallel universe, told the *New York Times* that alien abductors are from another dimension and are trying to send us a message about our destruction of society and the environment.

'Abduction lore has become so prevalent in our society that if you simply asked someone to imagine what would happen if they were abducted, they would concoct an identical scenario'

SCULLY

Jose Chung's 'From Outer Space'

Season three's *Jose Chung* also featured the abduction phenomenon in a cunningly crafted tale which, like the phenomenon itself, raised fascinating questions about the nature of perception, memory and objective reality.

Alien-abduction reports have never been as abundant as they are today. In the 1950s, 'contactees' told of being whisked away in glittering spaceships, where they were entertained by wise and benevolent 'space brothers' (usually from Mars or Venus), plied with blue cocktails and sometimes enticed into lovemaking. In more recent reports, the aliens have changed their *modus operandi*. They stopped saying they were from Mars or Venus, witheld the blue cocktails, and got decidedly frosty. Lovemaking was out. Clinical procedures and sexual assault were in.

The couple credited with bringing abduction into the Atomic Age were Betty and Barney Hill, who, under hypnosis, supposedly realised years later that in 1961 they had been snatched from their car as they drove through New Hampshire and examined by small entities in a spacecraft. Their story was serialised in 1966 by *Look*, a now defunct high-circulation general-interest magazine. By the time the article was adapted for a film, *The UFO Incident*, interest in the subject was skyrocketing, and the scenario the Hills described had apparently been experienced by others many times over. As Scully notes, the details are familiar to all of us, thanks to such best-selling chronicles as Whitley Strieber's *Communion*, John Mack's *Abduction* and Budd Hopkins's *Intruders*, not to mention a plethora of TV and big-screen movies.

Betty and Barney Hill

If such reports are taken literally, we must assume that extraterrestrial visitors have embarked on a mission to study mankind, their methods unfettered by ethical concerns. David Jacobs, author of the abduction treatise *Secret Life* asserts that the mission is more specific. He told *Fortean Times*: 'The whole focus is on the reproductive function, to produce babies which are hybrids – part human, part alien. We don't know why.

'There are four distinct types of beings involved. About 90% of cases involve the notorious "greys", described as small and hairless with thin limbs, a large bulbous cranium without nose or ears, big black eyes, and a slit for a mouth. The others are said to be reptilian, insect-like, and even humanoid.'

> *'How do they find you each time?'*
> MULDER
> *'Implants. In my gums. Here in my sinus cavity.*
> *And right here, in my belly.'*
> DUANE BARRY
> *Duane Barry*

As real as the abductions seem to their victims, no tangible evidence has ever been obtained. Abductees have reported inexplicable scars, and many claim to have been implanted with tracking devices, but X-rays and medical examinations have proved inconclusive.

'When people talk about hard evidence,' says Jacobs, 'they usually mean artifacts . . . like stealing an alien ashtray. With abductions, though, there is physiological evidence to back up the anecdotal kind. I attest to this myself, having seen people develop scars within a few days. Natural wounds could not heal and scar in such a short space of time.

'There are also implants – objects that have been placed inside the abductees. We have seen little white dots on MRI and CAT scans, and an X-ray of a very complex object lodged inside a woman's nose.'

However, Peter Brookesmith, a respected researcher, believes 'there is no good reason to suppose that the magnetic resonance imaging and other scanned images of "implants" passing around in ufological circles are anything but artifacts of the imaging process itself. And there is nothing to indicate that genuinely mysterious-seeming objects that have popped out of people's bodies are not the byproduct of natural, if not particularly common, events. One no more needs aliens in the explanations than one does in accounting for a limp. The only reason aliens enter the equation is because abduction investigators have put them there.'

Although many abductees claim to have discovered foreign objects under their skin, no record exists of such an object being submitted for analysis and identified as an alien implant. A UFO buff named Richard Price claimed that in September 1955, near a cemetery in Troy, New York, he had encountered two humanoids who took him aboard their craft and injected an implant into his penis. In 1989, whatever was in there finally came out. Price turned over a portion of it to David Pritchard, a scientist at the Massachusetts Institute of Technology. Pritchard found that the object consisted of cotton fibres, presumably from Price's underwear, surrounded by calcified tissue.

An artist's impression of the uniformed beings encountered by Betty and Barney Hill, based on descriptions given by the couple during hypnotic regression

'Before I knew it, I was aboard the hover-vessel and was heading not into Outer Space, but into Inner Space, toward the Earth's molten core, for that is the domain of the third alien, whose name, he soon told me, was . . . Lord Kinbote'

MULDER,
READING FROM THE MANIFESTO OF ROKY CRICKENSON
Jose Chung's 'From Outer Space'

In *Jose Chung*, the hapless Roky carefully records the details of his alien encounter. (The name Lord Kinbote, incidentally, is from writer Darin Morgan's favourite book, Vladimir Nabokov's *Pale Fire*.) Roky's tale, with its Ray Harryhausen-esque beast, subsequent visit from a man-in-black bearing an uncanny resemblance to a well-known US game-show host and other preposterous details, fails spectacularly to fit into the accepted parameters of alien abduction. But in fact the absurd, the bizarre, and deviations from the standard scenario are commonplace.

Horror novelist turned abduction reporter Whitley Strieber (who himself claimed to have been taken by aliens to a locker room and led around by his penis) tells of one report he received: 'A psychiatrist described what she had seen as obvious aliens. She said they looked like the face on the cover of *Communion*. They came be-bopping out of her closet in a conga line, went around the room, and disappeared into the wall of an apartment building outside.'

In another first-person account, *The Alien Jigsaw*, Katharina Wilson describes 119 encounters with aliens over 26 years, which included meetings with the dead, time-travel, psychic experiences, and a vision of an eight-foot-tall floating penguin.

Patrick Huyghe, co-editor of distinguished periodical *The Anomalist*, feels that books like Katharina's are vitally important. He wrote in *Omni* magazine:

'. . . Hearing about alien abductions directly from experiencers reveals aspects of the phenomenon long ignored – or perhaps just swept under the carpet – by most researchers. And in the end, these regularly hidden details may be vital in determining the cause of the UFO abduction phenomenon.

Indeed, as a journalist who's investigated more than my fair share of UFO abductions, I've learned that many aspects of the so-called abduction phenomenon just don't make it into print. Instead, most investigators inevitably process the stories, molding the accounts to fit the theories they favor or the patterns they expect to find. Things that don't fit their preconceived notion of what's really happening 'out there' are often deliberately left out of subsequent retellings of the tale.

Generally lacking in the standard (abduction) scenario . . . is the wide variety of other phenomena that the person often claims to have experienced as well – the psychic perceptions, the premonitions, the bedroom encounters with dead relatives, the ghosts, the time travel, and more. Despite what is often a nearly mind-numbing

Chistopher Walken plays writer Whitley Strieber in the 1989 movie adaptation of Communion . . . Strieber clearly has some kind of potent intergalactic allure (he seems to have so many encounters, why, it's enough to fill the pages of several best-sellers) - a fact that has intrigued many. 'Maybe he's got the most adorable bum in the galaxy,' postulates futurist bon-motician Robert Anton Wilson 'but somehow I doubt that' display of high strangeness, you would be hard pressed to find such descriptions in the published accounts.

In the standard abduction scenario, as brought to us by the 'experts,' these messy details are summarily expunged. What we are left with is a cleaned-up story, a tale that stays unerringly "on mark," thus fitting the desired "alien" mold . . .'

Certainly the 'big three' of alien abduction research – David Jacobs, John Mack and Budd Hopkins – continue to present us with a neatly-defined phenomenon. Hopkins can look forward to another bestseller thanks to his investigation of a case known as 'the Brooklyn Bridge abduction'.

In 1988, New Yorker Linda Cortile read *Intruders* and came across the concept of alien implants. Having a strange lump on her nose and long suspecting the involvement of intergalactic hanky-panky, she contacted Hopkins and joined his abductee support group. On 30 November 1989 an agitated Linda called Hopkins to report she had been abducted again, sometime around 3.00 a.m.

Under hypnosis, Linda revealed that five creatures had led her out of the closed window of her twelfth-floor apartment. She levitated across the sky

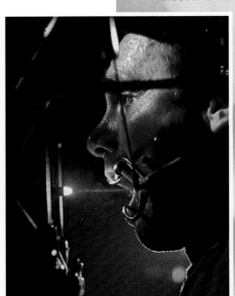

and into a spacecraft which hovered over the Brooklyn Bridge before plunging into the East River. Inside, creatures took skin samples and pounded an instrument up and down her spine.

The *pièce de resistance* concerns the incident's alleged witnesses, who included two government security agents and a man Hopkins will identify only as a 'very important political person' – but whom insiders say he has named as Javier Perez de Cuellar, secretary-general of the United Nations from 1982 to 1991.

Hopkins claims the two agents sent him a letter describing their sighting, and Linda says one, known as Dan, has been psychotically harrassing her ever since. Although they would not identify the VIP, the agents said they had been escorting him in a limousine to a helipad at the South Street Seaport at the time of Linda's abduction.

A United Nations spokesperson conceded that de Cuellar *had* been in New York on that date, but said he was unlikely to have been out at that time of the morning. No doubt Hopkins regards this as a cover-up, as well as reports that Linda, in the days before the alleged incident, had been reading *Nighteyes*, a science-fiction novel by Garfield Reeves-Stevens that bears striking resemblances to her tale.

'What's your opinion of hypnosis?'
JOSE CHUNG
'I know it has therapeutic value, but it's never been proven to enhance memory. In fact, it can actually worsen it, since people in that state are prone to confabulation'
SCULLY

Jose Chung's 'From Outer Space'

Very few abductees recall their experiences spontaneously. The vast majority 'recover' memories through regression hypnosis, although many say that once their 'repressed' memories are unblocked, they can recall the incidents clearly.

The story goes that the aliens block recollections of the occurrence, perhaps planting a false memory or two; apparently, some abductees seek help because of 'missing time', or a vague notion that *something* untoward has happened to them.

All this would be astonishing if repressed memory was an accepted phenomenon and hypnotic regression a dependable practice. They are not.

'Despite many attempts, not a single experiment has ever shown that repressed memories exist,' explains neuroscientist Dr Michael Persinger. 'If you look at examples in the clinical literature you find that there are only two or three cases . . . and they were non-verifiable. That's why most states in the US are now no longer accepting so-called recovered memories, information obtained in therapy, as objective evidence. But it's become a part of folk psychology.'

Alien abduction is not the only field of study whose findings depend heavily on the veracity of recovered memory. FBI Agent Ken Lanning spent years investigating a multitude of alleged Satanic ritual abuse incidents 'remembered' in the same way and found not a scrap of evidence that the incidents had taken place.

In both fields, we are meant to believe that thousands of people, with no prior recollection of what happened to them, have their memories unblocked by therapists. Some people recover memories of Satanic ritual abuse, others alien abduction. But miraculously, these two groups are neatly divided between the therapists who specialise in their particular trauma. Hopkins, Mack and Jacobs, for instance, don't seem to be finding any cases where patients turn out to have been abused by Satanists instead of aliens.

'There are certain indications that tell you that the memories are probably hyatrogenic,' says Persinger. 'That is, they're produced by the clinical process. In studies of all the verifiable traumas, *people don't forget*. If suddenly you have this entire epidemic of people who say "I don't remember anything and now I remember because I went to a clinician" then you're dealing with the very high likelihood that most of those cases were created by the therapy.

'One thing we know very clearly is that memory is not stored like a videotape. It is constantly reconstructed. A lot of people have tried this experiment: you take a metronome that's ticking once a second and tell someone under hypnosis that it's slowed down to once a minute. They will then experience sixty seconds as a whole hour. And if you ask the person to describe what they did, they'll give you an hour's worth of fantasy. The imagery generated under hypnosis has a great deal of believability.'

He adds that fantasies generated under hypnosis can have extreme emotional intensity and be accompanied by tears and panic. But what about the apparently spontaneous recall once the memories have been 'unblocked'?

'Once a piece of information is consolidated it's very difficult to change it. That's why the false memory is such a big problem: once it becomes true to the person, it's no different from any other kind of memory.

Mulder risks life and limb in his valiant attempt to save Scully from abduction in Ascension

'It's easy to produce pseudo memories. It's so easy it's scary. We have a thing called "village story" which is a five-minute narrative about a young kid who comes home and his sister is crying and he goes to bed and he wakes up in the middle of the night and he feels a presence and he smells a smell; he feels like something is trying to smother him, he feels vibrations on his body and he gets sick and then he feels pleasurable and he wants his Mom and he wakes up the next morning with some scars or erethemic reactions on his body and he goes to see his Dad, who tells him to be quiet.

'It's an ambiguous situation, and in fact it describes a complex partial seizure in a child (with some extraneous details), but all you have to do is put a label on it – imply that it was either sex abuse or an alien abduction – then ask people next week to remember the story, and they'll recall it according to the label you placed on it. It's remarkable. You can get pseudo memories like that and people are *convinced* they remember that Dad went in there and did it, or damn it, there was an alien – all because of the powerful effect of a label.

'The reason we do that is to recreate what happens in the therapeutic setting. If someone says, "I know why you're unhappy: this happened. Can you remember this the first time?" usually people say no. Then when they come back they say, "Yeah, I remember that now" and they do . . . and before you know it you've got a completely new memory.'

Psychologist Robert Baker's 'Lost In A Shopping Mall' study showed that childhood memories could be implanted by the power of suggestion. Patients who had never been lost as children were asked if they could remember such an incident and eventually 'recalled' it clearly, chattering away with details. Baker says hypnosis simply enhances suggestability. 'Hypnosis is nothing but the turning on of the human imagination. And that can be turned on best by getting them in a relaxed state and providing them with suggestions.'

'It doesn't have to be therapy, either,' adds Dr Persinger. 'It could be exposure to television, society, the media in general. No one is lying. It's just that memories are reconstructed. You change how you remember the past.'

Jody, a Florida housewife who has gone on television to describe a series of alien abductions, said her own 'recall' was prompted by reading Budd Hopkins' *Intruders*. 'I always knew that something had happened,' she says. 'There was a presence in my room. . . but I had no way to categorize it until I read the book.'

> *'Sometimes when you want to believe so badly. . . you end up looking too hard'*
>
> SCULLY
>
> *Duane Barry*

The results of a 1991 Roper Organization survey of almost 6000 Americans were widely interpreted as proof that a surprising number of citizens have been abducted by aliens. Designed by Jacobs and Hopkins, the poll allegedly pinpoints people who have been abducted but whose memories have been erased. The following were used as positive indicators; 0.3% of respondents, corresponding to 560,000 adult Americans, said at some point all five had happened to them:

- Waking up paralyzed with a sense of a strange person or presence or something else in the room.
- Experiencing a period of time of an hour or more in which you were apparently lost, but you could not remember why or where you had been.

- Feeling that you were actually flying through the air although you didn't know how or why.
- Seeing unusual lights or balls of light in a room without knowing what was causing them or where they came from.
- Finding puzzling scars on your body and neither you nor anyone else remembering how you received them or where you got them.

Several or all of these could as easily refer to normal phenomena associated with hypnogogic states, sleep paralysis, hallucinations or dreaming (see *Perchance to Dream*). Dr Persinger notes the close relationship between the abduction experience and the incubus/succubus visitation, and his own experiments have proven that electro-magnetic stimulation of the brain can reproduce a completely 'real' experience of this kind (see *In Search of the Truth*). He has also found that epileptic-type activity in the same area of the brain can lead to physical responses such as 'unexplained' scarring (see *Miraculous Wounds*) and posits that the Earth's natural electromagnetic charges – particularly at night – can trigger all of the aforementioned effects. Moreover, these natural forces are also responsible for balls of light.

But Jacobs, undeterred, backs up the survey's astounding numbers: 'This of course is consistent with what the abductees themselves tell us. They come into a room and see 50, 75, or 100 other people lying on tables, and they report a constant stream of people. And we figure it's twenty-four hours a day, seven days a week.'

If you expand these figures to the rest of the world, and try to factor in the number of aliens required for processing all these subjects, you end up with one of the largest industries on Earth going undetected by the majority of the populace. Dennis Stacy, editor of a monthly UFO publication, *The MUFON Journal*, crunched the numbers and refuted the poll's findings: 'Think of the logistics such a fantastic undertaking would involve. UFOs would be stacked up over the world's major metropolitan areas, awaiting landing and abduction rights, like so many 747s.'

'The government knows about it, y'know. They're even in on it sometimes. Right in the room when they come . . . The government knows why they're here but they can't dare let the truth out'
DUANE BARRY

Duane Barry voices *The X-Files* mythology, in which those in power might be cooperating with aliens in exchange for . . . what? Technology? Information? Campaign funds? Or are they simply being extorted; paying 'protection' in a sense?

Jacobs, who might be expected to be a prime target of a CIA disinformation campaign, asserts 'Neither Budd [Hopkins] nor myself, nor any of our abductees have ever been interfered with by any official of any kind . . . I believe the subject is, at best, regarded with indifference by the government because the scientific world is generally sceptical.'

> *'Some alien encounters are hoaxes, perpetrated by your government to manipulate the public. Some of these hoaxes are intentionally revealed to manipulate truth-seekers, who become discredited if they disclose the deliberately absurd deception'*
>
> MAN IN BLACK
> *Jose Chung's 'From Outer Space'*

There are plenty of conspiracy theorists who heartily support the scenario put forward in *Jose Chung*. Indeed, Barney Hill, father of all abductees is often cited as an 'example'. Hill was an active member of the civil rights group the NAACP (National Association for the Advancement of Coloured People) and the theory goes that some shadowy faction of the powers-that-be decided to bring Hill into disrepute by kidnapping him and his wife (using some kind of sonic weapon to knock them unconscious in their car), hypnotising them and implanting memories of something that at the time was outrageous and unheard of.

Whatever started the abduction syndrome epidemic, there is clearly *something* weird going on. Carl Sagan – author, Cornell University professor and internationally respected scientist – deconstructs the conundrum: 'There are two stories: One is we're being sexually abducted by beings from other worlds; and the other is that there's a pervasive, common hallucination that at least thousands of humans share. These are both disquieting possibilities.'

Another artist's impression of Barney and Betty Hill's abductors. Some have posited that the Hills were kidnapped not by aliens but by some all-too-earthly agency, who later implanted memories of aliens via hypnosis - a theory echoed in Jose Chung's 'From Outer Space'

INSIDE THE FBI

'No institution in America is as powerful. No institution generates as much curiosity, fear, and excitement. No institution holds as many secrets.'

When Ronald Kessler, author and premier authority on the Federal Bureau of Investigation, wrote these words at the start of 1993, it would have been hard to imagine that anything could make the FBI any *more* intriguing to the public. Or that by the end of the year, the names of Fox Mulder and Dana Scully would leap to mind in connection with the Bureau as readily as that of J. Edgar Hoover.

J. Edgar Hoover in 1936. On the right, appropriately, is Hoover's right-hand man, Clyde Tolson

'I heard reports of several UFO sightings here last night. Did you see anything?'

MULDER

'Not personally, sir, but we did receive a lot of calls . . . The FBI keeps tabs on this sort of thing?'

SHERIFF FRASS

'No'

MULDER

War of the Coprophages

As every dedicated X-Phile knows by now, the real FBI does not have an X-Files department. And no, they don't investigate alien cases. There's one simple reason, according to an inside source: 'It's a matter of jurisdiction. If aliens were to land in the US, it would be a case for Naturalization and Immigration. The aliens would have to be transporting stolen goods across the state lines for the FBI to get involved.'

'There seems to be a case developing around the elephant that escaped your zoo'

SCULLY

Fearful Symmetry

Of course, *The X-Files* is a drama, not a documentary series. The stories are not pulled from the files of the FBI, but from the imagination of Chris Carter and his talented team of writers. But for the benefit of

Mulder and X have a heated disagreement

any Lone-Gunmen types, suspicious of a cover-up, Colonel Robert Ressler, a twenty-year FBI veteran, confirms that neither he nor his colleagues have ever encountered a case resembling any of Mulder and Scully's. Particularly not, he adds (referring to *The Host*), 'some sort of a mutated slug coming out of the sewer'.

'Protocol requires any criminal investigation of military personnel to be conducted through military channels . . .'

CAPTAIN JANET DRAPER

'What? We didn't sign in at the front desk?'

MULDER

'You are in breach of code and procedure'

CAPTAIN DRAPER

The Walk

In order for Mulder and Scully to investigate some of the cases allocated to the X-Files, it becomes necessary for them to circumvent the limits of their jurisdiction. 'There's no business for the FBI to get involved in many of the things that these two get involved in,' says Ressler. In *War of the Coprophages*, for instance, 'Scully was in some sort of 7-11 store and there was some panicking going on. She says: "FBI! Everybody settle down! I'm in charge here!" I thought, "You're in charge of what? Panic in the 7-11?"'

But even real-life G-men and women are untroubled by the odd bit of artistic licence – the word is that many of them (including some high-ranking officials) are huge fans of the show. And for the layman, the skill of its writers ensures

X saves Mulder's life in 731

that the pretexts for the Agents' investigations are plausible.

Apparently, however, we know less about the FBI than we might imagine. 'I would say maybe 95% of people have no idea what the FBI is,' estimates Ressler. 'They have no idea who they work for. They don't know what they do. They don't know their jurisdiction.'

There would probably have been a great deal within The X-Files of which Hoover would not have approved, including the sometimes unorthodox actions of Mulder, Scully and Skinner and the powerful influence on FBI business of agents from shadowy factions, like Mr X

So what is the FBI? Who *do* they work for? What *do* they do? And what, if not the local 7-11, is their jurisdiction?

> *'A true piece of history, Scully, the very first X File . . .*
> *created by J. Edgar Hoover himself in 1946'*
>
> MULDER
>
> *Shapes*

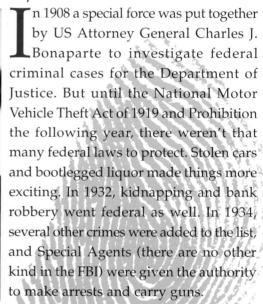

In 1908 a special force was put together by US Attorney General Charles J. Bonaparte to investigate federal criminal cases for the Department of Justice. But until the National Motor Vehicle Theft Act of 1919 and Prohibition the following year, there weren't that many federal laws to protect. Stolen cars and bootlegged liquor made things more exciting. In 1932, kidnapping and bank robbery went federal as well. In 1934, several other crimes were added to the list, and Special Agents (there are no other kind in the FBI) were given the authority to make arrests and carry guns.

In 1935, the organisation was officially dubbed the Federal Bureau of Investigation. Its motto: Fidelity, Bravery, Integrity.

By the end of World War II the FBI's tentacles stretched all the way down to South America. But it was in the 1950s and 60s that what had by then become known as 'Hoover's FBI' came into its own. J. Edgar Hoover began his 48-year tenure as Godfather of all Special Agents in 1924. For five decades, until his death in 1972, he was one of the most powerful men in America.

His prime directive was 'Don't embarrass the

Bureau'. Special Agents (invariably white males) had to fall within a certain height/weight ratio, wear dark-coloured suits, white shirts and never, ever sport argyle socks. (An odd rule indeed, coming from a man alleged to enjoy wearing dresses in his spare time.) It also meant that drug-related cases were ignored, because they might 'taint' Hoover's men.

Special Agents spent much of their time on auto theft cases (often over the heads of the local police who, as a result, still bear an anti-FBI grudge decades later) and on tracking draft dodgers, in order to impress Congress with the Bureau's crime-solving statistics and assure continued funding.

They also carried out 'background checks' on public figures and pursued both groups and individuals whom Hoover considered 'politically objectionable'. In the early civil rights era of the 1950s and the political turmoil of the 1960s, that meant anyone from religious leaders to actors, to doctors, newsmen, lawyers, and teachers. Ernest

Hemingway, Janis Joplin, Jane Fonda, William Kunstler, Martin Luther King and Charlie Chaplin were amongst those on whom the FBI held files. A 'Security Index' and a 'Communist Index' listed people who were to be arrested in a case of national emergency. At its peak the list included around 500,000 names. Nor was the information always compiled in a constitutional manner. 'Black Bag Jobs' (breaking in to a target's home or office to rifle through his belongings) and illegal phone taps were common.

'Hoover was a master of publicity and manipulation,' says Ressler. 'Under Hoover there would be no *X-Files*. Under Hoover they had *The FBI* with Efrem Zimbalist Junior. Every episode had to be approved by the FBI before it could even go on the air and Efrem Zimbalist Jr had to pass a background investigation. You could have nothing in your background that Hoover

A rare photograph of the FBI's training academy in Quantico, Virginia

would consider to be checkered. He just would not allow that person to be in that segment. Any of today's stars, like Jodie Foster [who portrayed Agent Clarice Starling in *Silence of the Lambs*] – if she'd ever smoked a joint, she'd be out. That's the way Hoover ran things.'

'Hoover kept a tight rein on Hollywood. On everything. Since Hoover's gone it's just up for grabs.'

'You could request a transfer to Quantico . . .'

SCULLY

The Host

On 5 May 1972, three days after Hoover's death, the FBI's legendary Academy opened at Quantico, Virginia. Not merely the place where new agents receive their 15-week training, Quantico was to become a centre for some of the most innovative crime-solving techniques ever developed. A 385-acre compound in the heart of the Quantico Marine base, the Academy consists of a 21-building complex housing all the tools (and toys) a budding crime solver could wish for.

Hogan's Alley, for example, is a perfect replica of a small American town, complete with a pool hall, a laundry, a restaurant, a hotel, a movie theater (showing *Manhattan Melodrama* – the flick that was playing when the G-Men shot Dillinger outside the Biograph in Chicago) and, most important of all, a bank. The town is used by FBI trainees to simulate foiling robberies, negotiating with hostage takers, enduring stake-outs and executing search warrants. Citizens of nearby real towns are paid an hourly rate to act as criminals.

'I'm constantly amazed by you. Working down here in the basement, sifting through files and transmissions that would end up in any other agent's garbage'
SCULLY
'That's why I'm in the basement, Scully'
MULDER
Piper Maru

'Hogan's Alley' – the pretend town nestling within the Quantico complex

If there were an X-Files unit in the FBI it almost certainly *would* be in the basement, and according to Robert Ressler, people like Mulder and Scully would indeed be regarded with some trepidation. 'Mulder and Scully are supposed to be in this secret unit that's even too weird for the Behavioral Science Unit . . . which a lot of people look at as being *very* weird . . .'

Ressler explains that in his own FBI career, just like Mulder and Scully, 'I was

A plaque presented to Colonel Robert Ressler on his retirement from the FBI

constantly under attack from the bureaucracy because I was doing things they couldn't understand.' The difference, he says, is that 'I could go to any field office and I could interface with my colleagues because I came from a similar background, a military background. I've got a lot of things under my belt which they could relate to. But within the FBI, Mulder and Scully would both be outcasts . . . They would definitely have problems with the normal agents.'

What was eventually to become the Behavioral Science Unit – Mulder's Alma Mater – was unofficially started at the FBI's Washington headquarters by Howard Teten and Pat Mullany (see *Looking Into the Abyss*). But the fledgling BSU really picked up speed when it found its new home in, yes, the basement at Quantico.

'A hierarchy exists in the FBI, isn't that right? A man has status, like yourself, the Assistant Director. Those under him obey his orders, right?'

MYSTERIOUS MEMBER OF THE INTELLIGENCE COMMUNITY

(TO SKINNER)

Piper Maru

In one sense a new era of crime detection had begun – but old problems remained. Many, like Ressler, think the very structure of the FBI is to blame. The Bureau is divided into support personnel – from secretaries to high level scientists – and the two classifications of Special Agent: administrators and investigators.

'Within the Agent classification,' says Ressler, 'it's pretty much the administrators against the investigators. What it amounts to is that a Street Agent has the same origin as the Assistant Directors of the FBI and all the other big shots. You all come in together on one plane and then the administrators will break away and go up the administrative ladder.

'The real problem is that a lot of the time the reason they break away is that the administrators cannot master the investigative skills . . . Successful investigators can go through a full career and retire as a Special Agent street investigator. A lot of the guys that have gone up the ladder did not get that fulfilment. They were poor investigators.

'You end up with guys up at headquarters that are just off the wall. I mean they couldn't find their ass with both hands in a well-lit room and yet they're telling guys in the field how to conduct their investigation. It provokes a lot of animosity between the guys in the street that are making the Bureau what it is and the guys that are up there pretending that they're running the show.'

> *'You still don't see, do you? Closing the X-Files, separating you and Scully . . . was just the opening gambit'*
>
> X
>
> *Sleepless*

The bureaucratic roadblocks that Mulder and Scully encounter so often in *The X-Files* do happen within the FBI. Confirms Ressler: 'There are people that will throw up roadblocks just because they don't like you.'

The BSU itself came in for its share of resentment from the kind of administrator 'who sits back and says, "Boy, that Behavioral Science Unit is getting too much attention. I think we need to shut them off. I think they have too many people."

Mulder and Scully at work in their basement office at FBI headquarters in Washington. Like the X-Files division, the Behavioral Science Unit was tucked away in the basement, and was at first regarded with suspicion

'Mullany was really visible for a period in 1977. He was in *Newsweek* and *US News* and *World Report*. A lot of media were trying to get hold of him. This guy down at the Academy – they used to call him the Empty Suit – he said "I think Mullany better take some vacation." He literally cut him off from the media because he was jealous of Mullany's accomplishment. You get a lot of that in the Bureau.

'This FBI is a hotbed of internal squabble. They spend more time fighting each other than they do fighting crime.'

'Let me take this down to ballistics. They'll clear this all up in a second'

SCULLY

Duane Barry

That is not to say that the FBI is no more than a petty, bureaucratic nightmare. There is some phenomenal work coming out of the Bureau. Their laboratory is one of the largest and most comprehensive in the world. It can work miracles, seemingly pulling vital clues out the air and lifting fingerprints off water. And the post-Hoover era has seen some very creative crime-solving. The FBI has worked with hypnotists, for example, to help witnesses remember licence plates and with psycholinguists to 'read between the lines' of ransom notes and letters to the police.

'The good thing about the FBI,' says Ressler 'is that it draws a lot of good people. And it sets up situations like the Behavioral Science Unit and the laboratory where they're for the most part left alone. The environment is conducive to doing good work and they've got the funds and resources.'

'There's been a mistake here. Another agent's been attached to the case'

MULDER

'That would be me. I'm Krycek. Alex Krycek'

KRYCEK

Sleepless

So what kind of 'good people' are drawn to the FBI? Still over 80% white males, the Bureau is actively recruiting women, minorities and the disabled. (Which might explain how Mulder got around the colour-blindness test.)

Applicants can expect to have everything from their credit rating to their academic record checked. Their neighbours will be questioned and applicants themselves have to pass not only a written test and an interview but a physical – with a drug test – as well.

New recruits must be between 23 and 37 and hold a degree from a four year college. The average age is 29. Only 1 in 20 applicants is accepted. The odds are better if you are an accountant or a lawyer – they make up over one third of all Special Agents.

'I'm Agent Dana Scully. This is Agent Mulder. We're with the FBI'

SCULLY

Fearful Symmetry

Would Mulder and Scully make the grade? Ressler isn't convinced. 'They make me nervous. They really do,' he says good-naturedly, stepping into a supervisorly mode. 'Mulder's always getting sick and falling down and getting hurt.'

But despite the Agents' weekly trials and tribulations, *The X-Files* seems to have become something of a recruitment campaign for the FBI. Interest has never been higher. Applications are up. And the Bureau isn't complaining.

Their only wish, however, is that helpful members of the public would refrain from telephoning to alert them to supernatural occurrences. If you have a paranormal problem and are wondering who you're gonna call, don't make it the FBI – they simply don't have the jurisdiction, the time or the resources to help out. Or, as a rather weary spokeswoman recently informed a journalist: 'We don't want your alien.'

IN SEARCH OF THE TRUTH

Sceptics in the paranormal field are quick to remind believers that extraordinary claims require extraordinary evidence. And many insist that the burden of proof rests with the believer. But not all. There are sceptics who, like Scully, wade boldly into the murky world of the unexplained, meticulously applying the scientific method in dogged pursuit of answers.

In Volume One, we met four real-life Mulders. Here, in their own words, four Scully counterparts describe their quests.

JAMES RANDI

For many years, James Randi, now 67, was best known as a magician, The Amazing Randi. Today he is one of the world's leading investigators of paranormal claims.

Randi's crusade for truth began at the age of 15 when he exposed the simple magic trick performed by a local evangelist who claimed miraculous powers. The young Randi was booed by the congregation and hauled to the police station.

A founding member of CSICOP – the Committee for the Scientific Investigation of Claims of the Paranormal – Randi has written several books exposing supernatural misinformation, formed an educational foundation, and travels the world conducting lectures and testing paranormal claims. He offers a standing bounty (now at $670,000) to anyone who can perform a paranormal feat under controlled conditions.

'I am an investigator of unusual things. I am not a debunker: that would mean having the attitude when I go in that I want to disprove. This is not so and it's a luxury that no scientific thinker can possibly afford. The ideal attitude is: I don't know if there is anything there. Let me take a look.

'My $670,000 is a way to put the money where the mouth is. I only have $10,000 in it: others have pledged various sums, and all, I think, are quite willing to lose it.

'I talked with one gentleman yesterday who told me "This will certainly be the best $5,000 I will have ever spent, because I will have had something to do with revealing something that has never been proven before – it would be very exciting." And then he added what I have always added: "I don't need this to make my life exciting. Sunsets are enough, and morning glories and newborn babies; but if it does come along it would make things just that little bit more interesting."

'I've tested hundreds of people – hundreds – and they all have fallen on their collective nose.

'There's always an excuse. Jupiter is in Sagittarius, it's too dark, too light, too hot, too cold, or "you are putting out negative vibrations". So I leave and have somebody else test them and apparently that person's putting out negative vibrations too. The reason is never, "I don't have the power".

'The vast majority aren't charlatans: they are self-deceived.

'Think about psychics. People never tell them: *No, that's absolutely 100% wrong, you are a terrible psychic.* They bear with it until the psychic gets round to something they *do* recognise and they sit there happily nodding and smiling and the psychic has reason to believe he has got the power.

'My foundation will be funding original parapsychological research. Things like dowsing and acupuncture have never been subjected to proper double-blind tests. People have always just accepted them: they're very old so they must be true. But the idea that the Earth is flat is also very old.

'I think that any misinformation has potential for damage. Things like astrology can be the thin end of the wedge. If you look at the astrology column and you don't bother to look at the other signs to see what might apply to you, or compare horoscopes from newspaper to newspaper – and often they are diametrically opposite – then you tend to accept it. You can say it's harmless fun, but it can lead you into the habit of accepting things without looking at them with a critical eye.

'People say it's like going from coffee to heroin. There are a lot of steps in between, but it *can* happen. I just got a letter from this poor woman who started out having her horoscope read at the local carnival, and has now been swindled out of all her savings by psychics.

'I would like to change the laws on fraud. Certainly people have the right to believe that they are psychic, but they don't have the right to sell psychic powers if it's shoddy goods. If a fellow is selling me a Stradivarius, I want to know that it's not a fiddle that he got out of his attic, and I can have him arrested and charged with fraud if it is. But I can't do that with psychics if they fail to do what they say they can.

'I'm trying to impress on legislators that this is an important matter. So far I have totally failed. Politicians tell me: "If people want to be stupid let them be stupid. People like to believe these things." They're in the business of getting re-elected and seem to think they don't have any responsibility.

'I'd also like to see legislation for truthfulness in the mass media. I just came back from Japan, where I tested this young girl psychic in a TV studio. It took 6 hours, because she insisted on taking breaks and just tiring the audience out until they weren't paying attention. But my eyes were glued on her, and they had a camera that went around behind her and caught her at her trickery. The audience giggled and pointed at the big screen in the studio where they could see her peeking at this little card to see what was written on it.

'I made a speech at the close of the programme in which I described how her trick was done and the host of the programme agreed. When the programme was broadcast they presented it that I had lost the challenge and she had won. They showed me saying hello and goodbye, and cut out my speech and the host's input.

'If a programme is clearly for purposes of entertainment, like *The X-Files*, I have no problem. Otherwise, it should be a legislated responsibility to tell the truth about these things.

'But my primary goal is to educate. We are setting courses for schools on critical thinking. I often do a little experiment: look over to some object at the left of your vision and focus on it, then look over to an object at the right. Did you see what was in between? Your eyes did but your brain didn't. You don't need it, that's not what you are concentrating on, so your brain says "don't process this". It's just an indication of how you are not seeing reality, just perceiving what you need of it in order to function.

'Of course the magician depends a great deal on that: you won't necessarily believe something he tells you, but you'll believe the conclusion you have come to on the evidence of your own senses. This is true of a lot of paranormal performers, too.

'I feel that people are being lied to, and cheated, and if, by speaking up, I can get someone into a process of thinking about things before accepting them, I've won a victory.'

DR MICHAEL PERSINGER

Dr Michael Persinger, Professor of Neuroscience at Laurentian University in Sudbury, Canada, was one of the first to put forward the theory that activity in the Earth's geomagnetic field may hold the key to a plethora of paranormal experiences. He has gone on to construct electro-magnetic devices with which he can stimulate the human brain, inducing many of these experiences at will in his subjects – a discovery with remarkable implications.

'Ultimately, all experience comes from the brain; so we want to determine what patterns of electrical activity in the brain generate certain experiences. The idea is that if we could reproduce those patterns artificially, we should be able to induce the same experiences. And we can. We can generate near death experiences. We can generate the sensation of a presence – that there's an entity with you. We can generate almost any kind of experience you want, including fear.

'There's no danger . . . the electro-magnetic fields we use are less than that generated by a hair drier. The critical thing is the information in them, translated into the language of the brain.

'We let nature show us how. If you look carefully at the geomagnetic data for the last forty or fifty years, you see that there are certain kinds of events

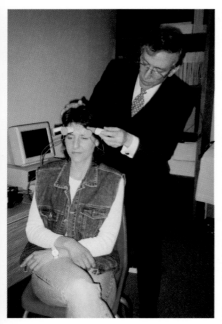

that occur with geomagnetic activity, including unusual phenomena. It would be inappropriate to say that geomagnetic activity does it all. But it's important because it influences the subtle processes that go on in the brain . . .

'We found in our studies, for instance, that the periods where there's an increase in geomagnetic activity during the night will produce what's called "post-mortem apparitional experiences". Not ghosts so much as one-off visitations by people who have just died. Studies have shown that when these occur, it's usually within three or four days of the death. And we've actually mapped out that if there's a geomagnetic storm or an increase in geomagnetic activity during those first three days after a bereavement, the likelihood of having a post-mortem apparition goes up. It's usually during the night; very vivid, and the person thinks it's real.

'This kind of "visitation" has a tremendous impact on the grieving process. The person feels better. That's one of the reasons we're studying it. Imagine if we could do the same thing therapeutically in a fifteen minute brain simulation . . .

'I don't think it's a major issue that people would know the experience was artificially created. These experiences are so intense that people will say: *yes, I know what you did, but I know what I feel.*

'The implications of this discovery are significant. It doesn't necessarily demean the importance of the experiences . . . but it tells us there's a brain basis to it. It also tells you that it's technically possible to manipulate it. Now, you can argue: Well, how do you know that it's not God doing it, or some other kind of extra-terrestrial process and the answer is you don't. And in the final analysis we're not really interested in that. We're interested in the part of the brain that mediates the experience.

'What we call telepathy or clairvoyance is another phenomenon that seems to be intrinsic to the species, and whatever it is, it is also tied to something in the geomagnetic field. When does it occur? Usually at night. What is the typical theme? Death and crisis. People say: I had a sudden vision in my mind's eye, or a gut feeling. Mostly it's about members of the immediate family; next most common is friends, then acquaintances. Rarely strangers. It's clearly tied to something we call bonding.

'Many species – fish for instance – communicate using electromagnetic fields. Is there anything that would allow all human beings to be enmeshed in the same environment? Yes – the geomagnetic field. Now, does that mean that all brains are interconnected? Well, yes, by definition. So therefore when someone dies who is significant to you, you might experience some sign of it.

'You would expect that if there was an interference in the geomagnetic field, that should decrease the number of cases where people get this kind of sign, and the answer is yes, that's one of the most profound things we found. We found it in all the data from this century and the last, and moreover we find it in the data from telepathy studies. In one study they had unbelievable "hits" some nights, other nights just nothing. They scratched their heads for many years until we looked at the data. Sure enough, the nights when there were magnetic storms were hopeless. The nights where they had unbelievable hits were the most quiet geomagnetically.'

BRENDA DUNNE

The Princeton Engineering Anomalies Research (PEAR) laboratory was established in 1979 by the University's Dean of Engineering and Applied Science, Professor Robert Jahn.

PEAR performs carefully controlled experiments in the fields of remote viewing – attempting to transmit the sights, sounds and smells of a remote location between two people – and psychokinesis, in which people try to influence the random output of specially designed machines, using their minds.

Undergraduate student Brenda Dunne was so sceptical about PEAR's reported successes that she decided to replicate some of their experiments. She detected a tiny but unlikely deviation from chance in her own results, and began to reconsider. Today Dunne is the Laboratory Manager at PEAR.

'Parapsychology has tended to have two major categories: ESP, where you acquire information [as with Remote Viewing], and psychokinesis where you are affecting what's out there [as with the human-machine experiments]. When we look at the results of these two classes of experiments, they showed remarkably similar characteristics. It leads us to suspect that they might be two aspects of a similar process.

'Whatever this process is – and remember we are talking about a very tiny effect – it seems that whatever is happening is not happening at the level of cognitive consciousness. People sometimes get results with the machines, for instance, when they are trying *not* to affect them. Others say things seem to work better if they don't try too hard, or if they distract themselves at the cognitive level by listening to music or reading a magazine.

'We wondered, given the small scale of the effect, what would happen if you had two people working on it. Would two people who were good do even better combined?

'There was no evidence of an overall effect. But when we were summarising the results, we noticed that the pairs that were getting better effects were the ones who were male and female as opposed to the same-sex pairs – and they actually did a bit better than they did as individuals.

Brenda Dunne with Professor Robert G. Jahn, Princeton University's Dean of Engineering and Applied Science who established the PEAR lab in 1979

'Then we looked at the opposite-sex pairs we call "bonded" pairs [people who are fond of each other and know each other well], and found that their effects were much stronger than those who were just acquaintances. It could be that when some resonance is established between people, the distinction our consciousness makes between "me" and "not me" lowers, as it does, say, when we fall in love.

'Bird migration, herd instincts, schools of fish . . . It may be that what we call resonance serves to amplify what would otherwise be a very minute signal. So one bird might not be able to find his way south: he might need to have a flock so that the group amplifies the subtle information that might otherwise go unobserved.

'It could also have something to do with shared emotional awareness. There were experiments done some years ago in the [then] Soviet Union where they took baby rabbits into a submarine so there was no way of any normal signal getting through to the mother rabbit on land. I find it rather abhorrent myself, but they would then kill one of the baby rabbits. And at the time that the baby was killed, the mother was wired up and they detected strong physiological responses. Human mothers seem to have those connections too – you know, waking up just before the baby starts to cry.

'What is it? That's the $64,000 question. We don't know what it is. We spent the first ten years of our seventeen-year program trying to answer the question "is it?" Responding to criticisms, eventually, we produced a database under what we believe are immaculate controls that testify to a very real, although very small, effect.

'Now we're trying to find something in the data that might give us an indication into what it is. We are dealing with something that we really don't understand yet. Given the nature of the topic, we certainly do not expect people to accept it on our say-so. I know how I felt when I first read it.

'Working in this area represents a certain professional risk. You lose your reputation real quick. I tell people who are thinking of going into the field that in addition to a well calibrated random source, careful protocols and controls etcetera, they should also maintain a good sense of humour. It's difficult. There's an intellectual dictatorship that tells you how you should think. Our program stands for the right to ask the question. Whether or not we ever find the answer, it's very important to ask it and not be told what questions you can and can't ask.

'Science is a method, not a body of knowledge. You can apply that method to any question. It's a way of asking a question carefully, systematically, and being open to whatever you find. Even if you find what you don't want, you have to be able to swallow hard and say "OK, maybe I was wrong".

'I push all scientists to practise every morning in front of the mirror saying "I don't know". And, in the evening before going to bed, saying "I was wrong". Theoretically, it's the attitude that guides science. Unfortunately, in practice, it frequently doesn't.'

DR SUSAN BLACKMORE

Dr Susan Blackmore is a psychologist who has spent the past twenty years conducting scientific parapsycological research. Based at the University of the West of England, she is a highly respected expert in the field of critical-thinking as well as the paranormal, and makes frequent appearances on television and in print. She is a member of the executive council of CSICOP.

'I'm very often called a sceptic, but I am not absolutely sceptical – in the popular sense – about the paranormal because I can imagine evidence that could make me change my mind. There are many sceptics whose attitude is that they know 'the truth' – that everything to do with spirtuality, the new age and the paranormal is bunkum and they want to do good to the world by proving it. I am not like that.

'Twenty years looking for paranormal phenomena has made me pretty doubtful, but I think we have to separate out the claims of the paranormal from claims of the extraordinary, and there is no doubt that people have extraordinary experiences that we don't understand. Out-of-body experiences, for example, which I've spent a lot of time researching, undoubtedly happen. I have had them myself.

'I was a student in my first term at Oxford studying psychology and I was running the psychical research society at the university. It was late one night after a meeting . . . I was seriously, seriously tired and I was smoking dope – not a lot – and sitting around listening to The Grateful Dead. Somebody said to me: where are you Sue? And then I was on the ceiling, looking down.

'I had the full-blown works: a nice, white, sort of fluffy, transparent, cloud-like body; a lovely, grey-silvery, snakey cord that went down into my head. I found that I could manipulate my so-called astral body to do anything I wanted. I flew out of the window and over the roofs of Oxford.

'The effect of the experience on my life was very dramatic. I felt: *I now know that there are things more important, more weird, than anything I've ever seen.* And I decided to become a parapsychologist.

'But it wasn't long before I became sceptical about the paranormal aspects of my own experience. I looked at the roofs of Oxford the next day, the gutters and chimney-pots, and I realised that they weren't as I had seen them. That sowed the seeds of doubt.

'I got myself a PhD and started doing experiments looking for the paranormal. There were several in which I really thought I'd found it, but there always turned out to be problems with the experiment. Gradually I started to think: *what if it's not there* ?

'It's difficult and uncomfortable, of course, to have that sort of intellectual conflict but if you have ever changed your mind in a really big way, you know that life goes on and that you are not your ideas and that you don't have to hang on to them.

'I know that a lot of people who claim to have paranormal abilities say that they can't be scientifically tested, because it is a not a scientific thing. It's a cop out. If they're just saying: *I can't do it to order in your laboratory,* that's perfectly reasonable – we know people often can't sleep very well in a lab, for instance. But to say that science can never, ever examine it is rubbish, because science is so open-ended.

'Quite early on in my research, though, I realised that parapsychology was asking the wrong questions. *Is there a paranormal? Are there paranormal powers?* You could go on looking for ever. I can only say: *I've done lots and lots of experiments, all of which showed negative results, so I don't think so.* But I can't prove it. You can never prove the *non*-existence of anything. A classic example people use is the existence of a white crow. I can say, *I've looked all my life and I've only seen black crows,* but there could be one somewhere and I just haven't found it.

'What I want to ask instead is: *what is the nature of the experiences?* And *what is the nature of the mind?* Those are difficult questions but much more interesting.

'I am a scientist, but I also spend a lot of my time and effort having experiences. I've been training in Zen meditation for 15 years, I've taken countless drugs, and over the years I have had out-of-body experiences, lucid dreams, sleep paralysis. I think a good scientist, in order to tackle questions about the nature of consciousness, needs to come at it from that angle as well as the laboratory-based, objective angle. And I have found that a lot of things that people say about their experiences are true. I just don't buy their theories.

'I think we will eventually be able to understand these experiences as mechanisms of the human mind, although it may take a long time. One thing I'm doing now is studying borderline states of consciousness, like lucid dreaming, in which reality and imagination fuse; because I want to better understand people's states when they think what they're seeing is real but actually its imagination.

'I love *The X-Files*. They do all the kind of weird, spine-chilling things that got me into all this in the first place. And I do identify with Scully. She's a woman and she's sceptical, which is rare and I like that. And of course, Scully is a sceptic who has experienced strange things herself – I identify with that too. She is prepared to think: *well hang on a minute, I did see that, didn't I? Aaaaaaaaargh!*'

EPISODE GUIDE – SEASONS 2 AND 3

2.1 Little Green Men
The X-Files division has been closed down, but Mulder secretly heads for Puerto Rico to investigate possible alien signals picked up by an abandoned NASA radio telescope.

2.2 The Host
Mulder discovers a genetically mutated creature – who appears to be half man, half fluke-worm – stalking the New Jersey sewer system.

2.3 Blood
When mild-mannered small-town residents launch inexplicable killing sprees, the only clues are a chemical used in covert crop dusting, and messages appearing on the digital readouts of everyday appliances.

2.4 Sleepless
Mulder investigates the unexplained deaths of men affiliated with a secret Vietnam-era experiment to turn a troop of soldiers into efficient killing machines who never sleep.

2.5 Duane Barry *(Part one of two)*
Mulder negotiates a hostage situation perpetrated by Duane Barry, an ex-FBI agent who claims he is a victim of alien abduction.

2.6 Ascension *(Part two of two)*
Duane Barry kidnaps Scully and disappears into the hills of Virginia. Mulder tracks him down to find that Scully has been taken from Barry's side by someone else. But who?

2.7 Three
The X-Files re-opened but Scully still missing, Mulder investigates a series of vampiric murders and finds himself falling for the prime suspect.

2.8 One Breath
Scully arrives at a Washington D.C. hospital under mysterious circumstances. Her family anxiously keep vigil as she lies comatose, but Mulder is driven to find those responsible for her condition.

2.9 Firewalker
Mulder and Scully stumble upon a deadly life-form when they investigate the mysterious deaths of several scientists studying an active volcano.

2.10 Red Museum
The agents find tensions running high in cattle country, following the arrival of a vegetarian religious sect and the disappearances of several teenagers who are later found wandering in their underwear with an ominous message scrawled on their backs.

2.11 Excelsius Dei
Mulder and Scully uncover strange goings-on in a nursing home after a nurse claims to have been raped by a supernatural entity.

2.12 Aubrey
The agents are led to ponder the possibility of genetic memory when an elderly serial killer appears to be back in business, and a disturbed policewoman knows more about his deeds than she should.

2.13 Irresistible
The hunt for a sick death-fetishist who escalates from corpse desecration to murder leaves Scully profoundly disturbed.

2.14 Die Hand Die Verletzt
Mulder and Scully investigate an apparent satanic ritual murder in a small New Hampshire town. But the town's secret devil-worship society appear to be victims themselves, and suspicion points to a substitute teacher who may be a diabolical force.

2.15 Fresh Bones
Following a series of apparent suicides at a Haitian refugee camp in North Carolina, the agents uncover a secret battle between the camp commander and a Voodoo priest.

2.16 Colony *(Part one of two)*
Mulder and Scully track an alien bounty-hunter who is murdering a colony of humanoid-looking clones. The stunning reappearance of Mulder's long-lost sister, Samantha, is no coincidence.

2.17 End Game *(Part two of two)*
When the bounty-hunter takes Scully hostage, Mulder is forced to make a painful choice which leads him to the dismaying truth about Samantha's 'return'.

2.18 Fearful Symmetry
Scully believes that the strange disappearances of animals from a zoo near a UFO 'hot spot' may be the work of animal liberationists. Mulder suspects alien abduction, and the statements of a sign language-literate gorilla lend credence to his beliefs.

2.19 Dod Kalm
Mulder and Scully travel to the Norwegian equivalent of the Bermuda Triangle to find out what happened to the crew of a Navy destroyer. They find their lives in danger when they fall victim to a peculiar phenomenon which causes them rapidly to age.

2.20 Humbug
The murder of a performer known as 'The Alligator Man' brings Mulder and Scully to a town populated by former circus and side-show acts.

2.21 The Calusari
The agents investigate the death of a toddler whom Mulder believes was lured to his doom by an unseen force. They must deduce whether the boy's superstitious Romanian grandmother is protecting his family or destroying it.

2.22 F. Emasculata
When a plague-like illness kills twelve men inside a prison facility, Mulder hunts two possibly-infected fugitives whilst Scully remains in the quarantine area. . . and discovers the horrifying truth.

2.23 Soft Light
Mulder and Scully help one of Scully's ex-students to trace a murderer, but it's the killer's shadow they have to keep an eye on.

2.24 Our Town
Investigating the disappearance of a federal poultry inspector in a small Arkansas town, the agents discover the town's dark secret – its citizens are eating more than just chicken.

2.25 Anasazi *(Part one of three)*
Mulder and Scully's lives, sanity and mutual trust are thrown into
jeopardy when a hacker gains access to secret government files.

3.1 The Blessing Way *(Part two of three)*
Mulder fights for his life with the help of Navajo elder Albert
Hosteen, Scully is stripped of her credentials and the FBI continues
its frantic search for the stolen files.

3.2 Paper Clip *(Part three of three)*
Reunited, Mulder and Scully continue their investigation without
the support of the FBI. Their discovery of an old Nazi scientist, given
sanctuary by the US government, leads them closer to the answers –
and to danger.

3.3 D.P.O.
A series of uncanny lightning-related deaths lead Mulder and Scully
to a teenage slacker who has survived a strike himself – and now
seems capable of controlling lightning.

3.4 Clyde Bruckman's Final Repose
Whilst tracking a serial killer who preys upon fortune tellers, the
agents meet a man whom Mulder believes to be a genuine psychic.

3.5 The List
A death-row prisoner vows that he will be reincarnated – and will
kill five men who have wronged him. When it appears that he is
keeping his promise, Mulder and Scully are called in to investigate.

3.6 2Shy
The strange MO of a serial killer stalking overweight woman via the
internet leads Mulder to suggest that he may be some kind of 'fat-
sucking vampire'.

3.7 The Walk
Mulder and Scully are called to a military hospital to investigate a
suicidal man claiming to be tormented by a 'phantom soldier'. The
prime suspect is a quadraplegic who may have discovered a
paranormal route to freedom.

3.8 Oubliette
The agents hunt for a kidnap victim, and meet a former victim of the
perpetrator whom Scully believes may be an accomplice. Mulder
suspects, however, that her knowledge of the crime is gained by
supernatural means.

3.9 Nisei *(Part one of two)*
Mulder and Scully unravel another thread in the conspiracy when
they uncover a faltering collusion between the government and a
Japanese war criminal.

3.10 731 *(Part two of two)*
The search for the truth is as dangerous as ever, when Mulder
boards a speeding train carrying a maybe-alien entity and Scully
discovers more about her own abduction.

3.11 Revelations
Each of the victims in a series of religiously-motivated murders
claimed to have been stigmatic – but turned out to be frauds. But a
little boy displaying wounds of religious significance seems genuine
– and likely to be the next victim.

3.12 War of the Coprophages
A town descends into mass hysteria after a series of deaths in which
the only common denominator is the presence of cockroaches.

3.13 Syzygy
The agents investigate a series of bizarre high-school deaths that
coincide, Mulder discovers, with a rare astrological event.

3.14 Grotesque
Mulder's former mentor, the FBI's chief profiler, requests his
assistance on a case involving a serial killer who claims to be
posessed by a demonic force.

3.15 Piper Maru *(Part one of two)*
A diving crew from a French salvage ship, sent to recover a
mysterious wreckage from World War II, fall prey to an odd
radiation illness.

3.16 Apocrypha *(Part two of two)*
The agents discover the astonishing truth about what was hidden in
the wreckage.

3.17 Pusher
Mulder and Scully assist on a case involving a hired killer who is
seemingly capable of bending people to his will.

3.18 Teso Dos Bichos
A series of deaths occurs after an ancient and sacred artifact is
removed from a South American excavation site by US
archaeologists.

3.19 Hell Money
The agents travel to San Francisco's Chinatown to investigate a
string of murders which, they discover, are linked to a deadly game.

3.20 Jose Chung's 'From Outer Space'
In an interview with a flamboyant author, Scully recalls the details of
a case of apparent alien abduction in which nothing is quite as it
seems.

3.21 Avatar
When Assistant Director Skinner is accused of murder, Mulder and
Scully join the investigation to clear their supervisor's name.

3.22 Quagmire
The agents investigate deaths and disappearances near a lake
rumoured to house a prehistoric monster.

3.23 Wetwired
The trust between Mulder and Scully is tested when they uncover a
dark conspiracy behind a series of murders in which the key appears
to lie with the suspects' TV-viewing habits.

3.24 Talitha Cumi *(Part one of two)*
Mulder and Scully's search for a man who seems to possess strange
powers leads to the discovery of a dangerous secret from Mulder's
past.

THE *X-FILES* MYTHOLOGY: THE STORY SO FAR...

Confused by the ongoing tale of covert operations and conspiracy in the *X-Files* universe? All that double-crossing making you dizzy? Think you may have missed an episode vital to the narrative? Look no further.

Warning: this guide contains 'spoilers': if you would prefer unseen episodes to remain a surprise, proceed with extreme caution.

Season One
1.1 *The X-Files*
Special Agent Dana Scully is drafted in to keep tabs on Fox Mulder, who specialises in unusual cases. During their first foray, Mulder confides that his sister, Samantha, was abducted during childhood, spurring his quest for the truth, and hints that a connection on Capitol Hill affords him some leeway in pursuing his unorthodox investigations.

Scully hands her superiors the strange nasal implant she removed from a suspected abduction victim. We see the ever-present Cigarette Smoking Man (CSM) enter a cavernous Pentagon storage room where he places the implant in a box with others like it.

1.2 *Deep Throat*
The agents stumble upon a project which seems to involve secret military aircraft built using UFO technology. Mulder meets the man we come to know as Deep Throat, an apparently benevolent ally with access to a vast bank of classified knowlege. We learn that those charged with guarding the government's secrets will stop at nothing to do so, and that they have an astounding array of resources: when Mulder breaks into the secret air-base, he is captured and subjected to some procedure which erases his memory of the experience.

1.10 *Fallen Angel*
Deep Throat tips Mulder off about a military operation to recover a crashed UFO. Telephone conversations between the operation's commander and an unseen superior hint that such matters fall under the auspices of some governing board.

1.17 *E.B.E.*
Another salvage operation takes place when a UFO is shot down, and a live Extraterrestrial Biological Entity (EBE) is recovered. Mulder's trust in Deep Throat is tested when he lies to throw Mulder off the scent. But perhaps his motives were just.

Deep Throat tells Mulder of a global agreement to kill recovered EBEs, and confesses that his desire to help Mulder stems from guilt over a distant incident in which he was called upon to murder an innocent visitor – a touching story the veracity of which has still not been confirmed.

1.24 *The Erlenmeyer Flask*
Thanks to Deep Throat the agents discover a project code-named Purity Control which aims to create alien-human hybrids. Scully finds one source of the alien DNA: an alien foetus. The hybrids can breathe under water, excel in strength and stamina, and have green blood which exudes a toxic miasma usually fatal to humans.

Mulder is captured by The Crewcut Man, a member of the security team for the faction overseeing the project. Deep Throat makes a deal: Mulder's safe return in exchange for the alien foetus. But we learn just how ruthless that faction really are when, after the exchange, Crewcut Man shoots Deep Throat dead.

Once again, we see CSM in the Pentagon warehouse, this time squirrelling away the alien foetus.

2.1 *Little Green Men*
The X-Files division has been shut down and the agents reassigned, but Mulder's quest is not forgotten. He has a flashback to Samantha's abduction, the details differing from his previous recollections: the siblings are alarmed by a bright light and tremors outside their home. Fox glimpses a strange entity and watches helplessly as his sister floats into the light.

Mulder is summoned to Capitol Hill by his patron, Senator Matheson. 'I know I've let you down,' Mulder tells him. 'You've supported me at great risk to your reputation. I realise when they shut us down there was nothing you could do. All I can say is, I think we were close. To what, I don't know.' Urging Mulder to investigate an incident, the senator warns him of 'The Blue Beret UFO Retrieval Team. . . authorised to display terminal force.'

At the close of the tale, the relationship between Skinner and CSM becomes clearer. When Mulder expresses his disgust at a wiretap placed on his telephone, Skinner shoots CSM a look suggesting his unawareness and disapproval of such an act. Moments later, CSM correctly deduces that Skinner's instruction to 'get the hell out' is directed at *him* and not Mulder.

2.4 *Sleepless*
Mulder recieves an anonymous tip-off on a case, but finds that an eager young agent called Alex Krycek has already signed off on it.

In the course of the investigation, Mulder meets his new informant, X, successor to the late Deep Throat. X's motives for helping Mulder are unclear. 'You think I want to be here?' X barks. 'I don't want to be here.' Is X beholden to Deep Throat? Was Deep Throat doing someone else's bidding – a job now carried out with greater reluctance by X? Or does X have an agenda of his own, for which Mulder is a useful pawn?

The plot thickens at the denouement, when we see a colder, harder Krycek delivering a report to a shadowy group presided over by CSM. 'He's either found another source, or another source has found him. . .' Krycek confirms, warning also that Scully is 'a much larger problem than you described'. 'Every problem has a solution,' CSM retorts.

2.5 *Duane Barry* and 2.6 *Ascension*
Although Mulder is alone in believing that Duane Barry is telling the truth about being abducted, medical examinations confirm Barry's claims of anomalous dental work and implants placed in his body. Scully discovers that the implants are electronic – possibly tracking devices – but her investigation is cut short when Barry escapes from custody and kidnaps her from her home. Mulder wonders how Barry obtained Scully's address, and indeed why he targeted her. He can't discount his suspicions that someone else may have led Barry to her.

We see Krycek at his most ruthless: reporting Mulder's every move to CSM and stopping at nothing – including the murder of an innocent man – to prevent Mulder from saving Scully. Krycek succeeds, and Scully is taken from Barry's side by parties unknown. 'That was the deal,' Barry explains later. 'Her instead of me.'

Krycek asks CSM why they do not have Mulder eliminated. 'That's not policy' replies CSM. 'Kill Mulder and you risk turning one man's religion into a crusade.' Asked about Scully, CSM will only assure Krycek, 'We've taken care of that,' adding that Krycek has no right to information, 'only orders to be carried out.' Krycek's next order, it seems, is to kill Duane Barry and frame Mulder.

Seeking Senator Matheson's help, Mulder is accosted by X, who insists that there is nothing the Senator can do – 'not without committing politcal suicide.' 'Do they have something on him?' asks Mulder. 'They have something on everyone,' X assures him. 'The question is when they'll use it.' Quizzed about

Scully's abduction, X insists that 'This reaches beyond any of us . . . even my predecessor.'

Mulder suggests to Skinner that Scully's abduction was orchestrated by 'some covert agency within the government. . . whoever it is that the man who smokes those cigarettes works for', because she 'got too close' and because she was involved in Mulder's own ongoing quest for truth. He also proves that Krycek works for the same faction and has murdered with impunity. Alas, no official action can be taken: Krycek has disappeared. 'There's only one thing that I *can* do,' fumes Skinner. 'As of right now I'm reopening The X-Files. That's what they fear the most.'

2.8 *One Breath*
Scully appears in the intensive care unit of a hospital, with no record of how she came to be there. Mulder summons X, but he doesn't come. Frohike of the Lone Gunmen sneaks Scully's medical charts out of the hospital; it is deduced that Scully may have been subjected to advanced genetic engineering experiments.

Back at the hospital, Mulder chases a man who is attempting to steal a sample of Scully's blood. His pursuit is scuppered by X, who insists that Mulder desist in his hunt for the people responsible for Scully's condition. 'You got him killed, you got her killed,' says X, referring to Deep Throat and Scully, 'That's not going to happen to me.' He goes on to clarify his relationship with Mulder ('You're *my* tool. . . I come to you when *I* need *you*.') and adds that 'I used to be you. I was where you are now.' When Mulder breaks away and apprehends the blood-thief, X shoots the man before Mulder is able to learn anything.

The 'no smoking' sign that Skinner has placed on his desk betrays his increasing displeasure at his enforced co-operation with CSM, and an unknown informant (sent by Skinner, we later learn) slips Mulder CSM's address. Mulder pays CSM an emotional visit, holding him at gunpoint. 'Don't try and threaten me, Mulder. I've watched presidents die,' CSM coolly informs him, adding that he has no wife, no family, some power, and is 'in the game because I believe what I'm doing [helping to conceal the truth?] is right. . . If people were to know of the things I know, it would all fall apart.'

Later, we learn more about Skinner, who refuses to accept Mulder's resignation, confiding that he had a near-death experience in Vietnam. 'I'm afraid to look any further beyond that. . .' he explains. 'You, you are not.'

Mulder encounters X again. 'I can't tell you why she was taken. It's too close to me,' says X, leading us to suspect that the faction responsible is small enough for a leak to be easily traced. Instead, X appears to have double-bluffed the organisation, telling them that Mulder is out of town and has information on Scully in his desk at home. 'I'm giving you the man who took her,' X promises. 'At 8.17 tonight they'll search your apartment. They will be armed, you will be waiting. . . to defend youself with terminal intensity. It's the only way Mulder. The law will not punish these people.'

Although Mulder's apartment is turned over that night as promised, we never learn whether X really planned the operation in Mulder's favour – or whether *Mulder* was the victim of a bluff – since Mulder cannot keep the appointment. He chooses instead to be at Scully's bedside, since the doctors have warned that her death is imminent.

2.10 *Red Museum*
After Scully's miraculous recovery, a case takes the agents to a town where an unknown substance injected into cattle seems linked to violence amongst the locals, and a local doctor has regularly injected a group of teenagers with the same substance since their infancy, pretending it is a vitamin supplement. These teens have never suffered illness, but seem aggressive.

The substance turns out to be the same one used in the

Purity Control project. 'It all makes sense,' Mulder concludes. 'They've been conducting an experiment. Somebody's been paying to have those kids injected with alien DNA to see how they'd react. It's been going on for years.' The link with Purity Control is further confirmed when Scully spots Crew Cut Man – Deep Throat's assassin – lurking in the vicinity. He appears to have been sent to exterminate those involved in the experiment, perhaps because its cover has been blown, but is himself killed by the local Sheriff.

2.16 *Colony* and 2.17 *End Game*
Mulder and Scully find themselves tracking an alien bounty hunter sent to kill a disparate colony of extra-terrestrial clones, who are humanoid in appearance and known as The Gregors. They can only be killed one way: a puncture wound to the back of the neck with a special weapon the bounty hunter has in his possession.

Mulder's long-lost sister, Samantha, miraculously returns, and confides that she is connected with the Gregors, having been adopted and raised by a pair of them after being returned, amnesiac, from her childhood abduction. But to Mulder's horror, it becomes apparent that this is not his sister, but a Gregor, one of many clones whose physical features were supplied by DNA from the real Samantha Mulder. 'We needed your help," another Samantha-clone coldly informs Mulder 'We knew you could be manipulated. . . We know where your sister is,' she adds. 'Ask yourself. . . How else would we know so much about her?'

It appears that the alien bounty-hunter successfully completes his mission to destroy the Gregors. Using information supplied by X, who is well up on the recent events, Mulder flees in pursuit of the killer. Scully, desperate to find her partner, summons X using Mulder's secret code – sticking an 'X' of masking-tape on the window of his apartment. As soon as X lays eyes on Scully, he leaves angrily, but is stopped in the elevator by Skinner – a nightmare for X, whose life no doubt depends on his liason with Mulder remaining secret. 'Did you tell her what she needed to know?' asks Skinner, before proving himself supremely ballsy by steaming into a violent tussle with X and demanding to know Mulder's whereabouts, which he passes on to Scully.

Tracked down by Mulder, the bounty-hunter confirms that Samantha is alive before he escapes.

2.25 *Anasazi*, 3.1 *The Blessing Way* and 3.2 *Paper Clip*
The Thinker, the Lone Gunmen's anarchist computer-hacker buddy, breaks into the Department of Defense's system, downloads their most sensitive files and hands them to Mulder in the name of truth and justice. The files, Mulder tells Scully, are 'The Holy Grail. . . Hard evidence that the government has known about the existence of Extraterrestrials for almost 50 years.' However their secrets remain elusive – they are encrypted in WWII Navajo-based code. We see officials in Italy, Japan and Germany fretting over the theft, and hear the files refered to as the 'MJ documents' – like the legendary MJ12 documents of UFO-conspiracy lore, the output of a secret council who deal with this highly classified knowledge. 'They must take care of it promptly,' insists the German official, before placing a call to a number we assume belongs to the nameless 'they' – which is answered by CSM.

In the course of this three-part story, we learn a great deal more about the people who are running the show, the way they operate, and the history of the operation. There is a council of 'Elders' based at a gentleman's club in New York City, which one later describes as 'A consortium representing certain global interests.' Purity Control is clearly one project overseen by the consortium, and their scientific methods involve experimentation on human subjects referred to in the files as 'the merchandise'.

The stack of apparently alien bodies that Mulder discovers

in a box-car buried in the New Mexico desert, and which bear smallpox vaccination scars, may well be a batch of one-time 'merchandise'. In a flashback, we see these unfortunates being gassed. The agents discover that one scientist involved in the project was a Nazi war criminal, Victor Klemper, now retired. 'Klemper was trying to create an alien-human hybrid,' posits Mulder. 'That's what I saw in the box car. He was using human test subjects.' We learn that CSM is either a member, or at least a prominent sub-contractor, of the consortium. He appears to be in charge of troubleshooting, damage-control and general dirty-work; his orders are carried out by a team that includes Alex Krycek. If The Lone Gunmen's assessment is right, this team is code-named Garnet, and is a 'multinational black ops unit. . . trained killers'.

Garnet's prime directives at this time seem to be to discredit Mulder and to recover the stolen files. The first plan begins with the tainting of the water supply at Mulder's home with psychoactive drugs, causing him to behave violently and irrationally. The foundations laid, Mulder's father is shot dead (by Krycek), in the knowledge that Mulder will be implicated. Krycek is subsequently sent to Mulder's appartment, clearly (unbeknownst to Krycek) in the hopes that Mulder will kill this expendable foot-soldier, ideally with the same weapon used to shoot Bill Mulder. This part of the scheme is scuppered by Scully, who, finding her partner poised to shoot Krycek, shoots Mulder in the shoulder.

We have learned, however, that Mulder's father, Bill, was more than an innocent pawn in the game. Later on Mulder will find an old photograph showing his father standing with a group of men which includes Klemper and, by the look of things, CSM, Deep Throat and Well-Manicured Man. Before his death, Bill Mulder also receives a visit from CSM and it is apparent that the two once worked closely together. Mulder Sr's primary concern seems to be that his son does not discover his involvement in the conspiracy, but he is also edgy at the thought that CSM and Co might harm Fox. 'I've protected him this long, haven't I?', retorts CSM, adding his old refrain: 'The last thing we need is a martyr of a crusade.'

Disregarding CSM's advice to 'deny everything', shortly before his demise Bill Mulder has a heart-to-heart with his son in which he hints at the shame and regret of being involved in the making of terrible decisions regarding the project involving 'the merchandise'. According to CSM, the project was in fact authorised by Bill Mulder.

In his frustration, CSM becomes careless, ordering the destruction of the box-car, knowing that Mulder is inside it, a conspicuous hit on The Thinker and another on Scully. The consortium is displeased, and one Elder, the Well-Manicured Man, warns Scully of the hit. 'I feel my colleagues are acting impulsively,' he explains. 'Your death will draw unnecesary attention to our group.' When the hit goes ahead, carried out by the bungling Krycek and an accomplice whom we later come to know as the Hispanic Man, Scully has fled to safety, and her sister, Melissa, is murdered in error.

Later, at the hospital, the same pair beat up Skinner, and Krycek takes the digital tape. CSM, hoping to salvage his reputation, attempts to blow up Krycek's car in the hopes of destroying the tape and killing Krycek, denoting the unacceptability of careless hits. But Krycek makes a lucky escape. Realising that his days at Garnet are over, he flees (with the tape), vowing revenge.

Assistant Director Skinner, we discover, is firmly on the side of Mulder and Scully, and of justice, and is prepared to risk his life and position for it. Forced though he is to endure CSM's presence, he is not afraid to stand up to him, and cleverly hatches a plan forcing CSM to guarantee some measure of safety for the agents, and to ensure the continuation of their work at the FBI.

Scully is unsettled to learn that her name appears in the stolen files, in a recent entry, next to that of Duane Barry. The context, she says, is unclear, 'but it has something to do with a test.' She edges closer to the truth when she discovers a tiny computer chip implanted in the back of her neck, but even a visit to a regressive hypnotherapist fails to help her recall the details of her abduction. Equally disturbing is the agents' strange experience in a vast, secret warehouse, where Mulder glimpses a huge craft and Scully sees entities moving past her. Moreover, they find row upon row of cabinets containing the medical files, smallpox vaccination forms and tissue samples of thousands of Americans, including Scully and Samantha Mulder. Mulder pegs them as 'records of abductions, of abductees', but makes the disquieting discovery that beneath the label on Samatha's file lies one bearing his own name.

According to Well Manicured Man, Bill Mulder objected strenuously to the project involving this data-gathering, and threatened to expose it. In response, Samantha was taken 'as insurance'. The horrible truth dawning on him, Mulder drives to his mother's house and demands to know whether his father had ever asked her if she had a favourite of her children, if he ever asked her to make a choice between them. 'I couldn't choose', sobs Mrs Mulder. 'It was your father's choice and I hated him for it.'

3.9 *Nisei* and 3.10 *731*

Mulder and Scully learn that Klemper was not the only war criminal to be given given sanctuary in America and work on purity-control-type projects: Dr Takeo Ishimaru, ex of Japan's nightmarish Unit 731, was until recently hard at work on the next generation of research. Their unpleasant business is conducted from a secluded leprosy research centre and on train cars travelling on secret railroads.

When Dr Ishimaru ceases to play ball, conducting work in secret and resfusing to share his results with the American faction who supported him, he and his cohorts are targetted for death. Before the enclave of corrupt Japanese scientists is wiped out, they kill a hapless UFO enthusiast who has been selling video tapes he pulled off a satellite feed which show them conducting an autopsy on what appears to be an alien.

When Ishimaru and the other staff flee the leprosy centre, death squads arrive and exterminate every test subject, dumping hundreds of bodies in open pits for removal. A survivor reveals to Scully that he was one of the few genuine lepers at the centre, and that hundreds of strange-looking people were brought in periodically, kept apart and subjected to tests from which they would return with burns. Ishimaru and Co also appear to have played a major part in the recent abductions of unsuspecting civilians for experimentation. Their notes include the address of a woman named Betsy Hagopian, where Scully finds members of an all-female abductee support-group. To her horror, the women claim to recognise Scully as 'one of us'. Like Scully, all have had implants removed from the backs of their necks, and Hagopian herself is in hospital, dying from unidentifiable tumours which her friends believe were caused by the experiments performed on her. 'We're all gonna end up like Betsy,' warns one, 'We're all dying because of what they do to us.' Scully has her implant analysed, and learns that it is a tiny computer chip.

Satellite images in the possession of the Japanese team show a boat called the*Talapus*, which salvaged what Scully belives to be the remains of a Russian submarine, and Mulder believes to be a UFO – so when Mulder sees Dr Ishimaru boarding a train with a living being, he is compelled to follow. This despite insistence from X that to do so is too dangerous – a message obviously so important that X relinquishes his cover to relay it via Scully.

Although we have not seen X at the gentleman's club, we know that he is the successor to Deep Throat, who was almost certainly a member of the consortium. X certainly knows most of what's going on. 'You wanna know what's on that train, who killed your sister?' he asks Scully. 'You find out what they put in your neck. It holds more than I could ever tell you. Maybe everything you need to know.' Scully duly discovers that the implanted chip could conceivably be used to 'know a person's every thought'. Moreover, it is of Japanese origin, and a shipment from the manufacturer is traced to the address of Dr Ishimaru. Later, Scully will begin to recall details of her abduction for the first time: strange tests conducted in a train car by a team that included Ishimaru.

Ishimaru is garotted by an assassin referred to in the script as The Red Haired Man. Though he holds an NSA badge, it seems likely that he is one of Garnet's boys. Twice he tries to kill Mulder. Through Red Haired Man's hints, Mulder is convinced that Ishimaru was trying to create alien-human hybrids to form a standing army immune to the effects of biological weapons. But Scully, who has been approached by a consortium member, insists that the creature on board, whilst the victim of horrific experiments related to biological warfare, was human. Whatever it was, the entity perishes on board the train car – along with Red-Haired Man – when a bomb, rigged by Ishimaru, explodes. Mulder is saved in the nick of time by X.

At the close, we see CSM sitting with a Japanese translator, studying the journals belonging to Dr Ishimaru.

3.15 *Piper Maru* and 3.16 *Apochrypha*

The crew of a French salvage ship searching the same spot of ocean explored by the *Talapus* are dying from acute radiation burns. It transpires that they were diving for the wreck of a World War II plane, the pilot of which appeared to be alive, but was in fact being used as a host body for a strange, probably extra-terrestrial organism which seems to be fluid in form. The organism hops from the pilot to the French diver and later to the diver's wife.

Mulder discovers that salvage broker Geraldine Kallenchuk is selling government secrets. It was she who gave the location of the wreck to the French, and her source, Mulder discovers, is Krycek, now operating alone, selling information from the stolen files. Krycek kills Kallenchuk when his cover is blown, but a brush with the diver's wife sees him invaded by the organism.

Scully learns that the crew of a US submarine sent to recover the same plane 50 years ago had suffered the same radiation damage – clearly a result of proximity to the organism – and most had died. In a flashback, we see a team of officials quizzing the survivors – a team comprising a young Bill Mulder, Deep Throat and CSM.

Meanwhile, the investigation into the murder of Melissa Scully has been made inactive, and Skinner's moves to re-open it lead to a visit from two be-suited men issuing thinly veiled threats which Skinner ignores. He is later the victim of an assassination attempt by the Hispanic Man. CSM is once again hauled up by the consortium, since he has apparently moved the salvaged UFO to a new location for security. Moreover, the hit on Skinner is deemed far too public, since a composite photo of the assassin has been released to the press. ('He's one of yours, isn't he?' notes Well-Manicured Man, confirming our suspicions that CSM is indeed head of Garnet, or whatever else this covert group of cold-blooded troubleshooters is called).

Scully apprehends Hispanic Man, but spares his life in exchange for Krycek's whereabouts – an abandoned missile site in North Dakota – before handing him over to the police. (However, Hispanic Man is later disposed of in his cell – at the behest of his boss, no doubt). At the missile site, deep underground, Mulder and Scully encounter CSM, who seems satisfied that things are back under control. 'The UFO's here. That's what Krycek was after, isn't it?' Mulder asks him, receiving no answer. Yet, we learn, it was not Krycek seeking the UFO, but the organism inside him. In a locked silo containing

Krycek and the UFO, we watch the alien leave its host body and seep into the craft. And we are left with the image of Krycek, pounding on the silo door in the darkness, deep below the earth; doomed.

3.24 *Talitha Cumi* (Part one of two)

In an episode containing some of the most earth-shattering revelations yet, Mulder and Scully trace a kind and gentle man, Jeremiah Smith, who turns out to be a non-human of the same kind as the alien bounty-hunter of *Colony* and *End Game*. Smith not only has the ability to change his appearance to that of any other person, but can perform miraculous feats, including the healing of humans. When an incident threatens to expose Smith's existence, CSM bursts into action, his first stop being the Mulder family's long-abandoned beach home, where he believes that the only weapon capable of killing the aliens (the one the bounty-hunter used to kill the colonists) is hidden. Spied on by X, CSM and Mrs Mulder have a heated argument, and after CSM's departure, Mrs Mulder collapses with a stroke.

Prior to this, however, we have seen CSM reminisce fondly to Mulder's mother about summers spent at her beach house, and hint at some personal history that may have passed between them. (Later, at the hospital, the intrigue deepens. 'I've known your mother since before you were born, Fox,' says CSM, as an inexplicably strange and awkward moment passes between the two men.)

CSM's next move is to incarcerate Smith, who is also being tailed by the bounty-hunter. In a stunning conversation, Smith tells CSM that he no longer believes in 'the greater purpose' and expresses disgust at the theft of human liberty embraced by CSM and his cohorts. 'Men can never be free because they are weak, corrupt, worthless and restless,' retorts CSM, whose next comment illuminates the reason why Mulder's work is perceived as such a threat. 'The people believe in authority. They have grown tired of waiting for miracle and mystery. Science is their religion. No greater explanation exists for them. They must never believe any differently if the project is to go ahead.'

He adds that no matter what the implications, 'The outcome is inevitable. The date is set.' 'What you're afraid of is they'll believe I am God,' says Smith, and, speaking of man, notes: 'You can't kill their love, which is what makes them who they are. Which makes them better than us. Than you. . . All you want is to be a part of it. To be one of the commandants when the process begins.' He reveals that CSM is dying of lung cancer, and the possibility arises that Smith's life might be spared in return for healing CSM.

Mulder turns the beach house over and finds the weapon, which X demands that he hand over. 'When the time comes, when the truth is finally determined, its value will soar,' X tells him, warning that 'they' will kill Mulder for possession of it, 'even if they have to martyr you and risk turning your work into a crusade'. 'What we're talking about here is colonisation. The date is set, isn't it?' asks Mulder, before refusing to relinquish the weapon in a move that nudges the meeting to descend into physical violence.

Smith approaches Mulder and Scully, promising information on Samantha Mulder and agreeing to heal Mulder's mother, whose life hangs in the balance. But before they can leave for the hospital, the trio are apprehended by the Bounty Hunter. What happens next? We'll have to wait until Season Four to find out. . .

Pictures courtesy of: Associated Press, Camera Press, Chimpanzee and Human Communication Institute, Fortean Picture Library, Genesis Space Photo Library, Images Colour Library, Mander & Mitchenson, Mary Evans Picture Library, MTV, Planet Earth Pictures, Prima Photos, Princeton University, Rex Features, Ronald Grant Archive, Science Photo Library, Syndication International, Topham Picture Library, Vampire Research Society

BIBLIOGRAPHY
SOURCES AND FURTHER READING

HALLUCINOGENIC JOURNEYS

Plants of the Gods, Richard Evans Schultes and Albert Hofmann; Healing Arts Press, Vermont, 1992

Tales of a Shaman's Apprentice, Mark J. Plotkin; Penguin, 1993

The Archaic Revival, Terrence McKenna; HarperCollins, 1991

Food of the Gods, Terrence McKenna; Bantam, 1992

One River, Wade Davis; Simon and Schuster, 1997

Hallucinogens and Shamanism, Michael J. Harner; Oxford University Press, 1973

The Way of the Shaman, Michael J. Harner; Bantam, 1986

Flesh of the Gods: The Ritual Use of Hallucinogens, PT Furst, ed.; Praeger, NY, 1972

Alternative Realities: The Paranormal, the Mystic and the Transcendant in Human Experience, Leonard George; Facts on File,1995

PERCHANCE TO DREAM

The Terror that Comes in the Night, David J. Hufford; University of Pennsylvania Press, 1982

The Weather Matrix and Human Behaviour, Michael A. Persinger; Praeger, New York, 1980

Unsolved Mysteries Past and Present, Colin Wilson and Damon Wilson; Contemporary Books, Chicago,1992

Alternative Realities: The Paranormal, the Mystic and the Transcendant in Human Experience – op. cit.

Ghosts, Peter Brooksmith; Orbis, London,1984

On the Nightmare, Ernest Jones; Liveright Publishing Co., New York, 1951

The Nature of Sleep and its Disorders, National Sleep Foundation (USA) Jan 25, 1994

The New York Times 16 January 1996

Omni 16:12 (1994)

Skeptical Inquirer 15:4 (Summer 1991)

Fortean Times #69

The Journal of Forensic Sciences #35

The Journal of the American Society for Psychical Research 66:3 (1972); 80 (1986)

The Journal of Nervous and Mental Disease 181:11 (1993)

BETWEEN TWO WORLDS

The Truth in the Light, Peter Fenwick and Elizabeth Fenwick; Headline, 1996

Dying to Live, Susan Blackmore; Grafton, 1993

Harpers Encyclopedia of Mystical and Paranormal Experience, Rosemary Ellen Guiley; HarperCollins, 1991

Parapsychology and Out-of-the-Body Experiences, Susan Blackmore; Transpersonal Books, London, 1978

Beyond the Body: an Investigation of Out-of-the-Body Experiences, Susan Blackmore; William Heinemann, London, 1982

The Near-Death Experience: Problems, Prospects, Perspectives, Bruce Greyson and Charles P. Flynn eds. Charles C. Thomas, Springfield, Illinois, 1984

Flight of the Mind: a Psychological Study of Out-of-Body Experiences, HJ Irwin; Scarecrow Press, Metuchen, NJ, 1985

Life at Death: a Scientific Investigation of the Near Death Experience, Kenneth Ring; Coward McCann and Geoghegan, 1980

The Astonishing Hypothesis: The Scientific Search for the Soul, Francis Crick; Scribner, 1994

Explaining Consciousness: the "Hard Problem" Special issue of The Journal of Consciousness Studies, Vol. 2, No. 3 (1995)

The Nature of Consciousness: Philosophical and Scientific Debates, Ned Block, Owen Flanagan and Guven Guzeldere, eds. MIT Press, 1996

The First CIA-selected Coordinate Remote Viewing Experiment, Ingo Swann, 1996 (On-line)

Journeys Out of the Body, Robert A Monroe; Doubleday, Garden City, New York, 1971

Far Journeys, Robert A Monroe; Dolphin/Doubleday, Garden City, New York, 1985

Recollections of Death – A Medical Investigation, Michael Sabom; Simon and Schuster, New York, 1982

Psychic Voyages, The Time-Life Editors; Time Life, 1987

Search for the Soul, The Time-Life Editors; Time Life, 1989

The Theory and Practice of Astral Projection, Anthony Martin; Aquarian Press, 1980

Apparitions, GNM Tyrrell; Duckworth, London, 1953

Coming Back to Life, PMH Atwater; Dodd Mead, New York, 1988

Natural Or Supernatural: A Casebook of True, Unexplained Mysteries, Martin S. Caidin; Contemporary Books, 1993

Strange But True, Jenny Randles and Peter Hough; Piatkus, 1994

Skeptical Inquirer – Spring 1979

Fortean Times #62

Omni 16:1 (1993); 16:2 (1993); 16:5 (1994)

Psychiatry 55:95 (1992)

Scientific American 271:1 (1994); 273:6 (1995)

Plants of the Gods, Richard Evans Schultes and Albert Hofmann; Healing Arts Press, Vermont, 1992

Tales of a Shaman's Apprentice, Mark J. Plotkin; Penguin, 1993

The Archaic Revival, Terrence McKenna; HarperCollins, 1991

Food of the Gods, Terrence McKenna; Bantam, 1992

One River, Wade Davis; Simon and Schuster, 1997

Hallucinogens and Shamanism, Michael J. Harner; Oxford University Press, 1973

The Way of the Shaman, Michael J. Harner; Bantam, 1986

Flesh of the Gods: The Ritual Use of Hallucinogens, PT Furst, ed.; Praeger, NY, 1972

Alternative Realities: The Paranormal, the Mystic and the Transcendant in Human Experience, Leonard George; Facts on File,1995

MIRACULOUS WOUNDS

The Bleeding Mind: An Investigation Into the Mysterious Phenomenon of Stigmata, Ian Wilson; George Weidenfeld & Nicholson Limited, London, 1988

Looking For a Miracle: Weeping Icons, Relics, Stigmata, Visions & Healing Cures, Joe Nickell; Prometheus Books, Amherst, New York,1993

La Stigmatisation, l'ecstase divine, les miracles de Lourdes, réponse aux libres penseurs,

2 Vols A. Imbert-Goubeyre; Bellet, Clermont, 1894

The Physical Phenomena of Mysticism, Herbert Thurston; H. Regnery Co., Chicago, 1952

Comparative Miracles, Robert D. Smith; B. Herder Book Co., St. Louis, 1965

Fortean Times # 71

LOOKING INTO THE ABYSS

Serial Slaughter: What's behind America's Murder Epidemic?, Michael Newton; Loompanics, 1992

Whoever Fights Monsters, Robert K. Ressler and Tom Shactman; Simon and Schuster, 1992

Justice is Served, Robert K. Ressler and Tom Shactman; St. Martins' Paperback, New York, 1994

I Have Lived in the Monster, Robert K. Ressler and Tom Shactman; Simon & Schuster, 1996

Sexual Homicide: Patterns and Motives, Robert K. Ressler,Ann W. Burgess and John E. Douglas; Lexington Books, NYC, 1988

Crime Classification Manual: The Standard System for Investigating and Classifying Violent Crime, Robert K. Ressler, Ann W. Burgess, Allen G. Burgess and John E. Douglas; Lexington Books, NYC, 1992

'Violent Crime' Issue, FBI Law Enforcement Bulletin, Federal Bureau of Investigation, Washington, August 1985

'VICAP Crime Analysis Report', FBI Law Enforcement Bulletin Federal Bureau of Investigation, Washington, December 1986

Criminal Investigative Analysis: Sexual Homicide, National Center for the Analysis of Violent Crime; NCAVC FBI Academy, Quantico Virginia 1990

PHYSICAL ANOMALIES

Freak Show – Presenting Human Oddities For Amusement And Profit, Robert Bogdan; University of Chicago Press,1988

Freaks: We Who Are Not As Others, Daniel P. Mannix; Pocket Books 1976; Re/Search publications 1990

Freak Like Me, Jim Rose; Dell,1995

Freaks – Myths and Images of the Secret Self, Leslie Fiedler; Doubleday, 1993

Anomalies and Curiosities of Medicine, George G Gould M.D. and Walter L. Pyle M.D., 1896

The Elephant Man, Ashley Montague; Outerbridge and Dienstfrey, New York, 1971

The World's Most Fantastic Freaks, Mike Parker; Hamlyn, 1994

Very Special People, Frederick Drimmer; Citadel Press, 1991

Hoaxes and Scams – A Compendium Of Deceptions, Ruses And Swindles, Carl Sifakis; Facts on File, 1993

Inside Teradome, Jack Hunter; Creation Books, 1995

P.T. Barnum – America's Greatest Showman, Philip B. Kunhardt Jr, Philip B. Kunhardt III, Peter W. Kunhardt; Knopf, 1995

Shocked and Amazed – On and Off the Midway (periodical publication).

Circus Lingo, Joe McKennon; Carnival Publishing, 1995

Strange #5, #9

PSYCHIC DETECTIVES

Psychic Sleuths, Joe Nickell, ed.; Prometheus Books, 1994

The Blue Sense: Psychic Detectives and Crime, Arthur Lyons and Marcello Truzzi; Mysterious Press, NY, 1982

Strange But True, Jenny Randles and Peter Hough; Piatkus, 1994

Skeptical Inquirer 12:4 (Summer 1988), 17:2 (Winter 1993)

Unexplained!, Jerome Clark; Visible Ink Press, 1993

Mysterious America, Loren Coleman; Faber and Faber, Boston, 1983

Alien Animals, Janet and Colin Bord; Granada-Elek, London, 1980

In the Wake of Sea Serpents, Bernard Heuvelmans; Rupert Hart-Davis, London, 1968

Lake Monster Traditions: ACross-Cultural Analysis, Michel Meurger;Fortean Times, London, 1988

Strange Life: A Sourcebook on the Mysteries of Organic Nature, William R. Corliss; The Sourcebook Project, 1976

Strange Northwest, Chris Bader; Hancock House, 1995

The Best of Fortean Times, Alan Sisman, ed.; Futura, 1991

Vancouver Sun 25 July 1990

Fortean Times #46, #49, #82

Strange #1, #2, #5

Cryptozoology #1 (1982)

ELECTRIC SKIES
MORE WEIRD NATURE

Tornadoes, Dark Days, Anomalous Precipitation and Related Weather Phenomena – A Catalogue of Geophysical Anomalies, William R. Corliss; The Sourcebook Project, 1983

Lightning, Auroras, Nocturnal Lights, And Related Luminous Phenomena – A Catalogue of Geophysical Anomalies, William R. Corliss; The Sourcebook Project, 1982

Science Frontiers: Some Anomalies and Curiosities of Nature, William R. Corliss; The Sourcebook Project, 1994

Handbook of Unusual Natural Phenomena, William R. Corliss;Arlington House, New York, 1986

Disneyland of the Gods, John A. Keel; Illuminet Press, 1995

Unexplained!, Jerome Clark; Visible Ink Press, 1993

Mysterious Fires and Lights, Vincent H. Gaddis; Dell, 1967

The Inexplicable Sky Arthur Constance; Citadel Press, New York, 1956
The Damned Universe of Charles Fort, Louis Kaplan; Autonomedia, New York, 1993

The Books of Charles Fort, Dover Publications, New York, 1974

The Cellular Slime Molds, John Tyler Binner; Princeton, New Jersey, 1967

Meteorological Magazine #67, #74

Monthly Weather Review #36, #45

Weather #28

The Quarterly Journal of the Royal Meteorological Society #17

Sky and Telescope magazine August 1993

Nature #125, #158,

Science #103, #110

Scientific American #21, # 57, #117

Scientific American Supplement #57

Popular Science Monthly #42

Fate 41:10

Fortean Times #45, #61, #62, #84, #45

Strange #1, #4, #6, #7, #8, #10

IS THERE INTELLIGENT LIFE ON EARTH?

Friends of Washoe Newsletter, Dr Roger S. Fouts and Deborah H. Fouts eds.; Central Washington University; Ellensburg, Washington (For subscriptions, donations and enquiries write to P.O. Box 728 Ellensburg Washington 98926, enclosing an international reply coupon)

Linguistics at Large, Noel Minnis, ed.; Granada Publishing, Hertfordshire, 1973

Speaking of Apes: A Critical Anthology of Two-Way Communication with Man, Thomas A. Sebeok and Jean Umiker-Sebeok, eds.; Plenum Press, New York, 1979

Aping Language, Joel Wallman; Cambridge University Press, 1992

Teaching Sign Language to Chimpanzee, R. Allen Gardner, Beatrix T. Gardner & Thomas E. Van Cantfort, eds.; State University of New York Press, 1989

The Ethological Roots of Culture, R. Allen Gardner, Beatrix T. Gardner, Brunetto Chiarelli & Frans X. Plooiji, eds.; NATO Advanced Science Institute Series, Kluwer Academic Publishers Norwell, MA, 1994

Can Chimps Talk? (Television documentary) Written and directed by Jenny Jones; Nova show # 2105, air-date February 15 1994

Human Evolution 9:4 (1994)

NATIVE AMERICAN WONDERS

The Navajo Code Talkers, Doris A. Paul; Dorrance Publishing, Pittsburgh, 1973

Warriors: Navajo Code Talkers, Kenji Kawano; Northland Publishing Company, Flagstaff, Arizona,1996

The Navajos, Peter Iverson; Chlesea House Publishers, New York, 1990

Native American Mythology, Page Bryant; Aquarian, 1991

The Native American Almanac, Arlene Hirshfelder and Martha Keipw de Montano; Prentice Hall, 1993

American Indian Myths and Legends, Richard Erdoes & Aldonso Ortiz, eds.; Pantheon Books, 1984

THE NIGHT STALKERS

The Vampire Book: The Encyclopedia of the Undead, J. Gordon Melton; Visible Ink Press, 1994

Vampire Encyclopedia, Mathew Bunson; Thames and Hudson,1993

The Living Dead: A Study of the Vampire in Romantic Literature, James B. Twitchell; Duke University Press, Durham,1981

Vampires, Burial and Death: Folklore and Reality, Paul Barber; Yale University Press, New Haven, 1988

The Vampire Companion,Katherine Ramsland; Ballantine Books, NY, 1993

Vampyres: Lord Byron to Count Dracula, Christopher Frayling; Faber and Faber, 1991

The Vampire, Montague Summers; Dorset Press, 1991 (orig. 1928)

American Vampires: Fans, Victims, Practitioners, Norine Dresser; WW Norton and Co., New York, 1989

The Highgate Vampire (Revised edition); Sean Manchester Gothic Press 1985 (Mail Order: PO Box 542 Highgate London N6 6BG)

Whoever Fights Monsters, Robert K. Ressler and Tom Shactman; Simon and Schuster, 1992

Fortean Times #64, #71, #80, #86

A DARK COLLUSION

Satanic, Occult, Ritualistic Crime: A Law Enforcement Perspective, Kenneth V.Lanning; National Center for the Analysis of Violent Crime, FBI Academy, Quantico, Virginia; October 1989

Satanic Panic: The Creation of a Contemporary Legend, Jeffrey S. Victor; Open Court, Chicago and La Salle Illinois, 1993

Out of Darkness: Exploring Satanism and Ritual Abuse, David K. Sakheim and Susan E. Devine, eds.; Lexington Books, New York, 1992

The Encyclopedia of Occult and Supernatural Murder, Brian Lane; Headline, London, 1995

The Secret Life of a Satanist: the authorized biography of Anton LaVey, Blanche Barton; Feral House, Portland, 1990

Aleister Crowley: The Nature of the Beast, Colin Wilson; Aquarian Press, 1987

The Black Art, Rollo Ahmed; Arrow, 1966

At The Heart of Darkness: Witchcraft, Black Magic and Satanism Today, John Parker; Citadel Press, New York, 1993

Michelle Remembers, Michelle Smith and Lawrence Pazder; Congdon and Lattes, New York, 1980

Fortean Times #57

Skeptical Inquirer 14:3 (Spring 1990), 14:4 (Summer 1990)

VOODOO

The Serpent and the Rainbow, Wade Davis; HarperCollins,1986

Voodoo in Haiti, Alfred Metraux; Schocken Books, New York, 1972

The Magic Island, William Seabrook; George G. Harrap and Co., London,1929

Island Posessed, Katherine Dunham; Doubleday and Co.,Garden City, New York, 1969

The Divine Horsemen – The Living Gods of Haiti, Maya Deren; Thames and Hudson, London, 1953

Parapsychology and Anthropology: Proceedings of an International Conference held in London, England August 29-31 1973; Allan Angoff and Diana Barth, eds.; Parapsychology Foundation inc. New York.

Arthur C. Clarke's A-Z of Mysteries; Simon Welfare and John Fairley; HarperCollins, 1993

Les Zombis dans le contexte vodou et Haitien, Dr. Lamarque Douyon; Haiti Santé , 1980

The Unexplained (partwork), Orbis, 1983

American Anthropologist #44 (1942), #74 (1972)

Fortean Times #78, #82

WRITTEN IN THE STARS

Does Astrology need to be True? (parts I and II); Geoffrey Dean; The Hundredth Monkey and other Paradigms of the Paranormal, Kendrick Frasier, ed.; Prometheus Books, 1991

Synchronicity – An Acausal Connecting Principal, CG Jung; Ark, 1991

Jung and Astrology, Maggie Hyde; HarperCollins, 1992

Incredible Life: A Handbook of Biological Mysteries, William R. Corliss; The Sourcebook Project, 1981

Handbook of Biological Anomalies – Humans 1, William R. Corliss; The Sourcebook Project,1992

An Encyclopedia of Claims, Frauds and Hoaxes of the Occult and Supernatural, James Randi; St. Martin's Press, 1995

Voices, D. Skafte; The American Academy of Psychotherapists, 1969

The Value of Astrological Judgements and Forecasts, J. Reverchon; Yerres, France, 1971

Alternative Realities: The Paranormal, the Mystic and the Transcendant in Human Experience, Leonard George; Facts on File, 1995

American Journal of Psychotherapy #36

American Journal of Psychiatry #129

Journal of Clinical Psychology #36

Psychological Reports #67

Zetetic Scholar #3, #4

Astrological Journal #24

CONSPIRACY

Advisory Committee on Human Radiation Experiments – Final Report U.S. Government; 1996

50 Greatest Conspiracies of All Times: History's Biggest Mysteries, Coverups and Cabals, Jonathan Vankin & John Whalen; Citadel Press ,1995

The CIA's Greatest Hits, Mark Zepezauer; Odonian Press, 1994

Secret and Suppressed: Banned Ideas & Hidden History, Jim Keith, ed.; Feral House, 1993

Secret Agenda, Linda Hunt; St. Martins Press, 1991
The Paperclip Conspiracy: The Hunt for Nazi Scientists, Tom Bower; Little Brown, Boston, 1987

Blowback, Christopher Simpson; Weidenfeld & Nicholson, New York, 1988

Memorandum re: Post-World War II Reccruitment of German Scientists – Project Paperclip, The Advisory Committee Staff, Advisory Committee on Human Radiation Experiments, April 5, 1995

Unit 731: Japan's Secret Biological Warfare in World War II, Peter Williams & David Wallace; Hodder and Stoughton, 1989

Unit 731: Testimony, Hal Gold, Charles Tuttle Company, 1996

Japan's Secret War: Unit 731, David Tharp (On-line)

New York Times 17 March 1995

MIND CONTROL

The Search for the Manchurian Candidate: The CIA and Mind Control, John Marks; Norton, 1991

Subliminal Perception: The Nature of a Controversy, NF Dixon; McGraw Hill, London, 1971

Big Secrets, William Poundstone; Quill, New York, 1983

Bigger Secrets, William Poundstone; Houghton Mifflin, 1986

The Kennedy Subcommittee Hearings on Biomedical and Behavioral Research, U.S. Government; 1975

The Manipulation of Human Behavior, Albert Biderman and Herbert Zimmer, eds.; John Wiley and Sons, New York, 1961

The CIA's Greatest Hits – Op. Cit.

Advisory Committee on Human Radiation Experiments - Final Report, U.S. Government; 1996

Vance and Belknap v. Judas Priest and CBS Records, 86-5844/86-3939. Second District Court of Nevada, August 24 1990

The Battle for Your Mind: Persuasion and Brainwashing Techniques Being Used On The Public Today, Dick Sutphen, 1995 (On-line)

Hypnotism: Its History, Practice and Theory, J. Milne Bramwell; Grant Richards, London, 1903

Journal of Forensic Sciences #39

Psychology and Marketing #5 (1988)

Psychology Today September 1988

Skeptical Inquirer 16:3 (Spring 1992)

Advertising Age, October 15 1984; October 2 1989

American Psychologist #40 (1985)

URBAN LEGENDS

The Vanishing Hitchhiker: American Urban Legends and their Meanings, Jan Harold Brunvand; Norton 1981

The Choking Doberman and other "new" Urban Legends, Jan Harold Brunvand; Norton, 1984

The Mexican Pet: More "new" Urban Legends and Some Old Favourites, Jan Harold Brunvand; Norton, 1988

Curses! Broiled Again!, Jan Harold Brunvand; Norton, 1990

The Baby Train and Other Lusty Urban Legends, Jan Harold Brunvand; Norton, 1994

Contemporary Legend: A Reader, Dr Gillian Bennett and Dr Paul Smith; Garland, New York, 1996

The Tumour in the Whale, Rodney Dale; Gerald Duckworth and Co, London, 1978

Its True, It Happened to a Friend, Rodney Dale; Gerald Duckworth and Co, London, 1984

Knock-Out Dates: Flirting with Danger, James Schaefer and Murray A. Latzen; The FBI Law Enforcement Bulletin 62:1 (January 1993)

Losing Their Minds in Bogota, Anne Proenza and Isabel Vincent; World Press Review 41:10 (October 1994)

Sell Yourself to Science, Jim Hogshire; Loompanics, 1993

A Friend of a Friend (radio documentary), Producer: Mark Mason, BBC Radio 4, December 26, 1995

The Great Organ Hunt (television documentary)
Producer: Jenny Barraclough, BBC1 "Knife to the Heart", May 1996

The Observer 19 May 1996

The Guardian 2 May 1995

Fortean Times #75, #79, #85

The Anomalist #2

alt.folklore.urban FAQ (On-line)

MASS HYSTERIA AND THE BELIEF ENGINE

Alternative Realities: The Paranormal, the Mystic and the Transcendant in Human Experience, Leonard George; Facts on File, 1995

Hoaxes and Scams – a Compendium of Deceptions, Ruses and Swindles Carl Sifakis, Facts on File, 1993

Extraordinary Popular Delusions and The Madness of Crowds, Charles McKay; Harmony, 1980 (orig. 1890)

Anomalistic Psychology: A study of Magical Thinking
L. Zusne and WH Jones; Lawrence Erlbaum, New Jersey, 1989

The June Bug: A Study in Hysterical Contagion, AC Kerckhoff and KW Back; Appleton Century Crofts, New York, 1968

Sensation Seeking: Beyond the Optimal Level of Arousal, M. Zuckerman; Lawrence Erlbaum, New Jersey, 1979

Theory of Collective Behavior, NJ Smesler; Free Press, New York, 1962

Exploring the Paranormal: Perspectives on Belief and Experience, JR Stewart; Prism, 1989

Positive Illusion: Creative Self-Deception and the Healthy Mind, S. Taylor; Basic Books, New York, 1989

The Boston Globe 13 April 1996

Skeptical Inquirer 19:3 (May-June 1995)

Archives of Psychology 27:187 (1935)

Acta Psychiatrica Scandinavica Supplementum #252

Fortean Times #85

The Chupacabras Homepage (On-Line)

THE FRONTIERS OF REALITY

QED: The Strange Theory of Light and Matter, Richard P. Feynman; Penguin,1985

Understanding Physics, Isaac Asimov; Barnes and Noble, 1966

Science Frontiers: Some Anomalies and Curiosities of Nature, Compiled by William R. Corliss; The Sourcebook Project, 1994 (P.O. Box 107, Glen Arm MD 21057 USA)

Quantum Theory for Beginners, J.P McEvoy and Oscar Zarate; Icon Books, 1996

Quantum Physics and Parapsychology, Laura Oteri, ed; Parapsychology Foundation, New York, 1975

Margins of Reality: The Role of Consciousness in the Physical World, Robert G. Jahn and Brenda J. Dunne; Harcourt Brace Jordanovich, 1987

Atomic Physics and Human Knowledge, Niels Bohr; Wiley, 1958

Out of My Later Years, Albert Einstein; Citadel Press,1956

Physics and Philosophy, Werner Heisenberg; Harper Torchbooks, 1958

My View of The World, Erwin Schrödinger; Cambridge University Press, 1964

Quantum Theory, D. Bohm; Prentice-Hall, 1951

New Perspectives in Physics, Louis de Broglie; Basic Books,1962

The Universe in Light of Modern Physics, Max Planck; W.W. Norton, 1931

Flim-Flam! Psychics, ESP, Unicorns and Other Delusions, James Randi; Prometheus Books, 1982

Into Thin Air, Paul Begg; Sphere, 1981

The Philadelphia Experiment, Charles Berlitz & William Moore; Panther, 1979

The Bermuda Triangle, Charles Berlitz; Avon Books, New York, 1974

The Unexplained (partwork); Orbis 1983

The Bermuda Triangle – Solved!, Lawrence David Kusche; Warner Books, 1975

Invisible Residents: A Disquisition Upon Certain Matters Maritime, and the possibility of Intelligent Life under the Waters of this Earth, Ivan T Sanderson; World Publishing Company New York 1970

Physics Today 38:38 (1985)

Science # 256 (1992)

Science News 136:292 (1989)

THE SEARCH FOR EXTRA-TERRESTRIAL INTELLIGENCE

Murmurs of the Earth, Carl Sagan, Frank Drake, Lomberg et.al; Warner News Media 1992 (Publication includes CD-ROM replicating the Voyager record; Mail order through the American Planetary Society (818) 793-1675 or the Time-Warner Interactive Group, P.O. Box 61041, Tampa, Florida 33661-1041.)

Intelligent Life in the Universe, Frank D. Drake; from: Science and the Paranormal: Probing the Existence of the Supernatural George O. Abell and Barry Singer, eds.; Scribners 1983

National Aeronautics and Space Administration High Resolution Microwave Survey (HRMS) Press Kit, Jet Propulsion Laboratory, October 1992

Flying Saucers: Serious Business, Frank Edwards; Citadel Press 1992

The Observer 26 February 1995

The Times 19 May 1995

Sunday Express 21 January 1996

San Jose Mercury News 18 January 1996

Time 5 February 1996

Omni 16:3 (1993), 16:4 (1994), 16:9 (1994)

Nature 365:6448 (1993)

Scientific American 271:4 (1994), 273:2 (1995)

Technology Review (May/June 1994)

Astrophysical Journal 415:1 (1993)

Discover September 1994

BioScience 45:6 (1995)

Strange #11

Observatorium homepage; NASA (On-line)

The Voyager Mission Homepage; NASA (On-line)

The IM Group homepage; NASA (On-line)

San Francisco State University Observatory homepage (On-line)

Project Phoenix homepage (On-line)

Massachusetts Institute of Technology Leg Lab homepage (On-line)

Berkely University Poly-Pedal Lab homepage (On-line)

ALIEN ABDUCTION

Abduction – Human Encounters with Aliens, John E. Mack; Simon and Schuster 1994

Passport to Magonia, Jacques Vallee; Henry Regnery Co., 1969

Dimensions: A Casebook of Alien Contact, Jacques Vallee; Ballantine Books, NY 1988

Dark White: Aliens, Abductions and the UFO Obsession, Jim Schnabel; Penguin 1994

Grand Illusions, Dr Gregory L. Little; White Buffalo Books, 1994

UFO Abductions: A Dangerous Game, Philip J. Klass; Prometheus Books, 1989

Victims of Memory, Mark Pendergrast; Upper Access, Vermont, 1995

The Tectonic Strain Theory As An Explanation For UFO Phenomena: A Non-Techinical Review of the Research, 1970-1990; Michael A. Persinger; Journal of UFO Studies # 2, (1990)

Neurophychological Profiles of Adults Who Report 'Sudden Remembering' of Early Childhood Memories: Implications For Claims of Sex Abuse And Alien Visitation/Abduction Experiences; Michael A. Persinger; Perceptual and Motor Skills #75 (1992)

MUFON UFO Journal #293 (1992), #296 (1992)

New York Times 4 May 1995

Washington Post 9 May 1995, August 4 1995

Fortean Times #69, #71, #79, #83, #85

High Times #240 (August 1995)

Omni: 16:7 (1994), 16:9 (1994), 17:7 (1995), 17:9 (1996),

INSIDE THE FBI

The FBI, Ronald Kessler; Pocket Star Books, New York, 1993

FBI Secrets: An Agent's Expose, M. Wesley Swearingen; South End Press, Boston, 1995

The Federal Bureau of Investigation World-Wide-Web Site (On-line)

Type & Graphic Design - Jake Siney, Paul Hill & Dean McCallam